CCENT®
Cisco Certified Entry Networking Technician
Study Guide
Second Edition

CCENT®

Cisco Certified Entry Networking Technician

Study Guide

Second Edition

Todd Lammle

WILEY

John Wiley & Sons, Inc.

Senior Acquisitions Editor: Jeff Kellum
Development Editor: Tom Cirtin
Technical Editors: Troy McMillan and Dax Mickelson
Production Editor: Christine O'Connor
Copy Editor: Kim Wimpsett
Editorial Manager: Pete Gaughan
Production Manager: Tim Tate
Vice President and Executive Group Publisher: Richard Swadley
Vice President and Publisher: Neil Edde
Media Project Manager 1: Laura Moss-Hollister
Media Associate Producer: Josh Frank
Media Quality Assurance: Doug Kuhn
Book Designers: Judy Fung and Bill Gibson
Compositor: Craig Johnson, Happenstance Type-O-Rama
Proofreader: Rebecca Rider
Indexer: Nancy Guenther
Project Coordinator, Cover: Katherine Crocker
Cover Designer: Ryan Sneed

Dear Reader,

Thank you for choosing *CCENT: Cisco Certified Entry Networking Technician Study Guide, Second Edition*. This book is part of a family of premium-quality Sybex books, all of which are written by outstanding authors who combine practical experience with a gift for teaching.

Sybex was founded in 1976. More than 30 years later, we're still committed to producing consistently exceptional books. With each of our titles, we're working hard to set a new standard for the industry. From the paper we print on, to the authors we work with, our goal is to bring you the best books available.

I hope you see all that reflected in these pages. I'd be very interested to hear your comments and get your feedback on how we're doing. Feel free to let me know what you think about this or any other Sybex book by sending me an email at nedde@wiley.com. If you think you've found a technical error in this book, please visit http://sybex.custhelp.com. Customer feedback is critical to our efforts at Sybex.

Best regards,

Neil Edde
Vice President and Publisher
Sybex, an Imprint of Wiley

Acknowledgments

For trying to keep me going in a straight line, I need to thank my acquisitions editor, Jeff Kellum. It is no small accomplishment, and I applaud him for his patience and dedication to our vision. Jeff Kellum was instrumental in the success of this book, as well as my CCNA series.

Working with Thomas Cirtin as my developmental editor was a first, and it was a smooth, pleasant experience. Thank you, Tom!

In addition, Kim Wimpsett and Christine O'Connor made the editorial process a breeze. I was very happy when I heard they were working with me on this book again!

I also want to thank my technical editor, Troy McMillan. His dedicated, concise comments have been invaluable and have made this a better book. I also don't want to forget my newest forum administrator and hard worker, Jim Frye from Tennessee! He not only added some great ideas to this book, my forum, and web site, but he also provided the great additional study tools on the extra material provided with this book. Check it out!

Thanks also to the media team, whose hard work has resulted in a power-packed, good-looking test engine. And last but not least, thanks to proofreader Rebecca Rider, indexer Nancy Guenther, and compositor Craig Johnson at Happenstance Type-O-Rama.

About the Author

Todd Lammle, CCSI, CCNA/CCNP/Cisco Security and Voice, MCSE, CEH/CHFI, FCC RF Licensed, is the authority on Cisco Certification internetworking. He is a world-renowned author, speaker, trainer and consultant. Todd has more than 30 years of experience working with LANs, WANs, and large licensed and unlicensed wireless networks. He is president of GlobalNet Training and Consulting, Inc., a network integration and training firm based in Dallas, San Francisco, and Boulder. You can reach Todd through his forum at www.lammle.com.

Contents at a Glance

Contents

Introduction

Welcome to the exciting world of Cisco certification! You have picked up this book because you want something better—namely, a better job with more satisfaction. Rest assured that you have made a good decision. Cisco certification can help you get your first networking job, or more money and a promotion if you are already in the field.

Cisco certification can also improve your understanding of the internetworking of more than just Cisco products: you will develop a complete understanding of networking and how different network topologies work together to form a network. This is beneficial to every networking job and is the reason Cisco certification is in such high demand, even at companies with few Cisco devices.

Cisco is the king of routing and switching. The Cisco certifications reach beyond popular certifications such as the Microsoft certifications to provide you with an indispensable factor in understanding today's network—insight into the Cisco world of internetworking. By deciding that you want to become Cisco certified, you are saying that you want to be the best—the best at routing and the best at switching. This book will lead you in that direction.

 For updates covering additions or modifications to the Cisco certification exams, as well as additional study tools for other Cisco certifications, be sure to visit the Todd Lammle website at www.lammle.com.

Cisco's Network Support Certifications

Initially, Cisco started with the coveted Cisco Certified Internetwork Expert (CCIE) certification. You took only one written test and then you were faced with the (extremely difficult) hands-on lab, an all-or-nothing approach that made it tough to succeed.

In response, Cisco created a series of new certifications to help you get the coveted CCIE as well as aid prospective employers in measuring skill levels. With these new certifications, which make for a better approach to preparing for that almighty lab, Cisco opened doors that few were allowed through before.

Cisco Certifications

You don't need to achieve the CCENT, CCNA, or even the higher professional certifications to go for the CCIE, but it is extremely unlikely that you will pass the CCIE unless you go through the step-by-step certification process that Cisco created. It's not impossible, just improbable.

Here is the beginning process Cisco has in mind for you.

Cisco Certified Entry Network Technician (CCENT)

The Cisco CCENT (Cisco Certified Entry Networking Technician) certification validates the skills required for entry-level network support positions, the starting point for many successful careers in networking. This new certification is an entry-level certification that was needed as the CCNA certification objectives grew and grew.

Candidates should have the knowledge and skills to install, operate, and troubleshoot a small enterprise branch network, including basic network security. CCENT certification is the first step toward achieving CCNA, which covers medium-size enterprise branch networks with more complex connections.

This book is geared toward the CCENT certification and helping you self-study for the ICND1 exam (640-822). To achieve this certification, you can read this book, take a hands-on course if needed, and then take one written exam for $150.

Cisco Certified Network Associate (CCNA)

The CCNA certification was the first in the new line of Cisco certifications and was the precursor to all higher Cisco certifications. The CCNA is no longer an entry-level certification, which is why Cisco created the CCENT certification. After you pass the ICND1 exam, which provides you with a CCENT certification, you can take just one more test, the ICND2 (640-816), and you will receive your CCNA certification.

However, the Cisco Certified Network Associate can be achieved by taking either one test at $295 (640-802) or two tests at $150 each (ICND1 and ICND2). All the CCNA exams are extremely hard and cover a lot of material, so you have to really know your stuff! Taking a Cisco class or spending months with hands-on experience is not out of the norm.

And once you have your CCNA, you don't have to stop there—you can choose to continue with your studies and achieve a higher certification, called the Cisco Certified Network Professional (CCNP). Someone with a CCNP has all the skills and knowledge they need to attempt the Routing and Switching CCIE lab. Just becoming a CCNA can land you that job you've dreamed about.

> This book covers everything CCENT/ICND1 related. For up-to-date information on Todd Lammle Cisco Authorized CCENT/CCNA, CCNP, Security, Voice, Data Center, and CCIE bootcamps, please see www.lammle.com.

Why Become CCENT Certified?

Cisco, not unlike Microsoft and other networking vendors, has created the certification process to give administrators a set of skills and to equip prospective employers with a way to measure skills or match certain criteria. Becoming Cisco certified can be the initial step of a successful journey toward a new, highly rewarding and sustainable career.

The certification program was created to provide a solid introduction not only to the Cisco Internetwork Operating System (IOS) and Cisco hardware but also to internetworking in general, making it helpful to you in areas that are not exclusively Cisco's. At this point in the certification process, it's not unrealistic that network managers—even those without Cisco equipment—require Cisco certifications for their job applicants.

If you make it through the CCENT and are still interested in Cisco and internetworking, you're headed down a path to certain success.

Where Do You Take the Exams?

You may take the CCENT exam at any Pearson VUE authorized center; go to www.vue.com or call (877) 404-EXAM (3926).

Here's how to register for any Cisco exam:

1. Determine the number of the exam you want to take. (The CCENT exam number is 640-822.)

2. Register with the nearest Pearson VUE testing center. At this point, you will be asked to pay in advance for the exam. At the time of this writing, the CCENT (ICND1) exam is $150 (CCNA 640-802 is $295) and must be taken within one year of payment. You can schedule exams up to six weeks in advance or as late as the same day you want to take it—but if you fail a Cisco exam, you must wait five days before you will be allowed to retake it. If something comes up and you need to cancel or reschedule your exam appointment, contact Pearson VUE at least 24 hours in advance.

3. When you schedule the exam, you'll get instructions regarding all appointment and cancellation procedures, the ID requirements, and information about the testing center location.

Tips for Taking Your CCENT Exam

The CCENT test contains about 40 to 50 questions, to be completed in about 90 minutes or less. This can change per exam. You must get a score of about 85 percent to pass this exam, but again, each exam can be different.

To pass the exam, the candidate must have the knowledge and skills required to successfully install, operate, and troubleshoot a small branch office network. The exam includes questions on the following:

- Networking fundamentals
- Connecting to a WAN
- Basic security and wireless concepts
- Routing and switching fundamentals
- TCP/IP and OSI models
- IP addressing

- WAN technologies
- Operating and configuring IOS devices
- Configuring RIPv2, static, and default routing
- Implementing NAT and DHCP
- Configuring simple networks

Many questions on the exam have answer choices that at first glance look identical—especially the syntax questions! Remember to read through the choices carefully because close doesn't cut it. If you get commands in the wrong order or forget one measly character, you'll get the question wrong. So, to practice, do the hands-on exercises at the end of the chapters over and over again until they feel natural to you.

Also, never forget that the right answer is the Cisco answer. In many cases, more than one appropriate answer is presented, but the *correct* answer is the one that Cisco recommends. On the exam, the instructions are always to pick one, two, or three, never to "choose all that apply."

The CCNA 640-822 exam includes the following test formats:

- Multiple-choice single answer
- Multiple-choice multiple answer
- Drag-and-drop
- Fill-in-the-blank
- Router simulations

In addition to multiple-choice, fill-in-the-blank, and drag-and-drop response questions, Cisco certification exams may include performance simulation exam items.

Here are some general tips for exam success:

- Arrive early at the exam center so you can relax and review your study materials.
- Read the questions *carefully*. Don't jump to conclusions. Make sure you're clear about *exactly* what each question asks.
- When answering multiple-choice questions that you're not sure about, use the process of elimination to get rid of the obviously incorrect answers first. Doing this greatly improves your odds if you need to make an educated guess.
- You can no longer move forward and backward through the Cisco exams, so double-check your answer before clicking Next since you can't change your mind.

After you complete an exam, you'll get immediate, online notification of your pass or fail status, a printed Examination Score Report that indicates your pass or fail status, and your exam results by section. (The test administrator will give you the printed score report.) Test scores are automatically forwarded to Cisco within five working days after you take the test, so you don't need to send your score to Cisco. If you pass the exam, you'll receive confirmation from Cisco, typically within two to four weeks.

What Does This Book Cover?

This book covers everything you need to know in order to pass the CCENT/ICND1 exam. However, taking the time to study and practice with routers or a router simulator is the real key to success. Please see www.lammle.com/forum for more information on labs, lab equipment, and suggested router simulators.

This book's chapters cover all the CCENT objectives:

- Chapter 1, "Internetworking," introduces you to internetworking. You will learn the basics of the Open Systems Interconnection (OSI) model the way Cisco wants you to learn it. Ethernet networking and standards are discussed in detail in this chapter as well. There are written labs and plenty of review questions to help you. Do not skip the written labs in this chapter!

- Chapter 2, "Internet Protocols," provides you with the background necessary for success on the exam as well as in the real world by discussing TCP/IP. This in-depth chapter covers the very beginnings of the Internet Protocol stack, moves on to IP addressing and understanding the difference between a network address and broadcast address, and ends with network troubleshooting.

- Chapter 3, "IP Subnetting, Troubleshooting IP, and Introduction to NAT," introduces you to subnetting. You will be able to subnet a network in your head after reading this chapter. In addition, you'll learn how to troubleshoot IP networks. Plenty of help is found in this chapter if you do not skip the written lab and review questions.

- Chapter 4, "Cisco's Internetworking Operating System (IOS)," introduces you to the Cisco Internetwork Operating System (IOS) and command-line interface (CLI). In this chapter, you will learn how to turn on a router and configure the basics of the IOS, including setting passwords, banners, and more. IP configuration will be discussed and hands-on labs will help you gain a firm grasp of the concepts taught in the chapter. Before you go through the hands-on labs, be sure to complete the written lab and review questions.

- Chapter 5, "Managing a Cisco Internetwork," provides you with the management skills needed to run a Cisco IOS network. Backing up and restoring the IOS and router configuration are covered, as are the troubleshooting tools necessary to keep a network up and running. Before performing the hands-on labs in this chapter, complete the written lab and review questions.

- Chapter 6, "IP Routing," teaches you about IP routing. This is a fun chapter because you will begin to build your network, add IP addresses, and route data between routers. You will also learn about static, default, and RIP routing. The written lab, hands-on labs, and review questions will help you master IP routing.

- Chapter 7, "Layer 2 Switching," gives you a background on layer 2 switching and how switches perform address learning and make forwarding and filtering decisions. Be sure to go through the written lab and review questions in this chapter.

- Chapter 8, "Wireless Technologies," covers the new wireless objectives. Study the technology covered in this section and make sure you understand basic service sets as well as wireless security. The written lab and review questions will help you fine-tune your study of this chapter.

- Chapter 9, "Security," provides you with the information you need to nail the new security objectives covered in the CCENT exam. Access lists are not covered in the CCENT objectives, but basic security is. Study the chapter carefully, and then go through the written and review questions at the end of the chapter.

- Chapter 10, "Introduction to Wide Area Networks," concentrates on Cisco wide area network (WAN) protocols. This chapter covers the basics of WAN protocols and goes into detail about HDLC and PPP. Do not skip the written lab, review questions, and hands-on labs found in this chapter.

How to Use This Book

If you want a solid foundation for the serious effort of preparing for the Cisco CCENT exam, then look no further. I have spent hundreds of hours putting together this book with the sole intention of helping you pass the CCENT exam and learn how to configure Cisco routers and switches.

This book is loaded with valuable information, and to help you get the most out of your studying time, I recommend the following study method:

1. Take the assessment test immediately following this introduction. (The answers are at the end of the test.) It's okay if you don't know any of the answers; that is why you bought this book! Carefully read over the explanations for any question you get wrong and note which chapters the material comes from. This information should help you plan your study strategy.

2. Study each chapter carefully, making sure you fully understand the information and the test objectives listed at the beginning. Pay extra-close attention to chapters from which questions you missed in the assessment test were taken.

3. Complete each written lab at the end of each chapter. Do *not* skip the written exercises; they directly relate to the CCENT/ICND1 exam and what you must glean from the chapter you just read. Do not just skim these labs! Make sure you understand completely the reason for each answer. You can find the answers in Appendix A.

4. Complete all hands-on labs in the chapter, referring to the text of the chapter so that you understand the reason for each step you take. If you do not have Cisco equipment available, look for a router simulator that will cover all the labs needed for all your Cisco certification needs.

If you have Cisco's Packet Tracer, you're set, and if so, you can email me for preconfigured Packet Tracer labs. Please see www.lammle.com/forum for more information.

5. Answer all of the review questions related to each chapter. (The answers to the review questions appear in Appendix B.) Note the questions that confuse you and study the corresponding sections of the book again. Do not just skim these questions! Make sure you understand completely the reason for each answer.

6. Try your hand at the bonus exams that are included on the companion website at www .sybex.com/go/ccent2e. The questions in these exams appear only on the website. This will give you a complete overview of the type of questions you can expect to see on the real CCENT exam. Check out www.lammle.com for more Cisco exam prep questions.

7. Test yourself using all the flashcards on the website. These are new and include an updated flashcard program to help you prepare for the CCENT/CCNA exams. This is a great study tool!

To learn every bit of the material covered in this book, you'll have to apply yourself regularly and with discipline. Try to set aside the same time period every day to study, and select a comfortable and quiet place to do so. If you work hard, you will be surprised at how quickly you learn this material.

If you follow these steps and really study and practice the review questions, the bonus exams, the electronic flashcards, and all the written and hands-on labs, it would be hard to fail the CCENT exam.

Additional Study Tools

I worked hard to provide some really great tools to help you with your certification process. All of the following tools should be loaded on your workstation when studying for the test.

 Readers can get access to the following tools by visiting www.sybex.com/ ccent2e.

The Sybex Test Preparation Software

The test preparation software prepares you to pass the CCENT/ICND1 exam. In the test engine, you will find all the review and assessment questions from the book, plus two additional bonus exams that appear exclusively with this book.

 Additional bonus exams can be found at www.lammle.com.

Electronic Flashcards

To prepare for the exam, you can read this book, study the review questions at the end of each chapter, and work through the practice exams included in the book and with companion study tools. But wait, there's more! You can also test yourself with the flashcards. If you can get through these difficult questions and understand the answers, you'll know you're ready for the CCENT/ICND1 exam.

The flashcards include more than 150 questions specifically written to hit you hard and make sure you are ready for the exam. Between the review questions, bonus exams, and flashcards, you'll be more than prepared for the exam.

Glossary

The glossary is a handy resource for Cisco terms. This is a great tool for understanding some of the more obscure terms used in this book.

> To get up-to-the-minute CCENT and other Cisco exam information, please see www.lammle.com and www.sybex.com/go/ccent2e.

Todd Lammle Videos

I have created a full CCNA series of videos that can be purchased in either DVD or online streaming format from www.lammle.com. However, as a bonus included with this book, the first module of this series is included in its entirety. The video is more than one hour of informative CCENT/CCNA information. This bonus module alone has a value of $149! Do not skip this video because it covers the internetworking objectives, which are very important to the CCENT/CCNA exam.

Todd Lammle Audios

In addition to the section of videos included for free on the companion website, I have included one full section from my CCNA audio series—almost one hour of audio! The full CCNA audio series has a value of $199 and can be found at www.lammle.com. This is a great tool to add to your arsenal of study material to help you pass the CCENT/CCNA exam.

How to Contact the Author

You can reach CCSI Todd Lammle through GlobalNet Training & Consulting, Inc., at www.lammle.com.

CCENT Exam Objectives

OBJECTIVE	CHAPTER
Describe the Operation of Data Networks	
Describe the purpose and functions of various network devices	1
Select the components required to meet a given network specification	1
Use the OSI and TCP/IP models and their associated protocols to explain how data flows in a network	1
Describe common networking applications including web applications	1, 2
Describe the purpose and basic operation of the protocols in the OSI and TCP models	1, 2
Describe the impact of applications (Voice Over IP and Video Over IP) on a network	2
Interpret network diagrams	6
Determine the path between two hosts across a network	6
Describe the components required for network and Internet communications	1
Identify and correct common network problems at layers 1, 2, 3 and 7 using a layered model approach	1
Differentiate between LAN/WAN operation and features	1, 10
Implement a Small Switched Network	
Select the appropriate media, cables, ports, and connectors to connect switches to other network devices and hosts	1
Explain the technology and media access control method for Ethernet technologies	1
Explain network segmentation and basic traffic management concepts	1, 7
Explain the operation of Cisco switches and basic switching concepts	7
Perform, save and verify initial switch configuration tasks including remote access management	7
Verify network status and switch operation using basic utilities (including: ping, traceroute, telnet, SSH, arp, ipconfig), SHOW & DEBUG commands	7

OBJECTIVE	CHAPTER
Implement and verify basic security for a switch (port security, deactivate ports)	7
Identify, prescribe, and resolve common switched network media issues, configuration issues, autonegotiation, and switch hardware failures	1, 7
Implement an IP Addressing Scheme and IP Services to Meet Network Requirements for a Small Branch Office	
Describe the need and role of addressing in a network	2, 3, 4
Create and apply an addressing scheme to a network	2, 3, 4
Assign and verify valid IP addresses to hosts, servers, and networking devices in a LAN environment	2, 3
Explain the basic uses and operation of NAT in a small network connecting to one ISP	3
Describe and verify DNS operation	2, 3, 4
Describe the operation and benefits of using private and public IP addressing	2, 3
Enable NAT for a small network with a single ISP and connection using SDM and verify operation using CLI and ping	3
Configure, verify and troubleshoot DHCP and DNS operation on a router (including: CLI/SDM)	3, 4
Implement static and dynamic addressing services for hosts in a LAN environment	3
Identify and correct IP addressing issues	3
Implement a Small Routed Network	
Describe basic routing concepts (including: packet forwarding, router lookup process)	6
Describe the operation of Cisco routers (including: router bootup process, POST, router components)	5
Select the appropriate media, cables, ports, and connectors to connect routers to other network devices and hosts	1
Configure, verify, and troubleshoot RIPv2	6
Access and utilize the router CLI to set basic parameters	4

Assessment Test

1. Which of the following describes a Class A address? (Choose three.)
    A. The decimal value of the first octet can range from 1 to 126.
    B. The decimal value of the first octet can range from 1 to 192.
    C. The first octet represents the entire network portion of the address.
    D. The default mask for a Class A network is 255.255.0.0.
    E. The value of the first binary place in the first octet must be 0.

2. What does the command `routerA(config)#line cons 0` allow you to perform next?
    A. Set the Telnet password.
    B. Shut down the router.
    C. Set your console password.
    D. Disable console connections.

3. Which of the following is the valid host range for the subnet on which the IP address 192.168.168.188 255.255.255.192 resides?
    A. 192.168.168.129–190
    B. 192.168.168.129–191
    C. 192.168.168.128–190
    D. 192.168.168.128–192

4. What does the `passive` command provide to dynamic routing protocols?
    A. Stops an interface from sending or receiving periodic dynamic updates
    B. Stops an interface from sending periodic dynamic updates but not from receiving updates
    C. Stops the router from receiving any dynamic updates
    D. Stops the router from sending any dynamic updates

5. Which protocol does Ping use?
    A. TCP
    B. ARP
    C. ICMP
    D. BootP

6. How many collision domains are created when you segment a network with a 12-port switch?
    A. 1
    B. 2
    C. 5
    D. 12

7. Which of the following commands will allow you to set your Telnet password on a Cisco router?

   A. `line telnet 0 4`

   B. `line aux 0 4`

   C. `line vty 0 4`

   D. `line con 0`

8. If you wanted to delete the configuration stored in NVRAM, what would you type?

   A. `erase startup`

   B. `erase nvram`

   C. `delete nvram`

   D. `erase running`

9. Which protocol is used to send a destination network unreachable message back to originating hosts?

   A. TCP

   B. ARP

   C. ICMP

   D. BootP

10. Which class of IP address has the most host addresses available by default?

   A. A

   B. B

   C. C

   D. A and B

11. What is the subnet address of 172.16.159.159/22?

   A. 172.16.0.0

   B. 172.16.128.0

   C. 172.16.156.0

   D. 172.16.192.0

12. How many broadcast domains are created when you segment a network with a 12-port switch?

   A. 1

   B. 2

   C. 5

   D. 12

13. What PDU is at the Transport layer?

    A. User data

    B. Session

    C. Segment

    D. Frame

14. What is a stub network?

    A. A network with more than one exit point

    B. A network with more than one exit and entry point

    C. A network with only one entry and no exit point

    D. A network that has only one entry and exit point

15. Where is a hub specified in the OSI model?

    A. Session layer

    B. Physical layer

    C. Data Link layer

    D. Application layer

16. What does the command `show controllers s 0` provide?

    A. The type of serial port connection (e.g., Ethernet or Token Ring)

    B. The type of connection (e.g., DTE or DCE)

    C. The configuration of the interface, including the IP address and clock rate

    D. The controlling processor of that interface

17. What is the main reason the OSI model was created?

    A. To create a layered model larger than the DoD model

    B. So application developers can change only one layer's protocols at a time

    C. So different networks could communicate

    D. So Cisco could use the model

18. Which layer of the OSI model creates a virtual circuit between hosts before transmitting data?

    A. Application

    B. Session

    C. Transport

    D. Network

    E. Data Link

19. Which protocol does DHCP use at the Transport layer?

   A. IP

   B. TCP

   C. UDP

   D. ARP

20. How do you copy a router IOS to a TFTP host?

   A. `copy run starting`

   B. `copy start running`

   C. `copy running tftp`

   D. `copy flash tftp`

21. If your router is facilitating a CSU/DSU, which of the following commands do you need to use to provide the router with a 64Kbps serial link?

   A. `RouterA(config)#bandwidth 64`

   B. `RouterA(config-if)#bandwidth 64000`

   C. `RouterA(config)#clockrate 64000`

   D. `RouterA(config-if)#clock rate 64`

   E. `RouterA(config-if)#clock rate 64000`

22. Which of the following commands will set your prompt so you can set your Telnet password on a Cisco router?

   A. `line telnet 0 4`

   B. `line aux 0 4`

   C. `line vty 0 4`

   D. `line con 0`

23. What command do you use to set the enable secret password on a Cisco router to *todd*?

   A. `RouterA(config)#enable password todd`

   B. `RouterA(config)#enable secret todd`

   C. `RouterA(config)#enable secret password todd`

   D. `RouterA(config-if)#enable secret todd`

24. Which two statements best describe the wireless security standard that is defined by WPA? (Choose two.)

   A. It specifies use of a static encryption key that must be changed frequently to enhance security.

   B. It requires use of an open authentication method.

   C. It specifies the use of dynamic encryption keys that change each time a client establishes a connection.

   D. It requires that all access points and wireless devices use the same encryption key.

   E. It includes authentication by PSK.

25. Which protocol is used to find an Ethernet address from a known IP address?

   A. IP

   B. ARP

   C. RARP

   D. BootP

26. Which command is used to enable RIP on a Cisco router?

   A. `copy tftp rip`

   B. `router rip on`

   C. `router rip`

   D. `on rip routing`

27. Which additional configuration step is necessary in order to connect to an AP that has SSID broadcasting disabled?

   A. Set the SSID value in the client software to `public`.

   B. Configure open authentication on the AP and the client.

   C. Set the SSID value on the client to the SSID configured on the AP.

   D. Configure MAC address filtering to permit the client to connect to the AP.

28. Which encryption type does WPA2 use?

   A. AES-CCMP

   B. PPK via IV

   C. PSK

   D. TKIP/MIC

29. What are two security appliances that can be installed in a network? (Choose two.)

   A. ATM

   B. IDS

   C. IOS

   D. IPS

30. What are two recommended ways of protecting network device configuration files from outside network security threats? (Choose two.)

   A. Allow unrestricted access to the console or VTY ports.

   B. Use a firewall to restrict access from the outside to the network devices.

   C. Use SSH or another encrypted and authenticated transport to access device configurations.

   D. Always use Telnet to access the device command line because it is automatically encrypted.

Answers to Assessment Test

1. A, C, E. To define a Class A address, the first bit in the first byte must be a zero. The range is 1 to 126, and the first octet represents the entire network portion of the address. See Chapter 2 for more information.

2. C. The command `line console 0` places you at a prompt where you can then set your console user-mode password. See Chapter 4 for more information.

3. A. 256 – 192 = 64. 64 + 64 = 128. 128 + 64 = 192. The subnet is 128, the broadcast address is 191, and the valid host range is the numbers in between, or 129–190. See Chapter 3 for more information.

4. B. The `passive` command, short for `passive-interface`, stops regular updates from being sent out of an interface. However, the interface can still receive updates. See Chapter 6 for more information.

5. C. Internet Control Message Protocol (ICMP) is the protocol at the Network layer that is used to send echo requests and replies. See Chapter 2 for more information.

6. D. Layer 2 switching creates individual collision domains. See Chapter 7 for more information.

7. C. The command `line vty 0 4` places you in a prompt that will allow you to set or change your Telnet password. See Chapter 4 for more information.

8. A. The command `erase-startup-config` deletes the configuration stored in NVRAM. See Chapter 4 for more information.

9. C. ICMP is the protocol at the Network layer that is used to send messages back to an originating router. See Chapter 2 for more information.

10. A. Class A addressing provides 24 bits for hosts addressing. See Chapter 3 for more information.

11. C. First, a /22 mask is 255.255.252.0, meaning you have a block size of four in the third octet. The subnet is 172.16.156.0. See Chapter 3 for more information.

12. A. By default, switches break up collision domains but are one large broadcast domain. See Chapter 1 for more information.

13. C. Segmentation happens at the Transport layer. See Chapter 1 for more information.

14. D. Stub networks have only one connection to an internetwork. Only default routes can be set on a stub network or network loops may occur. See Chapter 6 for more information.

15. B. A hub is a Physical layer device. See Chapter 1 for more information.

16. B. The command show controllers s 0 tells you what type of serial connection you have. If it is a DCE, you need to provide the clock rate. See Chapter 4 for more information.

17. C. The primary reason the OSI model was created was so that different networks could interoperate. See Chapter 1 for more information.

18. C. The Transport layer creates virtual circuits between hosts before transmitting any data. See Chapter 1 for more information.

19. C. User Datagram Protocol is a connection network service at the Transport layer, and DHCP uses this connectionless service. See Chapter 2 for more information.

20. D. The command used to copy a configuration from a router to a TFTP host is copy flash tftp. See Chapter 8 for more information.

21. E. The clock rate command is two words, and the speed of the line is in bits per second (bps). See Chapter 5 for more information.

22. C. The command line vty 0 4 places you in a prompt that will allow you to set or change your Telnet password. See Chapter 4 for more information.

23. B. The command enable secret todd sets the enable secret password to *todd*. See Chapter 4 for more information.

24. C, E. WPA uses PSK to include authentication and can use either static or dynamic encryption keys. The benefit of WPA over a static WEP key is that WPA can change dynamically while the system is used. See Chapter 8 for more information.

25. B. If a device knows the IP address of where it wants to send a packet but doesn't know the hardware address, it will send an ARP broadcast looking for the hardware address or, in this case, the Ethernet address. See Chapter 2 for more information.

26. C. To enable RIP routing on a Cisco router, use the global config command router rip. See Chapter 6 for more information.

27. D. If an AP does have SSID broadcasting disabled, the client needs to set the SSID value of the AP on the client software in order to connect to the AP. See Chapter 8 for more information.

28. A. WPA2 uses the Advanced Encryption Standard (AES) known as the Counter Mode Cipher Block Chaining-Message Authentication Code (CBC-MAC) protocol (CCMP). See Chapter 8 for more information.

29. B, D. Intrusion detection systems (IDSs) and intrusion prevention systems (IPSs). These tools help prevent threats by watching for trends, particular patterns, and other factors. See Chapter 9 for more information.

30. B, C. You should always have a firewall on your network to block access from outside devices. In addition, Cisco recommends always using Secure Shell (SSH) instead of Telnet to configure your devices in-band. See Chapter 9 for more information.

CCENT®
Cisco Certified Entry Networking Technician
Study Guide
Second Edition

Chapter 1

Internetworking

THE CCENT EXAM OBJECTIVES COVERED IN THIS CHAPTER INCLUDE THE FOLLOWING:

✓ **Describe the operation of data networks**

- Describe the purpose and functions of various network devices

- Select the components required to meet a given network specification

- Use the OSI and TCP/IP models and their associated protocols to explain how data flows in a network

- Describe common networking applications including web applications

- Describe the purpose and basic operation of the protocols in the OSI and TCP models

- Describe the components required for network and Internet communications

- Identify and correct common network problems at layers 1, 2, 3 and 7 using a layered model approach

✓ **Implement a small switched network**

- Select the appropriate media, cables, ports, and connectors to connect switches to other network devices and hosts

- Explain the technology and media access control method for Ethernet technologies

- Explain network segmentation and basic traffic management concepts

- Identify, prescribe, and resolve common switched network media issues, configuration issues, autonegotiation, and switch hardware failures

Welcome to the exciting world of internetworking. This first chapter will really help you understand the basics of internetworking by focusing on how to connect networks using Cisco routers and switches. First, you need to know exactly what an internetwork is, right? You create an internetwork when you connect two or more networks to a router and configure a logical network addressing scheme with a protocol, such as IP on the router interfaces. I'll be covering these four topics in this chapter:

- Internetworking basics
- Network segmentation
- How bridges, switches, and routers are used to physically segment a network
- How routers are employed to create an internetwork

I'm also going to dissect the Open Systems Interconnection (OSI) model and describe each part in detail because you really need a good grasp of OSI for a solid foundation to build your networking knowledge upon. The OSI model has seven hierarchical layers that were developed to enable networks to communicate reliably between disparate systems. Since this book centers on all things CCENT, it's crucial for you to understand the OSI model as Cisco sees it, so that's how I'll be presenting the seven layers to you.

Since there are a bunch of different types of devices specified in the different layers of the OSI model, it's also very important to understand the many types of cables and connectors used for connecting all those devices to a network. I'll go over cabling Cisco devices, discussing how to connect to a router or switch (along with Ethernet LAN technologies) and even how to connect a router or switch with a console connection.

After you finish reading this chapter, take the time to answer the review questions and complete the written labs. These are given to you to really lock the information from this chapter into your memory. Don't skip them!

To find up-to-the-minute updates for this chapter, please see www.lammle.com/forum and/or www.sybex.com/go/ccent2e.

Internetworking Basics

Before I explore internetworking models and the specifications of the OSI reference model, you have to understand the big picture and learn the answer to this key question: why is it so important to learn Cisco internetworking?

Networks and networking have grown exponentially over the past 15 years—understandably so. They've had to evolve at light speed just to keep up with huge increases in basic, mission-critical user needs, such as sharing data and printers, as well as more advanced demands, such as videoconferencing. Unless everyone who needs to share network resources is located in the same office area (an increasingly uncommon situation), the challenge is to connect the relevant networks so all users can share the networks' wealth.

Addressing

Starting with a look at Figure 1.1, you get a picture of a basic local area network (LAN) that's connected using a hub. This network is actually one collision domain and one broadcast domain—but no worries if you have no idea what this means because I'm going to talk about both collision and broadcast domains so much throughout this whole chapter that you'll probably even dream about them!

 **FIGURE 1.1** The basic network

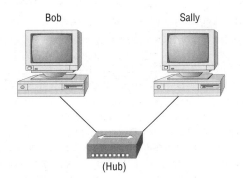

Bob   Sally

(Hub)

The basic network allows devices to share information.
The term computer language refers to binary code (0s or 1s).
The two hosts above communicate using hardware or MAC addresses.

Okay, about Figure 1.1—how would you say the PC named Bob communicates with the PC named Sally? Well, they're both on the same LAN connected with a multiport repeater (a hub). Does Bob just send out a data message, "Hey Sally, you there?" or does Bob use Sally's Internet Protocol (IP) address and put things more like, "Hey 192.168.0.3, are you there?" I hope you picked the IP address option, but even if you did, the news is still bad—both answers are wrong! Why? Because Bob is actually going to use Sally's *Media Access Control (MAC) address* (known as a hardware address), which is burned right into the network card of Sally's PC, to get ahold of her.

Great, but how does Bob get Sally's MAC address since Bob knows only Sally's name and doesn't even have her IP address yet? Bob is going to start with name resolution (hostname to IP address resolution), something that's usually accomplished using Domain Name Service (DNS). And of note, if these two are on the same LAN, Bob can just broadcast to Sally asking her for the information (no DNS needed)—welcome to Microsoft Windows!

Here's an output from a network analyzer depicting a simple name resolution process from Bob to Sally:

```
Source      Destination   Protocol   Info
192.168.0.2  192.168.0.255   NBNS   Name query NB SALLY<00>
```

As I already mentioned, since the two hosts are on a local LAN, Windows (Bob) will just broadcast to resolve the name Sally (the destination 192.168.0.255 is a broadcast address), and Sally will let Bob know her address was 192.16.0.3 (analyzer output not shown). Let's take a look at the rest of the information:

```
EthernetII,Src:192.168.0.2(00:14:22:be:18:3b),Dst:Broadcast
 (ff:ff:ff:ff:ff:ff)
```

What this output shows is that Bob knows his own MAC address and source IP address but not Sally's IP address or MAC address, so Bob sends a broadcast address of all *f*s for the MAC address (a Data Link layer broadcast) and an IP LAN broadcast of 192.168.0.255. Again, don't freak—you're going to learn all about broadcasts in Chapter 3, "IP Subnetting, Troubleshooting IP, and Introduction to NAT."

Now Bob has to broadcast on the LAN to get Sally's MAC address so he can finally communicate to her PC and send data:

```
Source      Destination Protocol Info
192.168.0.2 Broadcast   ARP Who has 192.168.0.3? Tell 192.168.0.2
```

Next, check out Sally's response:

```
Source      Destination   Protocol   Info
192.168.0.3 192.168.0.2   ARP   192.168.0.3 is at 00:0b:db:99:d3:5e
192.168.0.3 192.168.0.2 NBNS Name query response NB 192.168.0.3
```

Sweet—Bob now has both Sally's IP address and her MAC address! Both are listed as the source address at this point because this information was sent from Sally back to Bob. So, *finally*, Bob has all the goods he needs to communicate with Sally. And just so you know, I'm going to tell you all about Address Resolution Protocol (ARP) and show you exactly how Sally's IP address was resolved to a MAC address a little later in Chapter 6, "IP Routing."

To complicate things further, it's also likely that at some point you'll have to break up one large network into a bunch of smaller ones because user response times will have dwindled to a slow crawl as the network grew and grew. And with all that growth, your LAN's traffic congestion will have reached epic proportions. The answer to this problem is breaking up that really big network into a number of smaller ones—something called *network segmentation*. You do this by using devices like *routers*, *switches*, and *bridges*. Figure 1.2 shows a network that's been segmented with a switch so each network segment connected to the switch is now a separate collision domain. But make note of the fact that this network is still one broadcast domain.

FIGURE 1.2   A switch can replace the hub, breaking up collision domains.

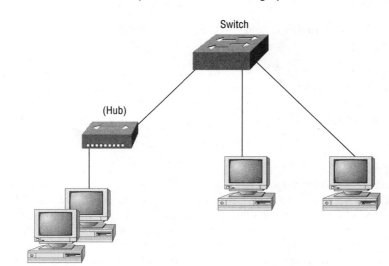

Keep in mind that the hub used in Figure 1.2 just extended the one collision domain from the switch port. Here's a list of some of the things that commonly cause LAN traffic congestion:

- Too many hosts in a collision or broadcast domain
- Broadcast storms
- Too much multicast traffic
- Low bandwidth
- Adding hubs for connectivity to the network
- A bunch of ARP broadcasts

Take another look at Figure 1.2. Did you notice that I replaced the main hub from Figure 1.1 with a switch? Whether you did or didn't, I did that because hubs don't segment a network; they just connect network segments. Basically, it's an inexpensive way to connect a couple of PCs, which is great for home use and troubleshooting, but that's about it!

Now, routers are used to connect networks and route packets of data from one network to another. Cisco became the de facto standard of routers because of its high-quality router products, great selection, and fantastic service. Routers, by default, break up a *broadcast domain*—the set of all devices on a network segment that hear all the broadcasts sent on that segment. Figure 1.3 shows a router in our little network that creates an internetwork and breaks up broadcast domains.

FIGURE 1.3   Routers create an internetwork.

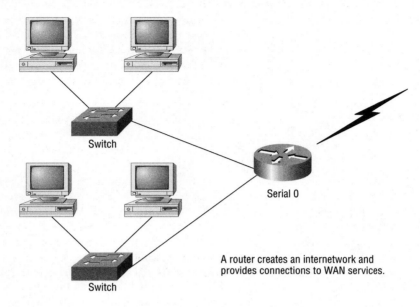

A router creates an internetwork and provides connections to WAN services.

The network in Figure 1.3 is a pretty cool network. Each host is connected to its own collision domain, and the router has created two broadcast domains. And don't forget that the router provides connections to wide area network (WAN) services as well! The router uses something called a serial interface for WAN connections, specifically, a V.35 physical interface on a Cisco router.

Breaking up a broadcast domain is important because when a host or server sends a network broadcast, every device on the network must read and process that broadcast—unless you have a router. When the router's interface receives this broadcast, it can respond by basically saying, "Thanks, but no thanks," and discard the broadcast without forwarding it on to other networks. Even though routers are known for breaking up broadcast domains by default, it's important to remember that they break up collision domains as well.

There are two advantages of using routers in your network.

- They don't forward broadcasts by default.
- They can filter the network based on layer 3 (Network layer) information (like the IP address).

Four router functions in your network can be listed as follows:

- Packet switching
- Packet filtering
- Internetwork communication
- Path selection

Remember, basically, that routers are really switches; they're actually what are called layer 3 switches (I'll talk about layers later in this chapter). Unlike layer 2 switches, which forward or filter frames, routers (layer 3 switches) use logical addressing and provide what is called *packet switching*. Routers can also provide packet filtering by using access lists, and when routers connect two or more networks together and use logical addressing (IP or IPv6), you have what is called an *internetwork*. Finally, routers use a routing table (map of the internetwork) to make path selections and to forward packets to remote networks.

> In this book, I'll just talk about IP addressing. If you'd like to know more about IPv6, pick up a copy of Sybex's *CCNA: Cisco Certified Network Associate Study Guide, 7th Edition*. There's a whole chapter on IPv6.

Conversely, layer 2 switches, the ones we usually call just plain switches, aren't used to create internetworks because they do not break up broadcast domains by default; they're employed to add functionality to a network LAN. The main purpose of these switches is to make a LAN work better—to optimize its performance—providing more bandwidth for the LAN's users. And these switches don't forward packets to other networks, as routers do. Instead, they only "switch" frames from one port to another within the switched network. Okay, you may be thinking, "Wait a minute, what are frames and packets?" I'll tell you all about them later in this chapter, I promise!

By default, switches break up collision domains. *Collision domain* is an Ethernet term used to describe a network scenario in which one device sends a packet on a network segment and every other device on the same segment is forced to pay attention to it. If, at the same time, a different device tries to transmit, a collision occurs, and both devices must retransmit—one at a time. Not very efficient! This situation is typically found in a hub environment, where each host segment connects to a hub that represents only one collision domain and only one broadcast domain. By contrast, each and every port on a switch represents its own collision domain.

> Switches create separate collision domains within a single broadcast domain. Routers provide a separate broadcast domain for each interface.

The term *bridging* was introduced before routers and hubs were implemented, so it's pretty common to hear people referring to switches as bridges. That's because bridges and switches basically do the same thing—break up collision domains on a LAN (in reality, you cannot buy a physical bridge these days, only LAN switches, but they use bridging technologies, so Cisco still calls them multiport bridges at times).

So, what this means is that a switch is basically just a multiple-port bridge with more brainpower, right? Well, pretty much, but there are differences. Switches do provide a bridging function, but they do so with greatly enhanced management ability and features. Plus, most of the time, bridges had only 2 or 4 ports. Yes, you could get your hands on a bridge with up to 16 ports, but that's nothing compared to the hundreds of ports available on some switches!

You would use a bridge in a network to reduce collisions within broadcast domains and to increase the number of collision domains in your network. Doing this provides more bandwidth for users. And keep in mind that using hubs in your Ethernet network can contribute to congestion. As always, plan your network design carefully!

Figure 1.4 shows how a network would look with all these internetwork devices in place. Remember that not only will the router break up broadcast domains for every LAN interface, it will break up collision domains as well.

FIGURE 1.4   Internetworking devices

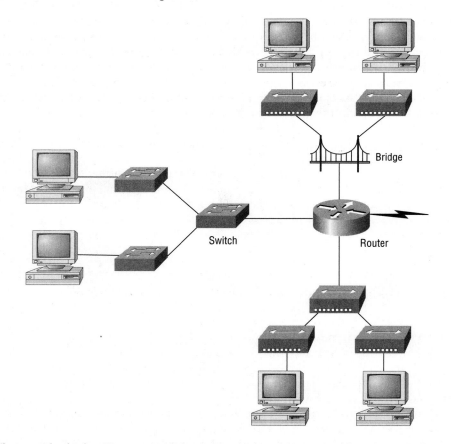

When you looked at Figure 1.4, did you notice that the router is found at center stage and that it connects each physical network together? I have to use this layout because of the older technologies involved—bridges and hubs.

On the top internetwork in Figure 1.4, you'll notice that a bridge was used to connect the hubs to a router. The bridge breaks up collision domains, but all the hosts connected to both hubs are still crammed into the same broadcast domain. Also, the bridge created only two collision domains, so each device connected to a hub is in the same collision domain as every other device connected to that same hub. This is actually pretty lame, but it's still better than having one collision domain for all hosts.

Notice something else: the three interconnected hubs at the bottom of the figure also connect to the router. This setup creates one collision domain and one broadcast domain and makes the bridged network, with its two collision domains, look much better indeed!

> Although bridges/switches are used to segment networks, they will not isolate broadcast or multicast packets.

The best network connected to the router is the LAN switch network on the left. Why? Because each port on that switch breaks up collision domains. But it's not all good—all devices are still in the same broadcast domain. Do you remember why this can be a really bad thing? Because all devices must listen to all broadcasts transmitted, that's why. And if your broadcast domains are too large, the users have less bandwidth and are required to process more broadcasts. Network response time eventually will slow to a level that could cause office riots.

Once I have only switches in the example network, things change a lot! Figure 1.5 shows the network that is typically found today.

FIGURE 1.5   Switched networks creating an internetwork

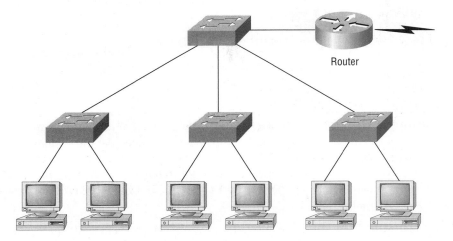

Router

Here I've placed the LAN switches at the center of the network world, and the routers are connecting the logical networks. If I implemented this kind of setup, I've created Virtual LANs (VLANs), something that you don't have to worry about in the ICND1 objectives. VLANs are covered in depth in *CCNA: Cisco Certified Network Associate Study Guide, Seventh Edition* (Sybex, 2011). But it is really important to understand that even in a switched network, you still need a router to provide your inter-VLAN communication, or internetworking. Don't forget that!

Obviously, the best network is one that's correctly configured to meet the business requirements of the company it serves. The best network design is one in which LAN switches with
routers are used and correctly placed in the network. This book will help you understand the
basics of routers and switches so you can make good, informed decisions on a case-by-case
basis.

Let's go back to Figure 1.4 again. Look at the figure. How many collision domains and
broadcast domains are in this internetwork? I hope you answered nine collision domains and
three broadcast domains! The broadcast domains are definitely the easiest to see because
only routers break up broadcast domains by default. And since there are three connections,
that gives you three broadcast domains. But do you see the nine collision domains? Just in
case that's a no, I'll explain. The all-hub network is one collision domain; the bridge network
equals three collision domains. Add in the switch network of five collision domains—one for
each switch port—and you have a total of nine.

Now, in Figure 1.5, each port on the switch is a separate collision domain, and each
VLAN is a separate broadcast domain. But you still need a router for routing between
VLANs. How many collision domains do you see here? I'm counting 10—remember that
connections between the switches are considered a collision domain!

So, now that you've gotten an introduction to internetworking and the various devices
that live in an internetwork, it's time to head into internetworking models.

🌐 Real World Scenario

Should I Replace My Existing 10/100Mbps Switches?

You're a network administrator at a large company in San Jose. The boss comes to
you and says that he got your requisition to buy all new switches and is not sure about
approving the expense; do you really need it?

Well, if you can, absolutely! The newest switches really add a lot of functionality to a
network that older 10/100 Mbps switches just don't have (yes, five-year-old switches are
considered just plain old today). But most of us don't have an unlimited budget to buy
all new gigabit switches. 10/100 Mbps switches can still create a nice network—that is, of
course, if you design and implement the network correctly—but you'll still have to replace
these switches eventually.

So, do you need 1Gbps or better switch ports for all your users, servers, and other devices?
Yes, you *absolutely* need new higher-end switches! With the new Windows networking
stack and the IPv6 revolution shortly ahead of us, the server and hosts are no longer the
bottlenecks of our internetworks—our routers and switches are! We need at a minimum
gigabit to the desktop and on every router interface; 10Gbps would be better, or even
higher if you can afford it.

So, go ahead! Put that requisition in to buy all new switches.

Now that you've gotten an introduction to internetworking and the various devices that live in an internetwork, it's time to head into internetworking models.

Internetworking Models

When networks first came into being, computers could typically communicate only with computers from the same manufacturer. For example, companies ran either a complete DECnet solution or an IBM solution—not both together. In the late 1970s, the *Open Systems Interconnection (OSI) reference model* was created by the International Organization for Standardization (ISO) to break this barrier.

The OSI model was meant to help vendors create interoperable network devices and software in the form of protocols so that different vendor networks could work with each other. Like world peace, it'll probably never happen completely, but it's still a great goal.

The OSI model is the primary architectural model for networks. It describes how data and network information are communicated from an application on one computer through the network media to an application on another computer. The OSI reference model breaks this approach into layers.

In the following section, I am going to explain the layered approach and how you can use this approach to help troubleshoot internetworks.

The Layered Approach

A *reference model* is a conceptual blueprint of how communications should take place. It addresses all the processes required for effective communication and divides these processes into logical groupings called *layers*. When a communication system is designed in this manner, it's known as *layered architecture*.

Think of it like this: you and some friends want to start a company. One of the first things you'll do is sit down and think through what tasks must be done, who will do them, the order in which they will be done, and how they relate to each other. Ultimately, you might group these tasks into departments. Let's say you decide to have an order-taking department, an inventory department, and a shipping department. Each of your departments has its own unique tasks, keeping its staff members busy and requiring them to focus on only their own duties.

In this scenario, I'm using departments as a metaphor for the layers in a communication system. For things to run smoothly, the staff of each department will have to trust and rely heavily upon the others to do their jobs and competently handle their unique responsibilities. In your planning sessions, you would probably take notes, recording the entire process to facilitate later discussions about standards of operation that will serve as your business blueprint, or reference model.

Once your business is launched, your department heads, each armed with the part of the blueprint relating to their own department, will need to develop practical methods to implement their assigned tasks. These practical methods, or protocols, will need to be compiled into a standard operating procedures manual and followed closely. Each of the various procedures in your manual will have been included for different reasons and have varying degrees of importance and implementation. If you form a partnership or acquire another company, it will be imperative that its business protocols—its business blueprint—match yours (or at least be compatible).

Similarly, software developers can use a reference model to understand computer communication processes and see what types of functions need to be accomplished on any one layer. If they are developing a protocol for a certain layer, all they need to concern themselves with is that specific layer's functions, not those of any other layer. Another layer and protocol will handle the other functions. The technical term for this idea is *binding*. The communication processes that are related to each other are bound, or grouped together, at a particular layer.

Advantages of Reference Models

One of the greatest functions of the reference model specifications is to assist in data transfer between disparate hosts—meaning, for example, that they enable you to transfer data between a Unix host and a PC or a Mac. The reference models aren't physical models, though. Rather, they're sets of guidelines that application developers can use to create and implement applications that run on a network. They also provide a framework for creating and implementing networking standards, devices, and internetworking schemes.

The Open Systems Interconnection (OSI) model is a hierarchical model, and the same benefits and advantages you gain from implementing OSI standards can apply to any layered model. The primary purpose of all such models, especially the OSI model, is to allow different vendors' networks to interoperate.

Advantages of using the OSI layered model include, but are not limited to, the following:

- It divides the network communication process into smaller and simpler components, thus aiding component development, design, and troubleshooting.
- It allows multiple-vendor development through standardization of network components.
- It encourages industry standardization by defining what functions occur at each layer of the model.
- It allows various types of network hardware and software to communicate.
- It prevents changes in one layer from affecting other layers, so it does not hamper hardware or software development.

The OSI Reference Model

Basically, the ISO is pretty much the Emily Post of the network protocol world. Just as Ms. Post wrote the book setting the standards—or protocols—for human social interaction, the ISO developed the OSI reference model as the precedent and guide for an open network protocol set. Defining the etiquette of communication models, it remains today the most popular means of comparison for protocol suites.

The OSI reference model has seven layers:

- Application layer (layer 7)
- Presentation layer (layer 6)
- Session layer (layer 5)
- Transport layer (layer 4)
- Network layer (layer 3)
- Data Link layer (layer 2)
- Physical layer (layer 1)

The OSI layers are divided into two groups. The top three layers define how the applications within the end stations communicate with each other and with users. The bottom four layers define how data is transmitted end to end. Figure 1.6 shows the three upper layers and their functions, and Figure 1.7 shows the four lower layers and their functions.

When you study Figure 1.6, understand that the user interfaces with the computer at the Application layer and also that the upper layers are responsible for applications communicating between hosts. Notice that none of the upper layers knows anything about networking or network addresses. That's the responsibility of the four bottom layers.

FIGURE 1.6   The upper layers

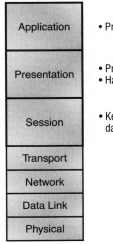

FIGURE 1.7   The lower layers

Transport	• Provides reliable or unreliable delivery • Performs error correction before retransmit
Network	• Provides logical addressing, which routers use for path determination
Data Link	• Combines packets into bytes and bytes into frames • Provides access to media using MAC address • Performs error detection not correction
Physical	• Moves bits between devices • Specifies voltage, wire speed, and pin-out of cables

In Figure 1.7, you can see that it's the four bottom layers that define how data is transferred through a physical wire or through switches and routers. These bottom layers also determine how to rebuild a data stream from a transmitting host to a destination host's application.

In this chapter I've discussed hubs, bridges, switches and routers, but where are these devices in relation to the OSI model? Hubs/repeaters are Physical layer devices, Bridges/Switches work at the Data Link layer, and Routers work at the Network layer. None of the network devices works at all seven of the OSI model's layer. The following network devices operate on all seven layers of the OSI model:

- Network management stations (NMSs)
- Web and application servers
- Gateways (not default gateways)
- Network hosts

Figure 1.8 summarizes the functions defined at each layer of the OSI model.

FIGURE 1.8   Layer functions

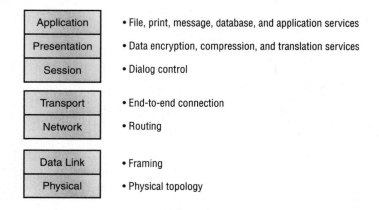

Application	• File, print, message, database, and application services
Presentation	• Data encryption, compression, and translation services
Session	• Dialog control
Transport	• End-to-end connection
Network	• Routing
Data Link	• Framing
Physical	• Physical topology

With this in hand, you're now ready to explore each layer's function in detail.

The Application Layer

The *Application layer* of the OSI model marks the spot where users actually communicate to the computer. This layer comes into play only when it's apparent that access to the network is going to be needed soon. Take the case of Internet Explorer (IE). You could uninstall every trace of networking components from a system, such as TCP/IP, the network interface card (NIC), and so on, and you could still use IE to view a local HTML document—no problem. But things would definitely get messy if you tried to do something like view an HTML document that must be retrieved using Hypertext Transfer Protocol (HTTP) or nab a file with File Transfer Protocol (FTP) or Trivial File Transfer Protocol (TFTP). That's because IE will respond to requests such as those by attempting to access the Application layer. And what's happening is that the Application layer is acting as an interface between the actual application program—which isn't at all part of the layered structure—and the next layer down by providing ways for the application to send information down through the protocol stack. In other words, IE doesn't truly reside within the Application layer; it interfaces with Application layer protocols when it needs to deal with remote resources.

The Application layer is also responsible for identifying and establishing the availability of the intended communication partner and determining whether sufficient resources for the intended communication exist.

These tasks are important because computer applications sometimes require more than only desktop resources. Often, they'll unite communicating components from more than one network application. Prime examples are file transfers and email, as well as enabling remote access, network management activities, client/server processes, and information location. Many network applications provide services for communication over enterprise networks, but for present and future internetworking, the need is fast developing to reach beyond the limits of current physical networking.

It's important to remember that the Application layer is acting as an interface between the actual application programs. This means that Microsoft Word, for example, does not reside at the Application layer but instead interfaces with the Application layer protocols. Chapter 2, "Internet Protocols," will present some programs that actually reside at the Application layer—for example, FTP and TFTP.

The Presentation Layer

The *Presentation layer* gets its name from its purpose: it presents data to the Application layer and is responsible for data translation and code formatting.

This layer is essentially a translator and provides coding and conversion functions. A successful data-transfer technique is to adapt the data into a standard format before transmission. Computers are configured to receive this generically formatted data and then convert the data into its native format for actual reading—for example, from Extended Binary

Coded Decimal Interchange Code (EBCDIC) to American Standard Code for Information Interchange (ASCII). By providing translation services, the Presentation layer ensures that data transferred from the Application layer of one system can be read by the Application layer of another one.

The OSI has protocol standards that define how standard data should be formatted. Tasks like data compression, decompression, encryption, and decryption are associated with this layer. Some Presentation layer standards are involved in multimedia operations too.

The Session Layer

The *Session layer* is responsible for setting up, managing, and then tearing down sessions between Presentation layer entities. This layer also provides dialogue control between devices, or nodes. It coordinates communication between systems and serves to organize their communication by offering three different modes: *simplex*, *half-duplex*, and *full duplex*. To sum up, the Session layer basically keeps one application's data separate from other applications' data.

The Transport Layer

The *Transport layer* segments and reassembles data into a data stream. Services located in the Transport layer segment and reassemble data from upper-layer applications and unite it onto the same data stream. They provide end-to-end data transport services and can establish a logical connection between the sending host and destination host on an internetwork.

Some of you are probably familiar with Transmission Control Protocol (TCP) and User Datagram Protocol (UDP) already. (But if you're not, no worries—I'll tell you all about them in Chapter 2.) If so, you know that both work at the Transport layer and that TCP is a reliable service and UDP is not. This means that application developers have more options because they have a choice between the two protocols when working with TCP/IP protocols.

The Transport layer is responsible for providing mechanisms for multiplexing upper-layer applications, establishing sessions, and tearing down virtual circuits. It also hides details of any network-dependent information from the higher layers by providing transparent data transfer.

> The term *reliable networking* can be used at the Transport layer. It means that acknowledgments, sequencing, and flow control will be used.

The Transport layer can be connectionless or connection-oriented. However, Cisco is mostly concerned with you understanding the connection-oriented portion of the Transport layer. The following sections provide the skinny on the connection-oriented (reliable) protocol of the Transport layer.

Flow Control

Data integrity is ensured at the Transport layer by maintaining *flow control* and by allowing applications to request reliable data transport between systems. Flow control prevents a sending host on one side of the connection from overflowing the buffers in the receiving host—an event that can result in lost data. Reliable data transport employs a connection-oriented communications session between systems, and the protocols involved ensure that the following will be achieved:

- The segments delivered are acknowledged back to the sender upon their reception.
- Any segments not acknowledged are retransmitted.
- Segments are sequenced back into their proper order upon arrival at their destination.
- A manageable data flow is maintained in order to avoid congestion, overloading, and data loss.

Some types of flow control are buffering, congestion avoidance, and windowing.

The purpose of flow control is to provide a means for the receiver to govern the amount of data sent by the sender.

Connection-Oriented Communication

In reliable transport operation, a device that wants to transmit sets up a connection-oriented communication with a remote device by creating a session. The transmitting device first establishes a connection-oriented session, called a *call setup* or a *three-way handshake*, with its peer system. Data is then transferred; when the transfer is finished, a call termination takes place to tear down the virtual circuit.

Figure 1.9 depicts a typical reliable session taking place between sending and receiving systems. Looking at it, you can see that both hosts' application programs begin by notifying their individual operating systems that a connection is about to be initiated. The two operating systems communicate by sending messages over the network confirming that the transfer is approved and that both sides are ready for it to take place. After all of this required synchronization takes place, a connection is fully established, and the data transfer begins (this virtual circuit setup is called overhead!).

While the information is being transferred between hosts, the two machines periodically check in with each other, communicating through their protocol software to ensure that all is going well and that the data is being received properly.

FIGURE 1.9   Establishing a connection-oriented session

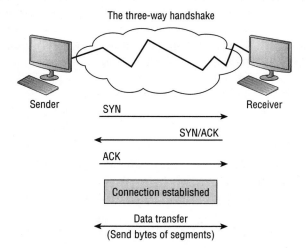

Here's a summary of the steps in the connection-oriented session—the three-way hand-shake—pictured in Figure 1.9:

1. The first "connection agreement" segment is a request for synchronization.

2. The second segments acknowledge the request and establish connection parameters—the rules—between hosts. These segments request that the receiver's sequencing is synchronized here as well so that a bidirectional connection is formed.

3. The final segment also is an acknowledgment. It notifies the destination host that the connection agreement has been accepted and that the actual connection has been established. Data transfer can now begin.

It sounds pretty simple, but things don't always flow so smoothly. Sometimes during a transfer, congestion can occur because a high-speed computer is generating data traffic a lot faster than the network can transfer. A bunch of computers simultaneously sending datagrams through a single gateway or destination can also botch things up nicely. In the latter case, a gateway or destination can become congested even though no single source caused the problem. In either case, the problem is basically akin to a freeway bottleneck—too much traffic for too small a capacity. It's not usually one car that's the problem; there are simply too many cars on that freeway.

So, what happens when a machine receives a flood of datagrams too quickly for it to process? It stores them in a memory section called a *buffer*. But this buffering action can solve the problem only if the datagrams are part of a small burst. If not and the datagram deluge continues, a device's memory will eventually be exhausted, its flood capacity will be exceeded, and it will react by discarding any additional datagrams that arrive.

No huge worries here, though. Because of the transport function, network flood control systems really work quite well. Instead of dumping data and allowing the data to be lost, the transport can issue a "not ready" indicator to the sender, or source, of the flood (as shown in Figure 1.10). This mechanism works kind of like a stoplight, signaling the sending device to stop transmitting segment traffic to its overwhelmed peer. After the peer receiver processes the segments already in its memory reservoir—its buffer—it sends out a "ready" transport indicator. When the machine waiting to transmit the rest of its datagrams receives this "go" indictor, it resumes its transmission.

FIGURE 1.10 Transmitting segments with flow control

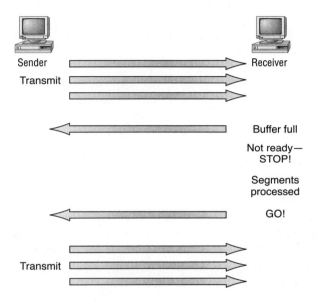

In fundamental, reliable, connection-oriented data transfer, datagrams are delivered to the receiving host in exactly the same sequence they're transmitted—and the transmission fails if this order is breached! If any data segments are lost, duplicated, or damaged along the way, a failure will occur. This problem is solved by having the receiving host acknowledge that it has received each and every data segment.

A service is considered connection-oriented if it has the following characteristics:

- A virtual circuit is set up (e.g., a three-way handshake).
- It uses sequencing.
- It uses acknowledgments.
- It uses flow control.

The types of flow control are buffering, windowing, and congestion avoidance.

Windowing

Ideally, data throughput happens quickly and efficiently. And as you can imagine, it would be slow if the transmitting machine had to wait for an acknowledgment after sending each segment. But because there's time available *after* the sender transmits the data segment and *before* it finishes processing acknowledgments from the receiving machine, the sender uses the break as an opportunity to transmit more data. The quantity of data segments (measured in bytes) that the transmitting machine is allowed to send without receiving an acknowledgment for them is called a *window*.

Windows are used to control the amount of outstanding, unacknowledged data segments.

So, the size of the window controls how much information is transferred from one end to the other. While some protocols quantify information by observing the number of packets, TCP/IP measures it by counting the number of bytes.

As you can see in Figure 1.11, there are two window sizes—one set to 1 and one set to 3.

FIGURE 1.11   Windowing

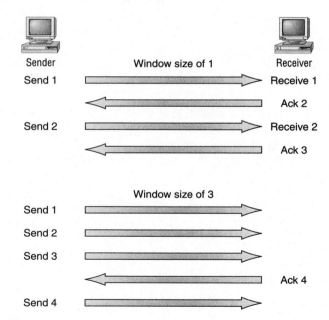

When you've configured a window size of 1, the sending machine waits for an acknowledgment for each data segment (measured in bytes) it transmits before transmitting another. If you've configured a window size of 3, it's allowed to transmit three bytes of data before an acknowledgment is received.

In this simplified example, both the sending and receiving machines are workstations. In reality, this is not done in simple, small numbers but in the amount of bytes that can be sent.

> If a receiving host fails to receive all the bytes that it should acknowledge, the host can improve the communication session by decreasing the window size.

Acknowledgments

Reliable data delivery ensures the integrity of a stream of data sent from one machine to the other through a fully functional data link. It guarantees that the data won't be duplicated or lost. This is achieved through something called *positive acknowledgment with retransmission*—a technique that requires a receiving machine to communicate with the transmitting source by sending an acknowledgment message back to the sender when it receives data. The sender documents each segment it sends and waits for this acknowledgment before sending the next segment. When it sends a segment, the transmitting machine starts a timer and retransmits if it expires before an acknowledgment is returned from the receiving end.

In Figure 1.12, the sending machine transmits segments 1, 2, and 3. The receiving node acknowledges it has received them by requesting segment 4. When it receives the acknowledgment, the sender then transmits segments 4, 5, and 6. If segment 5 doesn't make it to the destination, the receiving node acknowledges that event with a request for the segment to be resent. The sending machine will then resend the lost segment and wait for an acknowledgment, which it must receive in order to move on to the transmission of segment 7.

FIGURE 1.12   Transport layer reliable delivery

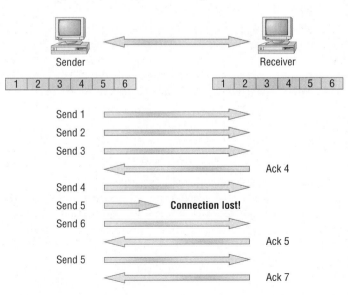

The Network Layer

The *Network layer* (also called layer 3) manages device addressing, tracks the location of devices on the network, and determines the best way to move data, which means that the Network layer must transport traffic between devices that aren't locally attached. Routers (layer 3 devices) are specified at the Network layer and provide the routing services within an internetwork.

It happens like this: First, when a packet is received on a router interface, the destination IP address is checked. If the packet isn't destined for that particular router, it will look up the destination network address in the routing table. Once the router chooses an exit interface, the packet will be sent to that interface to be framed and sent out on the local network. If the router can't find an entry for the packet's destination network in the routing table, the router drops the packet.

Two types of packets are used at the Network layer: data and route updates.

Data Packets   Data packets are used to transport user data through the internetwork. Protocols used to support data traffic are called *routed protocols*; examples of routed protocols are IP and IPv6. You'll learn about IP addressing in Chapters 2 and 3. (IPv6 is beyond the scope of this book. It is explained in *CCNA: Cisco Certified Network Associate Study Guide*.)

Route Update Packets   Route update packets are used to update neighboring routers about the networks connected to all routers within the internetwork. Protocols that send route update packets are called *routing protocols*; examples of some common ones are Routing Information Protocol (RIP), RIP version 2 (RIPv2), Enhanced Interior Gateway Routing Protocol (EIGRP), and Open Shortest Path First (OSPF). Route update packets are used to help build and maintain routing tables on each router.

In Figure 1.13, I've given you an example of a routing table. The routing table used in a router includes the following information:

Network Addresses   Protocol-specific network addresses. A router must maintain a routing table for individual routed protocols because each routing protocol keeps track of a network with a different addressing scheme (IP, IPv6, and Internetwork Packet Exchange [IPX], for example). Think of it as a street sign in each of the different languages spoken by the residents that live on a particular street. So, if there were American, Spanish, and French folks on a street named Cat, the sign would read Cat/Gato/Chat.

Interface   The exit interface a packet will take when destined for a specific network.

Metric   The distance to the remote network. Different routing protocols use different ways of computing this distance. I'm going to cover routing protocols in Chapter 6, but for now, know that some routing protocols (namely RIP) use something called a *hop count* (the number of routers a packet passes through en route to a remote network), while others use bandwidth, delay of the line, or even tick count ($1/18$ of a second).

FIGURE 1.13   Routing table used in a router

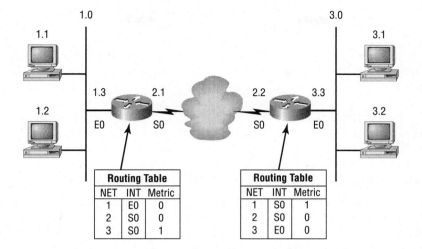

And as I mentioned earlier, routers break up broadcast domains, which means that by default, broadcasts aren't forwarded through a router. Do you remember why this is a good thing? Routers also break up collision domains, but you can also do that using layer 2 (Data Link layer) switches. Because each interface in a router represents a separate network, it must be assigned unique network identification numbers, and each host on the network connected to that router must use the same network number. Figure 1.14 shows how a router works in an internetwork.

FIGURE 1.14   A router in an internetwork

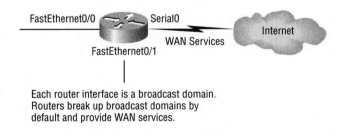

Here are some points about routers that you should really commit to memory:

- Routers, by default, will not forward any broadcast or multicast packets.
- Routers use the logical address in a Network layer header to determine the next hop router to forward the packet to.

- Routers can use access lists, created by an administrator, to control security on the types of packets that are allowed to enter or exit an interface.

- Routers can provide layer 2 bridging functions, if needed, and can simultaneously route through the same interface.

- Layer 3 devices (routers in this case) provide connections between VLANs.

- Routers can provide quality of service (QoS) for specific types of network traffic.

> **NOTE** Switching is covered in Chapter 7, "Layer 2 Switching."

The Data Link Layer

The *Data Link layer* provides the physical transmission of the data and handles error notification, network topology, and flow control. This means that the Data Link layer will ensure that messages are delivered to the proper device on a LAN using hardware addresses and will translate messages from the Network layer into bits for the Physical layer to transmit.

The Data Link layer formats the message into pieces, each called a *data frame*, and adds a customized header containing the hardware destination and source address. This added information forms a sort of capsule that surrounds the original message in much the same way that engines, navigational devices, and other tools were attached to the lunar modules of the Apollo project. These various pieces of equipment were useful only during certain stages of space flight and were stripped off the module and discarded when their designated stage was complete. Data traveling through networks is similar.

Figure 1.15 shows the Data Link layer with the Ethernet and Institute of Electrical and Electronics Engineers (IEEE) specifications. When you check it out, notice that the IEEE 802.2 standard is used in conjunction with and adds functionality to the other IEEE standards.

FIGURE 1.15 Data Link layer

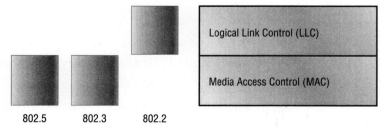

				Logical Link Control (LLC)
				Media Access Control (MAC)
802.5	802.3	802.2		

It's important for you to understand that routers, which work at the Network layer, don't care at all about where a particular host is located. They're concerned only about where networks are located and the best way to reach them—including remote ones. Routers are totally obsessive when it comes to networks. And for once, this is a good thing! It's the Data Link layer that's responsible for the actual unique identification of each device that resides on a local network.

To allow a host to send packets to individual hosts on a local network as well as transmit packets between routers, the Data Link layer uses hardware addressing. Each time a packet is sent between routers, it's framed with control information at the Data Link layer, but that information is stripped off at the receiving router, and only the original packet is left completely intact. This framing of the packet continues for each hop until the packet is finally delivered to the correct receiving host. It's really important to understand that the packet itself is never altered along the route; it's only encapsulated with the type of control information required for it to be properly passed on to the different media types.

The IEEE Ethernet Data Link layer has two sublayers:

Media Access Control (MAC) 802.3   Defines how packets are placed on the media. Contention media access is "first come/first served" access where everyone shares the same bandwidth—which is where the name comes from. Physical addressing is defined here, as well as logical topologies. What's a logical topology? It's the signal path through a physical topology. Line discipline, error notification (not correction), ordered delivery of frames, and optional flow control can also be used at this sublayer.

Logical Link Control (LLC) 802.2   Responsible for identifying Network layer protocols and then encapsulating them. An LLC header tells the Data Link layer what to do with a packet once a frame is received. It works like this: a host will receive a frame and look in the LLC header to find out where the packet is destined—say, the IP protocol at the Network layer. The LLC can also provide flow control and sequencing of control bits.

The switches and bridges I talked about near the beginning of the chapter both work at the Data Link layer and filter the network using hardware (MAC) addresses. You will look at these in the following section.

Switches and Bridges at the Data Link Layer

Layer 2 switching is considered hardware-based bridging because it uses specialized hardware called an *application-specific integrated circuit (ASIC)*. ASICs can run up to gigabit speeds with very low latency rates.

Latency is the time measured from when a frame enters a port to the time it exits a port.

Bridges and switches read each frame as it passes through the network. The layer 2 device then puts the source hardware address in a filter table and keeps track of which port the frame was received on. This information (logged in the bridge's or switch's filter table) is what helps the machine determine the location of the specific sending device. Figure 1.16 shows a switch in an internetwork.

FIGURE 1.16   A switch in an internetwork

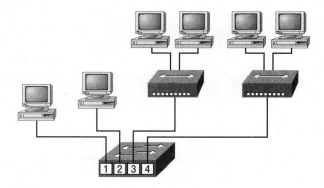

Each segment has its own collision domain.
All segments are in the same broadcast domain.

The real estate business is all about location, location, location, and it's the same way for both layer 2 and layer 3 devices. Though both need to be able to negotiate the network, it's crucial to remember that they're concerned with very different parts of it. Primarily, layer 3 machines (such as routers) need to locate specific networks, whereas layer 2 machines (switches and bridges) need to eventually locate specific devices. So, networks are to routers what individual devices are to switches and bridges. And routing tables that "map" the internetwork are for routers what filter tables that "map" individual devices are for switches and bridges.

After a filter table is built on the layer 2 device, it will forward frames only to the segment where the destination hardware address is located. If the destination device is on the same segment as the frame, the layer 2 device will block the frame from going to any other segments. If the destination is on a different segment, the frame can be transmitted only to that segment. This is called *transparent bridging.*

When a switch interface receives a frame with a destination hardware address that isn't found in the device's filter table, it forwards the frame to all connected segments. If the unknown device that was sent the "mystery frame" replies to this forwarding action, the switch updates its filter table regarding that device's location. But in the event the destination address of the transmitting frame is a broadcast address, the switch will forward all broadcasts to every connected segment by default.

All devices that the broadcast is forwarded to are considered to be in the same broadcast domain. This can be a problem; layer 2 devices propagate layer 2 broadcast storms that choke performance, and the only way to stop a broadcast storm from propagating through an internetwork is with a layer 3 device—a router.

The biggest benefit of using switches instead of hubs in your internetwork is that each switch port is actually its own collision domain. (Conversely, a hub creates one large collision domain.) But even armed with a switch, you still can't break up broadcast domains. Neither switches nor bridges will do that. They'll typically simply forward all broadcasts instead.

Another benefit of LAN switching over hub-centered implementations is that each device on every segment plugged into a switch can transmit simultaneously—at least, they can as long as there is only one host on each port and a hub isn't plugged into a switch port. As you might have guessed, hubs allow only one device per network segment to communicate at a time.

The Physical Layer

Finally, arriving at the bottom, you'll find that the *Physical layer* does two things: it sends bits and receives bits. Bits come in values of only 1 or 0—a Morse code with numerical values. The Physical layer communicates directly with the various types of actual communication media. Different kinds of media represent these bit values in different ways. Some use audio tones, while others employ *state transitions*—changes in voltage from high to low and low to high. Specific protocols are needed for each type of media to describe the proper bit patterns to be used, how data is encoded into media signals, and the various qualities of the physical media's attachment interface.

The Physical layer specifies the electrical, mechanical, procedural, and functional requirements for activating, maintaining, and deactivating a physical link between end systems. This layer is also where you identify the interface between the *data terminal equipment (DTE)* and the *data communication equipment (DCE)*. (Some old phone-company employees still call DCE data circuit-terminating equipment.) The DCE is usually located at the service provider, while the DTE is the attached device. The services available to the DTE are most often accessed via a modem or *channel service unit/data service unit (CSU/DSU)*.

The Physical layer's connectors and different physical topologies are defined by the OSI as standards, allowing disparate systems to communicate. The CCENT objectives are interested only in the IEEE Ethernet standards.

Hubs at the Physical Layer

A *hub* is really a multiple-port repeater. A repeater receives a digital signal and reamplifies or regenerates that signal and then forwards it out all active ports without looking at any data. An active hub does the same thing. Any digital signal received from a segment on a hub port is regenerated or reamplified and transmitted out all ports on the hub. This means all devices plugged into a hub are in the same collision domain as well as in the same broadcast domain. Figure 1.17 shows a hub in a network.

FIGURE 1.17   A hub in a network

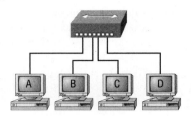

All devices in the same collision domain.
All devices in the same broadcast domain.
Devices share the same bandwidth.

Hubs, like repeaters, don't examine any of the traffic as it enters and is then transmitted out to the other parts of the physical media. Every device connected to the hub, or hubs, must listen if a device transmits. A physical star network—where the hub is a central device and cables extend in all directions out from it—is the type of topology a hub creates. Visually, the design really does resemble a star, whereas Ethernet networks run a logical bus topology, meaning that the signal has to run through the network from end to end.

Hubs and repeaters can be used to enlarge the area covered by a single LAN segment, although I do not recommend this. LAN switches are affordable for almost every situation.

Ethernet Networking

Ethernet is a contention-based media access method that allows all hosts on a network to share the same bandwidth of a link. Ethernet is popular because it's readily scalable, meaning that it's comparatively easy to integrate new technologies, such as upgrading from Fast Ethernet to Gigabit Ethernet, into an existing network infrastructure. It's also relatively simple to implement in the first place, and with it, troubleshooting is reasonably straightforward. Ethernet uses both Data Link and Physical layer specifications, and this chapter will give you both the Data Link layer and Physical layer information you need to effectively implement, troubleshoot, and maintain an Ethernet network.

Collision Domain

The term *collision domain* is an Ethernet term that refers to a particular network scenario wherein one device sends a packet out on a network segment, thereby forcing every other device on that same physical network segment to pay attention to it. This can be bad because if two devices on one physical segment transmit at the same time, a *collision event*—a situation where each device's digital signals interfere with another on the wire—occurs and forces the devices to retransmit later. Collisions can have a dramatically negative effect on network performance, so they're definitely something you want to avoid!

The situation I just described is typically found in a hub environment where each host segment connects to a hub that represents only one collision domain and one broadcast domain.

Broadcast Domain

Here's the written definition: a *broadcast domain* refers to the set of all devices on a network segment that hear all the broadcasts sent on that segment.

Even though a broadcast domain is typically a boundary delimited by physical media like switches and routers, it can also reference a logical division of a network segment where all hosts can reach each other via a Data Link layer (hardware address) broadcast.

That's the basic story, so now let's take a look at a collision detection mechanism used in half-duplex Ethernet.

CSMA/CD

Ethernet networking uses *Carrier Sense Multiple Access with Collision Detection (CSMA/CD)*, a protocol that helps devices share the bandwidth evenly without having two devices transmit at the same time on the network medium. CSMA/CD was created to overcome the problem of those collisions that occur when packets are transmitted simultaneously from different nodes. And trust me—good collision management is crucial, because when a node transmits in a CSMA/CD network, all the other nodes on the network receive and examine that transmission. Only bridges and routers can effectively prevent a transmission from propagating throughout the entire network!

So, how does the CSMA/CD protocol work? Let's start by taking a look at Figure 1.18.

When a host wants to transmit over the network, it first checks for the presence of a digital signal on the wire. If all is clear (no other host is transmitting), the host will then proceed with its transmission. But it doesn't stop there. The transmitting host constantly monitors the wire to make sure no other hosts begin transmitting. If the host detects another signal on the wire, it sends out an extended jam signal that causes all nodes on the segment to stop sending data (think busy signal). The nodes respond to that jam signal by waiting a while before attempting to transmit again. Backoff algorithms determine when the colliding stations can retransmit. If collisions keep occurring after 15 tries, the nodes attempting to transmit will then timeout. Pretty clean!

FIGURE 1.18 CSMA/CD

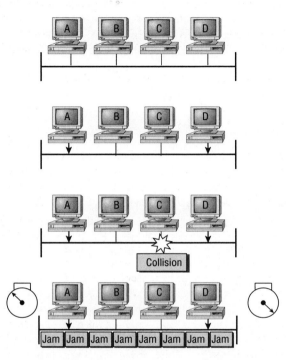

Carrier Sense Multiple Access with Collision Detection (CSMA/CD)

When a collision occurs on an Ethernet LAN, the following happens:

1. A jam signal informs all devices that a collision occurred.

2. The collision invokes a random backoff algorithm.

3. Each device on the Ethernet segment stops transmitting for a short time until their backoff timers expire.

4. All hosts have equal priority to transmit after the timers have expired.

The following are the effects of having a CSMA/CD network sustaining heavy collisions:

- Delay
- Low throughput
- Congestion

Backoff on an Ethernetnetwork is the retransmission delay that's enforced when a collision occurs. When a collision occurs, a host will resume transmission after the forced time delay has expired. After this backoff delay period has expired, all stations have equal priority to transmit data.

In the following sections, I am going to cover Ethernet in detail at both the Data Link layer (layer 2) and the Physical layer (layer 1).

Half- and Full-Duplex Ethernet

Half-duplex Ethernet is defined in the original IEEE 802.3 Ethernet; Cisco says it uses only one wire pair with a digital signal running in both directions on the wire. Certainly, the IEEE specifications discuss the process of half-duplex somewhat differently, but what Cisco is talking about is a general sense of what is happening here with Ethernet.

It also uses the CSMA/CD protocol to help prevent collisions and to permit retransmitting if a collision does occur. If a hub is attached to a switch, it must operate in half-duplex mode because the end stations must be able to detect collisions. Half-duplex Ethernet is only about 30 to 40 percent efficient as Cisco sees it because a large 100BaseT network will usually give you only 30Mbps to 40Mbps under heavy load, at most.

But full-duplex Ethernet uses two pairs of wires at the same time instead of one wire pair like half-duplex. And full duplex uses a point-to-point connection between the transmitter of the transmitting device and the receiver of the receiving device. This means that with full-duplex data transfer, you get a faster data transfer compared to half-duplex. And because the transmitted data is sent on a different set of wires than the received data, no collisions will occur.

The reason you don't need to worry about collisions is because now it's like a freeway with multiple lanes instead of the single-lane road provided by half duplex. Full-duplex Ethernet is supposed to offer 100 percent efficiency in both directions—for example, you can get 20Mbps with a 10Mbps Ethernet running full duplex or 200Mbps for Fast Ethernet. But this rate is something known as an *aggregate rate*, which translates as "you're supposed to get" 100 percent efficiency. There are no guarantees, in networking as in life.

Full-duplex Ethernet can be used in five situations:

- With a connection from a switch to a host
- With a connection from a switch to a switch
- With a connection from a host to a host using a crossover cable
- With a connection from a router to a router
- With a connection from a switch to a router

Full-duplex Ethernet requires a point-to-point connection when only two nodes are present. You can run full duplex with just about any device except a hub.

Now, if it's capable of all that speed, why wouldn't it deliver? Well, when a full-duplex Ethernet port is powered on, it first connects to the remote end and then negotiates with the other end of the Fast Ethernet link. This is called an *autodetect mechanism*. This mechanism first decides on the exchange capability, which means it checks to see whether it can run at 10Mbps or 100Mbps. It then checks to see whether it can run full duplex, and if it can't, it will run half duplex.

 Remember that half-duplex Ethernet shares a collision domain and provides a lower effective throughput than full-duplex Ethernet, which typically has a private per-port collision domain and a higher effective throughput.

Last, remember these important points:

- There are no collisions in full-duplex mode.
- A dedicated switch port is required for each full-duplex node.
- Both the host network card and the switch port must be capable of operating in full-duplex mode.

Now let's take a look at how Ethernet works at the Data Link layer.

Ethernet at the Data Link Layer

Ethernet at the Data Link layer is responsible for Ethernet addressing, commonly referred to as *hardware addressing* or *MAC addressing*. Ethernet is also responsible for framing packets received from the Network layer and preparing them for transmission on the local network through the Ethernet contention media access method.

Ethernet Addressing

Here's where I get into how Ethernet addressing works. It uses the MAC address burned into each and every Ethernet NIC. The MAC, or hardware, address is a 48-bit (6-byte) address written in a hexadecimal format.

Figure 1.19 shows the 48-bit MAC addresses and how the bits are divided.

FIGURE 1.19   Ethernet addressing using MAC addresses

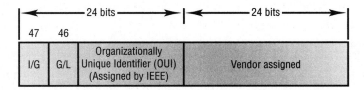

The *organizationally unique identifier (OUI)* is assigned by the IEEE to an organization. It's composed of 24 bits, or 3 bytes. The organization, in turn, assigns a globally administered address (24 bits, or 3 bytes) that is unique (supposedly) to each and every adapter it manufactures. Look closely at the figure. The high-order bit is the Individual/ Group (I/G) bit. When it has a value of 0, you can assume that the address is the MAC address of a device and may well appear in the source portion of the MAC header. When it is a 1, you can assume that the address represents either a broadcast or multicast address in Ethernet or a broadcast or functional address in Token Ring (TR) and Fiber Distributed Data Interface (FDDI).

The next bit is the global/local bit, or just G/L bit (also known as U/L, where *U* means *universal*). When set to zero, this bit represents a globally administered address (as in administered by the IEEE). When the bit is a 1, it represents a locally governed and administered address. The low-order 24 bits of an Ethernet address represent a locally administered or manufacturer-assigned code. This portion commonly starts with 24 zeros for the first card made and continues in order until there are 24 ones for the last (16,777,216th) card made. You'll find that many manufacturers use these same six hex digits as the last six characters of their serial number on the same card.

Before I get into working with the TCP/IP protocol and IP addressing (covered in Chapter 2), it's really important for you to truly understand the differences between binary, decimal, and hexadecimal numbers and how to convert one format into the other.

So, I'll start with binary numbering. It's pretty simple, really. The digits used are limited to either a 1 (one) or a 0 (zero), and each digit is called a bit (short for *bi*nary dig*it*). Typically, you count either 4 or 8 bits together, with these being referred to as a *nibble* and a *byte*, respectively.

What is interesting in binary numbering is the value represented in a decimal format— the typical decimal format being the base-10 number scheme that we've all used since kindergarten. The binary numbers are placed in a value spot: starting at the right and moving left, with each spot having double the value of the previous spot.

Table 1.1 shows the decimal values of each bit location in a nibble and a byte. Remember, a nibble is 4 bits and a byte is 8 bits.

TABLE 1.1   Binary values

Nibble values	Byte values
8 4 2 1	128 64 32 16 8 4 2 1

What all this means is that if a one digit (1) is placed in a value spot, then the nibble or byte takes on that decimal value and adds it to any other value spots that have a 1. And if a zero (0) is placed in a bit spot, you don't count that value.

Let me clarify things. If you have a 1 placed in each spot of your nibble, you would then add up 8 + 4 + 2 + 1, to give you a maximum value of 15. Another example for your nibble values would be 1010; that means that the 8 bit and the 2 bit are turned on, which equals a decimal value of 10. If you have a nibble binary value of 0110, then your decimal value would be 6, because the 4 and 2 bits are turned on.

But the byte values can add up to a value that's significantly higher than 15. This is how: if you counted every bit as a one (1), then the byte binary value would look like this (remember, 8 bits equal a byte): 11111111.

You would then count up every bit spot because each is turned on. It would look like this, which demonstrates the maximum value of a byte:

128 + 64 + 32 + 16 + 8 + 4 + 2 + 1 = 255

There are plenty of other decimal values that a binary number can equal. Let's work through a few examples:

10010110

Which bits are on? The 128, 16, 4, and 2 bits are on, so you just add them up: 128 + 16 + 4 + 2 = 150.

01101100

Which bits are on? The 64, 32, 8, and 4 bits are on, so you just need to add them up: 64 + 32 + 8 + 4 = 108.

11101000

Which bits are on? The 128, 64, 32, and 8 bits are on, so just add up the values: 128 + 64 + 32 + 8 = 232.

Table 1.2 is a table you should memorize before braving the IP sections in Chapter 3 and Chapter 4, "Cisco's Internetworking Operating System (IOS)."

TABLE 1.2   Binary to decimal memorization chart

Binary value	Decimal value
10000000	128
11000000	192
11100000	224
11110000	240
11111000	248
11111100	252
11111110	254
11111111	255

Hexadecimal addressing is completely different from binary or decimal—it's converted by reading nibbles, not bytes. By using a nibble, you can convert these bits to hex pretty simply. First, understand that the hexadecimal addressing scheme uses only the numbers 0 through 9. And since the numbers 10, 11, 12, and so on, can't be used (because they are two-digit numbers), the letters *A*, *B*, *C*, *D*, *E*, and *F* are used to represent 10, 11, 12, 13, 14, and 15, respectively.

Hex is short for *hexadecimal*, which is a numbering system that uses the first six letters of the alphabet (*A* through *F*) to extend beyond the available 10 digits in the decimal system.

Table 1.3 shows both the binary value and the decimal value for each hexadecimal digit.

TABLE 1.3 Hex to binary to decimal chart

Hexadecimal value	Binary value	Decimal value
0	0000	0
1	0001	1
2	0010	2
3	0011	3
4	0100	4
5	0101	5
6	0110	6
7	0111	7
8	1000	8
9	1001	9
A	1010	10
B	1011	11
C	1100	12

TABLE 1.3   Hex to binary to decimal chart *(continued)*

Hexadecimal value	Binary value	Decimal value
D	1101	13
E	1110	14
F	1111	15

Did you notice that the first 10 hexadecimal digits (0–9) are the same value as the decimal values? If not, look again. This handy fact makes those values super easy to convert.

So, suppose you have something like this: 0x6A. (Sometimes Cisco likes to put *0x* in front of characters so you know that they are a hex value. It doesn't have any other special meaning.) What are the binary and decimal values? All you have to remember is that each hex character is one nibble and two hex characters together make a byte. To figure out the binary value, you need to put the hex characters into two nibbles and then put them together into a byte; 6 = 0110 and A (which is 10 in hex) = 1010, so the complete byte would be 01101010.

To convert from binary to hex, just take the byte and break it into nibbles. Here's what I mean.

Say you have the binary number 01010101. First, break it into nibbles—0101 and 0101—with the value of each nibble being 5 since the 1 and 4 bits are on. This makes the hex answer 0x55. And in decimal format, the binary number is 01010101, which converts to 64 + 16 + 4 + 1 = 85.

Here's another binary number: 11001100

Your answer would be 1100 = 12 and 1100 = 12 (therefore, it's converted to CC in hex). The decimal conversion answer would be 128 + 64 + 8 + 4 = 204.

One more example, then you need to get working on the Physical layer. Suppose you had the following binary number:

10110101

The hex answer would be 0xB5, since 1011 converts to B and 0101 converts to 5 in hex value. The decimal equivalent is 128 + 32 + 16 + 4 + 1 = 181.

See Written Lab 1.4 for more practice with binary/hex/decimal conversion.

Ethernet Frames

The Data Link layer is responsible for combining bits into bytes and bytes into frames. Frames are used at the Data Link layer to encapsulate packets handed down from the Network layer for transmission on a type of media access.

The function of Ethernet stations is to pass data frames between each other using a group of bits known as a *MAC frame format*. This provides error detection from a cyclic redundancy check (CRC). But remember—this is error detection, not error correction. An 802.3 frame and Ethernet_II frame are shown in Figure 1.20.

FIGURE 1.20   802.3 and Ethernet frame formats

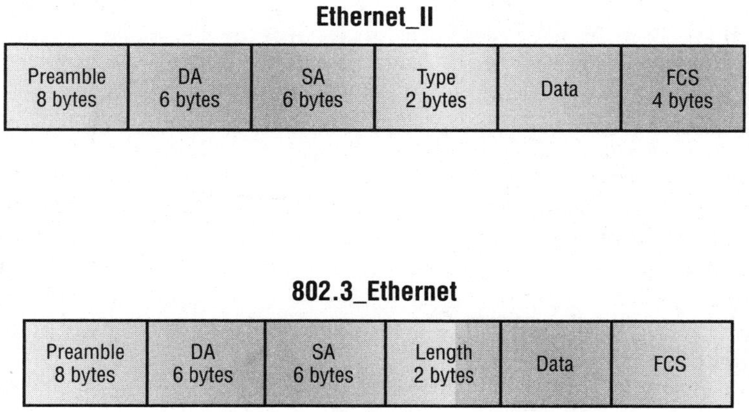

Ethernet_II

Preamble 8 bytes	DA 6 bytes	SA 6 bytes	Type 2 bytes	Data	FCS 4 bytes

802.3_Ethernet

Preamble 8 bytes	DA 6 bytes	SA 6 bytes	Length 2 bytes	Data	FCS

Encapsulating a frame within a different type of frame is called *tunneling*.

The following are the details of the different fields in the 802.3 and Ethernet frame types:

Preamble   An alternating 1,0 pattern provides a 5MHz clock at the start of each packet, which allows the receiving devices to lock the incoming bit stream. The preamble is seven octets.

Start Frame Delimiter (SFD)/Synch   The SFD is one octet (synch). The SFD is 10101011, where the last pair of 1s allows the receiver to come into the alternating 1,0 pattern somewhere in the middle and still sync up and detect the beginning of the data.

Destination Address (DA)   This transmits a 48-bit value using the least significant bit (LSB) first. The DA is used by receiving stations to determine whether an incoming packet is addressed to a particular node. The destination address can be an individual address or a broadcast or multicast MAC address. Remember that a broadcast is all 1s (or Fs in hex) and is sent to all devices, but a multicast is sent only to a similar subset of nodes on a network.

Source Address (SA)   The SA is a 48-bit MAC address used to identify the transmitting device, and it is transmitted LSB first. Broadcast and multicast address formats are illegal within the SA field.

Length or Type   802.3 uses a Length field, but the Ethernet frame uses a Type field to identify the Network layer protocol. 802.3 cannot identify the upper-layer protocol and must be used with a proprietary LAN—IPX, for example.

Data   This is a packet sent down to the Data Link layer from the Network layer. The size can vary from 46 to 1500 bytes.

Frame Check Sequence (FCS)   FCS is a field at the end of the frame that's used to store the Cyclic Redundancy Check (CRC) answer. The CRC is a mathematical algorithm that's run when each frame is built. When a receiving host receives the frame and runs the CRC, the answer should be the same. If not, the frame is discarded assuming errors have occurred. Let's pause here for a minute and take a look at some frames caught on a trusty network analyzer. You can see that the following frame has only three fields: Destination, Source, and Type (shown as Protocol Type on this analyzer):

```
Destination:    00:60:f5:00:1f:27
Source:         00:60:f5:00:1f:2c
Protocol Type: 08-00 IP
```

This is an Ethernet_II frame. Notice that the type field is IP, or 08-00 (mostly just referred to as 0x800) in hexadecimal.

The next frame has the same fields, so it must be an Ethernet_II frame too:

```
Destination:    ff:ff:ff:ff:ff:ff Ethernet Broadcast
Source:         02:07:01:22:de:a4
Protocol Type: 08-00 IP
```

Did you notice that this frame was a broadcast? You can tell because the destination hardware address is all 1s in binary or all *F*s in hexadecimal.

Let's take a look at one more Ethernet_II frame. You can see that the Ethernet frame is the same Ethernet_II frame you use with the IPv4 routed protocol, but the type field has 0x86dd when the frame is carrying IPv6 data, and when you have IPv4 data, the frame uses 0x0800 in the protocol field:

```
Destination: IPv6-Neighbor-Discovery_00:01:00:03 (33:33:00:01:00:03)
Source: Aopen_3e:7f:dd (00:01:80:3e:7f:dd)
Type: IPv6 (0x86dd)
```

This is the beauty of the Ethernet_II frame. Because of the protocol field, you can run any Network layer routed protocol, and it will carry the data because it can identify the Network layer protocol.

Ethernet at the Physical Layer

Ethernet was first implemented by a group called DIX (Digital, Intel, and Xerox). It created and implemented the first Ethernet LAN specification, which the IEEE used to create the

IEEE 802.3 Committee. This was a 10Mbps network that ran on coax and then eventually twisted-pair and fiber physical media.

The IEEE extended the 802.3 Committee to two new committees known as 802.3u (Fast Ethernet) and 802.3ab (Gigabit Ethernet on category 5) and then finally 802.3ae (10Gbps over fiber and coax).

Figure 1.21 shows the IEEE 802.3 and original Ethernet Physical layer specifications.

FIGURE 1.21   Ethernet Physical layer specifications

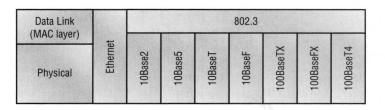

When designing your LAN, it's really important to understand the different types of Ethernet media available to you. Sure, it would be great to just run Gigabit Ethernet to each desktop and 10Gbps between switches, but that's not always feasible. But if you mix and match the different types of Ethernet media methods currently available, you can come up with a cost-effective network solution that works great.

The Electronic Industries Association and the newer Telecommunications Industry Alliance (EIA/TIA) is the standards body that creates the Physical layer specifications for Ethernet. The EIA/TIA specifies that Ethernet use a *registered jack (RJ) connector* on *unshielded twisted-pair (UTP)* cabling (RJ45). However, the industry is moving toward calling this just an 8-pin modular connector.

Each Ethernet cable type that is specified by the EIA/TIA has inherent attenuation, which is defined as the loss of signal strength as it travels the length of a cable and is measured in decibels (dB). The cabling used in corporate and home markets is measured in categories. A higher-quality cable will have a higher-rated category and lower attenuation. For example, category 5 is better than category 3 because category 5 cables have more wire twists per foot and therefore less crosstalk. Crosstalk is the unwanted signal interference from adjacent pairs in the cable.

Here are the original IEEE 802.3 standards:

10Base2   10Mbps, baseband technology, up to 185 meters in length. Known as *thinnet* and can support up to 30 workstations on a single segment. Uses a physical and logical bus with BNC connectors and thin coaxial cable. The 10 means 10Mbps, *Base* means baseband technology (which is a signaling method for communication on the network), and the 2 means almost 200 meters. 10Base2 Ethernet cards use BNC and T-connectors to connect to a network. (BNC stands for British Naval Connector, Bayonet Neill Concelman, or Bayonet Nut.)

10Base5   10Mbps, baseband technology, up to 500 meters in length using thick coaxial cable, known as *thicknet*. Uses a physical and logical bus with AUI connectors up to 2,500 meters with repeaters and 1,024 users for all segments.

10BaseT   10Mbps using category 3 Unshielded Twisted Pair (UTP) wiring for runs up to 100 meters. Unlike with the 10Base2 and 10Base5 networks, each device must connect into a hub or switch, and you can have only one host per segment or wire. Uses an RJ45 connector (8-pin modular connector) with a physical star topology and a logical bus.

Each of the 802.3 standards defines an AUI, which allows a one-bit-at-a-time transfer to the Physical layer from the Data Link media access method. This allows the MAC to remain constant but means the Physical layer can support any existing and new technologies. The original AUI interface was a 15-pin connector, which allowed a transceiver (transmitter/receiver) that provided a 15-pin-to-twisted-pair conversion or 15-pin-to-coax conversion.

There's an issue, though—the AUI interface can't support 100Mbps Ethernet because of the high frequencies involved. So, 100Base-T needed a new interface, and the 802.3u specifications created one called the Media Independent Interface (MII), which provides 100Mbps throughput. The MII uses a nibble, which you of course remember is defined as 4 bits. Gigabit Ethernet uses a Gigabit Media Independent Interface (GMII) and transmits 8 bits at a time. 802.3u (Fast Ethernet) is compatible with 802.3 Ethernet because they share the same physical characteristics. Fast Ethernet and Ethernet use the same maximum transmission unit (MTU) and the same MAC mechanisms, and they both preserve the frame format that is used by 10BaseT Ethernet. Basically, Fast Ethernet is just based on an extension to the IEEE 802.3 specification, and because of that, it offers a speed increase of 10 times that of 10BaseT.

Here are the expanded IEEE Ethernet 802.3 standards, starting with Fast Ethernet:

100Base-TX (IEEE 802.3u)   100Base-TX, most commonly known as Fast Ethernet, uses EIA/TIA category 5, 5E, or 6 UTP two-pair wiring. One user per segment; up to 100 meters long. It uses an RJ-45 connector with a physical star topology and a logical bus.

100Base-FX (IEEE 802.3u)   Uses fiber cabling 62.5/125-micron multimode fiber. Point-to-point topology; up to 412 meters long. It uses ST and SC connectors, which are media-interface connectors.

1000Base-CX (IEEE 802.3z)   Copper twisted-pair called *twinax* (a balanced coaxial pair) that can run only up to 25 meters and uses a special 9-pin connector known as the High Speed Serial Data Connector (HSSDC).

1000Base-T (IEEE 802.3ab)   Category 5, four-pair UTP wiring up to 100 meters long up to 1Gbps.

1000Base-SX (IEEE 802.3z)   The implementation of 1 Gigabit Ethernet running over multimode fiber-optic cable (instead of copper twisted-pair cable) and using short wavelength laser. Multimode fiber (MMF) using 62.5- and 50-micron core; uses an 850 nanometer (nm) laser and can go up to 220 meters with 62.5-micron or 550 meters with 50-micron.

1000Base-LX (IEEE 802.3z)   Single-mode fiber that uses a 9-micron core and 1300nm laser and can go from 3 kilometers up to 10 kilometers.

10GBase-T   10GBase-T is a standard proposed by the IEEE 802.3an committee to provide 10Gbps connections over conventional UTP cables (category 5e, 6, or 7 cables). 10GBase-T allows the conventional RJ-45 used for Ethernet LANs. It can support signal transmission at the full 100-meter distance specified for LAN wiring.

The following are all part of the IEEE 802.3ae standard:

10GBase-Short Range (SR) An implementation of 10 Gigabit Ethernet that uses short-wavelength lasers at 850nm over multimode fiber. It has a maximum transmission distance of between 2 and 300 meters, depending on the size and quality of the fiber.

10GBase-Long Range (LR) An implementation of 10 Gigabit Ethernet that uses long-wavelength lasers at 1,310nm over single-mode fiber. It also has a maximum transmission distance between 2 meters and 10km, depending on the size and quality of the fiber.

10GBase-Extended Range (ER) An implementation of 10 Gigabit Ethernet running over single-mode fiber. It uses extra-long-wavelength lasers at 1,550nm. It has the longest transmission distances possible of the 10Gb technologies: anywhere from 2 meters up to 40 kilometers, depending on the size and quality of the fiber used.

10GBase-Short Wavelength (SW) 10GBase-SW, as defined by IEEE 802.3ae, is a mode of 10GBase-S for MMF with a 850nm laser transceiver with a bandwidth of 10Gbps. It can support up to 300 meters of cable length. This media type is designed to connect to SONET equipment.

10GBase-Long Wavelength (LW) 10GBase-LW is a mode of 10GBase-L supporting a link length of 10km on standard single-mode fiber (SMF) (G.652). This media type is designed to connect to SONET equipment.

10GBase-Extra Long Wavelength (EW) 10GBase-EW is a mode of 10GBase-E supporting a link length of up to 40km on SMF based on G.652 using optical-wavelength 1550nm. This media type is designed to connect to SONET equipment.

 If you want to implement a network medium that is not susceptible to electromagnetic interference (EMI), fiber-optic cable provides a more secure, long-distance cable that is not susceptible to EMI at high speeds.

Table 1.4 summarizes the cable types.

TABLE 1.4 Common Ethernet cable types

Ethernet name	Cable type	Maximum speed	Maximum transmission distance	Notes
10Base-5	Coax	10Mbps	500 meters per segment	Also called *thicknet*, this cable type uses vampire taps to connect devices to cable.
10Base-2	Coax	10Mbps	185 meters per segment	Also called *thinnet*, a very popular implementation of Ethernet over coax.

TABLE 1.4   Common Ethernet cable types *(continued)*

Ethernet name	Cable type	Maximum speed	Maximum transmission distance	Notes
10Base-T	UTP	10Mbps	100 meters per segment	One of the most popular network cabling schemes.
100Base-TX	UTP, STP	100Mbps	100 meters per segment	Two pairs of category 5 UTP.
10Base-FL	Fiber	10Mbps	Varies (ranges from 500 meters to 2,000 meters)	Ethernet over fiber optics to the desktop.
100Base-FX	MMF	100Mbps	2,000 meters	100Mbps Ethernet over fiber optics.
1000Base-T	UTP	1000Mbps	100 meters	Four pairs of category 5e or higher.
1000Base-SX	MMF	1000Mbps	550 meters	Uses SC fiber connectors. Max length depends on fiber size.
1000Base-CX	Balanced, shielded copper	1000Mbps	25 meters	Uses a special connector, the HSSDC.
1000Base-LX	MMF and SMF	1000Mbps	550 meters multimode/ 2000 meters single mode	Uses longer wavelength laser than 1000Base-SX. Uses SC and LC connectors.
10GBase-T	UTP	10Gbps	100 meters	Connects to the network like a Fast Ethernet link using UTP.
10GBase-SR	MMF	10Gbps	300 meters	850nm laser. Max length depends on fiber size and quality.
10GBase-LR	SMF	10Gbps	10 kilometers	1310nm laser. Max length depends on fiber size and quality.
10GBase-ER	SMF	10Gpbs	40 kilometers	1550nm laser. Max length depends on fiber size and quality.

TABLE 1.4   Common Ethernet cable types *(continued)*

Ethernet name	Cable type	Maximum speed	Maximum transmission distance	Notes
10GBase-SW	MMF	10Gpbs	300 meters	850nm laser transceiver.
10GBase-LW	SMF	10Gpbs	10 kilometers	Typically used with SONET.
10GBase-EW	SMF	10Gpbs	40 kilometers	1550nm optical wavelength.

Armed with the basics covered in the chapter, you're equipped to go to the next level and put Ethernet to work using various Ethernet cabling.

Ethernet Cabling

Ethernet cabling is an important discussion, especially if you are planning on taking the Cisco exams. You need to really understand the following three types of cables:

- Straight-through cable
- Crossover cable
- Rolled cable

I will cover each in the following sections.

Straight-Through Cable

The *straight-through cable* is used to connect the following:

- Host to switch or hub
- Router to switch or hub

Four wires are used in straight-through cable to connect Ethernet devices. It is relatively simple to create this type; Figure 1.22 shows the four wires used in a straight-through Ethernet cable.

FIGURE 1.22   Straight-through Ethernet cable

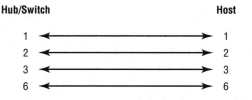

Notice that only pins 1, 2, 3, and 6 are used. Just connect 1 to 1, 2 to 2, 3 to 3, and 6 to 6, and you'll be up and networking in no time.

Crossover Cable

The *crossover cable* can be used to connect the following:

- Switch to switch
- Hub to hub
- Host to host
- Hub to switch
- Router direct to host

The same four wires are used in this cable as in the straight-through cable; you just connect different pins. Figure 1.23 shows how the four wires are used in a crossover Ethernet cable.

FIGURE 1.23   Crossover Ethernet cable

Notice that instead of connecting 1 to 1, 2 to 2, and so on, here you connect pins 1 to 3 and 2 to 6 on each side of the cable.

Rolled Cable

Although *rolled cable* isn't used to connect any Ethernet connections together, you can use a rolled Ethernet cable to connect a host EIA-TIA 232 interface to a router console serial communication (com) port.

If you have a Cisco router or switch, you would use this cable to connect your PC running HyperTerminal to the Cisco hardware. Eight wires are used in this cable to connect serial devices, although not all eight are used to send information, just as in Ethernet networking. Figure 1.24 shows the eight wires used in a rolled cable.

These are probably the easiest cables to make because you just cut the end off on one side of a straight-through cable, turn it over, and put it back on (with a new connector, of course).

FIGURE 1.24   Rolled Ethernet cable

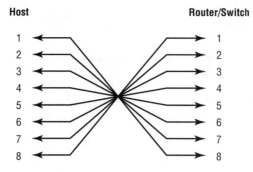

Once you have the correct cable connected from your PC to the Cisco router or switch console port, you can start HyperTerminal to create a console connection and configure the device. Set the configuration as follows:

1. Open HyperTerminal, and enter a name for the connection. It is irrelevant what you name it, but I always just use Cisco. Then click OK.

2. Choose the communications port—either COM1 or COM2, whichever is open on your PC.

3. Now set the port settings. The default values (2400bps and no flow control hardware) will not work; you must set the port settings as shown in Figure 1.25.

FIGURE 1.25 Port settings for a rolled cable connection

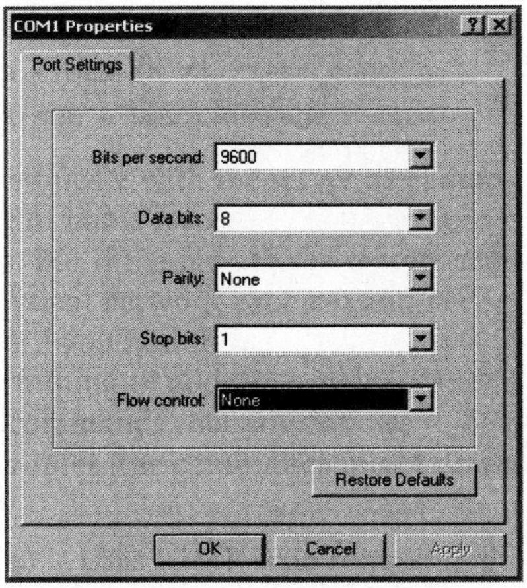

Notice that the bit rate is now set to 9600 and the flow control is set to None. At this point, you can click OK and press the Enter key, and you should be connected to your Cisco device console port.

You've taken a look at the various RJ45 unshielded twisted-pair (UTP) cables. Keeping this in mind, what cable is used between the switches in Figure 1.26?

FIGURE 1.26 RJ45 UTP cable question #1

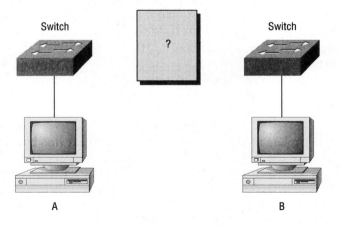

For host A to ping host B, you need a crossover cable to connect the two switches. But what types of cables are used in the network shown in Figure 1.27?

FIGURE 1.27   RJ45 UTP cable question #2

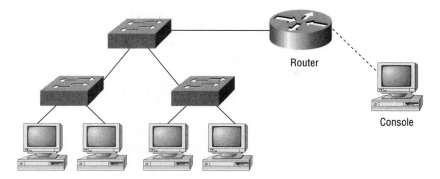

In Figure 1.27, there are a variety of cables in use. For the connection between the switches, you'd obviously use a crossover cable like you saw in Figure 1.23. The trouble is, you have a console connection that uses a rolled cable. Plus, the connection from the router to the switch is a straight-through cable, as is true for the hosts to the switches. Keep in mind that if you had a serial connection (which you don't), it would be a V.35 that you'd use to connect you to a WAN.

Data Encapsulation

When a host transmits data across a network to another device, the data goes through *encapsulation*: it is wrapped with protocol information at each layer of the OSI model. Each layer communicates only with its peer layer on the receiving device.

To communicate and exchange information, each layer uses *Protocol Data Units (PDUs)*. These hold the control information attached to the data at each layer of the model. They are usually attached to the header in front of the data field but can also be in the trailer, or end, of it.

Each PDU attaches to the data by encapsulating it at each layer of the OSI model, and each has a specific name depending on the information provided in each header. This PDU information is read only by the peer layer on the receiving device. After it's read, it's stripped off, and the data is then handed to the next layer up.

Figure 1.28 shows the PDUs and how they attach control information to each layer. This figure demonstrates how the upper-layer user data is converted for transmission on the network. The data stream is then handed down to the Transport layer, which sets up a virtual circuit to the receiving device by sending over a synch packet. Next, the data stream is broken up into smaller pieces, and a Transport layer header (a PDU) is created and attached to the header of the data field; now the piece of data is called a *segment*. Each segment is sequenced so the data stream can be put back together on the receiving side exactly as it was transmitted.

FIGURE 1.28   Data encapsulation

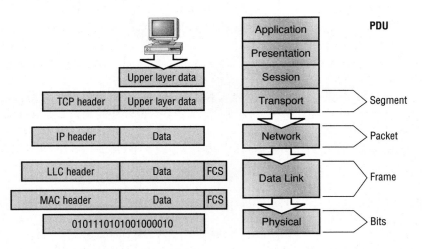

Each segment is then handed to the Network layer for network addressing and routing through the internetwork. Logical addressing (for example, IP) is used to get each segment to the correct network. The Network layer protocol adds a control header to the segment handed down from the Transport layer, and what you have now is called a *packet* or *datagram*. Remember that the Transport and Network layers work together to rebuild a data stream on a receiving host, but it's not part of their work to place their PDUs on a local network segment—which is the only way to get the information to a router or host.

It's the Data Link layer that's responsible for taking packets from the Network layer and placing them on the network medium (cable or wireless). The Data Link layer encapsulates each packet in a *frame*, and the frame's header carries the hardware address of the source and destination hosts. If the destination device is on a remote network, then the frame is sent to a router to be routed through an internetwork. Once it gets to the destination network, a new frame is used to get the packet to the destination host.

To put this frame on the network, it must first be put into a digital signal. Since a frame is really a logical group of 1s and 0s, the Physical layer is responsible for encoding these digits into a digital signal, which is read by devices on the same local network. The receiving devices will synchronize on the digital signal and extract (decode) the 1s and 0s from the digital signal. At this point, the devices build the frames, run a CRC, and then check their answer against the answer in the frame's FCS field. If it matches, the packet is pulled from the frame, and what's left of the frame is discarded. This process is called *de-encapsulation*. The packet is handed to the Network layer, where the address is checked. If the address matches, the segment is pulled from the packet, and what's left of the packet is discarded. The segment is processed at the Transport layer, which rebuilds the data stream and acknowledges to the transmitting station that it received each piece. It then happily hands the data stream to the upper-layer application.

At a transmitting device, the data encapsulation method works like this:

1. User information is converted to data for transmission on the network.

2. Data is converted to segments, and a reliable connection is set up between the transmitting and receiving hosts.

3. Segments are converted to packets or datagrams, and a logical address is placed in the header so each packet can be routed through an internetwork.

4. Packets or datagrams are converted to frames for transmission on the local network. Hardware (Ethernet) addresses are used to uniquely identify hosts on a local network segment.

5. Frames are converted to bits, and a digital encoding and clocking scheme is used.

To explain this in more detail using the layer addressing, I'll use Figure 1.29.

FIGURE 1.29   PDU and layer addressing

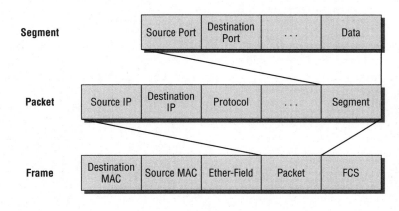

Bit   1011011100011110000

Remember that a data stream is handed down from the upper layer to the Transport layer. As technicians, we really don't care who the data stream comes from because that's really a programmer's problem. Our job is to rebuild the data stream reliably and hand it to the upper layers on the receiving device.

When the receiving host receives the data, a de-encapsulation will occur—meaning you'll start from the Physical layer and go up to the Application layer, removing headers as you go. For example, if a router receives a frame on an interface, the router will take the packet from the frame and then search the routing table to determine where to forward the packet, in other words, the exit interface.

Before I continue discussing Figure 1.29, I'll discuss port numbers and make sure you understand them. The Transport layer uses port numbers to define both the virtual circuit and the upper-layer process, as you can see from Figure 1.30.

FIGURE 1.30   Port numbers at the Transport layer

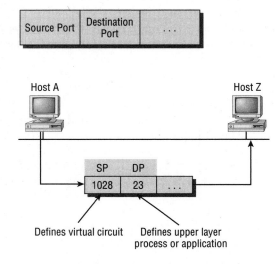

The Transport layer, when using a connection-oriented protocol (in other words, TCP), takes the data stream, makes segments out of it, and establishes a reliable session by creating a virtual circuit. It then sequences (numbers) each segment and uses acknowledgments and flow control. If you're using TCP, the virtual circuit is defined by the source and destination port number, as well as the source and destination IP address (this is called a *socket*). Remember, the host just makes this up starting at port number 1024 (0 through 1023 are reserved for use as well-known port numbers). The destination port number defines the upper-layer process (application) that the data stream is handed to when the data stream is reliably rebuilt on the receiving host.

Now that you understand port numbers and how they are used at the Transport layer, let's go back to Figure 1.29. Once the Transport layer header information is added to the piece of data, it becomes a segment and is handed down to the Network layer along with the destination IP address. (The destination IP address was handed down from the upper layers to the Transport layer with the data stream, and it was discovered through a name resolution method at the upper layers—probably DNS.)

The Network layer adds a header, and adds the logical addressing (IP addresses), to the front of each segment. Once the header is added to the segment, the PDU is called a *packet*. The packet has a protocol field that describes where the segment came from (either UDP or TCP) so it can hand the segment to the correct protocol at the Transport layer when it reaches the receiving host.

The Network layer is responsible for finding the destination hardware address that dictates where the packet should be sent on the local network. It does this by using the

Address Resolution Protocol (ARP)—something I'll talk about more in Chapter 3. IP at the Network layer looks at the destination IP address and compares that address to its own source IP address and subnet mask. If it turns out to be a local network request, the hardware address of the local host is requested via an ARP request. If the packet is destined for a remote host, IP will look for the IP address of the default gateway (router) instead.

The packet, along with the destination hardware address of either the local host or default gateway, is then handed down to the Data Link layer. The Data Link layer will add a header to the front of the packet, and the piece of data then becomes a frame. (We call it a *frame* because both a header and a trailer are added to the packet, which makes the data resemble bookends or a frame, if you will.) This is shown in Figure 1.29. The frame uses an Ether-Type field to describe which protocol the packet came from at the Network layer. Now a CRC is run on the frame, and the answer to the CRC is placed in the Frame Check Sequence field found in the trailer of the frame.

The frame is now ready to be handed down, one bit at a time, to the Physical layer, which will use bit timing rules to encode the data in a digital signal. Every device on the network segment will synchronize with the clock and extract the 1s and 0s from the digital signal and build a frame. After the frame is rebuilt, a CRC is run to make sure the frame is okay. If everything turns out to be all good, the hosts will check the destination MAC and IP addresses to see if the frame is for them.

If all this is making your eyes cross and your brain freeze, don't freak. I'll be going over exactly how data is encapsulated and routed through an internetwork in Chapter 6.

Summary

Whew! I know this seemed like the chapter that wouldn't end, but it did—and you made it through! You're now armed with a ton of fundamental information; you're ready to build upon it and are well on your way to certification.

I started by discussing simple, basic networking and the differences between collision and broadcast domains. I also discussed the various devices used in an internetwork.

I then discussed the OSI model—the seven-layer model used to help application developers design applications that can run on any type of system or network. Each layer has its special jobs and select responsibilities within the model to ensure that solid, effective communications do, in fact, occur. I provided you with complete details of each layer and discussed how Cisco views the specifications of the OSI model.

In addition, each layer in the OSI model specifies different types of devices. I described the different devices, cables, and connectors used at each layer. Remember that hubs are Physical layer devices and repeat the digital signal to all segments except the one from which it was received. Switches segment the network using hardware addresses and break up collision domains. Routers break up broadcast domains (and collision domains) and use logical addressing to send packets through an internetwork.

We are now going to move on to IP addressing in the next chapter.

Exam Essentials

Remember the possible causes of LAN traffic congestion.   Too many hosts in a broadcast domain, broadcast storms, multicasting, and low bandwidth are all possible causes of LAN traffic congestion.

Understand the difference between a collision domain and a broadcast domain.   Collision domain is an Ethernet term used to describe a network collection of devices in which one particular device sends a packet on a network segment, forcing every other device on that same segment to pay attention to it. On a broadcast domain, a set of all devices on a network segment hears all broadcasts sent on that segment.

Understand the difference between a hub, a bridge, a switch, and a router.   Hubs create one collision domain and one broadcast domain. Bridges break up collision domains but create one large broadcast domain. They use hardware addresses to filter the network. Switches are really just multiple port bridges with more intelligence. They break up collision domains but create one large broadcast domain by default. Switches use hardware addresses to filter the network. Routers break up broadcast domains (and collision domains) and use logical addressing to filter the network.

Remember the difference between connection-oriented and connectionless network services.   Connection-oriented services use acknowledgments and flow control to create a reliable session. More overhead is used than in a connectionless network service. Connectionless services are used to send data with no acknowledgments or flow control. This is considered unreliable.

Remember the OSI layers.   You must remember the seven layers of the OSI model and what function each layer provides. The Application, Presentation, and Session layers are upper layers and are responsible for communicating from a user interface to an application. The Transport layer provides segmentation, sequencing, and virtual circuits. The Network layer provides logical network addressing and routing through an internetwork. The Data Link layer provides framing and placing of data on the network medium. The Physical layer is responsible for taking 1s and 0s and encoding them into a digital signal for transmission on the network segment.

Understand how a three-way handshake creates a virtual circuit.   When a host starts a communication session to another host/server (when using TCP), a virtual circuit is created using three packets (which is why it's called a three-way handshake). The transmitting host makes up a source port number from 1024 to 65535. The destination port number will be that of the process or application that data is destined for, like port 80, for example (HTTP).

Remember the types of Ethernet cabling and when you would use them.   The three types of cables that can be created from an Ethernet cable are straight-through (to connect a PC's or a router's Ethernet interface to a hub or switch), crossover (to connect hub to hub, hub to switch, switch to switch, PC to router, or PC to PC), and rolled (for a console connection from a PC to a router or switch).

Understand how to connect a console cable from a PC to a router and start HyperTerminal. Take a rolled cable and connect it from the COM port of the host to the console port of a router. Start HyperTerminal and set the BPS to 9600 and flow control to None.

Written Lab 1

In this section, you'll complete the following labs to make sure you have the information and concepts contained within them fully dialed in:

- Lab 1.1: OSI Questions
- Lab 1.2: Defining the OSI Layers and Devices
- Lab 1.3: Identifying Collision and Broadcast Domains
- Lab 1.4: Binary/Decimal/Hexadecimal Conversion

   (The answers to the written labs can be found in Appendix A.)

Written Lab 1.1: OSI Questions

Answer the following questions about the OSI model:

1. Which layer chooses and determines the availability of communicating partners along with the resources necessary to make the connection, coordinates partnering applications, and forms a consensus on procedures for controlling data integrity and error recovery?

2. Which layer is responsible for converting data packets from the Data Link layer into electrical signals?

3. At which layer is routing implemented, enabling connections and path selection between two end systems?

4. Which layer defines how data is formatted, presented, encoded, and converted for use on the network?

5. Which layer is responsible for creating, managing, and terminating sessions between applications?

6. Which layer ensures the trustworthy transmission of data across a physical link and is primarily concerned with physical addressing, line discipline, network topology, error notification, ordered delivery of frames, and flow control?

7. Which layer is used for reliable communication between end nodes over the network and provides mechanisms for establishing, maintaining, and terminating virtual circuits; transport-fault detection and recovery; and controlling the flow of information?

8. Which layer provides logical addressing that routers will use for path determination?

9. Which layer specifies voltage, wire speed, and pinout cables and moves bits between devices?

10. Which layer combines bits into bytes and bytes into frames, uses MAC addressing, and provides error detection?

11. A Cisco router has received a frame on an interface that is connected to a local network segment. The router has de-encapsulated the frame. What step is next in processing the packet?

12. Which layer is represented by frames?

13. Which layer is represented by segments?

14. Which layer is represented by packets?

15. Which layer is represented by bits?

16. Put the following in order of encapsulation:
    - Packets
    - Frames
    - Bits
    - Segments

17. Which layer segments and reassembles data into a data stream?

18. Which layer provides the physical transmission of the data and handles error notification, network topology, and flow control?

19. Which layer manages device addressing, tracks the location of devices on the network, and determines the best way to move data?

20. What is the bit length and expression form of a MAC address?

Written Lab 1.2: Defining the OSI Layers and Devices

Fill in the blanks with the appropriate layer of the OSI or hub, switch, or router device.

Description	Device or OSI layer
This device sends and receives information about the Network layer.	
This layer creates a virtual circuit before transmitting between two end stations.	
This layer uses service access points.	
This device uses hardware addresses to filter a network.	
Ethernet is defined at these layers.	
This layer supports flow control and sequencing.	
This device can measure the distance to a remote network.	
Logical addressing is used at this layer.	
Hardware addresses are defined at this layer.	
This device creates one big collision domain and one large broadcast domain.	
This device creates many smaller collision domains, but the network is still one large broadcast domain.	
This device can never run full duplex.	
This device breaks up collision domains and broadcast domains.	

Written Lab 1.3: Identifying Collision and Broadcast Domains

Using the information shown in the following illustration, identify the number of collision domains and broadcast domains in each specified device. Each device is represented by a letter:

1. Hub
2. Bridge
3. Switch
4. Router

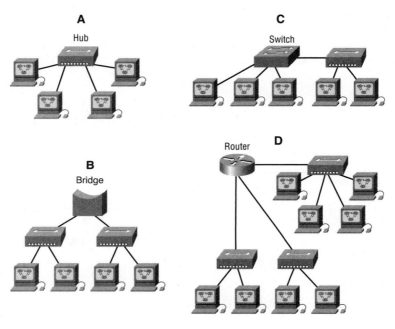

Written Lab 1.4: Binary/Decimal/Hexadecimal Conversion

1.   Convert from decimal IP address to binary format.

Complete the following table to express 192.168.10.15 in binary format:

128	64	32	16	8	4	2	1	Binary

Complete the following table to express 172.16.20.55 in binary format:

128	64	32	16	8	4	2	1	Binary

Complete the following table to express 10.11.12.99 in binary format:

128	64	32	16	8	4	2	1	Binary

2. Convert the following from binary format to decimal IP address:

Complete the following table to express 11001100.00110011.10101010.01010101 in decimal IP address format:

128	64	32	16	8	4	2	1	Decimal

Complete the following table to express 11000110.11010011.00111001.11010001 in decimal IP address format:

128	64	32	16	8	4	2	1	Decimal

Complete the following table to express 10000100.11010010.10111000.10100110 in decimal IP address format:

128	64	32	16	8	4	2	1	Decimal

3.   Convert the following from binary format to hexadecimal.

Complete the following table to express 11011000.00011011.00111101.01110110 in hexadecimal:

128	64	32	16	8	4	2	1	Hexa-decimal

Complete the following table to express 11001010.11110101.10000011.11101011 in hexadecimal:

128	64	32	16	8	4	2	1	Hexa-decimal

Complete the following table to express 10000100.11010010.01000011.10110011 in hexadecimal:

128	64	32	16	8	4	2	1	Hexa-decimal

Review Questions

You can find the answers in Appendix B.

 The following questions are designed to test your understanding of this chapter's material. For more information on how to get additional questions, please see this book's introduction.

1. A receiving host has failed to receive all of the segments that it should acknowledge. What can the host do to improve the reliability of this communication session?

   A. Send a different source port number.

   B. Restart the virtual circuit.

   C. Decrease the sequence number.

   D. Decrease the window size.

2. Which fields are contained within an IEEE Ethernet frame header? (Choose two.)

   A. Source and destination MAC address

   B. Source and destination network address

   C. Source and destination MAC address and source and destination network address

   D. FCS field

3. Which layer 1 devices can be used to enlarge the area covered by a single LAN segment? (Choose two.)

   A. Switch

   B. NIC

   C. Hub

   D. Repeater

   E. RJ45 transceiver

4. Segmentation of a data stream happens at which layer of the OSI model?

   A. Physical

   B. Data Link

   C. Network

   D. Transport

5. Which of the following describe router functions? (Choose four.)

    A. Packet switching

    B. Collision prevention

    C. Packet filtering

    D. Broadcast domain enlargement

    E. Internetwork communication

    F. Broadcast forwarding

    G. Path selection

6. Routers operate at layer __. LAN switches operate at layer __. Ethernet hubs operate at layer __. Word processing operates at layer __.

    A. 3, 3, 1, 7

    B. 3, 2, 1, none

    C. 3, 2, 1, 7

    D. 2, 3, 1, 7

    E. 3, 3, 2, none

7. When data is encapsulated, which is the correct order?

    A. Data, frame, packet, segment, bit

    B. Segment, data, packet, frame, bit

    C. Data, segment, packet, frame, bit

    D. Data, segment, frame, packet, bit

8. Why does the data communication industry use the layered OSI reference model? (Choose two.)

    A. It divides the network communication process into smaller and simpler components, thus aiding component development, design, and troubleshooting.

    B. It enables equipment from different vendors to use the same electronic components, thus saving research and development funds.

    C. It supports the evolution of multiple competing standards and thus provides business opportunities for equipment manufacturers.

    D. It encourages industry standardization by defining what functions occur at each layer of the model.

    E. It provides a framework by which changes in functionality in one layer require changes in other layers.

9. What are two purposes for segmentation with a bridge?

   A. To add more broadcast domains

   B. To create more collision domains

   C. To add more bandwidth for users

   D. To allow more broadcasts for users

10. Which of the following are unique characteristics of half-duplex Ethernet when compared to full-duplex Ethernet? (Choose two.)

    A. Half-duplex Ethernet operates in a shared collision domain.

    B. Half-duplex Ethernet operates in a private collision domain.

    C. Half-duplex Ethernet has higher effective throughput.

    D. Half-duplex Ethernet has lower effective throughput.

    E. Half-duplex Ethernet operates in a private broadcast domain.

11. You want to implement an Ethernet network medium that is not susceptible to EMI or voltage potential differences between two buildings. Which type of cabling should you use?

    A. Thicknet coax

    B. Thinnet coax

    C. Category 5 UTP cable

    D. Fiber-optic cable

12. Acknowledgments, sequencing, and flow control are characteristic of which OSI layer?

    A. Layer 2

    B. Layer 3

    C. Layer 4

    D. Layer 7

13. Which of the following are types of flow control? (Choose all that apply.)

    A. Buffering

    B. Cut-through

    C. Windowing

    D. Congestion avoidance

    E. VLANs

14. Which of the following types of connections can use full duplex? (Choose three.)

    A. Hub to hub

    B. Switch to switch

    C. Host to host

    D. Switch to hub

    E. Switch to host

15. What is the purpose of flow control?

   A. To ensure that data is retransmitted if an acknowledgment is not received

   B. To reassemble segments in the correct order at the destination device

   C. To provide a means for the receiver to govern the amount of data sent by the sender

   D. To regulate the size of each segment

16. Which three statements are true about the operation of a full-duplex Ethernet network?

   A. There are no collisions in full-duplex mode.

   B. A dedicated switch port is required for each full-duplex node.

   C. Ethernet hub ports are preconfigured for full-duplex mode.

   D. In a full-duplex environment, the host network card must check for the availability of the network media before transmitting.

   E. The host network card and the switch port must be capable of operating in full-duplex mode.

17. What type of RJ45 UTP cable is used between switches?

   A. Straight-through

   B. Crossover cable

   C. Crossover with a CSU/DSU

   D. Crossover with a router in between the two switches

18. How does a host on an Ethernet LAN know when to transmit after a collision has occurred? (Choose two.)

   A. In a CSMA/CD collision domain, multiple stations can successfully transmit data simultaneously.

   B. In a CSMA/CD collision domain, stations must wait until the media is not in use before transmitting.

   C. You can improve the CSMA/CD network by adding more hubs.

   D. After a collision, the station that detected the collision has first priority to resend the lost data.

   E. After a collision, all stations run a random backoff algorithm. When the backoff delay period has expired, all stations have equal priority to transmit data.

   F. After a collision, all stations involved run an identical backoff algorithm and then synchronize with each other prior to transmitting data.

19. What type of RJ45 UTP cable do you use to connect a PC's COM port to a router or switch console port?

   A. Straight-through

   B. Crossover cable

   C. Crossover with a CSU/DSU

   D. Rolled

20. You have the following binary number:

10110111

What are the decimal and hexadecimal equivalents?

A. 69/0x2102

B. 183/B7

C. 173/A6

D. 83/0xC5

Chapter

2

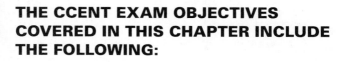

Internet Protocols

THE CCENT EXAM OBJECTIVES COVERED IN THIS CHAPTER INCLUDE THE FOLLOWING:

✓ **Describe the operation of data networks**

- Describe common networking applications including web applications

- Describe the purpose and basic operation of the protocols in the OSI and TCP models

- Describe the impact of applications (Voice Over IP and Video Over IP) on a network

✓ **Implement an IP addressing scheme and IP services to meet network requirements for a small branch office**

- Describe the need and role of addressing in a network

- Create and apply an addressing scheme to a network

- Assign and verify valid IP addresses to hosts, servers, and networking devices in a LAN environment

- Describe and verify DNS operation

- Describe the operation and benefits of using private and public IP addressing

- Configure, verify and troubleshoot DHCP and DNS operation on a router (using both CLI and SDM)

- Implement static and dynamic addressing services for hosts in a LAN environment

- Identify and correct IP addressing issues

The *Transmission Control Protocol/Internet Protocol (TCP/IP)* suite was created by the Department of Defense (DoD) to ensure and preserve data integrity, as well as to maintain communications in the event of catastrophic war. So, it follows that if designed and implemented correctly, a TCP/IP network can be a truly dependable and resilient one. In this chapter, I'll cover the protocols of TCP/IP, and throughout this book, you'll learn how to create a marvelous TCP/IP network—using Cisco routers, of course.

I'll begin by taking a look at the DoD's version of TCP/IP and then compare this version and its protocols with the OSI reference model discussed in Chapter 1, "Internetworking."

Once you understand the protocols used at the various levels of the DoD model, I'll cover IP addressing and the different classes of addresses used in networks today.

Subnetting will be covered in Chapter 3, "IP Subnetting, Troubleshooting IP, and Introduction to NAT."

Last, because IPv4 address types are so important to understanding IP addressing, as well as subnetting and Variable Length Subnet Masks (VLSMs), an understanding of the various flavors of IPv4 addresses is critical. I'll finish the chapter with various types of IPv4 addresses that you just must know. Internet Protocol version 6 (Ipv6) will not be discussed in this book; we will focus solely on IPv4. Also, references to Internet Protocol Version 4 usually are written as just IP, not typically IPv4.

For up-to-the-minute updates for this chapter, please see www.lammle.com/forum and/or www.sybex.com/go/ccent2e.

TCP/IP and the DoD Model

The DoD model is basically a condensed version of the OSI model—it's composed of four, instead of seven, layers:

- Process/Application layer
- Host-to-Host layer
- Internet layer
- Network Access layer

Figure 2.1 compares the DoD model and the OSI reference model. As you can see, the two are similar in concept, but each has a different number of layers with different names.

FIGURE 2.1 The DoD and OSI models

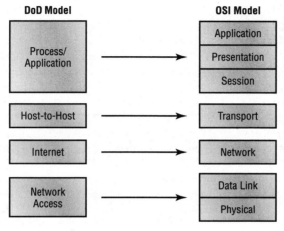

 When the different protocols in the IP stack are discussed, the layers of the OSI and DoD models are interchangeable. In other words, the Internet layer and the Network layer describe the same thing, as do the Host-to-Host layer and the Transport layer.

Process/Application Layer A vast array of protocols combine at the DoD model's *Process/ Application layer* to integrate the various activities and duties spanning the focus of the OSI's corresponding top three layers (Application, Presentation, and Session). You'll be looking closely at those protocols in the next part of this chapter. The Process/Application layer defines protocols for node-to-node application communication and also controls user-interface specifications.

Host-to-Host Layer The *Host-to-Host layer* parallels the functions of the OSI's Transport layer, defining protocols for setting up the level of transmission service for applications. It tackles issues such as creating reliable end-to-end communication and ensuring the error-free delivery of data. It handles packet sequencing and maintains data integrity.

Internet Layer The *Internet layer* corresponds to the OSI's Network layer, designating the protocols relating to the logical transmission of packets over the entire network. It takes care of the addressing of hosts by giving them an Internet Protocol (IP) address, and it handles the routing of packets among multiple networks.

Network Access Layer   At the bottom of the DoD model, the *Network Access layer* implements the data exchange between the host and the network. The equivalent of the Data Link and Physical layers of the OSI model, the Network Access layer oversees hardware addressing and defines protocols for the physical transmission of data.

The DoD and OSI models are alike in design and concept and have similar functions in similar layers. Figure 2.2 shows the TCP/IP protocol suite and how its protocols relate to the DoD model layers.

FIGURE 2.2   The TCP/IP protocol suite

DoD Model

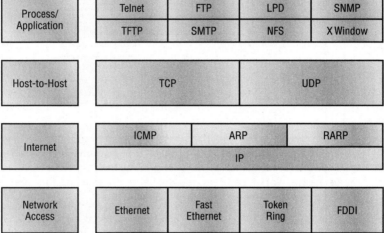

In the following sections, I will cover the different protocols in more detail, starting with the Process/Application layer protocols.

The Process/Application Layer Protocols

In this section, I'll describe the different applications and services typically used in IP networks. The following protocols and applications are covered in this section:

- Telnet
- File Transfer Protocol (FTP)
- Trivial File Transfer Protocol (TFTP)
- Network File System (NFS)

- Simple Mail Transfer Protocol (SMTP)
- Line Printer Daemon (LPD)
- X Window
- Simple Network Management Protocol (SNMP)
- Secure Shell (SSH)
- Domain Name Service (DNS)
- Dynamic Host Configuration Protocol/Bootstrap Protocol (DHCP/BootP)

Telnet

Telnet is the chameleon of protocols—its specialty is terminal emulation. It allows a user on a remote client machine, called a Telnet client, to access the resources of another machine, a Telnet server. Telnet achieves this by pulling a fast one on the Telnet server and making the client machine appear as though it were a terminal directly attached to the local network. This projection is actually a software image—a virtual terminal that can interact with the chosen remote host.

These emulated terminals are of the text-mode type and can execute refined procedures such as displaying menus that give users the opportunity to choose options and access the applications on the duped server. Users begin a Telnet session by running the Telnet client software and then logging into the Telnet server.

File Transfer Protocol

File Transfer Protocol (FTP) is the protocol that actually lets you transfer files, and it can accomplish this between any two machines using it. But FTP isn't just a protocol; it's also a program. Operating as a protocol, FTP is used by applications. As a program, it's employed by users to perform file tasks by hand. FTP also allows for access to both directories and files and can accomplish certain types of directory operations, such as moving to a different directory from the current one.

Accessing a host through FTP is only the first step, though. Users must then be subjected to an authentication login that's probably secured with passwords and usernames implemented by system administrators to restrict access. You can get around this somewhat by adopting the username *anonymous*—though what you'll gain access to will be limited.

Even when employed by users manually as a program, FTP's functions are limited to listing and manipulating directories, typing file contents, and copying files between hosts. It can't execute remote files as programs.

Trivial File Transfer Protocol

Trivial File Transfer Protocol (TFTP) is the stripped-down, stock version of FTP, but it's the protocol of choice if you know exactly what you want and where to find it; plus it's so easy to use, and it's fast, too! It doesn't give you the abundance of functions that FTP does, though. TFTP has no directory-browsing abilities; it can do nothing but send and receive files. This compact little protocol also skimps in the data department, sending much smaller blocks of data than FTP, and there's no authentication as with FTP, so it's even more insecure. Few sites support it because of the inherent security risks.

🌐 Real World Scenario

When Should You Use FTP?

The folks at your San Francisco office need a 100MB file emailed to them right away. What do you do? Most email servers would reject the email because they have size limits. Even if there's no size limit on the server, it still would take a while to send this big file to SF. FTP to the rescue!

If you need to give someone a large file or you need to get a large file from someone, FTP is a nice choice. Smaller files (less than 5MB) can just be sent via email if you have the bandwidth of DSL or a cable modem. However, most ISPs don't allow files larger than 5MB to be emailed, so FTP is an option you should consider if you need to send and receive large files. (Who doesn't these days?) To use FTP, you will need to set up an FTP server on the Internet so that the files can be shared.

Besides, FTP is faster than email, which is another reason to use FTP for sending or receiving large files. In addition, because it uses TCP and is connection-oriented, if the session dies, FTP can sometimes start up where it left off. Try that with your email client!

Network File System

Network File System (NFS) is a jewel of a protocol specializing in file sharing. It allows two different types of file systems to interoperate. It works like this: suppose the NFS server software is running on a Windows server and the NFS client software is running on a Unix host. NFS allows for a portion of the RAM on the NT server to transparently store Unix files, which can, in turn, be used by Unix users. Even though the Windows file system and Unix file system are not alike—they have different case sensitivity, filename lengths, security, and so on—both Unix users and NT users can access the same file with their normal file systems, in their normal way.

Simple Mail Transfer Protocol

Simple Mail Transfer Protocol (SMTP), answering our ubiquitous call to email, uses a spooled, or queued, method of mail delivery. Once a message has been sent to a destination, the message is spooled to a device, usually a disk. The server software at the destination posts a vigil, regularly checking the queue for messages. When it detects them, it proceeds to deliver them to their destination. SMTP is used to send mail; Post Office Protocol version 3 (POP3) or IMAP is used to receive mail.

SMTP is connection-oriented and uses TCP at the Transport layer.

Line Printer Daemon

The Line Printer Daemon (LPD) protocol is designed for printer sharing. The LPD, along with the Line Printer (LPR) program, allows print jobs to be spooled and sent to the network's printers using TCP/IP.

X Window

Designed for client-server operations, *X Window* defines a protocol for writing client-server applications based on a graphical user interface (GUI). The idea is to allow a program, called a *client*, to run on one computer and have it display things through a window server on another computer.

Simple Network Management Protocol

Simple Network Management Protocol (SNMP) collects and manipulates valuable network information. It gathers data by polling the devices on the network from a management station at fixed or random intervals, requiring them to disclose certain information. When all is well, SNMP receives something called a *baseline*—a report delimiting the operational traits of a healthy network. This protocol can also stand as a watchdog over the network, quickly notifying managers of any sudden turn of events. These network watchdogs are called *agents*, and when aberrations occur, agents send an alert called a *trap* to the management station.

SNMP 1, 2, and 3

SNMP 1 and 2 are pretty much obsolete. This doesn't mean you won't see them in a network at some time, but version 1 is super old and, well, obsolete. SNMPv2 provided improvements, especially in performance. But one of the best additions was what was called GETBULK, which allowed a host to retrieve a large amount of data at once. However, version 2 never really caught on in the networking world. SNMP 3 is now the standard and uses both TCP and UDP, unlike version 1, which used only UDP. Version 3 added even more security and message integrity, authentication, and encryption.

Secure Shell

The Secure Shell (SSH) protocol sets up a secure Telnet-like session over a standard TCP/IP connection and is employed for doing things such as logging into systems, running programs on remote systems, and moving files from one system to another. And it does all of this while maintaining a nice, strong, encrypted connection. You can think of it as the new-generation protocol that's now used in place of rsh and rlogin—even Telnet.

Domain Name Service

Domain Name Service (DNS) resolves hostnames—specifically, Internet names, such as www.lammle.com. You don't have to use DNS; you can just type in the IP address of any device you want to communicate with. An IP address identifies hosts on a network and the Internet. However, DNS was designed to make our lives easier. Think about this: what would happen if you wanted to move your web page to a different service provider? The IP address would change, and no one would know what the new one was. DNS allows you to use a domain name to specify an IP address. You can change the IP address as often as you want, and no one will know the difference as long as that IP address change is communicated to the DNS servers.

DNS is used to resolve a *fully qualified domain name (FQDN)*—for example, www.lammle.com or todd.lammle.com—to an IP address. The parts of an FQDN allow DNS to logically locate a system in a hierarchical structure based on its domain identifier.

Say you're working on a router and are in the command-line interface. (I'll tell you about the command-line interface in Chapter 4, "Cisco's Internetworking Operating System (IOS)." From the command line you can ping another router or a host with an IP address to test connectivity. With DNS and a Cisco router, you can save yourself the headache of memorizing each and every IP address or typing in the FQDN todd.lammle.com each time you want to ping. On a Cisco router, you can use the command ip domain-name lammle.com to append each request with the lammle.com domain. Then you can type in the name *todd*, and it resolves to the correct IP address for you.

If you want to resolve the name *todd*, you either must type in the FQDN of todd.lammle.com or have a device such as a PC or router add the suffix for you.

> An important thing to remember about DNS is that if you can ping a device with an IP address but cannot use its FQDN, then you might have some type of DNS configuration failure.

Dynamic Host Configuration Protocol/Bootstrap Protocol

Dynamic Host Configuration Protocol (DHCP) assigns IP addresses to hosts. It allows easier administration and works well in small to even very large network environments. All types of hardware can be used as a DHCP server, including a Cisco router.

DHCP differs from Bootstrap Protocol (BootP) in that BootP assigns an IP address to a host but the host's hardware address must be entered manually in a BootP table. You can think of DHCP as a dynamic BootP. But remember that BootP is also used to send an operating system that a host can boot from. DHCP can't do that.

But there is a lot of information a DHCP server can provide to a host when the host is requesting an IP address from the DHCP server. Here's a list of the information a DHCP server can provide:

- IP address
- Subnet mask
- Domain name
- Default gateway (routers)
- DNS server address

A DHCP server can give us even more information than this, but the items in the list are the most common.

A client that sends out a DHCP Discover message in order to receive an IP address sends out a broadcast at both layers 2 and 3.

- The layer 2 broadcast is all *F*s in hex, which looks like this: FF: FF: FF: FF: FF: FF.
- The layer 3 broadcast is *255.255.255.255*, which means all networks and all hosts.

DHCP is connectionless, which means it uses User Datagram Protocol (UDP) at the Transport layer, also known as the Host-to-Host layer, which I'll talk about next.

In case you don't believe me, here's an example of output from my trusty analyzer:

```
Ethernet II, Src: 192.168.0.3 (00:0b:db:99:d3:5e), Dst: BroadcastÂ
 (ff:ff:ff:ff:ff:ff)
Internet Protocol, Src: 0.0.0.0 (0.0.0.0), Dst: 255.255.255.255 (255.255.255.255)
```

The Data Link and Network layers are both sending out "all hands" broadcasts saying, "Help—I don't know my IP address!" Notice the source IP (Src) field is all zeros (0.0.0.0) because the host does not have an IP address.

NOTE   Broadcast addresses will be discussed in more detail at the end of this chapter.

Figure 2.3 shows the process of a client-server relationship using a DHCP connection.

FIGURE 2.3   DHCP client four-step process

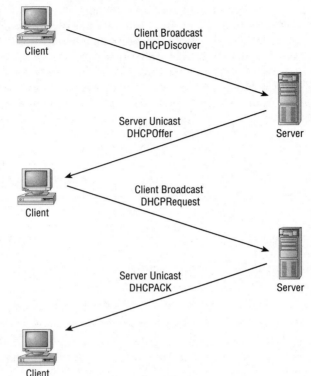

The following is the four-step process a client takes to receive an IP address from a DHCP server:

1. The DHCP client broadcasts a DHCP <u>Discover</u> message looking for a DHCP server (port 67).

2. The DHCP server that received the DHCP Discover message will send a unicast DHCP <u>Offer</u> message back to the host.

3. The client will then broadcast to the server a DHCP <u>Request</u> message asking for an IP address and possibly other information.

4. The server will finalize the exchange with a unicast DHCP <u>Acknowledgment</u> message.

DHCP Conflicts

A DHCP address conflict occurs when two hosts use the same IP address. This sounds bad, doesn't it? Well, of course it is! We'll never even have to discuss this problem when we start using IPv6!

During IP address assignment, a DHCP server checks for conflicts using the Ping program to test the availability of the address before it is assigned from the pool. If no host replies, then the DHCP server assumes that the IP address is not already allocated. This helps the server know that it is providing a good address, but what about the host? To provide extra protection against the all-so-terrible IP conflict issue, the host can broadcast for its own address.

A host uses something called a *gratuitous ARP* to help avoid a possible duplicate address. The DHCP client sends an ARP broadcast out on the local LAN or VLAN using its newly assigned address to solve conflicts before they occur.

So, if an IP address conflict is detected, the address is removed from the DHCP pool (scope), and it is all-so-important to remember that the address will not be assigned to a host until the administrator resolves the conflict by hand.

Automatic Private IP Addressing

So, what happens if you have a few hosts connected together with a switch or hub and you don't have a DHCP server? You can add IP information by hand (this is called *static IP addressing*; or, Windows provides what is called Automatic Private IP Addressing [APIPA], a feature of newer Windows operating systems). With APIPA, clients can automatically self-configure an IP address and subnet mask (basic IP information that hosts use to communicate) when a DHCP server isn't available. The IP address range for APIPA is 169.254.0.1 through 169.254.255.254. The client also configures itself with a default Class B subnet mask of 255.255.0.0.

However, when you're in your corporate network working and you have a DHCP server running and your host shows that it is using this IP address range, this means that either your DHCP client on the host is not working or the server is down or can't be reached because of a network issue. I don't know anyone who's seen a host in this address range and has been happy about it!

Now let's take a look at the Transport layer, or what the DoD calls the Host-to-Host layer.

The Host-to-Host Layer Protocols

The main purpose of the Host-to-Host layer is to shield the upper-layer applications from the complexities of the network. This layer says to the upper layer, "Just give me your data stream, with any instructions, and I'll begin the process of getting your information ready to send."

The following sections describe the two protocols at this layer:

- Transmission Control Protocol (TCP)

- User Datagram Protocol (UDP)

In addition, I'll cover some of the key host-to-host protocol concepts, as well as the port numbers.

Remember, this is still considered layer 4, and Cisco really likes the way layer 4 can use acknowledgments, sequencing, and flow control.

Transmission Control Protocol

Transmission Control Protocol (TCP) takes large blocks of information from an application and breaks them into segments. It numbers and sequences each segment so that the destination's TCP stack can put the segments back into the order the application intended. After these segments are sent, TCP (on the transmitting host) waits for an acknowledgment of the receiving end's TCP virtual circuit session and retransmits those that aren't acknowledged.

Before a transmitting host starts to send segments down the model, the sender's TCP stack contacts the destination's TCP stack to establish a connection. What is created is known as a *virtual circuit*. This type of communication is called *connection-oriented*. During this initial handshake, the two TCP layers also agree on the amount of information that's going to be sent before the recipient's TCP sends back an acknowledgment. With everything agreed upon in advance, the path is paved for reliable communication to take place.

TCP is a full-duplex, connection-oriented, reliable, and accurate protocol, but establishing all these terms and conditions, in addition to error checking, is no small task. TCP is very complicated and, not surprisingly, costly in terms of network overhead. And since today's networks are much more reliable than those of yore, this added reliability is often unnecessary; however, most programmers use it because it removes a lot of work programming. For example, real-time video over IP and voice over IP (VoIP) uses UDP because they can't afford the overhead, but yet it keeps working better and better because the physical networks are getting more reliable.

TCP Segment Format

Since the upper layers just send a data stream to the protocols in the Transport layers, I'll demonstrate how TCP segments a data stream and prepares it for the Internet layer. When the Internet layer receives the data stream, it routes the segments as packets through an internetwork. The segments are handed to the receiving host's Host-to-Host layer protocol, which rebuilds the data stream to hand to the upper-layer applications or protocols.

Figure 2.4 shows the TCP segment format. The figure shows the different fields within the TCP header.

FIGURE 2.4   TCP segment format

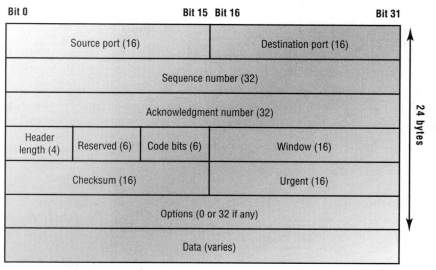

The TCP header is 20 bytes long, or up to 24 bytes with options. You need to understand what each field in the TCP segment is.

Source Port   The port number of the application on the host sending the data. (Port numbers will be explained a little later in this section.)

Destination Port   The port number of the application requested on the destination host.

Sequence Number   A number used by TCP to put the data back in the correct order or retransmit missing or damaged data, a process called *sequencing*.

Acknowledgment Number   The TCP octet that is expected next.

Header Length   The number of 32-bit words in the TCP header. This indicates where the data begins. The TCP header (even one including options) is an integral number, 32 bits in length.

Reserved   Always set to zero.

Code Bits/Flags   Control functions used to set up and terminate a session.

Window   The window size the sender is willing to accept, in octets before an acknowledgment is required.

Checksum   The cyclic redundancy check (CRC), because TCP doesn't trust the lower layers and checks everything to make sure the segment is not corrupted. The CRC checks the header and data fields.

Urgent   A valid field only if the Urgent pointer in the code bits is set. If so, this value indicates the offset from the current sequence number, in octets, where the segment of non-urgent data begins.

Options   May be 0 or a multiple of 32 bits, if needed. What this means is that no options have to be present (option size of 0). However, if any options are used that do not cause the option field to total a multiple of 32 bits, padding 0s must be used to make sure the data begins on a 32-bit boundary.

Data   Handed down to the TCP protocol at the Transport layer, which includes the upper-layer headers.

Let's take a look at a TCP segment copied from a network analyzer.

```
TCP - Transport Control Protocol
  Source Port:        5973
  Destination Port: 23
  Sequence Number:   1456389907
  Ack Number:        1242056456
  Offset:            5
  Reserved:          %000000
  Code:              %011000
        Ack is valid
        Push Request
  Window:            61320
  Checksum:          0x61a6
  Urgent Pointer:    0
  No TCP Options
  TCP Data Area:
  vL.5.+.5.+.5.+.5  76 4c 19 35 11 2b 19 35 11 2b 19 35 11
   2b 19 35 +. 11 2b 19
Frame Check Sequence: 0x0d00000f
```

Did you notice that everything I talked about earlier is in the segment? As you can see from the number of fields in the header, TCP creates a lot of overhead. Application developers may opt for efficiency over reliability to save overhead, so User Datagram Protocol was also defined at the Transport layer as an alternative.

User Datagram Protocol

If you were to compare *User Datagram Protocol (UDP)* with TCP, you'd find that the former is basically the scaled-down economy model that's sometimes referred to as a *thin protocol.* Like a thin person on a park bench, a thin protocol doesn't take up a lot of room—or in this case, much bandwidth on a network.

UDP doesn't offer all the bells and whistles of TCP either, but it does do a fabulous job of transporting information that doesn't require reliable delivery—and it does so using far fewer network resources. (UDP is covered thoroughly in Request for Comments 768.)

> **NOTE** The Requests for Comments (RFCs) form a series of notes, started in 1969, about the Internet (originally the ARPAnet). The notes discuss many aspects of computer communication; they focus on networking protocols, procedures, programs, and concepts but also include meeting notes, opinion, and sometimes humor.

There are some situations in which it would definitely be wise for developers to opt for UDP rather than TCP. Remember the watchdog SNMP up there at the Process/Application layer? SNMP monitors the network, sending intermittent messages and a fairly steady flow of status updates and alerts, especially when running on a large network. The cost in overhead to establish, maintain, and close a TCP connection for each one of those little messages would reduce what would be an otherwise healthy, efficient network to a dammed-up bog in no time!

Another circumstance calling for UDP over TCP is when reliability is already handled at the Process/Application layer. Network File System (NFS) handles its own reliability issues, making the use of TCP both impractical and redundant. But ultimately, it's up to the application developer to decide whether to use UDP or TCP, not the user who wants to transfer data faster.

UDP does *not* sequence the segments and does not care in which order the segments arrive at the destination and when the packets are received at the Network layer; IP just hands the segments up to the Transport layer in the order they are received. UDP sends the segments up and forgets about them. It doesn't follow through, check up on them, or even allow for an acknowledgment of safe arrival—complete abandonment. Because of this, it's referred to as an *unreliable* protocol. This does not mean that UDP is ineffective, only that it doesn't handle issues of reliability.

Further, UDP doesn't create a virtual circuit, nor does it contact the destination before delivering information to it. Because of this, it's also considered a *connectionless* protocol. Since UDP assumes that the application will use its own reliability method, it doesn't use any. This gives an application developer a choice when running the Internet Protocol stack: TCP for reliability or UDP for faster transfers.

UDP Segment Format

Figure 2.5 clearly illustrates UDP's markedly low overhead as compared to TCP's hungry usage. Look at the figure carefully—can you see that UDP doesn't use windowing or provide for acknowledgments in the UDP header?

FIGURE 2.5   UDP segment

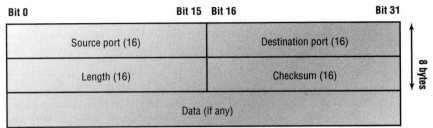

It's important for you to understand what each field in the UDP segment is.

Source Port   Port number of the application on the host sending the data

Destination Port   Port number of the application requested on the destination host

Length   Length of UDP header and UDP data

Checksum   Checksum of both the UDP header and UDP data fields

Data   Upper-layer data

UDP, like TCP, doesn't trust the lower layers and runs its own CRC to verify segment integrity. Remember that the Frame Check Sequence (FCS) is the field that houses the CRC, which is why you can see the FCS information.

The following shows a UDP segment caught on a network analyzer:

```
UDP - User Datagram Protocol
  Source Port:       1085
  Destination Port: 5136
  Length:            41
  Checksum:          0x7a3c
  UDP Data Area:
  ..Z......00 01 5a 96 00 01 00 00 00 00 00 11 0000 00
  ...C..2._C._C  2e 03 00 43 02 1e 32 0a 00 0a 00 80 43 00 80
Frame Check Sequence: 0x00000000
```

Notice that low overhead! Try to find the sequence number, ack number, and window size in the UDP segment. You can't because they just aren't there!

Key Concepts of Host-to-Host Protocols

Since you've seen both a connection-oriented (TCP) and connectionless (UDP) protocol in action, it would be good to summarize the two here. Table 2.1 highlights some of the key concepts that you should keep in mind regarding these two protocols. You should memorize this table.

TABLE 2.1 Key features of TCP and UDP

TCP	UDP
Sequenced	Unsequenced
Reliable	Unreliable
Connection-oriented	Connectionless
Virtual circuit	Low overhead
Acknowledgments	No acknowledgment
Windowing flow control	No windowing or flow control

A telephone analogy can really help you understand how TCP works. Most of us know that before you speak to someone on a phone, you must first establish a connection with that other person—wherever they are. This is like a virtual circuit with the TCP protocol. If you were giving someone important information during your conversation, you might say, "You know?" or ask, "Did you get that?" Saying something like this is a lot like a TCP acknowledgment—it's designed to get you verification. From time to time (especially on cell phones), people also ask, "Are you still there?" They end their conversations with a "Goodbye" of some kind, putting closure on the phone call. TCP also performs these types of functions.

Alternately, using UDP is like sending a postcard. To do that, you don't need to contact the other party first. You simply write your message, address the postcard, and mail it. This is analogous to UDP's connectionless orientation. Since the message on the postcard is probably not a matter of life or death, you don't need an acknowledgment of its receipt. Similarly, UDP does not involve acknowledgments.

Let's discuss TCP, UDP, and the applications and processes associated with each protocol.

Port Numbers

TCP and UDP must use *port numbers* to communicate with the upper layers because they're what keep track of different conversations crossing the network simultaneously. Originating-source port numbers are dynamically assigned by the source host and will equal some number starting at 1024 up to 65535. Port numbers 1023 and below are defined in RFC 3232 (or just see www.iana.org), which discusses what are called *well-known* port numbers.

Virtual circuits that don't use an application with a well-known port number are assigned port numbers randomly from a specific range instead. These port numbers identify the source and destination application or process in the TCP segment.

Figure 2.6 illustrates how both TCP and UDP use port numbers.

FIGURE 2.6   Port numbers for TCP and UDP

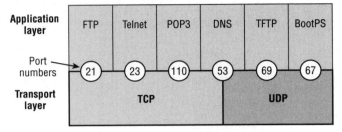

The different port numbers that can be used are explained next:

- Numbers below 1024 are considered well-known port numbers and are defined in RFC 3232.
- Numbers 1024 and above are used by the upper layers to set up sessions with other hosts and by TCP to use as source and destination addresses in the TCP and UDP segment.

In the following sections, you'll take a look at an analyzer output showing a TCP session.

TCP Session: Source Port

The following listing shows a TCP session captured with OmniPeek analyzer software:

```
TCP - Transport Control Protocol
 Source Port:        5973
 Destination Port:   23
 Sequence Number:    1456389907
 Ack Number:         1242056456
 Offset:             5
 Reserved:           %000000
 Code:               %011000
      Ack is valid
      Push Request
 Window:             61320
 Checksum:           0x61a6
 Urgent Pointer:     0
 No TCP Options
 TCP Data Area:
 vL.5.+.5.+.5.+.5  76 4c 19 35 11 2b 19 35 11 2b 19 35 11
  2b 19 35 +. 11 2b 19
Frame Check Sequence: 0x0d00000f
```

Notice that the source host makes up the source port, which in this case is 5973. The destination port is 23, which is used to tell the receiving host the purpose of the intended connection (Telnet).

By looking at this session, you can see that the source host makes up the source port by using numbers from 1024 to 65535. But why does the source make up a port number? To differentiate between sessions with different hosts, my friend. How would a server know where information is coming from if it didn't have a different number from a sending host? TCP and the upper layers don't use hardware and logical addresses to understand the sending host's address as the Data Link and Network layer protocols do. Instead, they use port numbers.

TCP Session: Destination Port

You'll sometimes look at an analyzer and see that only the source port is above 1024 and the destination port is a well-known port, as shown in the following trace:

```
TCP - Transport Control Protocol
  Source Port:      1144
  Destination Port: 80 World Wide Web HTTP
  Sequence Number:  9356570
  Ack Number:       0
  Offset:           7
  Reserved:         %000000
  Code:             %000010
        Synch Sequence
  Window:           8192
  Checksum:         0x57E7
  Urgent Pointer:   0
  TCP Options:
   Option Type: 2 Maximum Segment Size
     Length:    4
     MSS:         536
   Option Type: 1 No Operation
   Option Type: 1 No Operation
   Option Type: 4
     Length:    2
     Opt Value:
  No More HTTP Data
Frame Check Sequence: 0x43697363
```

And sure enough, the source port is greater than 1024, but the destination port is 80, or HTTP service. The server, or receiving host, will change the destination port if it needs to do so.

In the preceding trace, a "syn" packet is sent to the destination device. The sync sequence is what's telling the remote destination device that it wants to create a session.

TCP Session: Syn Packet Acknowledgment

The next trace shows an acknowledgment to the syn packet:

```
TCP - Transport Control Protocol
  Source Port:       80 World Wide Web HTTP
  Destination Port: 1144
  Sequence Number:  2873580788
  Ack Number:       9356571
  Offset:           6
  Reserved:         %000000
  Code:             %010010
       Ack is valid
       Synch Sequence
  Window:           8576
  Checksum:         0x5F85
  Urgent Pointer:   0
  TCP Options:
   Option Type: 2 Maximum Segment Size
     Length:    4
     MSS:       1460
  No More HTTP Data
Frame Check Sequence: 0x6E203132
```

Notice the *Ack is valid*, which means that the source port was accepted and the device agreed to create a virtual circuit with the originating host.

And here again, you can see that the response from the server shows that the source is 80 and the destination is the 1144 sent from the originating host—all's well. The next packet (not shown) would be a sync/ack that will establish the three-way handshake.

Table 2.2 lists the typical applications used in the TCP/IP suite, their well-known port numbers, and the Transport layer protocols used by each application or process. It's important that you study and memorize this table.

TABLE 2.2   Key protocols that use TCP and UDP

TCP	UDP
Telnet 23	SNMP 161
SMTP 25	TFTP 69

TABLE 2.2   Key protocols that use TCP and UDP *(continued)*

TCP	UDP
HTTP 80	DNS 53
FTP 21	BOOTPS/DHCP 67
DNS 53	
HTTPS 443	
SSH 22	

Notice that DNS uses both TCP and UDP. Whether it opts for one or the other depends on what it's trying to do. Even though it's not the only application that can use both protocols, it's certainly one that you should remember in your studies.

 What makes TCP reliable is sequencing, acknowledgments, and flow control (windowing). UDP does not have reliability.

The Internet Layer Protocols

In the DoD model, there are two main reasons for the Internet layer's existence: routing and providing a single network interface to the upper layers.

None of the other upper- or lower-layer protocols has any functions relating to routing—that complex and important task belongs entirely to the Internet layer. The Internet layer's second duty is to provide a single network interface to the upper-layer protocols. Without this layer, application programmers would need to write "hooks" into every one of their applications for each different Network Access protocol. Not only would this be a pain in the neck, but it would lead to different versions of each application—one for Ethernet, another one for Token Ring, and so on. To prevent this, IP provides one single network interface for the upper-layer protocols. That accomplished, it's then the job of IP and the various Network Access protocols to get along and work together.

All network roads don't lead to Rome—they lead to IP. And all the other protocols at this layer, as well as all those at the upper layers, use it. Never forget that. All paths through the DoD model go through IP. The following sections describe the protocols at the Internet layer:

- Internet Protocol (IP)
- Internet Control Message Protocol (ICMP)
- Address Resolution Protocol (ARP)
- Reverse Address Resolution Protocol (RARP)
- Proxy ARP

Internet Protocol

Internet Protocol (IP) essentially is the Internet layer. The other protocols found here merely exist to support it. IP holds the big picture and could be said to "see all," in that it's aware of all the interconnected networks. It can do this because all the machines on the network have a software, or logical, address called an IP address, which I'll cover more thoroughly later in this chapter.

IP looks at each packet's address. Then, using a routing table, it decides where a packet is to be sent next, choosing the best path. The protocols of the Network Access layer at the bottom of the DoD model don't possess IP's enlightened scope of the entire network; they deal only with physical links (local networks).

Identifying devices on networks requires answering these two questions: which network is it on, and what is its ID on that network? The first answer is the *software address*, or *logical address* (the correct street). The second answer is the hardware address (the correct mailbox). All hosts on a network have a logical ID called an *IP address*. This is the software, or logical, address and contains valuable encoded information, greatly simplifying the complex task of routing. (IP is discussed in RFC 791.)

IP receives segments from the Host-to-Host layer and fragments them into datagrams (packets) if necessary. IP then reassembles datagrams back into segments on the receiving side. Each datagram is assigned the IP address of the sender and of the recipient. Each router (layer 3 device) that receives a datagram makes routing decisions based on the packet's destination IP address.

Figure 2.7 shows an IP header. This will give you an idea of what the IP protocol has to go through every time user data is sent from the upper layers and is to be sent to a remote network.

FIGURE 2.7   IP header

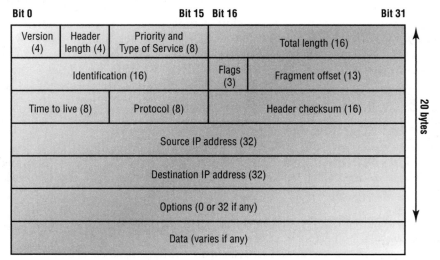

The following fields make up the IP header:

Version   IP version number.

Header Length   Header length (HLEN) in 32-bit words.

Priority and Type of Service   Type of Service tells how the datagram should be handled. The first 3 bits are the priority bits.

Total Length   Length of the packet including header and data.

Identification   Unique IP-packet value.

Flags   Specifies whether fragmentation should occur.

Fragment Offset   Provides fragmentation and reassembly if the packet is too large to put in a frame. It also allows different maximum transmission units (MTUs) on the Internet.

Time to Live   The time to live is set into a packet when it is originally generated. If the packet doesn't get to where it wants to go before the TTL expires, boom—it's gone. This stops IP packets from continuously circling the network looking for a home.

Protocol   Port of upper-layer protocol (TCP is port 6; UDP is port 17). Also supports Network layer protocols, like ARP and ICMP. Can be called Type field in some analyzers. I'll talk about this field in more detail in a minute.

Header Checksum   Cyclic redundancy check (CRC) on header only.

Source IP Address   32-bit IP address of sending station.

Destination IP Address   32-bit IP address of the station this packet is destined for.

Options   Used for network testing, debugging, security, and more.

Data   After the IP option field will be the upper-layer data.

Here's a snapshot of an IP packet caught on a network analyzer (notice that all the header information discussed previously appears here):

```
IP Header - Internet Protocol Datagram
 Version:              4
 Header Length:        5
 Precedence:           0
 Type of Service:      %000
 Unused:               %00
 Total Length:         187
 Identifier:           22486
 Fragmentation Flags:  %010 Do Not Fragment
 Fragment Offset:      0
 Time To Live:         60
 IP Type:              0x06 TCP
 Header Checksum:      0xd031
 Source IP Address:    10.7.1.30
 Dest. IP Address:     10.7.1.10
 No Internet Datagram Options
```

The Type field—it's typically a Protocol field, but this analyzer sees it as an IP Type field—is important. If the header didn't carry the protocol information for the next layer, IP wouldn't know what to do with the data carried in the packet. The preceding example tells IP to hand the segment to TCP.

Figure 2.8 demonstrates how the Network layer sees the protocols at the Transport layer when it needs to hand a packet to the upper-layer protocols.

FIGURE 2.8   The Protocol field in an IP header

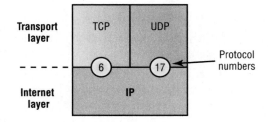

In this example, the Protocol field tells IP to send the data to either TCP port 6 or UDP port 17. But it will be UDP or TCP only if the data is part of a data stream headed for an upper-layer service or application. It could just as easily be destined for Internet Control Message Protocol (ICMP), Address Resolution Protocol (ARP), or some other type of Network layer protocol.

Table 2.3 lists some other popular protocols that can be specified in the Protocol field.

TABLE 2.3   Possible protocols found in the Protocol field of an IP header

Protocol	Protocol number
Internet Control Message Protocol (ICMP)	1
IP in IP (tunneling)	4
TCP	6
Interior Gateway Routing Protocol (IGRP)	9
UDP	17
Enhanced IGRP (EIGRP)	88
Open Shortest Path First (OSPF)	89
Internet Protocol version 6 (IPv6)	41
Generic Routing Encapsulation (GRE)	47
Layer 2 Tunnel Protocol (L2TP)	115

You can find a complete list of protocol field numbers at www.iana.org/
assignments/protocol-numbers.

Internet Control Message Protocol

Internet Control Message Protocol (ICMP) works at the Network layer and is used by IP
for many different services. ICMP is a management protocol and messaging service provider for IP. Its messages are carried as IP datagrams.

ICMP packets have the following characteristics:

- They can provide hosts with information about network problems.
- They are encapsulated within IP datagrams.

The following are some common events and messages that ICMP relates to:

Destination Unreachable   If a router can't send an IP datagram any further because a remote
route is down, it uses ICMP to send a message back to the sender, advising it of the situation.
For example, take a look at Figure 2.9, which shows that interface E0 of the Lab_B router
is down.

FIGURE 2.9   ICMP error message is sent to the sending host from the remote router.

E0 on Lab B is down. Host A is trying to communicate to Host B. What happens?

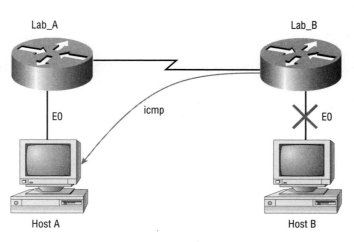

When Host A sends a packet destined for Host B, the Lab_B router will send an ICMP destination unreachable message back to the sending device (Host A in this example).

Buffer Full/Source Quench   If a router's memory buffer for receiving incoming datagrams
is full, it will use ICMP to send out this message until the congestion abates.

Hops/Time Exceeded Each IP datagram is allotted a certain number of routers, called *hops*, to pass through. If it reaches its limit of hops before arriving at its destination, the last router to receive that datagram deletes it. The executioner router then uses ICMP to send an obituary message, informing the sending machine of the demise of its datagram.

Ping Packet Internet Groper (Ping) is a program that uses ICMP echo request and reply messages to check the physical and logical connectivity of machines on an internetwork. For example, a network administrator will use Ping (which uses the ICMP protocol) to check basic connectivity from a workstation to a server.

Traceroute Using ICMP time-outs, the Traceroute program is used to discover the path a packet takes as it traverses an internetwork.

Both Ping and Traceroute (also just called Trace; Microsoft Windows uses tracert) allow you to verify address configurations in your internetwork.

The following data is from a network analyzer catching an ICMP echo request:

```
Flags:          0x00
 Status:         0x00
 Packet Length: 78
 Timestamp:      14:04:25.967000 12/20/03
Ethernet Header
 Destination: 00:a0:24:6e:0f:a8
 Source:      00:80:c7:a8:f0:3d
 Ether-Type:  08-00 IP
IP Header - Internet Protocol Datagram
 Version:            4
 Header Length:      5
 Precedence:         0
 Type of Service:    %000
 Unused:             %00
 Total Length:       60
 Identifier:         56325
 Fragmentation Flags: %000
 Fragment Offset:    0
 Time To Live:       32
 IP Type:            0x01 ICMP
 Header Checksum:    0x2df0
 Source IP Address:  100.100.100.2
 Dest. IP Address:   100.100.100.1
 No Internet Datagram Options
ICMP - Internet Control Messages Protocol
 ICMP Type:      8 Echo Request
 Code:           0
```

```
Checksum:          0x395c
Identifier:        0x0300
Sequence Number:   4352
ICMP Data Area:
abcdefghijklmnop   61 62 63 64 65 66 67 68 69 6a 6b 6c 6d
qrstuvwabcdefghi   71 72 73 74 75 76 77 61 62 63 64 65 66
Frame Check Sequence: 0x00000000
```

Notice anything unusual? Did you catch the fact that even though ICMP works at the Internet (Network) layer, it still uses IP to do the Ping request? The Type field in the IP header is 0x01, which specifies that the data being carried is owned by the ICMP protocol. Remember, just as all roads lead to Rome, all segments or data *must* go through IP!

The Ping program uses the alphabet in the data portion of the packet as a payload, typically around 100 bytes by default, unless, of course, you are pinging from a Windows device, which thinks the alphabet stops at the letter *W* and doesn't include *X*, *Y*, or *Z* and then starts at *A* again as shown in the analyzer output. Go figure!

Before I get into the ARP protocol, let's take another look at ICMP in action. Figure 2.10 shows an internetwork (it has a router, so it's an internetwork, right?).

FIGURE 2.10   ICMP in action

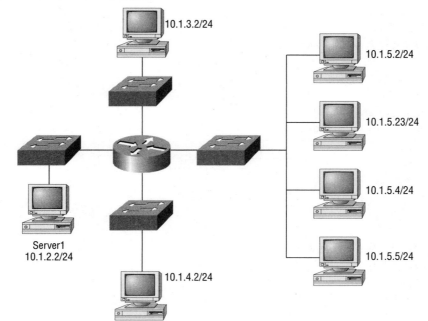

The router is configured with the IP addresses 10.1.2.1, 10.1.3.1, and 10.1.4.1. The 10.1.5.0 subnet is connected but is not configured on the router interface.

Server1 (10.1.2.2) telnets to 10.1.1.5 from a DOS prompt. What do you think Server1 will receive as a response? Since Server1 will send the Telnet data to the default gateway, which is the router, the router will drop the packet because there isn't a network 10.1.1.0 in the routing table. Because of this, Server1 will receive a destination unreachable back from ICMP.

Address Resolution Protocol

Address Resolution Protocol (ARP) finds the hardware address of a host from a known IP address. Here's how it works: When IP has a datagram to send, it must inform a Network Access protocol, such as Ethernet, of the destination's hardware address on the local network. (It has already been informed by upper-layer protocols of the destination's IP address.) If IP doesn't find the destination host's hardware address in the ARP cache, it uses ARP to find this information.

As IP's detective, ARP interrogates the local network by sending out a broadcast asking the machine with the specified IP address to reply with its hardware address. So, basically, ARP translates the software (IP) address into a hardware address—for example, the destination machine's Ethernet board address—and, from it, deduces its whereabouts on the LAN by broadcasting for this address. Figure 2.11 shows how an ARP looks to a local network.

FIGURE 2.11   Local ARP broadcast

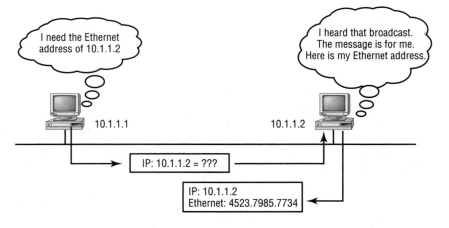

ARP resolves IP addresses to Ethernet (MAC) addresses.

The following trace shows an ARP broadcast—notice that the destination hardware address is unknown, is all *F*s in hex (all 1s in binary), and is a hardware address broadcast:

```
Flags:            0x00
Status:           0x00
Packet Length: 64
Timestamp:        09:17:29.574000 12/06/03
Ethernet Header
Destination:      FF:FF:FF:FF:FF:FF Ethernet Broadcast
Source:           00:A0:24:48:60:A5
Protocol Type: 0x0806 IP ARP
ARP - Address Resolution Protocol
Hardware:                  1 Ethernet (10Mb)
Protocol:                  0x0800 IP
Hardware Address Length: 6
Protocol Address Length: 4
Operation:                 1 ARP Request
Sender Hardware Address: 00:A0:24:48:60:A5
Sender Internet Address: 172.16.10.3
Target Hardware Address: 00:00:00:00:00:00 (ignored)
Target Internet Address: 172.16.10.10
Extra bytes (Padding):
................ 0A 0A 0A 0A 0A 0A 0A 0A 0A 0A 0A 0A 0A
  0A 0A 0A 0A 0A
Frame Check Sequence: 0x00000000
```

Reverse Address Resolution Protocol

When an IP machine happens to be a diskless machine, it has no way of initially knowing its IP address. But it does know its MAC address. *Reverse Address Resolution Protocol (RARP)* discovers the identity of the IP address for diskless machines by sending out a packet that includes its MAC address and a request for the IP address assigned to that MAC address. A designated machine, called a *RARP server*, responds with the answer, and the identity crisis is over. RARP uses the information it does know about the machine's MAC address to learn its IP address and complete the machine's ID portrait.

Figure 2.12 shows a diskless workstation asking for its IP address with a RARP broadcast.

FIGURE 2.12   RARP broadcast example

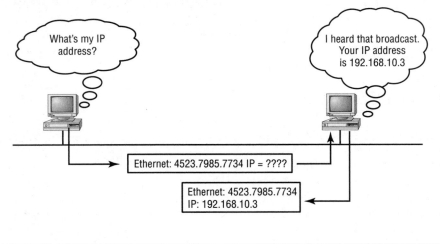

    RARP resolves Ethernet (MAC) addresses to IP addresses.

Proxy Address Resolution Protocol

On a network, your hosts can't have more than one default gateway configured. Think about this…what if the default gateway (router) happens to go down? The host won't just start sending to another router automatically—you have to reconfigure that host. But Proxy ARP can actually help machines on a subnet reach remote subnets without configuring routing or even a default gateway.

One advantage of using Proxy ARP is that it can be added to a single router on a network without disturbing the routing tables of all the other routers that live there too. But there's a serious downside to using Proxy ARP. Using Proxy ARP will definitely increase the amount of traffic on your network segment, and hosts will have a larger ARP table than usual in order to handle all the IP-to-MAC-address mappings. And Proxy ARP is configured on all Cisco routers by default—you should disable it if you don't think you're going to use it.

One last thought on Proxy ARP: Proxy ARP isn't really a separate protocol. It is a service run by routers on behalf of other devices (usually PCs) that are separated from their query to another device by a router, although they think they share the subnet with the remote device. This lets the router provide its own MAC address in response to ARP queries attempting to resolve a distant IP address to a functional MAC address.

If you can afford it, use Cisco's Hot Standby Router Protocol (HSRP) instead. It means you have to buy two or more of your Cisco device(s), but it is well worth it. Check out the Cisco website for more information on HSRP.

IP Addressing

One of the most important topics in any discussion of TCP/IP is IP addressing. An *IP address* is a numeric identifier assigned to each machine on an IP network. It designates the specific location of a device on the network.

An IP address is a software address, not a hardware address—the latter is hard-coded on a network interface card (NIC) and used for finding hosts on a local network. IP addressing was designed to allow hosts on one network to communicate with a host on a different network regardless of the type of LANs the hosts are participating in.

Before I get into the more complicated aspects of IP addressing, you need to understand some of the basics. First I'm going to explain some of the fundamentals of IP addressing and its terminology. Then you'll learn about the hierarchical IP addressing scheme and private IP addresses.

IP Terminology

In the rest of this chapter you'll learn several important terms vital to your understanding of the Internet Protocol. Here are a few to get you started:

Bit   A *bit* is one digit, either a 1 or a 0.

Byte   A *byte* is 7 or 8 bits, depending on whether parity is used. For the rest of this chapter, always assume a byte is 8 bits.

Octet   An octet, made up of 8 bits, is just an ordinary 8-bit binary number. In this chapter, the terms *byte* and *octet* are completely interchangeable.

Network Address   This is the designation used in routing to send packets to a remote network—for example, 10.0.0.0, 172.16.0.0, and 192.168.10.0.

Broadcast Address   The address used by applications and hosts to send information to all nodes on a network is called the *broadcast address*. Examples include 255.255.255.255, which is any network, all nodes; 172.16.255.255, which is all subnets and hosts on network 172.16.0.0; and 10.255.255.255, which broadcasts to all subnets and hosts on network 10.0.0.0.

The Hierarchical IP Addressing Scheme

An IP address consists of 32 bits of information. These bits are divided into four sections, referred to as *octets* or bytes, each containing 1 byte (8 bits). You can depict an IP address using one of three methods:

- Dotted-decimal, as in 172.16.30.56
- Binary, as in 10101100.00010000.00011110.00111000
- Hexadecimal, as in AC.10.1E.38

All these examples truly represent the same IP address. Hexadecimal isn't used as often as dotted-decimal or binary when IP addressing is discussed, but you still might find an IP address stored in hexadecimal in some programs. The Windows Registry is a good example of a program that stores a machine's IP address in hex.

The 32-bit IP address is a structured or hierarchical address, as opposed to a flat or nonhierarchical address. Although either type of addressing scheme could have been used, *hierarchical addressing* was chosen for a good reason. The advantage of this scheme is that it can handle a large number of addresses, namely, 4.3 billion (a 32-bit address space with two possible values for each position—either 0 or 1—gives you 2^{32}, or 4,294,967,296). The disadvantage of the flat addressing scheme, and the reason it's not used for IP addressing, relates to routing. If every address were unique, all routers on the Internet would need to store the address of each and every machine on the Internet. This would make efficient routing impossible, even if only a fraction of the possible addresses were used.

The solution to this problem is to use a two- or three-level hierarchical addressing scheme that is structured by network and host or by network, subnet, and host.

This two- or three-level scheme is comparable to a telephone number. The first section, the area code, designates a very large area. The second section, the prefix, narrows the scope to a local calling area. The final segment, the customer number, zooms in on the specific connection. IP addresses use the same type of layered structure. Rather than all 32 bits being treated as a unique identifier, as in flat addressing, part of the address is designated as the network address, and the other part is designated as either the subnet and host or just the node address.

In the following sections, I'll discuss IP network addressing and the different classes of address you can use to address your networks.

Network Addressing

The *network address* (which can also be called the *network number*) uniquely identifies each network. Every machine on the same network shares that network address as part of its IP address. In the IP address 172.16.30.56, for example, 172.16 is the network address.

The *node address* is assigned to, and uniquely identifies, each machine on a network. This part of the address must be unique because it identifies a particular machine—an individual—as opposed to a network, which is a group. This number can also be referred to as a *host address*. In the sample IP address 172.16.30.56, the 30.56 is the node address.

The designers of the Internet decided to create classes of networks based on network size. For the small number of networks possessing a very large number of nodes, they created the rank *Class A network*. At the other extreme is the *Class C network*, which is reserved for the numerous networks with a small number of nodes. The class distinction for networks between very large and very small is predictably called the *Class B network*.

Subdividing an IP address into a network and node address is determined by the class designation of one's network. Figure 2.13 summarizes the three classes of networks used to address hosts with—a subject I'll explain in much greater detail throughout the rest of this chapter.

FIGURE 2.13   Summary of the three classes of networks

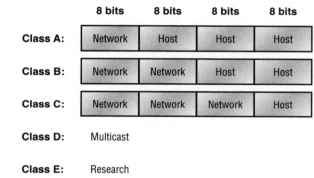

To ensure efficient routing, Internet designers defined a mandate for the leading-bits section of the address for each different network class. For example, since a router knows that a Class A network address always starts with a 0, the router might be able to speed a packet on its way after reading only the first bit of its address. This is where the address schemes define the difference between a Class A, a Class B, and a Class C address. In the next sections, I'll discuss the differences between these three classes, followed by a discussion of the Class D and Class E addresses (Classes A, B, and C are the only ranges that are used to address hosts in your networks).

Network Address Range: Class A

The designers of the IP address scheme said that the first bit of the first byte in a Class A network address must always be off, or 0. This means a Class A address must be between 0 and 127 in the first byte, inclusive.

Consider the following first byte of a network address:

0xxxxxxx

If you turn the other 7 bits all off and then turn them all on, you'll find the Class A range of network addresses.

00000000 = 0
01111111 = 127

So, a Class A network is defined in the first octet between 0 and 127, and it can't be less or more. (Yes, I know 0 and 127 are not valid in a Class A network. I'll talk about reserved addresses in a minute.)

Network Address Range: Class B

In a Class B network, the RFCs state that the first bit of the first byte must always be turned on, but the second bit must always be turned off. If you turn the other 6 bits all off and then all on, you will find the range for a Class B network.

10000000 = 128
10111111 = 191

As you can see, a Class B network is defined when the first byte is configured from 128 to 191.

Network Address Range: Class C

For Class C networks, the RFCs define the first 2 bits of the first octet as always turned on, but the third bit can never be on. Following the same process used with the previous classes, convert from binary to decimal to find the range. Here's the range for a Class C network:

11000000 = 192
11011111 = 223

So, if you see an IP address that starts at 192 and goes to 223 in the first octet, you'll know it is a Class C IP address.

Network Address Ranges: Classes D and E

The addresses between 224 to 255 in the first octet are reserved for Class D and E networks. Class D (224–239) is used for multicast addresses and Class E (240–255) for scientific purposes, but I'm not going into these types of addresses in this book (and you don't need to know them).

Network Addresses: Special Purpose

Some IP addresses are reserved for special purposes, so network administrators can't ever assign these addresses to nodes. Table 2.4 lists the members of this exclusive little club and the reasons why they're included in it.

TABLE 2.4   Reserved IP addresses

Address	Function
Network address of all 0s	Interpreted to mean "this network or segment."
Network address of all 1s	Interpreted to mean "all networks."
Network 127.0.0.1	Reserved for loopback tests. Designates the local node and allows that node to send a test packet to itself without generating network traffic.

TABLE 2.4   Reserved IP addresses *(continued)*

Address	Function
Node address of all 0s	Interpreted to mean "network address" or any host on specified network.
Node address of all 1s	Interpreted to mean "all nodes" on the specified network; for example, 128.2.255.255 means "all nodes" on network 128.2 (Class B address).
Entire IP address set to all 0s	Used by Cisco routers to designate the default route. Could also mean "any network."
Entire IP address set to all 1s (same as 255.255.255.255)	Broadcast to all nodes on the current network; sometimes called an "all 1s broadcast" or limited broadcast.

Class A Addresses

In a Class A network address, the first byte is assigned to the network address, and the three remaining bytes are used for the node addresses. The Class A format is as follows:

network.node.node.node

For example, in the IP address 49.22.102.70, the 49 is the network address, and 22.102.70 is the node address. Every machine on this particular network would have the distinctive network address of 49.

Class A network addresses are 1 byte long, with the first bit of that byte reserved and the 7 remaining bits available for manipulation (addressing). As a result, the maximum number of Class A networks that can be created is 128. Why? Because each of the 7 bit positions can be either a 0 or a 1, thus 2^7, or 128.

To complicate matters further, the network address of all 0s (00000000) is reserved to designate the default route (see Table 2.4 in the previous section). Additionally, the address 127, which is reserved for diagnostics, can't be used either, which means you can really only use the numbers 1 to 126 to designate Class A network addresses. This means the actual number of usable Class A network addresses is 128 minus 2, or 126.

The IP address 127.0.0.1 is used to test the IP stack on an individual node and cannot be used as a valid host address. However, the loopback address creates a shortcut method for TCP/IP applications and services that run on the same device to communicate with each other.

Each Class A address has 3 bytes (24-bit positions) for the node address of a machine. This means there are 2^{24}—or 16,777,216—unique combinations and, therefore, precisely that many possible unique node addresses for each Class A network. Because node addresses with the two patterns of all 0s and all 1s are reserved, the actual maximum usable number of nodes for a Class A network is 2^{24} minus 2, which equals 16,777,214. Either way, that's a huge amount of hosts on a network segment!

Class A Valid Host IDs

Here's an example of how to figure out the valid host IDs in a Class A network address:

- All host bits off is the network address: 10.0.0.0.
- All host bits on is the broadcast address: 10.255.255.255.

The valid hosts are the numbers in between the network address and the broadcast address: 10.0.0.1 through 10.255.255.254. Notice that with the exception of the two IP addresses in the bullets above, 0s and 255s can be used as valid host ID values. All you need to remember when trying to find valid host addresses is that the host bits can't all be turned off or all be on at the same time.

Class B Addresses

In a Class B network address, the first 2 bytes are assigned to the network address, and the remaining 2 bytes are used for node addresses. The format is as follows:

`network.network.node.node`

For example, in the IP address 172.16.30.56, the network address is 172.16, and the node address is 30.56.

With a network address being 2 bytes (8 bits each), there would be 2^{16} unique combinations. But the Internet designers decided that all Class B network addresses should start with the binary digit 1 and then 0. This leaves 14 bit positions to manipulate, which is 16,384 (that is, 2^{14}) unique Class B network addresses.

A Class B address uses 2 bytes for node addresses. This is 2^{16} minus the two reserved patterns (all 0s and all 1s), for a total of 65,534 possible node addresses for each Class B network.

Class B Valid Host IDs

Here's an example of how to find the valid hosts in a Class B network:

- All host bits turned off is the network address: 172.16.0.0.
- All host bits turned on is the broadcast address: 172.16.255.255.

The valid hosts would be the numbers in between the network address and the broadcast address: 172.16.0.1 through 172.16.255.254.

Class C Addresses

The first 3 bytes of a Class C network address are dedicated to the network portion of the address, with only 1 measly byte remaining for the node address. Here's the format:

`network.network.network.node`

Using the example IP address 192.168.100.102, the network address is 192.168.100, and the node address is 102.

In a Class C network address, the first three bit positions are always the binary 110. The calculation is as follows: 3 bytes, or 24 bits, minus 3 reserved positions leaves 21 positions. Hence, there are 2^{21}, or 2,097,152, possible Class C networks.

Each unique Class C network has 1 byte to use for node addresses. This leads to 2^8 or 256, minus the two reserved patterns of all 0s and all 1s, for a total of 254 node addresses for each Class C network.

Class C Valid Host IDs

Here's an example of how to find a valid host ID in a Class C network:

- All host bits turned off is the network ID: 192.168.100.0.
- All host bits turned on is the broadcast address: 192.168.100.255.

The valid hosts would be the numbers in between the network address and the broadcast address: 192.168.100.1 through 192.168.100.254.

Private IP Addresses

The people who created the IP addressing scheme also created what we call *private IP addresses*. These addresses can be used on a private network, but they're not routable through the Internet. This is designed for the purpose of creating a measure of well-needed security, but it also conveniently saves valuable IP address space.

If every host on every network had to have real routable IP addresses, we would have run out of IP addresses to hand out years ago. But by using private IP addresses, ISPs, corporations, and home users need only a relatively tiny group of bona fide IP addresses to connect their networks to the Internet. This is economical because they can use private IP addresses on their inside networks and get along just fine.

To accomplish this task, the ISP and the corporation—the end user, no matter who they are—need to use something called *Network Address Translation (NAT)*, which basically takes a private IP address and converts it for use on the Internet. (Chapter 3 includes an introduction to NAT.) Many people can use the same real IP address to transmit out onto the Internet. Doing things this way saves megatons of address space—good for us all!

Table 2.5 lists the reserved private addresses.

TABLE 2.5   Reserved IP address space

Address class	Reserved address space
Class A	10.0.0.0 through 10.255.255.255
Class B	172.16.0.0 through 172.31.255.255
Class C	192.168.0.0 through 192.168.255.255

You must know your private address spaces!

According to Cisco, private IP addresses are used for the following reasons:

- To create addresses that cannot be routed through the public Internet
- To conserve public addresses

🌐 **Real World Scenario**

So, What Private IP Address Should I Use?

That's a really great question. Should you use Class A, Class B, or even Class C private addressing when setting up your network? Let's take Acme Corporation in San Francisco as an example. This company is moving into a new building and needs a whole new network (what a treat this is!). It has 14 departments, with about 70 users in each. You could probably squeeze one or two Class C addresses to use, or maybe you could use a Class B or even a Class A just for fun.

The rule of thumb in the consulting world is, when you're setting up a corporate network—regardless of how small it is—you should use a Class A network address because it gives you the most flexibility and growth options. For example, if you used the 10.0.0.0 network address with a /24 mask, then you'd have 65,536 networks, each with 254 hosts. Lots of room for growth with that network!

But if you're setting up a home network, you'd opt for a Class C address because it is the easiest for people to understand and configure. Using the default Class C mask gives you one network with 254 hosts—plenty for a home network.

With the Acme Corporation, a nice 10.1.*x*.0 with a /24 mask (the *x* is the subnet for each department) makes this easy to design, install, and troubleshoot.

IPv4 Address Types

Most people use the term *broadcast* as a generic term, and most of the time, we understand what they mean. But not always. For example, you might say, "The host broadcasted through a router to a DHCP server," but, well, it's pretty unlikely that this would ever really happen. What you probably mean—using the correct technical jargon—is, "The DHCP client broadcasted for an IP address; a router then forwarded this as a unicast packet to the DHCP server."

Okay, I've referred to broadcast addresses throughout Chapters 1 and 2 and even showed you some examples. But I really haven't gone into the different terms and uses associated with them yet, and it's about time I did. So, here are the four IPv4 address types that I'd like to define for you:

Layer 2 Broadcasts   These are sent to all nodes on a LAN.

Layer 3 Broadcasts   These are sent to all nodes on the network.

Unicast   This is an address for a single interface, and it is used to send packets to a single destination host.

Multicast   Multicast packets are sent from a single source and transmitted to many devices on different networks. It's referred to as one-to-many.

Layer 2 Broadcasts

First, understand that layer 2 broadcasts are also known as *hardware broadcasts*—they go out only on a LAN, and they don't go past the LAN boundary (router).

The typical hardware address is 6 bytes (48 bits) and looks something like 0c:43:a4:f3:12:c2. The broadcast would be all 1s in binary, which would be all *F*s in hexadecimal, as in FF.FF.FF.FF.FF.FF.

Layer 3 Broadcasts

Then there are the plain old broadcast addresses at layer 3. Broadcast messages are meant to reach all hosts on a broadcast domain. These are the network broadcasts that have all host bits on.

Here's an example that you're already familiar with: the network address of 172.16.0.0 255.255.0.0 would have a broadcast address of 172.16.255.255—all host bits on. Broadcasts can also be "any network and all hosts," as indicated by 255.255.255.255.

A good example of a broadcast message is an Address Resolution Protocol (ARP) request. When a host has a packet, it knows the logical address (IP) of the destination. To get the packet to the destination, the host needs to forward the packet to a default gateway if the destination resides on a different IP network. If the destination is on the local network, the source will forward the packet directly to the destination. Because the source doesn't have the MAC address to which it needs to forward the frame, it sends out a broadcast, something that every device in the local broadcast domain will listen to. This broadcast says, in essence, "If you are the owner of IP address 192.168.2.3, please forward your MAC address to me," with the source giving the appropriate information.

Unicast Address

Unicast is the definition of an IP address on a node. It defines a destination address.

In addition, a unicast can be relayed from a destination address of 255.255.255.255 to an actual destination IP address; in other words, it's directed to a specific host (unicast). A DHCP client request is a good example of how this works.

Here's an example. Your host on a LAN sends out a layer 2 broadcast (FF.FF.FF.FF.FF.FF) and layer 3 (255.255.255.255) broadcast, looking for a DHCP server on the LAN. The router will see that this is a broadcast meant for the DHCP server because it has a destination port number of 67 (BootP server) and will forward the request to the IP address of the DHCP server on another LAN. So, basically, if your DHCP server IP address is 172.16.10.1, your host just sends out a 255.255.255.255 DHCP client broadcast request, and the router changes that broadcast to the specific destination address of 172.16.10.1. (For the router to provide this service, you need to configure the interfaces with the `ip helper-address` command—this is not a default service.)

Multicast Address

Multicast is a different beast entirely. At first glance, it appears to be a hybrid of unicast and broadcast communication, but that isn't quite the case. Multicast does allow point-to-multipoint communication, which is similar to broadcasts, but it happens in a different manner. The crux of *multicast* is that it enables multiple recipients to receive messages without flooding the messages to all hosts on a broadcast domain. However, this is not the default behavior—it's what you *can* do with multicasting if it's configured correctly!

Multicast works by sending messages or data to IP *multicast group* addresses. Routers then forward copies (unlike broadcasts, which are not forwarded) of the packet out every interface that has hosts *subscribed* to that group address. This is where multicast differs from broadcast messages—with multicast communication, copies of packets, in theory, are sent only to subscribed destinations. For example, this means that the routers will receive a multicast packet destined for 224.0.0.9 (this is an EIGRP packet, and only a router running the EIGRP protocol will read these). All hosts on the broadcast LAN (Ethernet is a broadcast multi-access LAN technology) will pick up the frame, read the destination address, and immediately discard the frame, unless they are in the multicast group. This saves PC processing, not LAN bandwidth. Multicasting can cause severe LAN congestion, in some instances, if not implemented carefully.

Users or applications can subscribe to several different groups. The range of multicast addresses starts with 224.0.0.0 and goes through 239.255.255.255. As you can see, this range of addresses falls within IP Class D address space based on classful IP assignment.

Summary

If you made it this far and understood everything the first time through, you should be proud of yourself. I really covered a lot of ground in this chapter, but understand that the information in this chapter is key to being able to navigate through the rest of this book.

And even if you didn't get a complete understanding the first time around, don't stress. It really wouldn't hurt you to read this chapter more than once. There is still a lot of ground to cover, so make sure you've got it all down, and get ready for more. What I'm doing is building a foundation, and you want a strong foundation, right?

After you learned about the DoD model, the layers, and associated protocols, you learned about the oh-so-important IP addressing. I discussed in detail the difference between each class of address and how to find a network address, broadcast address, and valid host range, which is critical information to understand before going on to Chapter 3.

Since you've already come this far, there's no reason to stop now and waste all those brain waves and new neurons. So, don't stop—go through the written lab and review questions at the end of this chapter and make sure you understand each answer's explanation. The best is yet to come!

Exam Essentials

Differentiate the DoD and the OSI network models.   The DoD model is a condensed version of the OSI model, composed of four layers instead of seven, but is nonetheless like the OSI model in that it can be used to describe packet creation and devices and in that protocols can be mapped to its layers.

Identify Process/Application layer protocols.   Telnet is a terminal emulation program that allows you to log into a remote host and run programs. File Transfer Protocol (FTP) is a connection-oriented service that allows you to transfer files. Trivial FTP (TFTP) is a connectionless file transfer program. Simple Mail Transfer Protocol (SMTP) is a send-mail program.

Identify Host-to-Host layer protocols.   Transmission Control Protocol (TCP) is a connection-oriented protocol that provides reliable network service by using acknowledgments and flow control. User Datagram Protocol (UDP) is a connectionless protocol that provides low overhead and is considered unreliable.

Identify Internet layer protocols.   Internet Protocol (IP) is a connectionless protocol that provides network address and routing through an internetwork. Address Resolution Protocol (ARP) finds a hardware address from a known IP address. Reverse ARP (RARP) finds an IP address from a known hardware address. Internet Control Message Protocol (ICMP) provides diagnostics and destination unreachable messages.

Remember which Host-to-Host layer protocol the upper layer process or applications use.   You need to remember that Telnet uses port 23 and is connection-oriented, meaning it uses TCP at the Host-to-Host layer. FTP uses port 21 and TCP. SMTP uses port 25 and TCP. TFTP uses port 69 and UDP, so it is connectionless. SNMP uses port 161 and is connectionless.

Remember the Internet layer protocols   Internet Protocol (IP) is a connectionless protocol that provides network address and routing through an internetwork. Address Resolution Protocol (ARP) finds a hardware address from a known IP address. Reverse ARP (RARP) finds an IP address from a known hardware address. Internet Control Message Protocol (ICMP) provides diagnostics and destination unreachable messages.

Describe the functions of DNS and DHCP in the network.   *Dynamic Host Configuration Protocol (DHCP)* provides network configuration information (including IP addresses) to hosts, eliminating the need to perform the configurations manually. *Domain Name Service (DNS)* resolves hostnames—both Internet names such as `www.routersim.com` and device names such as Workstation2—to IP addresses, eliminating the need to know the IP address of a device for connection purposes.

Identify what is contained in the TCP header of a connection-oriented transmission.   The fields in the TCP header include the source port, the destination port, the sequence number, the acknowledgment number, the header length, a field reserved for future use, code bits, the window size, the checksum, the urgent pointer, the options field, and finally the data field.

Identify what is contained in the UDP header of a connectionless transmission.   The fields in the UDP header include only the source port, destination port, length, checksum, and data. The smaller number of fields as compared to the TCP header come at the expense of providing none of the more advanced functions of the TCP frame.

Identify what is contained in the IP header.   The fields of an IP header include version, header length, priority or type of service, total length, identification, flags, fragment offset, time to live, protocol, header checksum, source IP address, destination IP address, options, and, finally, data.

Compare and contrast UDP and TCP characteristics and features.   TCP is connection-oriented, acknowledged, and sequenced and has flow and error control, while UDP is connectionless, unacknowledged, and not sequenced and provides no error or flow control.

Understand the role of port numbers.   Port numbers are used to identify the protocol or service that is to be used in the transmission.

Identify the role of ICMP.   *Internet Control Message Protocol (ICMP)* works at the Network layer and is used by IP for many different services. ICMP is a management protocol and messaging service provider for IP.

Remember the Class A range.   The IP range for a Class A network is 1–126. This provides 8 bits of network addressing and 24 bits of host addressing by default. The first two bits of the first byte are always 01.

Remember the Class B range.   The IP range for a Class B network is 128–191. Class B addressing provides 16 bits of network addressing and 16 bits of host addressing by default. The first two bits of the first byte are always 10.

Remember the Class C range.   The IP range for a Class C network is 192–223. Class C addressing provides 24 bits of network addressing and 8 bits of host addressing by default. The first three bits of the first byte are always 110.

Remember the Private IP ranges.   Class A private address range is 10.0.0.0 through 10.255.255.255. Class B private address range is 172.16.0.0 through 172.31.255.255. Class C private address range is 192.168.0.0 through 192.168.255.255.

Understand the difference between a broadcast, unicast, and multicast transmission. A broadcast is to all devices in a subnet (one-to-all), a unicast is to an address on a single device, and a multicast is to some but not all devices (one-to-many).

Written Lab 2

Write the answers to the following questions.

1.   What is the range of the first octet of all Class C addresses in decimal and in binary?

2.   What layer of the DoD model is equivalent to the Transport layer of the OSI model?

3.   What is the valid range of the first octet of all Class A addresses in decimal?

4.   What is the 127.0.0.1 address used for?

5.   How do you find the network address from a listed IP address?

6.   How do you find the broadcast address from a listed IP address?

7.   What is the Class A private IP address space?

8.   What is the Class B private IP address space?

9.   What is the Class C private IP address space?

10.   What are all the available characters that you can use in hexadecimal addressing?

   (The answers to Written Lab 2 can be found in Appendix A.)

Review Questions

You can find the answers in Appendix B.

The following questions are designed to test your understanding of this chapter's material. For more information on how to get additional questions, please see this book's introduction.

1. Data on your host is being encapsulated. What are the correct layers and protocols used when sending email messages? (Choose four.)
    A. Application layer/SMTP
    B. Application layer/SNMP
    C. Transport layer/UDP
    D. Transport layer/TCP
    E. Internet layer/IP
    F. Internet layer/ARP
    G. Network Access/Ethernet
    H. Network Access/ARP

2. Which of the following allows a router to respond to an ARP request that is intended for a remote host?
    A. Gateway DP
    B. Reverse ARP (RARP)
    C. Proxy ARP
    D. Inverse ARP (IARP)
    E. Address Resolution Protocol (ARP)

3. You want to implement a mechanism that automates the IP configuration, including IP address, subnet mask, default gateway, and DNS information. Which protocol will you use to accomplish this?
    A. SMTP
    B. SNMP
    C. DHCP
    D. ARP

4. What protocol is used to find the hardware address of a local device?
    A. RARP
    B. ARP
    C. IP
    D. ICMP
    E. BootP

5. Which of the following are layers in the TCP/IP model? (Choose three.)

   A. Application

   B. Session

   C. Transport

   D. Internet

   E. Data Link

   F. Physical

6. Which class of IP address provides a maximum of only 254 host addresses per network ID?

   A. Class A

   B. Class B

   C. Class C

   D. Class D

   E. Class E

7. Which of the following describe the DHCP Discover message? (Choose two.)

   A. It uses FF:FF:FF:FF:FF:FF as a layer 2 broadcast.

   B. It uses UDP as the Transport layer protocol.

   C. It uses TCP as the Transport layer protocol.

   D. It does not use a layer 2 destination address.

8. Which layer 4 protocol is used for a Telnet connection?

   A. IP

   B. TCP

   C. TCP/IP

   D. UDP

   E. ICMP

9. Which statements are true regarding ICMP packets? (Choose two.)

   A. They acknowledge receipt of a TCP segment.

   B. They guarantee datagram delivery.

   C. They can provide hosts with information about network problems.

   D. They are encapsulated within IP datagrams.

   E. They are encapsulated within UDP datagrams.

10. Which of the following services use TCP? (Choose three.)

   A. DHCP

   B. SMTP

   C. SNMP

   D. FTP

   E. HTTP

   F. TFTP

11. Which of the following services use UDP? (Choose three.)

    A. DHCP

    B. SMTP

    C. SNMP

    D. FTP

    E. HTTP

    F. TFTP

12. Which of the following are found in a TCP header but not in a UDP header? (Choose three.)

    A. Sequence number

    B. Acknowledgment number

    C. Source port

    D. Destination port

    E. Window size

    F. Checksum

13. The following illustration shows a data structure header. What protocol is this header from?

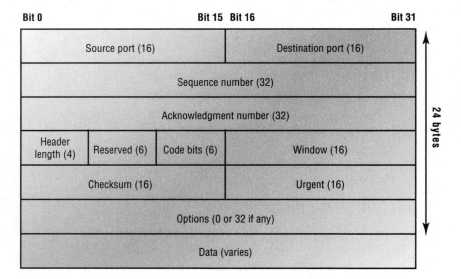

    A. IP

    B. ICMP

    C. TCP

    D. UDP

    E. ARP

    F. RARP

14. If you use either Telnet or FTP, which is the highest layer you are using to transmit data?

 A. Application

 B. Presentation

 C. Session

 D. Transport

15. The DoD model (also called the TCP/IP stack) has four layers. Which layer of the DoD model is equivalent to the Network layer of the OSI model?

 A. Application

 B. Host-to-Host

 C. Internet

 D. Network Access

16. Which two of the following are private IP addresses?

 A. 12.0.0.1

 B. 168.172.19.39

 C. 172.20.14.36

 D. 172.33.194.30

 E. 192.168.24.43

17. What layer in the TCP/IP stack is equivalent to the Transport layer of the OSI model?

 A. Application

 B. Host-to-Host

 C. Internet

 D. Network Access

18. Which of the following are the *four* steps that are required for a host to receive an IP address from a DHCP server?

 A. Step 1: DHCPDiscover/unicast

 B. Step 1: DHCPDiscover/broadcast

 C. Step 2: DHCPOffer/unicast

 D. Step 2: DHCPOffer/broadcast

 E. Step 3: DHCPRequest/unicast

 F. Step 3: DHCPRequest/broadcast

 G. Step 4: DHCPACK/unicast

 H. Step 4: DHCPACK/broadcast

19. When files are transferred between a host and an FTP server, the data is divided into smaller pieces for transmission. As these pieces arrive at the destination host, they must be reassembled to reconstruct the original file. What provides for the reassembly of these pieces into the correct order?

    A. The TTL in the IP header

    B. The frame check sequence in the Ethernet frame trailer

    C. The sequence number in the TCP header

    D. The Start Frame Delimiter in the 802.3 preamble

    E. The acknowledgment number in the segment header

20. Which of the following protocols uses both TCP and UDP?

    A. FTP

    B. SMTP

    C. Telnet

    D. DNS

Chapter 3

IP Subnetting, Troubleshooting IP, and Introduction to NAT

THE CCENT EXAM OBJECTIVES COVERED IN THIS CHAPTER INCLUDE THE FOLLOWING:

✓ **Implement an IP addressing scheme and IP services to meet network requirements for a small branch office**

- Describe the need and role of addressing in a network

- Create and apply an addressing scheme to a network

- Assign and verify valid IP addresses to hosts, servers, and networking devices in a LAN environment

- Explain the basic uses and operation of NAT in a small network connecting to one ISP

- Describe and verify DNS operation

- Describe the operation and benefits of using private and public IP addressing

- Enable NAT for a small network with a single ISP and connection using SDM and verify operation using CLI and ping

- Configure, verify and troubleshoot DHCP and DNS operation on a router (including: CLI/SDM)

- Implement static and dynamic addressing services for hosts in a LAN environment

- Identify and correct IP addressing issues

This chapter will pick up right where I left off in the previous chapter. I will continue the discussion of IP addressing.

I'll start with subnetting an IP network. You're going to have to really apply yourself, because subnetting takes time and practice in order to nail it. So, be patient. Do whatever it takes to get this stuff dialed in. This chapter truly is important—possibly the most important chapter in this book for you to understand.

I'll thoroughly cover IP subnetting from the very beginning. I know this might sound weird to you, but I think you'll be much better off if you can try to forget everything you've learned about subnetting before reading this chapter, especially if you've been to a Microsoft class!

After the discussion of IP subnetting, I'm going to tell you all about IP address troubleshooting and take you through the steps Cisco recommends when troubleshooting an IP network.

I'll wrap up the chapter by going over an introduction to network address translation (NAT), which has the great benefit of helping conserve address space. You'll learn the basics of the various types of NAT.

So, get psyched—you're about to go for quite a ride! This chapter will truly help you understand IP addressing and networking, so don't get discouraged or give up. If you stick with it, I promise that one day you'll look back on this, and you'll be really glad you decided to hang on. It's one of those things that after you understand it, you'll wonder why you once thought it was so hard. Ready? Let's go!

For up-to-the-minute updates for this chapter, please see www.lammle.com/forum and/or www.sybex.com/go/ccent2e.

Subnetting Basics

In Chapter 2, "Internet Protocols," you learned how to define and find the valid host ranges used in a Class A, Class B, and Class C network address by turning the host bits all off and then all on. This is very good, but here's the catch: you were defining only one network. What happens if you wanted to take one network address and create six networks from it?

You would have to do something called *subnetting*, because that's what allows you to take one larger network and break it into a bunch of smaller networks.

There are loads of reasons in favor of subnetting, including the following benefits:

Reduced Network Traffic　We all appreciate less traffic of any kind. Networks are no different. Without trusty routers, packet traffic could grind the entire network down to a near standstill. With routers, most traffic will stay on the local network; only packets destined for other networks will pass through the router. Routers create broadcast domains. The more broadcast domains you create, the smaller the broadcast domains and the less network traffic on each network segment.

Optimized Network Performance　This is a result of reduced network traffic.

Simplified Management　It's easier to identify and isolate network problems in a group of smaller connected networks than it is within one gigantic network.

Facilitated Spanning of Large Geographical Distances　Because WAN links are considerably slower and more expensive than LAN links, a single large network that spans long distances can create problems in every area previously listed. Connecting multiple smaller networks makes the system more efficient.

In the following sections, I am going to move to subnetting a network address. This is the good part—ready?

IP Subnet-Zero

ip subnet-zero is not a new command, but in the past, Cisco courseware and Cisco exam objectives didn't cover it—but they certainly do now! This command allows you to use the first and last subnets in your network design. For example, the Class C mask of 192 provides subnets 64 and 128 (discussed thoroughly later in this chapter), but with the ip subnet-zero command, you now get to use subnets 0, 64, 128, and 192. That is two more subnets for every subnet mask you use.

Even though I don't discuss the command-line interface (CLI) until the next chapter, "Cisco's Internetworking Operating System (IOS)," it's important for you to be familiar with this command:

```
Router#sh running-config
Building configuration...
!
hostname Pod1R1
!
ip subnet-zero
!
```

This router output shows that the command ip subnet-zero is enabled on the router. Cisco has turned this command on by default starting with Cisco IOS version 12.*x*.

> When studying for your Cisco exams, make sure you read very carefully and understand if Cisco is asking you *not* to use ip subnet-zero. There are instances where this may happen.

How to Create Subnets

To create subnetworks, you take bits from the host portion of the IP address and reserve them to define the subnet address. This means fewer bits for hosts, so the more subnets, the fewer bits available for defining hosts.

Later in this chapter, you'll learn how to create subnets, starting with Class C addresses. But before you actually implement subnetting, you need to determine your current requirements, as well as plan for future conditions.

> Before moving on to designing and creating a subnet mask, you need to understand that in this first section, I will be discussing classful routing, which means that all hosts (all nodes) in the network use the same subnet mask. When moving on to variable-length subnet masks (VLSMs), I'll discuss classless routing, which means that each network segment *can* use a different subnet mask.

To create a subnet, follow these steps:

1. Determine the number of required network IDs:
   - One for each subnet
   - One for each wide area network connection
2. Determine the number of required host IDs per subnet:
   - One for each TCP/IP host
   - One for each router interface
3. Based on these requirements, create the following:
   - One subnet mask for your entire network
   - A unique subnet ID for each physical segment
   - A range of host IDs for each subnet

Understanding the Powers of 2

Powers of 2 are important to understand and memorize for use with IP subnetting. To review powers of 2, remember that when you see a number with another number to its upper right (called an *exponent*), this means you should multiply the number by itself as many times as the upper number specifies. For example, 2^3 is $2 \times 2 \times 2$, which equals 8. Here's a list of powers of 2 that you should commit to memory:

$2^1 = 2$

$2^2 = 4$

$2^3 = 8$

$2^4 = 16$

$2^5 = 32$

$2^6 = 64$

$2^7 = 128$

$2^8 = 256$

$2^9 = 512$

$2^{10} = 1,024$

$2^{11} = 2,048$

$2^{12} = 4,096$

$2^{13} = 8,192$

$2^{14} = 16,384$

Before you get stressed out about knowing all these exponents, remember that it's helpful to know them, but it's not absolutely necessary. Here's a little trick since you're working with 2s: each successive power of 2 is double the previous one.

For example, all you have to do to remember the value of 2^9 is to first know that $2^8 = 256$. Why? Because when you double 2 to the eighth power (256), you get 2^9 (or 512). To determine the value of 2^{10}, simply start at $2^8 = 256$, and then double it twice.

You can go the other way as well. If you needed to know what 2^6 is, for example, you just cut 256 in half two times: once to reach 2^7 and then one more time to reach 2^6.

Subnet Masks

For the subnet address scheme to work, every machine on the network must know which part of the host address will be used as the subnet address. This is accomplished by assigning a *subnet mask* to each machine. A subnet mask is a 32-bit value that allows the recipient of IP packets to distinguish the network ID portion of the IP address from the host ID portion of the IP address.

The network administrator creates a 32-bit subnet mask composed of 1s and 0s. The 1s in the subnet mask represent the positions that refer to the network or subnet addresses.

Not all networks need subnets, meaning they use the default subnet mask. This is basically the same as saying that a network doesn't have a subnet address. Table 3.1 shows the default subnet masks for Classes A, B, and C. These default masks cannot change. In other words, you can't make a Class B subnet mask read 255.0.0.0. If you try, the host will read that address as invalid and usually won't even let you type it in. For a Class A network, you can't change the first byte in a subnet mask; it must read 255.0.0.0 at a minimum. Similarly, you cannot assign 255.255.255.255, because this is all 1s—a broadcast address. A Class B address must start with 255.255.0.0, and a Class C has to start with 255.255.255.0.

TABLE 3.1   Default subnet mask

Class	Format	Default Subnet Mask
A	*network.node.node.node*	255.0.0.0
B	*network.network.node.node*	255.255.0.0
C	*network.network.network.node*	255.255.255.0

Classless Inter-Domain Routing (CIDR)

Another term you need to familiarize yourself with is *Classless Inter-Domain Routing (CIDR)*. It's basically the method that Internet service providers (ISPs) use to allocate an amount of addresses to a company, a home, or a customer. They provide addresses in a certain block size, something I'll be going into in greater detail later in this chapter.

When you receive a block of addresses from an ISP, what you get will look something like this: 192.168.10.32/28. This is telling you what your subnet mask is. The slash notation (/) means how many bits are turned on (1s). Obviously, the maximum could only be /32 because a byte is 8 bits and there are 4 bytes in an IP address: (4 × 8 = 32). But keep in mind that the largest subnet mask available (regardless of the class of address) can only be a /30 because you have to keep at least 2 bits for host bits.

Take, for example, a Class A default subnet mask, which is 255.0.0.0. This means that the first byte of the subnet mask is all ones (1s), or 11111111. When referring to a slash notation, you need to count all the 1s bits to figure out your mask. The 255.0.0.0 is considered a /8 because it has 8 bits that are 1s—that is, 8 bits that are turned on.

A Class B default mask would be 255.255.0.0, which is a /16 because 16 bits are ones (1s): 11111111.11111111.00000000.00000000.

Table 3.2 lists every available subnet mask and its equivalent CIDR slash notation.

TABLE 3.2   CIDR values

Subnet mask	CIDR value
255.0.0.0	/8
255.128.0.0	/9
255.192.0.0	/10
255.224.0.0	/11
255.240.0.0	/12
255.248.0.0	/13
255.252.0.0	/14
255.254.0.0	/15
255.255.0.0	/16
255.255.128.0	/17
255.255.192.0	/18
255.255.224.0	/19
255.255.240.0	/20
255.255.248.0	/21
255.255.252.0	/22
255.255.254.0	/23
255.255.255.0	/24
255.255.255.128	/25
255.255.255.192	/26

TABLE 3.2   CIDR values *(continued)*

Subnet mask	CIDR value
255.255.255.224	/27
255.255.255.240	/28
255.255.255.248	/29
255.255.255.252	/30

The /8 through /15 can be used only with Class A network addresses. /16 through /23 can be used by Class A and B network addresses. /24 through /30 can be used by Class A, B, and C network addresses. This is a big reason why most companies use Class A network addresses. Since they can use all subnet masks, they get the maximum flexibility in network design.

 No, you cannot configure a Cisco router using this slash format. But wouldn't that be nice? Nevertheless, it's *really* important for you to know subnet masks in the slash notation (CIDR).

Subnetting Class C Addresses

There are many different ways to subnet a network. The right way is the way that works best for you. In a Class C address, only 8 bits are available for defining the hosts. Remember that subnet bits start at the left and go to the right, without skipping bits. This means that Class C subnet masks can only be the following:

```
Binary      Decimal   CIDR
-------------------------------
00000000 = 0          /24
10000000 = 128        /25
11000000 = 192        /26
11100000 = 224        /27
11110000 = 240        /28
11111000 = 248        /29
11111100 = 252        /30
```

You can't use a /31 or /32 because you have to have at least 2 host bits for assigning IP addresses to hosts. In the past, I never discussed the /25 in a Class C network. Cisco always had been concerned with having at least 2 subnet bits, but now, because of Cisco recognizing the `ip subnet-zero` command in its curriculum and exam objectives, you can use just one subnet bit.

In the following sections, I'm going to teach you an alternate method of subnetting that makes it easier to subnet larger numbers in no time. Trust me, you need to be able to subnet fast!

Subnetting a Class C Address: The Fast Way!

When you've chosen a possible subnet mask for your network and need to determine the number of subnets, valid hosts, and broadcast addresses of each subnet that the mask provides, all you need to do is answer five simple questions.

- How many subnets does the chosen subnet mask produce?
- How many valid hosts per subnet are available?
- What are the valid subnets?
- What's the broadcast address of each subnet?
- What are the valid hosts in each subnet?

At this point, it's important that you both understand and have memorized your powers of 2. Please refer to the sidebar "Understanding the Powers of 2" earlier in this chapter if you need some help. Here's how you get the answers to those five big questions:

- *How many subnets?* $2x$ = number of subnets. x is the number of masked bits, or the 1s. For example, in 11000000, the number of 1s gives you 2^2 subnets. In this example, there are 4 subnets.

- *How many hosts per subnet?* $2y - 2$ = number of hosts per subnet. y is the number of unmasked bits, or the 0s. For example, in 11000000, the number of 0s gives you $2^6 - 2$ hosts. In this example, there are 62 hosts per subnet. You need to subtract 2 for the subnet address and the broadcast address, which are not valid hosts.

- *What are the valid subnets?* 256 – subnet mask = block size, or increment number. An example would be 256 – 192 = 64. The block size of a 192 mask is always 64. Start counting at zero in blocks of 64 until you reach the subnet mask value and these are your subnets: 0, 64, 128, 192. Easy, huh?

- *What's the broadcast address for each subnet?* Now here's the really easy part. Since you counted your subnets in the previous section as 0, 64, 128, and 192, the broadcast address is always the number right before the next subnet. For example, the 0 subnet has a broadcast address of 63 because the next subnet is 64. The 64 subnet has a broadcast address of 127 because the next subnet is 128. And so on. And remember, the broadcast of the last subnet is always 255.

- *What are the valid hosts?* Valid hosts are the numbers between the subnets, omitting all 0s and all 1s. For example, if 64 is the subnet number and 127 is the broadcast address, then 65–126 is the valid host range—it's *always* the numbers between the subnet address and the broadcast address.

I know this can truly seem confusing. But it really isn't as hard as it seems to be at first—just hang in there! Why not try a few and see for yourself?

Subnetting Practice Examples: Class C Addresses

Here's your opportunity to practice subnetting Class C addresses using the method I just described. Exciting, isn't it? You're going to start with the first Class C subnet mask and work through every subnet that you can using a Class C address. When you're done, I'll show you how easy this is with Class A and B networks too!

Practice Example #1C: 255.255.255.128 (/25)

Since 128 is 10000000 in binary, there is only 1 bit for subnetting and 7 bits for hosts. You're going to subnet the Class C network address 192.168.10.0.

192.168.10.0 = Network address

255.255.255.128 = Subnet mask

Now, let's answer the big five:

- *How many subnets?* Since 128 is 1 bit on (10000000), the answer would be $2^1 = 2$.
- *How many hosts per subnet?* You have 7 host bits off (**10000000**), so the equation would be $2^7 - 2 = 126$ hosts.
- *What are the valid subnets?* 256 – 128 = 128. Remember, you'll start at zero and count in your block size, so your subnets are 0, 128.
- *What's the broadcast address for each subnet?* The number right before the value of the next subnet is all host bits turned on and equals the broadcast address. For the zero subnet, the next subnet is 128, so the broadcast of the 0 subnet is 127.
- *What are the valid hosts?* These are the numbers between the subnet and broadcast address. The easiest way to find the hosts is to write out the subnet address and the broadcast address. This way, the valid hosts are obvious. The following table shows the 0 and 128 subnets, the valid host ranges of each, and the broadcast address of both subnets:

Subnet	0	128
First host	1	129
Last host	126	254
Broadcast	127	255

Before moving on to the next example, take a look at Figure 3.1. Okay, looking at a Class C /25, it's pretty clear there are two subnets. But so what—why is this significant? Well actually, it's not, but that's not the right question. What you really want to know is what you would do with this information!

FIGURE 3.1 Implementing a Class C /25 logical network

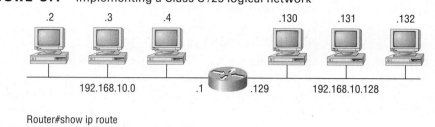

```
Router#show ip route
[output cut]
C 192.168.10.0 is directly connected to Ethernet 0.
C 192.168.10.128 is directly connected to Ethernet 1.
```

I know this isn't exactly everyone's favorite pastime, but it's really important, so just hang in there; I'm going to talk about subnetting—period. You need to know that the key to understanding subnetting is to understand the very reason you need to do it. And I'm going to demonstrate this by going through the process of building a physical network—and let's add a router. (You now have an internetwork, as I truly hope you already know!)

All right, because you added that router, in order for the hosts on our internetwork to communicate, they must now have a logical network addressing scheme. You could use IPX or IPv6, but IPv4 is still the most popular, and it also just happens to be what you're studying at the moment, so that's what you're going to go with. Okay—now take a look back to Figure 3.1. There are two physical networks, so you're going to implement a logical addressing scheme that allows for two logical networks. As always, it's a really good idea to look ahead and consider likely growth scenarios—both short and long term—but for this example, a /25 will do the trick.

Practice Example #2C: 255.255.255.192 (/26)

In this second example, you're going to subnet the network address 192.168.10.0 using the subnet mask 255.255.255.192.

> 192.168.10.0 = Network address

> 255.255.255.192 = Subnet mask

Now, let's answer the big five:

- *How many subnets?* Since 192 is 2 bits on (**11000000**), the answer would be $2^2 = 4$ subnets.

- *How many hosts per subnet?* You have 6 host bits off (**11000000**), so the equation would be $2^6 - 2 = 62$ hosts.

- *What are the valid subnets?* 256 – 192 = 64. Remember, you start at zero and count in your block size, so your subnets are 0, 64, 128, and 192.

- *What's the broadcast address for each subnet?* The number right before the value of the next subnet is all host bits turned on and equals the broadcast address. For the zero subnet, the next subnet is 64, so the broadcast address for the zero subnet is 63.

- *What are the valid hosts?* These are the numbers between the subnet and broadcast address. The easiest way to find the hosts is to write out the subnet address and the broadcast address. This way, the valid hosts are obvious. The following table shows the 0, 64, 128, and 192 subnets, the valid host ranges of each, and the broadcast address of each subnet:

The subnets (do this first)	0	64	128	192
Our first host (perform host addressing last)	1	65	129	193
Our last host	62	126	190	254
The broadcast address (do this second)	63	127	191	255

Okay, again, before getting into the next example, you can see that you can now subnet a /26. And what are you going to do with this fascinating information? Implement it! You'll use Figure 3.2 to practice a /26 network implementation.

FIGURE 3.2   Implementing a Class C /26 logical network

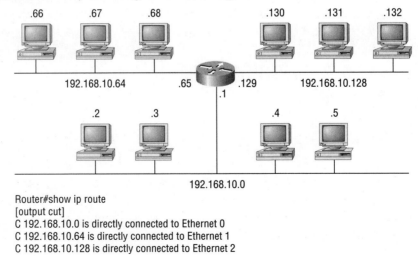

```
Router#show ip route
[output cut]
C 192.168.10.0 is directly connected to Ethernet 0
C 192.168.10.64 is directly connected to Ethernet 1
C 192.168.10.128 is directly connected to Ethernet 2
```

The /26 mask provides four subnetworks, and you need a subnet for each router interface. With this mask, in this example, you actually have room to add another router interface.

Practice Example #3C: 255.255.255.224 (/27)

This time, you'll subnet the network address 192.168.10.0 and subnet mask 255.255.255.224.

> 192.168.10.0 = Network address
>
> 255.255.255.224 = Subnet mask

- *How many subnets?* 224 is 11100000, so your equation would be $2^3 = 8$.
- *How many hosts?* $2^5 - 2 = 30$.
- *What are the valid subnets?* 256 − 224 = 32. You just start at zero and count to the subnet mask value in blocks (increments) of 32: 0, 32, 64, 96, 128, 160, 192, and 224.
- *What's the broadcast address for each subnet (always the number right before the next subnet)?*
- *What are the valid hosts (the numbers between the subnet number and the broadcast address)?*

To answer the last two questions, first just write out the subnets, and then write out the broadcast addresses—the number right before the next subnet. Last, fill in the host addresses. The following table gives you all the subnets for the 255.255.255.224 Class C subnet mask:

The subnet address	0	32	64	96	128	160	192	224
The first valid host	1	33	65	97	129	161	193	225
The last valid host	30	62	94	126	158	190	222	254
The broadcast address	31	63	95	127	159	191	223	255

Practice Example #4C: 255.255.255.240 (/28)

Let's practice on another one:

> 192.168.10.0 = Network address
>
> 255.255.255.240 = Subnet mask

- *Subnets?* 240 is 11110000 in binary. $2^4 = 16$.
- *Hosts?* 4 host bits, or $2^4 - 2 = 14$.
- *Valid subnets?* 256 − 240 = 16. Start at 0 and keep counting in increments of 16: 0, 16, 32, 48, 64, 80, 96, 112, 128, 144, 160, 176, 192, 208, 224, and 240.
- *Broadcast address for each subnet?*
- *Valid hosts?*

To answer the last two questions, check out the following table. It gives you the subnets, valid hosts, and broadcast addresses for each subnet. First, find the address of each subnet using the block size (increment). Second, find the broadcast address of each subnet increment (it's always the number right before the next valid subnet), and then just fill in the host addresses. The following table shows the available subnets, hosts, and broadcast addresses provided from a Class C 255.255.255.240 mask:

Subnet	0	16	32	48	64	80	96	112	128	144	160	176	192	208	224	240
First host	1	17	33	49	65	81	97	113	129	145	161	177	193	209	225	241
Last host		14	30	46	62	78	94	110	126	142	158	174	190	206	222	238	254
Broad-cast		15	31	47	63	79	95	111	127	143	159	175	191	207	223	239	255

Cisco has figured out that most people cannot count in 16s and therefore have a hard time finding valid subnets, hosts, and broadcast addresses with the Class C 255.255.255.240 mask. You'd be wise to study this mask.

Practice Example #5C: 255.255.255.248 (/29)

Let's keep practicing:

> 192.168.10.0 = Network address
>
> 255.255.255.248 = Subnet mask

- *Subnets?* 248 in binary = 11111000. 2^5 = 32.
- *Hosts?* $2^3 - 2 = 6$.
- *Valid subnets?* 256 – 248 = 0, 8, 16, 24, 32, 40, 48, 56, 64, 72, 80, 88, 96, 104, 112, 120, 128, 136, 144, 152, 160, 168, 176, 184, 192, 200, 208, 216, 224, 232, 240, and 248.
- *Broadcast address for each subnet?*
- *Valid hosts?*

Take a look at the following table. It shows some of the subnets (first four and last four only), valid hosts, and broadcast addresses for the Class C 255.255.255.248 mask:

Subnet	0	8	16	24	...	224	232	240	248
First host	1	9	17	25	...	225	233	241	249
Last host	6	14	22	30	...	230	238	246	254
Broadcast	7	15	23	31	...	231	239	247	255

Practice Example #6C: 255.255.255.252 (/30)

Just one more:

>   192.168.10.0 = Network address
>   255.255.255.252 = Subnet mask

- *Subnets?* 64.
- *Hosts?* 2.
- *Valid subnets?* 0, 4, 8, 12, and so on, all the way to 252.
- *Broadcast address for each subnet?*
- *Valid hosts?*

The following table shows you the subnet, valid host, and broadcast address of the first four and last four subnets in the 255.255.255.252 Class C subnet:

Subnet	0	4	8	12	...	240	244	248	252
First host	1	5	9	13	...	241	245	249	253
Last host	2	6	10	14	...	242	246	250	254
Broadcast	3	7	11	15	...	243	247	251	255

🌐 Real World Scenario

Should You Really Use This Mask That Provides Only Two Hosts?

You are the network administrator for Acme Corporation in San Francisco, with dozens of WAN links connecting to your corporate office. Right now your network is a classful network, which means that the same subnet mask is on each host and router interface. You've read about classless routing where you can have different size masks but don't know what to use on your point-to-point WAN links. Is the 255.255.255.252 (/30) a helpful mask in this situation?

Yes, this is a very helpful mask in wide area networks.

If you use the 255.255.255.0 mask, then each network would have 254 hosts, but you only use 2 addresses with a WAN link! That is a waste of 252 hosts per subnet. If you use the 255.255.255.252 mask, then each subnet has only 2 hosts and you don't waste precious addresses.

Subnetting in Your Head: Class C Addresses

It really is possible to subnet in your head. Even if you don't believe me, I'll show you how. And it's not all that hard either—take the following example:

192.168.10.33 = Node address

255.255.255.224 = Subnet mask

First, determine the subnet and broadcast address of the previous IP address. You can do this by answering question 3 of the big five questions: 256 − 224 = 32. 0, 32, 64. The address of 33 falls between the two subnets of 32 and 64 and must be part of the 192.168.10.32 subnet. The next subnet is 64, so the broadcast address of the 32 subnet is 63. (Remember that the broadcast address of a subnet is always the number right before the next subnet.) The valid host range is 33–62 (the numbers between the subnet and broadcast address). This is too easy!

Okay, let's try another one. You'll subnet another Class C address:

192.168.10.33 = Node address

255.255.255.240 = Subnet mask

What subnet and broadcast address is the previous IP address a member of? 256 − 240 = 16. 0, 16, 32, 48. Bingo—the host address is between the 32 and 48 subnets. The subnet is 192.168.10.32, and the broadcast address is 47 (the next subnet is 48). The valid host range is 33–46 (the numbers between the subnet number and the broadcast address).

Okay, you need to do more, just to make sure you have this down.

You have a node address of 192.168.10.174 with a mask of 255.255.255.240. What is the valid host range?

The mask is 240, so you'd do 256 − 240 = 16. This is your block size. Just keep adding 16 until you pass the host address of 174, starting at zero, of course: 0, 16, 32, 48, 64, 80, 96, 112, 128, 144, 160, 176. The host address of 174 is between 160 and 176, so the subnet is 160. The broadcast address is 175; the valid host range is 161–174. That was a tough one.

One more—just for fun. This is the easiest one of all Class C subnetting:

192.168.10.17 = Node address

255.255.255.252 = Subnet mask

What subnet and broadcast address is the previous IP address a member of? 256 − 252 = 0 (always start at zero unless told otherwise), 4, 8, 12, 16, 20, and so on. You've got it! The host address is between the 16 and 20 subnets. The subnet is 192.168.10.16, and the broadcast address is 19. The valid host range is 17–18.

Now that you're all over Class C subnetting, I'll move on to Class B subnetting. But before I do, let's have a quick review.

What Do You Know?

Okay—here's where you can really apply what you've learned so far and begin committing it all to memory. This is a very cool section that I've been using in my classes for years. It will really help you nail down subnetting!

When you see a subnet mask or slash notation (CIDR), you should know the following:

/25 What do you know about a /25?

- 128 mask
- 1 bit on and 7 bits off (10000000)
- Block size of 128
- 2 subnets, each with 126 hosts

/26 What do you know about a /26?

- 192 mask
- 2 bits on and 6 bits off (11000000)
- Block size of 64
- 4 subnets, each with 62 hosts

/27 What do you know about a /27?

- 224 mask
- 3 bits on and 5 bits off (11100000)
- Block size of 32
- 8 subnets, each with 30 hosts

/28 What do you know about a /28?

- 240 mask
- 4 bits on and 4 bits off
- Block size of 16
- 16 subnets, each with 14 hosts

/29 What do you know about a /29?

- 248 mask
- 5 bits on and 3 bits off
- Block size of 8
- 32 subnets, each with 6 hosts

/30 What do you know about a /30?

- 252 mask
- 6 bits on and 2 bits off
- Block size of 4
- 64 subnets, each with 2 hosts

Regardless of whether you have a Class A, Class B, or Class C address, the /30 mask will provide you with only two hosts, ever. This mask is suited almost exclusively—as well as suggested by Cisco—for use on point-to-point links.

If you can memorize this "What Do You Know?" section, you'll be much better off in your day-to-day job and in your studies. Try saying it out loud, which helps you memorize things—yes, your significant other and/or co-workers will think you've lost it, but they probably already do if you are in the networking field. And if you're not yet in the networking field but are studying all this to break into it, you might as well have people start thinking you're an odd bird now since they will eventually anyway.

It's also helpful to write these on some type of flashcards and have people test your skill. You'd be amazed at how fast you can get subnetting down if you memorize block sizes as well as this "What Do You Know?" section.

Subnetting Class B Addresses

Before diving into this, let's look at all the possible Class B subnet masks first. Notice that you have a lot more possible subnet masks than you do with a Class C network address.

```
255.255.0.0      (/16)
255.255.128.0    (/17)     255.255.255.0      (/24)
255.255.192.0    (/18)     255.255.255.128    (/25)
255.255.224.0    (/19)     255.255.255.192    (/26)
255.255.240.0    (/20)     255.255.255.224    (/27)
255.255.248.0    (/21)     255.255.255.240    (/28)
255.255.252.0    (/22)     255.255.255.248    (/29)
255.255.254.0    (/23)     255.255.255.252    (/30)
```

You know the Class B network address has 16 bits available for host addressing. This means you can use up to 14 bits for subnetting (because you have to leave at least 2 bits for host addressing). Using a /16 means you are not subnetting with Class B, but it is a mask you can use.

By the way, do you notice anything interesting about that list of subnet values—a pattern, maybe? Ah-ha! That's exactly why I had you memorize the binary-to-decimal numbers at the beginning of this section. Since subnet mask bits start on the left and move to the right and bits can't be skipped, the numbers are always the same regardless of the class of address. Memorize this pattern.

The process of subnetting a Class B network is pretty much the same as it is for a Class C, except that you just have more host bits and you start in the third octet.

Use the same subnet numbers for the third octet with Class B that you used for the fourth octet with Class C, but add a zero to the network portion and a 255 to the broadcast section in the fourth octet. The following table shows you an example host range of two subnets used in a Class B 240 (/20) subnet mask:

Subnetsubnet   16.0   32.0

Broadcasts   31.255   47.255

Just add the valid hosts between the numbers, and you're set!

Subnetting Practice Examples: Class B Addresses

This section will give you an opportunity to practice subnetting Class B addresses. Again, I have to mention that this is the same as subnetting with Class C, except you start in the third octet—with the exact same numbers!

Practice Example #1B: 255.255.128.0 (/17)

> 172.16.0.0 = Network address
>
> 255.255.128.0 = Subnet mask

- *Subnets?* 2^1 = 2 (same as Class C).
- *Hosts?* $2^{15} - 2$ = 32,766 (7 bits in the third octet, and 8 in the fourth).
- *Valid subnets?* 256 – 128 = 128. 0, 128. Remember that subnetting is performed in the third octet, so the subnet numbers are really 0.0 and 128.0, as shown in the next table. These are the exact numbers you used with Class C; you use them in the third octet and add a 0 in the fourth octet for the network address.
- *Broadcast address for each subnet?*
- *Valid hosts?*

The following table shows the two subnets available, the valid host range, and the broadcast address of each:

Subnet	0.0	128.0
First host	0.1	128.1
Last host	127.254	255.254
Broadcast	127.255	255.255

Okay, notice that you just added the fourth octet's lowest and highest values and came up with the answers. And again, it's done exactly the same way as for a Class C subnet. You just use the same numbers in the third octet and add 0 and 255 in the fourth octet—pretty simple, huh? I really can't say this enough: it's just not hard. The numbers never change; you just use them in different octets!

Practice Example #2B: 255.255.192.0 (/18)

> 172.16.0.0 = Network address
>
> 255.255.192.0 = Subnet mask

- *Subnets?* $2^2 = 4$.
- *Hosts?* $2^{14} - 2 = 16,382$ (6 bits in the third octet, and 8 in the fourth).
- *Valid subnets?* 256 − 192 = 64. 0, 64, 128, 192. Remember that the subnetting is performed in the third octet, so the subnet numbers are really 0.0, 64.0, 128.0, and 192.0, as shown in the next table.
- *Broadcast address for each subnet?*
- *Valid hosts?*

The following table shows the four subnets available, the valid host range, and the broadcast address of each:

Subnet	0.0	64.0	128.0	192.0
First host	0.1	64.1	128.1	192.1
Last host	63.254	127.254	191.254	255.254
Broadcast	63.255	127.255	191.255	255.255

Again, it's pretty much the same as it is for a Class C subnet—you just added 0 and 255 in the fourth octet for each subnet in the third octet.

Practice Example #3B: 255.255.240.0 (/20)

> 172.16.0.0 = Network address
>
> 255.255.240.0 = Subnet mask

- *Subnets?* $2^4 = 16$.
- *Hosts?* $2^{12} - 2 = 4094$.
- *Valid subnets?* 256 − 240 = 0, 16, 32, 48, and so on, up to 240. Notice that these are the same numbers as a Class C 240 mask—you just put them in the third octet and add a 0 and 255 in the fourth octet.
- *Broadcast address for each subnet?*
- *Valid hosts?*

The following table shows the first four subnets, valid hosts, and broadcast addresses in a Class B 255.255.240.0 mask:

Subnet	0.0	16.0	32.0	48.0
First host	0.1	16.1	32.1	48.1
Last host	15.254	31.254	47.254	63.254
Broadcast	15.255	31.255	47.255	63.255

Practice Example #4B: 255.255.254.0 (/23)

   172.16.0.0 = Network address

   255.255.254.0 = Subnet mask

- *Subnets?* $2^7 = 128$.
- *Hosts?* $2^9 - 2 = 510$.
- *Valid subnets?* $256 - 254 = 0, 2, 4, 6, 8$, and so on, up to 254.
- *Broadcast address for each subnet?*
- *Valid hosts?*

   The following table shows the first five subnets, valid hosts, and broadcast addresses in a Class B 255.255.254.0 mask:

Subnet	0.0	2.0	4.0	6.0	8.0
First host	0.1	2.1	4.1	6.1	8.1
Last host	1.254	3.254	5.254	7.254	9.254
Broadcast	1.255	3.255	5.255	7.255	9.255

Practice Example #5B: 255.255.255.0 (/24)

Contrary to popular belief, 255.255.255.0 used with a Class B network address is not called a Class B network with a Class C subnet mask. It's amazing how many people see this mask used in a Class B network and think it's a Class C subnet mask. This is a Class B subnet mask with 8 bits of subnetting—it's considerably different from a Class C mask. Subnetting this address is fairly simple.

   172.16.0.0 = Network address

   255.255.255.0 = Subnet mask

- *Subnets?* $2^8 = 256$.
- *Hosts?* $2^8 - 2 = 254$.
- *Valid subnets?* $256 - 255 = 1$. 0, 1, 2, 3, and so on, all the way to 255.
- *Broadcast address for each subnet?*
- *Valid hosts?*

   The following table shows the first four and last two subnets, the valid hosts, and the broadcast addresses in a Class B 255.255.255.0 mask:

Subnet	0.0	1.0	2.0	3.0	...	254.0	255.0
First host	0.1	1.1	2.1	3.1	...	254.1	255.1
Last host	0.254	1.254	2.254	3.254	...	254.254	255.254
Broadcast	0.255	1.255	2.255	3.255	...	254.255	255.255

Practice Example #6B: 255.255.255.128 (/25)

This is one of the hardest subnet masks you can play with. And worse, it actually is a really good subnet to use in production because it creates more than 500 subnets with 126 hosts for each subnet—a nice mixture. So, don't skip over it!

> 172.16.0.0 = Network address

> 255.255.255.128 = Subnet mask

- *Subnets?* $2^9 = 512$.
- *Hosts?* $2^7 - 2 = 126$.
- *Valid subnets?* Okay, now for the tricky part. $256 - 255 = 1$. 0, 1, 2, 3, and so on, for the third octet. But you can't forget the one subnet bit used in the fourth octet. Remember when I showed you how to figure one subnet bit with a Class C mask? You figure this the same way. (Now you know why I showed you the 1-bit subnet mask in the Class C section—to make this part easier.) You actually get 2 subnets for each third octet value, which is the reason for the 512 subnets. For example, if the third octet is showing subnet 3, the 2 subnets would actually be 3.0 and 3.128.
- *Broadcast address for each subnet?*
- *Valid hosts?*

The following table shows how you can create subnets, valid hosts, and broadcast addresses using the Class B 255.255.255.128 subnet mask (the first eight subnets are shown and then the last two subnets):

Subnet	0.0	0.128	1.0	1.128	2.0	2.128	3.0	3.128	...	255.0	255.128
First host	0.1	0.129	1.1	1.129	2.1	2.129	3.1	3.129	...	255.1	255.129
Last host	0.126	0.254	1.126	1.254	2.126	2.254	3.126	3.254	...	255.126	255.254
Broadcast	0.127	0.255	1.127	1.255	2.127	2.255	3.127	3.255	...	255.127	255.255

Practice Example #7B: 255.255.255.192 (/26)

Now, this is where Class B subnetting gets easy. Since the third octet has a 255 in the mask section, whatever number is listed in the third octet is a subnet number. However, now that you have a subnet number in the fourth octet, you can subnet this octet just as you did with Class C subnetting. Let's try it:

> 172.16.0.0 = Network address

> 255.255.255.192 = Subnet mask

- *Subnets?* $2^{10} = 1024$.
- *Hosts?* $2^6 - 2 = 62$.

- *Valid subnets?* 256 – 192 = 64. The subnets are shown in the following table. Do these numbers look familiar?
- *Broadcast address for each subnet?*
- *Valid hosts?*

The following table shows the first eight subnet ranges, valid hosts, and broadcast addresses:

Subnet	0.0	0.64	0.128	0.192	1.0	1.64	1.128	1.192
First host	0.1	0.65	0.129	0.193	1.1	1.65	1.129	1.193
Last host	0.62	0.126	0.190	0.254	1.62	1.126	1.190	1.254
Broadcast	0.63	0.127	0.191	0.255	1.63	1.127	1.191	1.255

Notice that for each subnet value in the third octet, you get subnets 0, 64, 128, and 192 in the fourth octet.

Practice Example #8B: 255.255.255.224 (/27)

This is done the same way as the preceding subnet mask, except that you just have more subnets and fewer hosts per subnet available.

172.16.0.0 = Network address

255.255.255.224 = Subnet mask

- *Subnets?* 2^{11} = 2048.
- *Hosts?* $2^5 - 2$ = 30.
- *Valid subnets?* 256 – 224 = 32. 0, 32, 64, 96, 128, 160, 192, 224.
- *Broadcast address for each subnet?*
- *Valid hosts?*

The following table shows the first eight subnets:

Subnet	0.0	0.32	0.64	0.96	0.128	0.160	0.192	0.224
First host	0.1	0.33	0.65	0.97	0.129	0.161	0.193	0.225
Last host	0.30	0.62	0.94	0.126	0.158	0.190	0.222	0.254
Broadcast	0.31	0.63	0.95	0.127	0.159	0.191	0.223	0.255

This next table shows the last eight subnets:

Subnet	255.0	255.32	255.64	255.96	255.128	255.160	255.192	255.224
First host	255.1	255.33	255.65	255.97	255.129	255.161	255.193	255.225
Last host	255.30	255.62	255.94	255.126	255.158	255.190	255.222	255.254
Broadcast	255.31	255.63	255.95	255.127	255.159	255.191	255.223	255.255

Subnetting in Your Head: Class B Addresses

Are you nuts? Subnet Class B addresses in your head? It's actually easier than writing it out—I'm not kidding! Let me show you how:

Question: What subnet and broadcast address is the IP address 172.16.10.33 255.255.255.224 (/27) a member of?

Answer: The interesting octet (the octet that you care about) is the fourth octet. 256 – 224 = 32. 32 + 32 = 64. Bingo: 33 is between 32 and 64. However, remember that the third octet is considered part of the subnet, so the answer would be the 10.32 subnet. The broadcast is 10.63, since 10.64 is the next subnet. That was a pretty easy one.

Question: What subnet and broadcast address is the IP address 172.16.66.10 255.255.192.0 (/18) a member of?

Answer: The interesting octet is the third octet instead of the fourth octet. 256 – 192 = 64. 0, 64, 128. The subnet is 172.16.64.0. The broadcast must be 172.16.127.255 since 128.0 is the next subnet.

Question: What subnet and broadcast address is the IP address 172.16.50.10 255.255.224.0 (/19) a member of?

Answer: 256 – 224 = 0, 32, 64 (remember, you always start counting at zero). The subnet is 172.16.32.0, and the broadcast must be 172.16.63.25 since 64.0 is the next subnet.

Question: What subnet and broadcast address is the IP address 172.16.46.255 255.255.240.0 (/20) a member of?

Answer: 256 – 240 = 16. The third octet is interesting. 0, 16, 32, 48. This subnet address must be in the 172.16.32.0 subnet, and the broadcast must be 172.16.47.255 since 48.0 is the next subnet. So, yes, 172.16.46.255 is a valid host.

Question: What subnet and broadcast address is the IP address 172.16.45.14 255.255.255.252 (/30) a member of?

Answer: Where is the interesting octet? (in the fourth octet). 256 – 252 = 0, 4, 8, 12, 16. The subnet is 172.16.45.12, with a broadcast of 172.16.45.15 because the next subnet is 172.16.45.16.

Question: What is the subnet and broadcast address of the host 172.16.88.255/20?

Answer: What is a /20? If you can't answer this, you can't answer this question, can you? A /20 is 255.255.240.0, which gives us a block size of 16 in the third octet, and since no subnet bits are on in the fourth octet, the answer is always 0 and 255 in the fourth octet. 0, 16, 32, 48, 64, 80, 96...bingo. 88 is between 80 and 96, so the subnet is 80.0 and the broadcast address is 95.255.

Question: A router receives a packet on an interface with a destination address of 172.16.46.191/26. What will the router do with this packet?

Answer: Discard it. Do you know why? 172.16.46.191/26 is a 255.255.255.192 mask, which gives you a block size of 64. Your subnets are then 0, 64, 128, and 192. 191 is the broadcast address of the 128 subnet, so a router, by default, will discard any broadcast packets.

Subnetting Class A Addresses

Class A subnetting is not performed any differently than Classes B and C, but there are 24 bits to play with instead of the 16 in a Class B address and the 8 in a Class C address.

Let's start by listing all the Class A masks.

```
255.0.0.0      (/8)
255.128.0.0    (/9)          255.255.240.0    (/20)
255.192.0.0    (/10)         255.255.248.0    (/21)
255.224.0.0    (/11)         255.255.252.0    (/22)
255.240.0.0    (/12)         255.255.254.0    (/23)
255.248.0.0    (/13)         255.255.255.0    (/24)
255.252.0.0    (/14)         255.255.255.128  (/25)
255.254.0.0    (/15)         255.255.255.192  (/26)
255.255.0.0    (/16)         255.255.255.224  (/27)
255.255.128.0  (/17)         255.255.255.240  (/28)
255.255.192.0  (/18)         255.255.255.248  (/29)
255.255.224.0  (/19)         255.255.255.252  (/30)
```

That's it. You must leave at least 2 bits for defining hosts. And I hope you can see the pattern by now. Remember, you're going to do this the same way as a Class B or C subnet. It's just that, again, you simply have more host bits, and you just use the same subnet numbers you used with Class B and C, but you start using these numbers in the second octet.

Subnetting Practice Examples: Class A Addresses

When you look at an IP address and a subnet mask, you must be able to distinguish the bits used for subnets from the bits used for determining hosts. This is imperative. If you're still struggling with this concept, please reread the section "IP Addressing" in Chapter 2. It shows you how to determine the difference between the subnet and host bits and should help clear things up.

Practice Example #1A: 255.255.0.0 (/16)

Class A addresses use a default mask of 255.0.0.0, which leaves 22 bits for subnetting since you must leave 2 bits for host addressing. The 255.255.0.0 mask with a Class A address is using 8 subnet bits.

- *Subnets?* $2^8 = 256$.
- *Hosts?* $2^{16} - 2 = 65,534$.
- *Valid subnets?* What is the interesting octet? $256 - 255 = 1$. 0, 1, 2, 3, and so on (all in the second octet). The subnets would be 10.0.0.0, 10.1.0.0, 10.2.0.0, 10.3.0.0, and so on, up to 10.255.0.0.

- *Broadcast address for each subnet?*
- *Valid hosts?*

The following table shows the first two and last two subnets, valid host range, and broadcast addresses for the private Class A 10.0.0.0 network:

Subnet	10.0.0.0	10.1.0.0	...	10.254.0.0	10.255.0.0
First host	10.0.0.1	10.1.0.1	...	10.254.0.1	10.255.0.1
Last host	10.0.255.254	10.1.255.254	...	10.254.255.254	10.255.255.254
Broadcast	10.0.255.255	10.1.255.255	...	10.254.255.255	10.255.255.255

Practice Example #2A: 255.255.240.0 (/20)

255.255.240.0 gives you 12 bits of subnetting and leaves you 12 bits for host addressing.

- *Subnets?* $2^{12} = 4096$.
- *Hosts?* $2^{12} - 2 = 4094$.
- *Valid subnets?* What is your interesting octet? $256 - 240 = 16$. The subnets in the second octet are a block size of 1 and the subnets in the third octet are 0, 16, 32, and so on.
- *Broadcast address for each subnet?*
- *Valid hosts?*

The following table shows some examples of the host ranges—the first three and the last subnets:

Subnet	10.0.0.0	10.0.16.0	10.0.32.0	...	10.255.240.0
First host	10.0.0.1	10.0.16.1	10.0.32.1	...	10.255.240.1
Last host	10.0.15.254	10.0.31.254	10.0.47.254	...	10.255.255.254
Broadcast	10.0.15.255	10.0.31.255	10.0.47.255	...	10.255.255.255

Practice Example #3A: 255.255.254.0 (/23)

255.255.254.0 gives you 15 bits of subnetting and leaves you 9 bits for host addressing.

- *Subnets?* $2^{15} = 32{,}766$.
- *Hosts?* $2^9 - 2 = 510$.
- *Valid subnets?* What is your interesting octet? $256 - 254 = 2$. The subnets in the second octet are a block size of 1, and the subnets in the third octet are a block size of 2. Starting at 0, the subnets are 0, 2, 4, 6, and so on.
- *Broadcast address for each subnet?*
- *Valid hosts?*

The following table shows some examples of the host ranges—the first three and the last subnets:

Subnet	10.0.0.0	10.0.2.0	10.0.4.0	...	10.255.254.0
First host	10.0.0.1	10.0.2.1	10.0.4.1	...	10.255.254.1
Last host	10.0.1.254	10.0.3.254	10.0.5.254	...	10.255.255.254
Broadcast	10.0.1.255	10.0.3.255	10.0.5.255	...	10.255.255.255

Practice Example #4A: 255.255.255.192 (/26)

Let's do one more example using the second, third, and fourth octets for subnetting.

- *Subnets?* 2^{18} = 262,144.
- *Hosts?* $2^6 - 2$ = 62.
- *Valid subnets?* In the second and third octet, the block size is 1, and in the fourth octet, the block size is 64.
- *Broadcast address for each subnet?*
- *Valid hosts?*

The following table shows the first four subnets and their valid hosts and broadcast addresses in the Class A 255.255.255.192 mask:

Subnet	10.0.0.0	10.0.0.64	10.0.0.128	10.0.0.192
First host	10.0.0.1	10.0.0.65	10.0.0.129	10.0.0.193
Last host	10.0.0.62	10.0.0.126	10.0.0.190	10.0.0.254
Broadcast	10.0.0.63	10.0.0.127	10.0.0.191	10.0.0.255

The following table shows the last four subnets and their valid hosts and broadcast addresses:

Subnet	10.255.255.0	10.255.255.64	10.255.255.128	10.255.255.192
First host	10.255.255.1	10.255.255.65	10.255.255.129	10.255.255.193
Last host	10.255.255.62	10.255.255.126	10.255.255.190	10.255.255.254
Broadcast	10.255.255.63	10.255.255.127	10.255.255.191	10.255.255.255

Subnetting in Your Head: Class A Addresses

This sounds hard, but as with Class C and Class B, the numbers are the same; you just start in the second octet. What makes this easy? You only need to worry about the octet that has the largest block size (typically called the interesting octet; one that is something other than 0 or 255)—for example, 255.255.240.0 (/20) with a Class A network. The second octet has a block size of 1, so any number listed in that octet is a subnet. The third octet is a 240 mask, which means you have a block size of 16 in the third octet. If your host ID is 10.20.80.30, what is your subnet, broadcast address, and valid host range?

The subnet in the second octet is 20 with a block size of 1, but the third octet is in block sizes of 16, so you'll just count them out: 0, 16, 32, 48, 64, 80, 96...*voilà*! (By the way, you can count by 16s by now, right?) This makes your subnet 10.20.80.0, with a broadcast of 10.20.95.255 because the next subnet is 10.20.96.0. The valid host range is 10.20.80.1 through 10.20.95.254. And yes, no lie! You really can do this in your head if you just get your block sizes nailed!

Okay, let's practice on one more, just for fun (please study this one!).

Host IP: 10.16.3.65/23

First, you can't answer this question if you don't know what a /23, is. It's 255.255.254.0. The interesting octet here is the third one: 256 − 254 = 2. Our subnets in the third octet are 0, 2, 4, 6, and so on. The host in this question is in subnet 2.0, and the next subnet is 4.0, so that makes the broadcast address 3.255. And any address between 10.16.2.1 and 10.16.3.254 is considered a valid host.

Troubleshooting IP Addressing

Troubleshooting IP addressing is obviously an important skill because running into trouble somewhere along the way is pretty much a sure thing, and it's going to happen to you. No, I'm not a pessimist; I'm just keeping it real. Because of this nasty fact, it will be great when you can save the day because you can both figure out (diagnose) the problem and fix it on an IP network whether you're at work or at home!

So, this is where I'm going to show you the "Cisco way" of troubleshooting IP addressing. Let's use the following as an example of your basic IP troubleshooting—poor Sally can't log in to the Windows server. Do you deal with this by calling the Microsoft team to tell them their server is a pile of junk and causing all your problems? Probably not such a great idea—let's first double-check our network instead.

Okay, let's get started by going over the troubleshooting steps that Cisco follows. They're pretty simple but important nonetheless. Pretend you're at a customer host, and they're complaining that they can't communicate to a server that just happens to be on a remote network. Here are the four troubleshooting steps Cisco recommends:

1. Open a command prompt window and ping 127.0.0.1. This is the diagnostic, or loopback, address, and if you get a successful ping, your IP stack is considered to be initialized. If it fails, then you have an IP stack failure and need to reinstall TCP/IP on the host.

```
C:\>ping 127.0.0.1
Pinging 127.0.0.1 with 32 bytes of data:
Reply from 127.0.0.1: bytes=32 time<1ms TTL=128
Reply from 127.0.0.1: bytes=32 time<1ms TTL=128
```

```
Reply from 127.0.0.1: bytes=32 time<1ms TTL=128
Reply from 127.0.0.1: bytes=32 time<1ms TTL=128
Ping statistics for 127.0.0.1:
    Packets: Sent = 4, Received = 4, Lost = 0 (0% loss),
Approximate round trip times in milli-seconds:
    Minimum = 0ms, Maximum = 0ms, Average = 0ms
```

2. From the command window, ping the IP address of the local host. If that's successful, your network interface card (NIC) is functioning. If it fails, there is a problem with the NIC. Success here doesn't mean that a cable is plugged into the NIC, only that the IP protocol stack on the host can communicate to the NIC (via the LAN driver).

```
C:\>ping 172.16.10.2
Pinging 172.16.10.2 with 32 bytes of data:
Reply from 172.16.10.2: bytes=32 time<1ms TTL=128
Reply from 172.16.10.2: bytes=32 time<1ms TTL=128
Reply from 172.16.10.2: bytes=32 time<1ms TTL=128
Reply from 172.16.10.2: bytes=32 time<1ms TTL=128
Ping statistics for 172.16.10.2:
    Packets: Sent = 4, Received = 4, Lost = 0 (0% loss),
Approximate round trip times in milli-seconds:
    Minimum = 0ms, Maximum = 0ms, Average = 0ms
```

3. From the command prompt window, ping the default gateway (router). If the ping works, it means that the NIC is plugged into the network and can communicate on the local network. If it fails, you have a local physical network problem that could be anywhere from the NIC to the router.

```
C:\>ping 172.16.10.1
Pinging 172.16.10.1 with 32 bytes of data:
Reply from 172.16.10.1: bytes=32 time<1ms TTL=128
Reply from 172.16.10.1: bytes=32 time<1ms TTL=128
Reply from 172.16.10.1: bytes=32 time<1ms TTL=128
Reply from 172.16.10.1: bytes=32 time<1ms TTL=128
Ping statistics for 172.16.10.1:
    Packets: Sent = 4, Received = 4, Lost = 0 (0% loss),
Approximate round trip times in milli-seconds:
    Minimum = 0ms, Maximum = 0ms, Average = 0ms
```

4. If steps 1 through 3 were successful, try to ping the remote server. If that works, then you know that you have IP communication between the local host and the remote server. You also know that the remote physical network is working.

```
C:\>ping 172.16.20.2
Pinging 172.16.20.2 with 32 bytes of data:
```

```
Reply from 172.16.20.2: bytes=32 time<1ms TTL=128
Reply from 172.16.20.2: bytes=32 time<1ms TTL=128
Reply from 172.16.20.2: bytes=32 time<1ms TTL=128
Reply from 172.16.20.2: bytes=32 time<1ms TTL=128
Ping statistics for 172.16.20.2:
    Packets: Sent = 4, Received = 4, Lost = 0 (0% loss),
Approximate round trip times in milli-seconds:
    Minimum = 0ms, Maximum = 0ms, Average = 0ms
```

If the user still can't communicate with the server after steps 1 through 4 are successful, you probably have some type of name resolution problem and need to check your Domain Name System (DNS) settings. But if the ping to the remote server fails, then you know you have some type of remote physical network problem and need to go to the server and work through steps 1 through 3 until you find the snag.

Before moving on to determining IP address problems and how to fix them, I just want to mention some basic DOS commands that you can use to help troubleshoot your network from both a PC and a Cisco router (the commands might do the same thing, but they are implemented differently).

Packet InterNet Groper (`ping`)   Uses ICMP echo request and replies to test if a node IP stack is initialized and alive on the network. Does a basic test of the host's TCP/IP protocol stack. If you want to test your host's IP stack, you would ping 127.0.0.1.

`traceroute`   Displays the list of routers on a path to a network destination by using TTL timeouts and ICMP error messages. This command will not work from a command prompt.

`tracert`   Same command as `traceroute`, but it's a Microsoft Windows command and will not work on a Cisco router. It is critical that you remember where the commands `traceroute` and `tracert` are used.

`telnet`   Tests the virtual teletype (VTY) configuration. Makes your host a dumb host and allows you to run programs on a remote host. If you can telnet from one host to another, both hosts have good TCP/IP connectivity.

`arp -a`   Displays IP-to-MAC-address mappings on a Windows PC.

`show ip arp`   Same command as `arp -a`, but displays the ARP table on a Cisco router. Like the commands `traceroute` and `tracert`, they are not interchangeable through DOS and Cisco.

`ipconfig /all`   Used only from a Windows command prompt and displays the PC network configuration.

Once you've gone through all these steps and used the appropriate commands, if necessary, what do you do if you find a problem? How do you go about fixing an IP address configuration error? Let's move on and discuss how to determine the IP address problems and how to fix them.

Determining IP Address Problems

It's common for a host, router, or other network device to be configured with the wrong IP address, subnet mask, or default gateway. Because this happens way too often, I'm going to teach you how to both determine and fix IP address configuration errors.

Once you've worked through the four basic steps of troubleshooting and determined there's a problem, you obviously then need to find and fix it. It really helps to draw out the network and IP addressing scheme. If it's already done, consider yourself lucky and go buy a lottery ticket, because although it should be done, it rarely is. And if it is, it's usually outdated or inaccurate anyway. Typically it is not done, and you'll probably just have to bite the bullet and start from scratch.

I'll show you how to draw out your network using CDP in Chapter 5, "Managing a Cisco Internetwork."

Once you have your network accurately drawn out, including the IP addressing scheme, you need to verify each host's IP address, mask, and default gateway address to determine the problem. (I'm assuming that you don't have a physical problem or that if you did, you've already fixed it.)

Let's check out the example illustrated in Figure 3.3. A user in the sales department calls and tells you that she can't get to ServerA in the marketing department. You ask her if she can get to ServerB in the marketing department, but she doesn't know because she doesn't have rights to log on to that server. What do you do?

FIGURE 3.3 IP address problem 1

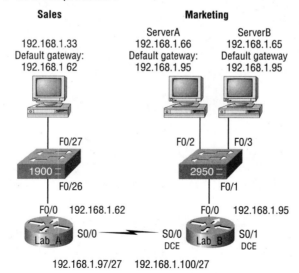

You ask the client to go through the four troubleshooting steps that you learned about in the preceding section. Steps 1 through 3 work, but step 4 fails. By looking at the figure, can you determine the problem? Look for clues in the network drawing. First, the WAN link between the Lab_A router and the Lab_B router shows the mask as a /27. You should already know that this mask is 255.255.255.224 and then determine that all networks are using this mask. The network address that is subnetted is 192.168.1.0. What are our valid subnets and hosts? 256 − 224 = 32, so this makes our subnets 32, 64, 96, 128, and so on. So, by looking at the figure, you can see that subnet 32 is being used by the sales department, the WAN link is using subnet 96, and the marketing department is using subnet 64.

Now you have to determine what the valid host ranges are for each subnet. From what you learned at the beginning of this chapter, you should now be able to easily determine the subnet address, broadcast addresses, and valid host ranges. The valid hosts for the Sales LAN are 33 through 62—the broadcast address is 63 because the next subnet is 64, right? For the Marketing LAN, the valid hosts are 65 through 94 (broadcast 95), and for the WAN link, 97 through 126 (broadcast 127). By looking at the figure, you can determine that the default gateway on the Lab_B router is incorrect. That address is the broadcast address of the 64 subnet, so there's no way it could be a valid host.

Did you get all that? Maybe you should try another one, just to make sure. Figure 3.4 shows a network problem. A user in the Sales LAN can't get to ServerB. You have the user run through the four basic troubleshooting steps and find that the host can communicate to the local network but not to the remote network. Find and define the IP addressing problem.

FIGURE 3.4   IP address problem 2

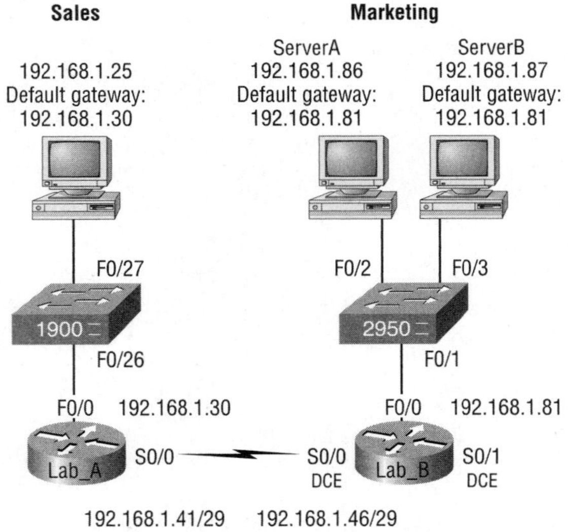

If you use the same steps used to solve the previous problem, you can see first that the WAN link again provides the subnet mask to use— /29, or 255.255.255.248. You need to determine what the valid subnets, broadcast addresses, and valid host ranges are to solve this problem.

The 248 mask is a block size of 8 (256 − 248 = 8), so the subnets both start and increment in multiples of 8. By looking at the figure, you see that the Sales LAN is in the 24 subnet, the WAN is in the 40 subnet, and the Marketing LAN is in the 80 subnet. Can you see the problem yet? The valid host range for the Sales LAN is 25–30, and the configuration appears correct. The valid host range for the WAN link is 41–46, and this also appears correct. The valid host range for the 80 subnet is 81–86, with a broadcast address of 87 because the next subnet is 88. ServerB has been configured with the broadcast address of the subnet.

Okay, now that you can figure out misconfigured IP addresses on hosts, what do you do if a host doesn't have an IP address and you need to assign one? What you need to do is look at other hosts on the LAN and figure out the network, mask, and default gateway. Let's take a look at a couple of examples of how to find and apply valid IP addresses to hosts.

You need to assign a server and router IP addresses on a LAN. The subnet assigned on that segment is 192.168.20.24/29, and the router needs to be assigned the first usable address and the server the last valid host ID. What are the IP address, mask, and default gateway assigned to the server?

To answer this, you must know that a /29 is a 255.255.255.248 mask, which provides a block size of 8. The subnet is known as 24, the next subnet in a block of 8 is 32, so the broadcast address of the 24 subnet is 31, which makes the valid host range 25–30.

Server IP address: 192.168.20.30

Server mask: 255.255.255.248

Default gateway: 192.168.20.25 (router's IP address)

As another example, let's take a look at Figure 3.5 and solve this problem.

FIGURE 3.5   Find the valid host.

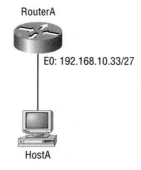

RouterA

E0: 192.168.10.33/27

HostA

Look at the router's IP address on Ethernet0. What IP address, subnet mask, and valid host range could be assigned to the host?

The IP address of the router's Ethernet0 is 192.168.10.33/27. As you already know, a /27 is a 224 mask with a block size of 32. The router's interface is in the 32 subnet. The next subnet is 64, so that makes the broadcast address of the 32 subnet 63 and the valid host range 33–62.

Host IP address: 192.168.10.34–62 (any address in the range except for 33, which is assigned to the router)

Mask: 255.255.255.224

Default gateway: 192.168.10.33

Figure 3.6 shows two routers with Ethernet configurations already assigned. What are the possible host addresses and subnet masks of hosts A and B?

FIGURE 3.6   Find the valid host (#2).

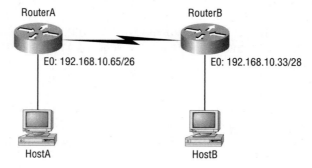

RouterA has an IP address of 192.168.10.65/26, and RouterB has an IP address of 192.168.10.33/28. What are the host configurations? RouterA Ethernet0 is in the 192.168.10.64 subnet, and RouterB Ethernet0 is in the 192.168.10.32 network.

HostA IP address: 192.168.10.66–126

HostA mask: 255.255.255.192

HostA default gateway: 192.168.10.65

HostB IP address: 192.168.10.34–46

HostB mask: 255.255.255.240

HostB default gateway: 192.168.10.33

Just a couple more examples, and then this chapter is history. Hang in there!

Figure 3.7 shows two routers; you need to configure the S0/0 interface on RouterA. The network assigned to the serial link is 172.16.17.0/22. What IP address can be assigned?

FIGURE 3.7   Find the valid host address (#3).

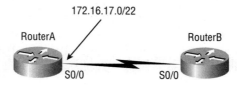

First, you must know that a /22 CIDR is 255.255.252.0, which makes a block size of 4 in the third octet. Since 17 is listed (and you know that can't be the actual subnet address, but Cisco is trying to trick you), the available range is 16.1 through 19.254; so, for example, the IP address S0/0 could be 172.16.18.255 since that's within the range.

In Figure 3.8, why can't HostA communicate with HostB?

FIGURE 3.8 IP communication problem

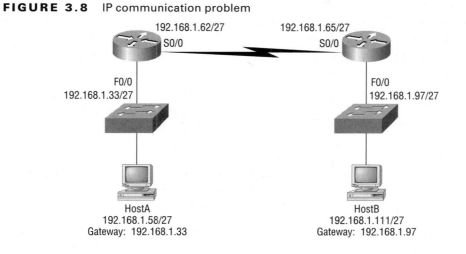

Again, what is your mask? That is always how you should start. Then you want to figure out the block size in the interesting octet. A /27 is 255.255.255.224, which is a block size of 32 in the fourth octet. The subnets are 0, 32, 64, 96, and so on. By looking at the figure, you can see that the HostA LAN is in the 32 subnet, the WAN is in the 64 subnet, and the HostB LAN is connected to the 96 subnet. Right away you should see that the WAN connection is not configured correctly. RouterA's serial 0/0 is configured with an IP address in the HostA LAN subnet range.

Okay, last one! You have one Class C network ID, and you need to provide one usable subnet per city while allowing enough usable host addresses for each city specified in Figure 3.9. What is your mask?

FIGURE 3.9 Find the valid subnet mask.

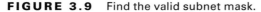

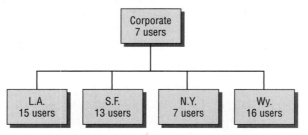

Actually, this is probably the easiest thing you've done all day! I count 5 subnets needed and the Wyoming office needs 16 users (always look for the network that needs the most hosts). What block size is needed for the Wyoming office? 32. (Remember, you cannot use a block size of 16 because you always have to subtract 2!) What mask provides you with a block size of 32? 224. Bingo! This provides 8 subnets, each with 30 hosts.

Introduction to Network Address Translation (NAT)

Similar to Classless Inter-Domain Routing (CIDR), the original intention for NAT was to slow the depletion of the available IP address space by allowing many private IP addresses to be represented by some smaller number of public IP addresses.

Since then, it's been discovered that NAT is also a useful tool for network migrations and mergers, server load sharing, and creating "virtual servers." So in this section, I'm going to describe the basics of NAT functionality and the terminology common to NAT.

At times, NAT really decreases the overwhelming amount of public IP addresses required in your networking environment. And NAT comes in really handy when two companies that have duplicate internal addressing schemes merge. NAT is also great to have around when an organization changes its Internet service provider and the networking manager doesn't want the hassle of changing the internal address scheme.

Here's a list of situations when it's best to have NAT on your side:

- You need to connect to the Internet, and your hosts don't have globally unique IP addresses.

- You change to a new ISP that requires you to renumber your network.

- You need to merge two intranets with duplicate addresses.

You typically use NAT on a border router. For an illustration of this, see Figure 3.10.

FIGURE 3.10   Where to configure NAT

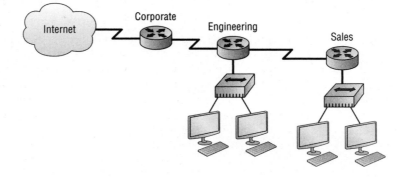

Now you may be thinking, "NAT's totally cool. It's the grooviest greatest network gadget, and I just gotta have it." Well, hang on a minute. There are truly some serious snags related to NAT use. Oh, don't get me wrong: it really can save you sometimes, but there's a dark side you need to know about, too. For a visual of the pros and cons linked to using NAT, check out Table 3.3.

TABLE 3.3   Advantages and disadvantages of implementing NAT

Advantages	Disadvantages
Conserves legally registered addresses.	Translation introduces switching path delays.
Reduces address overlap occurrence.	Loss of end-to-end IP traceability.
Increases flexibility when connecting to Internet.	Certain applications will not function with NAT enabled.
Eliminates address renumbering as network changes.	

Types of Network Address Translation

In this section, I'll go over the three types of NAT with you.

Static NAT   This type of NAT is designed to allow one-to-one mapping between local and global addresses. Keep in mind that the static version requires you to have one real Internet IP address for every host on your network.

Dynamic NAT   This version gives you the ability to map an unregistered IP address to a registered IP address from out of a pool of registered IP addresses. You don't have to statically configure your router to map an inside to an outside address as you would using static NAT, but you do have to have enough real, bona fide IP addresses for everyone who's going to be sending packets to and receiving them from the Internet.

Overloading   This is the most popular type of NAT configuration. Understand that overloading really is a form of dynamic NAT that maps multiple unregistered IP addresses to a single registered IP address—many-to-one—by using different ports. Now, why is this so special? Well, because it's also known as *Port Address Translation (PAT)*. And by using PAT (NAT Overload), you get to have thousands of users connect to the Internet using only one real global IP address—pretty slick, yeah? Seriously, NAT Overload is the real reason we haven't run out of valid IP address on the Internet. Really, I'm not joking.

NAT Names

The names you use to describe the addresses used with NAT are pretty simple. Addresses used after NAT translations are called *global* addresses. These are usually the public addresses used on the Internet, but remember, you don't need public addresses if you aren't going on the Internet.

Local addresses are the ones you use before NAT translation. So, the inside local address is actually the private address of the sending host that's trying to get to the Internet, while the outside local address is the address of your router's interface connected to the Internet.

After translation, the inside local address is called the *inside global address*, and the outside global address then becomes the name of the destination host. Check out Table 3.4, which lists all this terminology, for a clear picture of the various names used with NAT.

TABLE 3.4   NAT terms

Names	Meaning
Inside local	Name of inside source address before translation
Outside local	Your router interface IP address connected to the Internet
Inside global	Name of inside host after translation
Outside global	Name of outside destination host after translation

How NAT Works

Okay, now it's time to look at how this whole NAT thing works. I'm going to start by using Figure 3.11 to describe the basic translation of NAT.

In the example shown in Figure 3.11, host 10.1.1.1 sends an outbound packet to the border router configured with NAT. The router identifies the IP address as an inside local IP address destined for an outside network, translates the address, and documents the translation in the NAT table.

The packet is sent to the outside interface with the new translated source address. The external host returns the packet to the destination host, and the NAT router translates the inside global IP address back to the inside local IP address using the NAT table. This is as simple as it gets.

Let's take a look at a more complex configuration using overloading, or what is also referred to as Port Address Translation (PAT). I'll use Figure 3.12 to demonstrate how PAT works.

FIGURE 3.11   Basic NAT translation

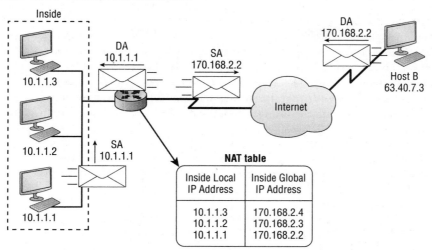

FIGURE 3.12   NAT overloading example (PAT)

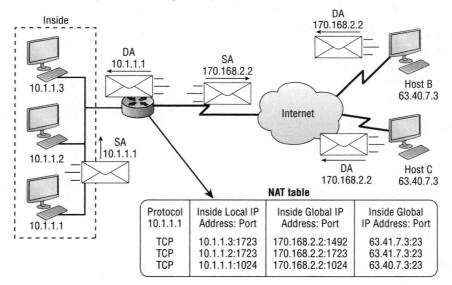

With overloading, all inside hosts get translated to one single IP address, which is why it's called *overloading*. Again, the reason we have not run out of available IP addresses on the Internet is because of overloading (PAT).

Take a look at the NAT table in Figure 3.12 again. In addition to the inside local IP address and outside global IP address, we now have port numbers. These port numbers help the router identify which host should receive the return traffic.

Port numbers are used at the Transport layer to identify the local host in this example. If we had to use IP addresses to identify the source hosts, that would be called *static NAT*, and we would run out of addresses. PAT allows us to use the Transport layer to identify the hosts, which in turn allows us to use (theoretically) up to 65,000 hosts with one real IP address.

You're done, the diva has sung, the chicken has crossed the road...whew! Take a good break (but skip the shot and the beer for now), and then come back and go through the written labs and review questions.

Summary

Did you read Chapters 2 and 3 and understand everything on the first pass? If so, that is fantastic—congratulations! The thing is, you probably got lost a couple of times, and as I told you, that's what usually happens, so don't stress. Don't feel bad if you have to read each chapter more than once, or even 10 times, before you're truly good to go.

This chapter provided you with an important understanding of IP subnetting. After reading this chapter, you should be able to subnet IP addresses in your head.

You should also understand the Cisco troubleshooting methods. You must remember the four steps that Cisco recommends you take when trying to narrow down exactly where a network/IP addressing problem is and then know how to proceed systematically in order to fix it. In addition, you should be able to find valid IP addresses and subnet masks by looking at a network diagram.

Exam Essentials

Remember the steps to subnet in your head.   Understand how IP addressing and subnetting work. First, determine your block size by using the 256-subnet mask math. Then count your subnets and determine the broadcast address of each subnet—it is always the number right before the next subnet. Your valid hosts are the numbers between the subnet address and the broadcast address.

Understand the various block sizes.   This is an important part of understanding IP addressing and subnetting. The valid block sizes are always 4, 8, 16, 32, 64, 128, and so on. You can determine your block size by using the 256-subnet mask math.

Remember the four diagnostic steps.   The four simple steps that Cisco recommends for troubleshooting are ping the loopback address, ping the NIC, ping the default gateway, and ping the remote device.

You must be able to find and fix an IP addressing problem.   Once you go through the four troubleshooting steps that Cisco recommends, you must be able to determine the IP addressing problem by drawing out the network and finding the valid and invalid hosts addressed in your network.

Understand the troubleshooting tools that you can use from your host and a Cisco router. `ping 127.0.0.1` tests your local IP stack. `tracert` is a Windows DOS command to track the path a packet takes through an internetwork to a destination. Cisco routers use the command `traceroute`, or just `trace` for short. Don't confuse the Windows and Cisco commands. Although they produce the same output, they don't work from the same prompts. `ipconfig /all` will display your PC network configuration from a command prompt, and `arp -a` (again from a DOS prompt) will display IP-to-MAC-address mapping on a Windows PC.

Understand basic NAT terminology.   You must know the difference between *inside local* and *inside global*. This is mandatory! Inside local is before translation, and inside global is after translation. Inside global is defined as a registered address that represents an inside host to an outside network. You must also understand PAT and how it works by mapping multiple private IP addresses to a single registered IP address by using a different port number.

Written Labs 3

In this section, you'll complete the following labs to make sure you have the information and concepts contained within them fully dialed in:

- Lab 3.1: Written Subnet Practice #1
- Lab 3.2: Written Subnet Practice #2
- Lab 3.3: Written Subnet Practice #3

(The answers to the written labs can be found in Appendix A.)

Written Lab 3.1: Written Subnet Practice #1

Write the subnet, broadcast address, and valid host range for question 1 through question 6 and then answer the questions that follow:

1. 192.168.100.25/30
2. 192.168.100.37/28
3. 192.168.100.66/27
4. 192.168.100.17/29
5. 192.168.100.99/26
6. 192.168.100.99/25
7. You have a Class B network and need 29 subnets. What is your mask?
8. What is the broadcast address of 192.168.192.10/29?
9. How many hosts are available with a Class C /29 mask?
10. What is the subnet for host ID 10.16.3.65/23?
11. What form of NAT maps multiple private IP addresses to a single registered IP address by using different ports?
12. What does the term *inside global address* represent in the configuration of NAT?
13. What diagnostic tool will you use to test a remote host's IP stack?
14. What diagnostic tool will you use to display IP-to-MAC addressing on a Windows PC?
15. What is the IP address range for subnet 192.168.2.64/26?
16. How many hosts does the subnet 172.16.112.0/20 provide?
17. What is the subnet address of 172.16.159.159/22?
18. What is the subnet for the host ID of 10.16.3.65/23?
19. What is the broadcast address the host 10.16.3.65/23 will use?
20. Two routers are connected with a serial connection. One is configured with IP address 192.168.10.82/30, and the other is 192.168.10.85/30. Why won't the two routers communicate?

Written Lab 3.2: Written Subnet Practice #2

Given a Class B network and the net bits identified (CIDR), complete the following table to identify the subnet mask and the number of host addresses possible for each mask:

Classful address	Subnet mask	Number of hosts per subnet ($2x - 2$)
/16		
/17		
/18		
/19		
/20		
/21		
/22		
/23		
/24		
/25		
/26		
/27		
/28		
/29		
/30		

Written Lab 3.3: Written Subnet Practice #3

Decimal IP address	Address class	Number of subnet and host bits	Number of subnets ($2x$)	Number of hosts ($2x - 2$)
10.25.66.154/23				
172.31.254.12/24				
192.168.20.123/28				
63.24.89.21/18				
128.1.1.254/20				
208.100.54.209/30				

Review Questions

You can find the answers in Appendix B.

 The following questions are designed to test your understanding of this chapter's material. For more information on how to get additional questions, please see this book's introduction.

1. What is the maximum number of IP addresses that can be assigned to hosts on a local subnet that uses the 255.255.255.224 subnet mask?
    A. 14
    B. 15
    C. 16
    D. 30
    E. 31
    F. 62

2. You have a network that needs 29 subnets while maximizing the number of host addresses available on each subnet. How many bits must you borrow from the host field to provide the correct subnet mask?
    A. 2
    B. 3
    C. 4
    D. 5
    E. 6
    F. 7

3. What is the subnetwork address for a host with the IP address 200.10.5.68/28?
    A. 200.10.5.56
    B. 200.10.5.32
    C. 200.10.5.64
    D. 200.10.5.0

4. The network address of 172.16.0.0/19 provides how many subnets and hosts?
    A. 7 subnets, 30 hosts each
    B. 7 subnets, 2,046 hosts each
    C. 7 subnets, 8,190 hosts each
    D. 8 subnets, 30 hosts each
    E. 8 subnets, 2,046 hosts each
    F. 8 subnets, 8,190 hosts each

5. Which *two* statements describe the IP address 10.16.3.65/23?

    A. The subnet address is 10.16.3.0 255.255.254.0.

    B. The lowest host address in the subnet is 10.16.2.1 255.255.254.0.

    C. The last valid host address in the subnet is 10.16.2.254 255.255.254.0.

    D. The broadcast address of the subnet is 10.16.3.255 255.255.254.0.

    E. The network is not subnetted.

6. If a host on a network has the address 172.16.45.14/30, what is the subnetwork this host belongs to?

    A. 172.16.45.0

    B. 172.16.45.4

    C. 172.16.45.8

    D. 172.16.45.12

    E. 172.16.45.16

7. On a VLSM network, which mask should you use on point-to-point WAN links in order to reduce the waste of IP addresses?

    A. /27

    B. /28

    C. /29

    D. /30

    E. /31

8. What is the subnetwork number of a host with an IP address of 172.16.66.0/21?

    A. 172.16.36.0

    B. 172.16.48.0

    C. 172.16.64.0

    D. 172.16.0.0

9. You have an interface on a router with the IP address of 192.168.192.10/29. Including the router interface, how many hosts can have IP addresses on the LAN attached to the router interface?

    A. 6

    B. 8

    C. 30

    D. 62

    E. 126

10. You need to configure a server that is on the subnet 192.168.19.24/29. The router has the first available host address. Which of the following should you assign to the server?

    A.   192.168.19.0 255.255.255.0

    B.   192.168.19.33 255.255.255.240

    C.   192.168.19.26 255.255.255.248

    D.   192.168.19.31 255.255.255.248

    E.   192.168.19.34 255.255.255.240

11. You have an interface on a router with the IP address of 192.168.192.10/29. What is the broadcast address the hosts will use on this LAN?

    A.   192.168.192.15

    B.   192.168.192.31

    C.   192.168.192.63

    D.   192.168.192.127

    E.   192.168.192.255

12. You need to subnet a network that has 5 subnets, each with at least 16 hosts. Which classful subnet mask would you use?

    A.   255.255.255.192

    B.   255.255.255.224

    C.   255.255.255.240

    D.   255.255.255.248

13. A network administrator is connecting hosts A and B directly through their Ethernet interfaces, as shown in the illustration. Ping attempts between the hosts are unsuccessful. What can be done to provide connectivity between the hosts? (Choose two.)

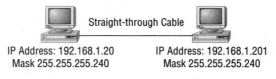

    A.   A crossover cable should be used in place of the straight-through cable.

    B.   A rollover cable should be used in place of the straight-though cable.

    C.   The subnet masks should be set to 255.255.255.192.

    D.   A default gateway needs to be set on each host.

    E.   The subnet masks should be set to 255.255.255.0.

14. If an Ethernet port on a router were assigned an IP address of 172.16.112.1/25, what would be the valid subnet address of this host?

A. 172.16.112.0

B. 172.16.0.0

C. 172.16.96.0

D. 172.16.255.0

E. 172.16.128.0

15. You are using the network ID of 192.168.10.0/28 and need to use the last available IP address in the range in the eighth subnet for a host. The zero subnet should not be considered valid for this question. Which of the following meet your business requirements?

A. 192.168.10.142

B. 192.168.10.66

C. 192.168.100.254

D. 192.168.10.143

E. 192.168.10.126

16. Using the example from the previous question, what would be the IP address if you were using the first subnet? The network ID is 192.168.10.0/28, and you need to use the last available IP address in the range. Again, the zero subnet should not be considered valid for this question.

A. 192.168.10.24

B. 192.168.10.62

C. 192.168.10.30

D. 192.168.10.127

17. Which configuration command must be in effect to allow the use of 8 subnets if the Class C subnet mask is 255.255.255.224?

A. Router(config)#`ip classless`

B. Router(config)#`ip version 6`

C. Router(config)#`no ip classful`

D. Router(config)#`ip unnumbered`

E. Router(config)#`ip subnet-zero`

F. Router(config)#`ip all-nets`

18. You have a network with a host address of 172.16.17.0/22. Which is another valid host address in the same subnet?

   A.   172.16.17.1 255.255.255.252

   B.   172.16.0.1 255.255.240.0

   C.   172.16.20.1 255.255.254.0

   D.   172.16.16.1 255.255.255.240

   E.   172.16.18.255 255.255.252.0

   F.   172.16.0.1 255.255.255.0

19. Your router has the following IP address on Ethernet0: 172.16.2.1/23. Which of the following can be valid host IDs on the LAN interface attached to the router? (Choose two.)

   A.   172.16.0.5

   B.   172.16.1.100

   C.   172.16.1.198

   D.   172.16.2.255

   E.   172.16.3.0

   F.   172.16.3.255

20. What does the "inside global" address represent in the configuration of NAT?

   A.   The summarized address for all of the internal subnetted addresses

   B.   The MAC address of the router used by inside hosts to connect to the Internet

   C.   A globally unique, private address assigned to a host on the inside network

   D.   A registered address that represents an inside host to an outside network

Chapter 4

Cisco's Internetworking Operating System (IOS)

THE CCENT EXAM OBJECTIVES COVERED IN THIS CHAPTER INCLUDE THE FOLLOWING:

✓ **Implement a small routed network**

- Access and utilize the router CLI to set basic parameters

- Connect, configure, and verify operation status of a device interface

- Verify device configuration and network connectivity using ping, traceroute, telnet, SSH or other utilities

- Implement password and physical security

- Verify network status and router operation using basic utilities (including: ping, traceroute, telnet, SSH, arp, ipconfig), SHOW & DEBUG commands

✓ **Implement an IP addressing scheme and IP services to meet network requirements for a small branch office**

- Describe the need and role of addressing in a network

- Create and apply an addressing scheme to a network

- Describe and verify DNS operation

- Configure, verify and troubleshoot DHCP and DNS operation on a router (including: CLI/SDM)

The time has come to introduce you to the Cisco Internetwork Operating System (IOS). The IOS is what runs Cisco routers as well as Cisco's switches, and it's what allows you to configure the devices.

So, that's what you're going to learn about in this chapter. I'll show you how to configure a Cisco IOS router using the Cisco IOS command-line interface (CLI). When you become proficient with this interface, you'll be able to configure hostnames, banners, passwords, and more, as well as troubleshoot using the Cisco IOS.

I'm also going to get you up to speed on the vital basics of router configurations and command verifications. Here's a list of the subjects I'll be covering in this chapter:

- Understanding and configuring the Cisco Internetwork Operating System
- Connecting to a router
- Bringing up a router
- Logging into a router
- Understanding the router prompts
- Understanding the CLI prompts
- Performing editing and help features
- Gathering basic routing information
- Setting administrative functions
- Setting hostnames
- Setting banners
- Setting passwords
- Setting interface descriptions
- Performing interface configurations
- Viewing, saving, and erasing configurations
- Verifying routing configurations

And just as it was with preceding chapters, the fundamentals that you'll learn in this chapter are foundational building blocks that really need to be in place before you go on to the next chapters in the book.

For up-to-the-minute updates for this chapter, please see www.lammle.com/forum or www.sybex.com/go/ccent2e.

The IOS User Interface

The *Cisco Internetwork Operating System (IOS)* is the kernel of Cisco routers and most switches. In case you didn't know, a kernel is the basic, indispensable part of an operating system that allocates resources and manages things such as low-level hardware interfaces and security.

In the following sections, I'll show you the Cisco IOS and how to configure a Cisco router using the command-line interface (CLI).

I'm going to save Cisco switch configurations for Chapter 7, "Layer 2 Switching."

Cisco Router IOS

The Cisco IOS is a proprietary kernel that provides routing, switching, internetworking, and telecommunications features. The first IOS was written by William Yeager in 1986, and it enabled networked applications. It runs on most Cisco routers as well as an ever-increasing number of Cisco Catalyst switches, like the Catalyst 2960 and 3560 series switches.

These are some important things that the Cisco router IOS software is responsible for:

- Carrying network protocols and functions
- Connecting high-speed traffic between devices
- Adding security to control access and stop unauthorized network use
- Providing scalability for ease of network growth and redundancy
- Supplying network reliability for connecting to network resources

You can access the Cisco IOS through the console port of a router, from a modem into the auxiliary (or Aux) port, or even through Telnet. Access to the IOS command line is called an *EXEC session*.

Connecting to a Cisco Router

You can connect to a Cisco router to configure it, verify its configuration, and check statistics. There are different ways to do this, but most often, the first place you would connect to is the console port. The *console port* is usually an RJ-45 (8-pin modular) connection located at the back of the router—by default, there may or may not be a password set. The new ISR routers use *cisco* as the username and *cisco* as the password by default.

See Chapter 1, "Internetworking," for an explanation of how to configure a PC to connect to a router console port.

You can also connect to a Cisco router through an *auxiliary port*—which is really the same thing as a console port, so it follows that you can use it as one. But an auxiliary port also allows you to configure modem commands so that a modem can be connected to the router. This is a cool feature—it lets you dial up a remote router and attach to the auxiliary port if the router is down and you need to configure it *out-of-band* (meaning from outside the network).

The third way to connect to a Cisco router is in-band, through the program *Telnet*. (*In-band* means configuring the router through the network, the opposite of *out-of-band*.) Telnet is a terminal emulation program that acts as though it's a dumb terminal. You can use Telnet to connect to any active interface on a router, such as an Ethernet or serial port. I'll discuss something called Secure Shell (SSH) later in this chapter, which is a more secure way to connect in-band through the network.

Figure 4.1 illustrates a Cisco 2600 series modular router, which is a cut above routers populating the 2500 series because it has a faster processor and can handle many more interfaces. Both the 2500 and 2600 series routers are end of life (EOL), and you can buy them only used. However, many 2600 series routers are still found in production, so it's important to understand them. Pay close attention to all the different kinds of interfaces and connections.

FIGURE 4.1   A Cisco 2600 router

Cisco 2610 router

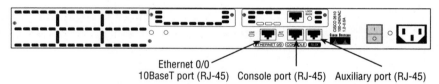

Ethernet 0/0
10BaseT port (RJ-45)   Console port (RJ-45)   Auxiliary port (RJ-45)

The 2600 series router can have multiple types of serial interfaces, which can be used for connecting a T1 using a serial V.35 WAN connection into a CSU/DSU. The modular card in the top slot is an actual CSU/DSU, which is pretty normal to see today. Multiple Ethernet or Fast Ethernet ports can be used on the router, depending on the model. This router also has one console and one auxiliary connection via RJ-45 connectors.

Another router I want to talk about is the 2800/2900 series (shown in Figure 4.2). This router replaced the 2600 series router and is referred to as an Integrated Services Router (ISR). The ISR series gets its name because many of the services, like security, are built into it. It's a modular device like the 2600, but it's much faster and a lot sleeker—it's elegantly designed to support a broad new range of interface options.

You need to keep in mind that for the most part, you get some serious bang for your buck with the 2800/2900—unless you start adding a lot of interfaces to it. You have to pony up for each one of those little beauties, and things can really start to add up—fast!

There are a couple of other series of routers that are less expensive than the 2800/2900 series: the 1800/1900 and 800/900 series. You may want to look into these routers if you're looking for a less-expensive alternative to the 2800/2900 but still want to run the same IOS.

FIGURE 4.2 A Cisco 2800 router

Figure 4.3 shows an 1841 router that holds most of the same interfaces as the 2800, but it's smaller and less expensive. The real reason you would opt for a 2800/2900 instead of an 1800/1900 series router comes down to the more advanced interfaces you can run on the 2800/2900—things like the wireless controller and switching modules.

FIGURE 4.3 A Cisco 1841 router

As a heads up, I'm going to be using mostly 2800, 1800, and 800 series routers throughout this book to demonstrate examples of router configurations. But understand that you can use the 2600 and even the older 2500 routers to practice routing principles.

 You can find more information about all Cisco routers at www.cisco.com/en/US/products/hw/routers/index.html.

Bringing Up a Router

When you first bring up a Cisco router, it will run a power-on self-test (POST). If it passes, it will then look for and load the Cisco IOS from flash memory. If an IOS file is present, the bootstrap expands it into RAM. (Just in case you don't know, flash memory is electronically erasable programmable read-only memory—an EEPROM.) After that, the IOS loads and looks for a valid configuration—the startup-config—that's stored in nonvolatile RAM, or NVRAM (which is a partition of flash memory).

The following messages appear when you first boot or reload a router (I am using my 2811 router):

```
System Bootstrap, Version 12.4(13r)T, RELEASE SOFTWARE (fc1)
Technical Support: http://www.cisco.com/techsupport
Copyright (c) 2006 by cisco Systems, Inc.
Initializing memory for ECC
c2811 platform with 262144 Kbytes of main memory
Main memory is configured to 64 bit mode with ECC enabled
```

```
Upgrade ROMMON initialized
program load complete, entry point: 0x8000f000, size: 0xcb80
program load complete, entry point: 0x8000f000, size: 0xcb80
```

This is the first part of the router boot process output. It's information about the bootstrap program that first runs the POST. It then tells the router how to load, which by default is to find the IOS in flash memory. It also lists the amount of RAM in the router.

The next part shows that the IOS is being decompressed into RAM:

```
program load complete, entry point: 0x8000f000, size: 0x14b45f8
Self decompressing the image :
  ###############################################################
  ######################################### [OK]
```

The pound signs are telling you that the IOS is being decompressed into RAM. After it is decompressed into RAM, the IOS is loaded and starts running the router, as shown here. Notice that the IOS version is stated as advanced security version 12.4(12):

```
[some output cut]
Cisco IOS Software, 2800 Software (C2800NM-ADVSECURITYK9-M), Version
   12.4(12), RELEASE SOFTWARE (fc1)
Technical Support: http://www.cisco.com/techsupport
Copyright (c) 1986-2006 by Cisco Systems, Inc.
Compiled Fri 17-Nov-06 12:02 by prod_rel_team
Image text-base: 0x40093160, data-base: 0x41AA0000
```

A sweet new feature of the new ISR routers is that the IOS name is no longer cryptic. The filename actually tells you what the IOS can do, as in Advanced Security (C2800NM-ADVSECURITYK9-M in this example). Once the IOS is loaded, the information learned from the POST will be displayed next, as you can see here:

```
[some output cut]
Cisco 2811 (revision 49.46) with 249856K/12288K bytes of memory.
Processor board ID FTX1049A1AB
2 FastEthernet interfaces
4 Serial(sync/async) interfaces
1 Virtual Private Network (VPN) Module
DRAM configuration is 64 bits wide with parity enabled.
239K bytes of non-volatile configuration memory.
62720K bytes of ATA CompactFlash (Read/Write)
```

There are two Fast Ethernet interfaces, four serial interfaces, plus a VPN module. The amount of RAM, NVRAM, and flash are also displayed. The previous router output shows that there's 256MB of RAM, 239K of NVRAM, and 64MB of flash. When it comes to figuring out the amount of RAM and flash, you typically will average up.

When the IOS is loaded and up and running, a configuration file (called `startup-config`) will be copied from NVRAM into RAM. The copy of this file that will be placed in RAM and is called `running-config`.

 My 1841 and 871W routers boot exactly the same as the 2811 router. They do show less memory and different interfaces, but other than that, they have the same bootup procedure.

Bringing Up a Non-ISR Router (a 2600 in This Example)

As you're about to see, the boot cycle is about the same for non-ISR routers as for the ISR routers. The following messages appear when you first boot or reload a 2600 router:

```
System Bootstrap, Version 11.3(2)XA4, RELEASE SOFTWARE (fc1)
Copyright (c) 1999 by cisco Systems, Inc.
TAC:Home:SW:IOS:Specials for info
C2600 platform with 65536 Kbytes of main memory
```

The next part shows that the IOS is being decompressed into RAM:

```
program load complete, entry point:0x80008000, size:0x43b7fc
Self decompressing the image :
####################################################
[some output cut]
################################################################### [OK]
```

So far, everything is pretty much the same. Notice here that the IOS version is stated as version 12.3(20):

```
Cisco Internetwork Operating System Software
IOS (tm) C2600 Software (C2600-IK9O3S3-M), Version 12.3(20), RELEASE
    SOFTWARE (fc2)
Technical Support: http://www.cisco.com/techsupport
Copyright (c) 1986-2006 by cisco Systems, Inc.
Compiled Tue 08-Aug-06 20:50 by kesnyder
Image text-base: 0x80008098, data-base: 0x81A0E7A8
```

Just as with the 2800 series, once the IOS is loaded, the information learned from the POST will be displayed.

```
cisco 2610 (MPC860) processor (revision 0x202) with 61440K/4096K bytes
    of memory.
Processor board ID JAD03348593 (1529298102)
M860 processor: part number 0, mask 49
```

```
Bridging software.
X.25 software, Version 3.0.0.
1 Ethernet/IEEE 802.3 interface(s)
1 Serial network interface(s)
2 Serial(sync/async) network interface(s)
32K bytes of non-volatile configuration memory.
16384K bytes of processor board System flash (Read/Write)
```

Okay—finally, what we see here is one Ethernet interface and three serial interfaces. The amount of RAM and flash is also displayed; the top line of the previous router output shows there are 64MB of RAM, and the last line shows 16MB of flash.

And as I mentioned, when the IOS is loaded and up and running, a valid configuration called the startup-config will be loaded from NVRAM. But here's where it differs from the default bootup of the ISR routers—if there isn't a configuration in NVRAM, the router will broadcast looking for a valid one on a TFTP host. (This can happen only if the router senses carrier detect, or CD, on any LAN interface.) If the broadcast fails, it will then go into what is called *setup mode*—a step-by-step process to help you configure the router. So, you need to remember that if you plug any interface of your router into your network and then boot your router, you may have to wait a couple minutes while the router searches for the configuration.

You can also enter setup mode at any time from the command line by typing the command **setup** from something called privileged mode, which I'll get to in a minute. Setup mode allows only some commands and is generally just unhelpful. Here is an example of setup mode:

```
Would you like to enter the initial configuration dialog? [yes/no]: y


At any point you may enter a question mark '?' for help.
Use ctrl-c to abort configuration dialog at any prompt.
Default settings are in square brackets '[]'.


Basic management setup configures only enough connectivity
for management of the system, extended setup will ask you
to configure each interface on the system


Would you like to enter basic management setup? [yes/no]: y
Configuring global parameters:


  Enter host name [Router]: Ctrl+C
Configuration aborted, no changes made.
```

You can exit setup mode at any time by pressing Ctrl+C.

I highly recommend using setup mode once for Cisco objective purposes and then never again. You should always use the CLI.

Command-Line Interface (CLI)

I sometimes refer to the CLI as "Cash-Line Interface" because if you can create advanced configurations on Cisco routers and switches using the CLI, then you'll get the cash!

Entering the CLI

After the interface status messages appear and you press Enter, the Router> prompt will appear. This is called *user exec mode* (user mode), and it's mostly used to view statistics, but it's also a stepping stone to logging in to privileged mode.

You can only view and change the configuration of a Cisco router starting in *privileged exec mode* (privileged mode), which you can enter with the enable command.

Here's how:

```
Router>enable
Router#
```

You now end up with a Router# prompt, which indicates that you're in *privileged mode*, where you can both view and change the router's configuration. You can go back from privileged mode into user mode by using the disable command, as shown here:

```
Router#disable
Router>
```

At this point, you can type **logout** from either mode to exit the console.

```
Router>logout


Router con0 is now available
Press RETURN to get started.
```

In the following sections, I am going to show you how to perform some basic administrative configurations.

Overview of Router Modes

To configure from a CLI, you can make global changes to the router by typing **configure terminal** (or **config t** for short), which puts you in global configuration mode and change what's known as the running-config. A global command (a command run from global config) is set only once and affects the entire router.

You can type config from the privileged-mode prompt and then just press Enter to take the default of terminal, as shown here:

```
Router#config
Configuring from terminal, memory, or network [terminal]? [press enter]
Enter configuration commands, one per line.  End with CNTL/Z.
Router(config)#
```

At this point, you make changes that affect the router as a whole (globally), which is why it's called *global configuration mode*. To change the running-config—the current configuration running in dynamic RAM (DRAM)—you use the configure terminal command, as I just demonstrated.

Here are some of the other options under the configure command:

```
Router(config)#exit or press cntl-z
Router#config ?
  memory             Configure from NV memory
  network            Configure from a TFTP network host
  overwrite-network  Overwrite NV memory from TFTP network host
  terminal           Configure from the terminal
  <cr>
```

I'll go through these commands in Chapter 5, "Managing a Cisco Internetwork."

CLI Prompts

It's really important that you understand the different prompts you can use when configuring a router. Knowing these well will help you navigate and recognize where you are at any time within configuration mode. In the following sections, I'll demonstrate the prompts that are used on a Cisco router and discuss the various terms used. (Always check your prompts before making any changes to a router's configuration!)

I won't go into every different command prompt offered because doing that would be reaching beyond the scope of this book. Instead, I'll describe all the different prompts you'll see throughout this chapter and the rest of the book. These command prompts really are the ones you'll use most in real life anyway; plus, they're the ones you'll need to know for the exam.

Don't freak! It's not important that you understand what each of these command prompts accomplishes yet because I'm going to completely fill you in on all of them really soon. So, right now, just relax and focus on becoming familiar with the different prompts available, and all will be well!

Interfaces

To make changes to an interface, you use the `interface` command from global configuration mode.

```
Router(config)#interface ?
  Async              Async interface
  BVI                Bridge-Group Virtual Interface
  CDMA-Ix            CDMA Ix interface
  CTunnel            CTunnel interface
  Dialer             Dialer interface
  FastEthernet       FastEthernet IEEE 802.3
  Group-Async        Async Group interface
  Lex                Lex interface
  Loopback           Loopback interface
  MFR                Multilink Frame Relay bundle interface
  Multilink          Multilink-group interface
  Null               Null interface
  Port-channel       Ethernet Channel of interfaces
  Serial             Serial
  Tunnel             Tunnel interface
  Vif                PGM Multicast Host interface
  Virtual-PPP        Virtual PPP interface
  Virtual-Template   Virtual Template interface
  Virtual-TokenRing  Virtual TokenRing
  range              interface range command
Router(config)#interface fastEthernet 0/0
Router(config-if)#
```

Did you notice that the prompt changed to `Router(config-if)#`? This tells you that you're in *interface configuration mode*. And wouldn't it be nice if the prompt also gave you an indication of what interface you were configuring? Well, at least for now you'll have to live without that prompt information, because it doesn't provide that. One thing is for sure: you really have to pay attention when configuring a router!

Subinterfaces

Subinterfaces allow you to create logical interfaces within the router. The prompt then changes to Router(config-subif)#.

```
Router(config-if)#interface f0/0.1
Router(config-subif)#
```

Line Commands

To configure user-mode passwords, use the line command. The prompt then becomes Router(config-line)#.

```
Router#config t
Enter configuration commands, one per line.  End with CNTL/Z.
Router(config)#line ?
  <0-337>  First Line number
  aux      Auxiliary line
  console  Primary terminal line
  tty      Terminal controller
  vty      Virtual terminal
```

The line console 0 command is known as a *major command* (also called a *global command*), and any command typed from the (config-line) prompt is known as a *subcommand*.

Routing Protocol Configurations

To configure routing protocols such as RIP and EIGRP, you'll use the prompt Router(config-router#).

```
Router#config t
Enter configuration commands, one per line.  End with CNTL/Z.
Router(config)#router rip
Router(config-router)#version 2
Router(config-router)#
```

Defining Router Terms

Table 4.1 defines some of the terms I've used so far.

TABLE 4.1   Router terms

Mode	Definition
User EXEC mode	Limited to basic monitoring commands
Privileged EXEC mode	Provides access to all other router commands

TABLE 4.1   Router terms *(continued)*

Mode	Definition
Global configuration mode	Commands that affect the entire system
Specific configuration modes	Commands that affect interfaces/processes only
Setup mode	Interactive configuration dialog

Editing and Help Features

You can use the Cisco advanced editing features to help you configure your router. If you type in a question mark (?) at any prompt, you'll be given a list of all the commands available from that prompt.

```
Router#?
Exec commands:
  access-enable      Create a temporary Access-List entry
  access-profile     Apply user-profile to interface
  access-template    Create a temporary Access-List entry
  archive            manage archive files
  auto               Exec level Automation
  bfe                For manual emergency modes setting
  calendar           Manage the hardware calendar
  cd                 Change current directory
  clear              Reset functions
  clock              Manage the system clock
  cns                CNS agents
  configure          Enter configuration mode
  connect            Open a terminal connection
  copy               Copy from one file to another
  crypto             Encryption related commands.
  ct-isdn            Run an ISDN component test command
  debug              Debugging functions (see also 'undebug')
  delete             Delete a file
  dir                List files on a filesystem
  disable            Turn off privileged commands
  disconnect         Disconnect an existing network connection
-More-
```

Plus, at this point you can press the spacebar to get another page of information, or you can press Enter to go one command at a time. You can also press Q (or any other key, for that matter) to quit and return to the prompt.

Here's a shortcut: to find commands that start with a certain letter, use the letter and the question mark with no space between them.

```
Router#c?
calendar  cd         clear    clock
cns       configure  connect  copy
crypto    ct-isdn
```

```
Router#c
```

By typing **c?**, I received a response listing all the commands that start with *c*. Also notice that the Router#c prompt reappears after the list of commands is displayed. This can be helpful when you have long commands and need the next possible command. It would be pretty lame if you had to retype the entire command every time you used a question mark!

To find the next parameters of a command string, type the first command and then a question mark.

```
Router#clock ?
  read-calendar    Read the hardware calendar into the clock
  set              Set the time and date
  update-calendar  Update the hardware calendar from the clock
Router#clock set ?
  hh:mm:ss  Current Time
Router#clock set 11:15:11 ?
  <1-31>  Day of the month
  MONTH   Month of the year
Router#clock set 11:15:11 25 april ?
  <1993-2035>  Year
Router#clock set 11:15:11 25 april 2011 ?
  <cr>
Router#clock set 11:15:11 25 april 2011
*April 25 11:15:11.000: %SYS-6-CLOCKUPDATE: System clock has been
updated from 18:52:53 UTC Wed Feb 28 2011 to 11:15:11 UTC Sat April 25 2011,
configured from console by cisco on console.
```

By typing the **clock ?** command, you'll get a list of the next possible parameters and what they do. Notice that you should just keep typing a command, a space, and then a question mark until <cr> (carriage return) is your only option.

If you're typing commands and receive

```
Router#clock set 11:15:11
% Incomplete command.
```

you'll know that the command string isn't done yet. Just press the up arrow key to redisplay the last command entered, and then continue with the command by using your question mark.

And if you receive the error

```
Router(config)#access-list 110 permit host 1.1.1.1
                                           ^
% Invalid input detected at '^' marker.
```

you've entered a command incorrectly. See that little caret—the ^? It's a very helpful tool that marks the exact point where you blew it and entered the command incorrectly. Here's another example of when you'll see the caret:

```
Router#sh serial 0/0/0
           ^
% Invalid input detected at '^' marker.
```

This command looks right, but be careful! The problem is that the full command is show interface serial 0/0/0.

Now if you receive the error

```
Router#sh ru
% Ambiguous command:  "sh ru"
```

it means there are multiple commands that begin with the string you entered and it's not unique. Use the question mark to find the command you need.

```
Router#sh ru?
rudpv1  running-config
```

As you can see, there are two commands that start with show ru.

Table 4.2 lists the enhanced editing commands available on a Cisco router.

TABLE 4.2 Enhanced editing commands

Command	Meaning
Ctrl+A	Moves your cursor to the beginning of the line
Ctrl+E	Moves your cursor to the end of the line

TABLE 4.2   Enhanced editing commands *(continued)*

Command	Meaning
Esc+B	Moves back one word
Ctrl+B	Moves back one character
Ctrl+F	Moves forward one character
Esc+F	Moves forward one word
Ctrl+D	Deletes a single character
Backspace	Deletes a single character
Ctrl+R	Redisplays a line
Ctrl+U	Erases a line
Ctrl+W	Erases a word
Ctrl+Z	Ends configuration mode and returns to EXEC
Tab	Finishes typing a command for you

Another cool editing feature I want to show you is the automatic scrolling of long lines. In the following example, the command typed had reached the right margin and automatically moved 11 spaces to the left (the dollar sign [$] indicates that the line has been scrolled to the left):

```
Router#config t
Enter configuration commands, one per line. End with CNTL/Z.
Router(config)#$110 permit tcp host 10.1.1.1 171.10.10.10 0.0.0.0 eq 23
```

You can review the router-command history with the commands shown in Table 4.3.

TABLE 4.3   Router-command history

Command	Meaning
Ctrl+P or up arrow	Shows last command entered
Ctrl+N or down arrow	Shows previous commands entered
show history	Shows last 10 commands entered by default

TABLE 4.3   Router-command history *(continued)*

Command	Meaning
show terminal	Shows terminal configurations and history buffer size
terminal history size	Changes buffer size (max 256)

The following example demonstrates the show history command and how to change the history size as well as how to verify it with the show terminal command. First, use the show history command to see the last 10 commands that were entered on the router, as shown here:

```
Router#show history
 en
 sh history
 show terminal
 sh cdp neig
 sh ver
 sh flash
 sh int fa0
 sh history
 sh int s0/0
 sh int s0/1
```

Now use the show terminal command to verify the terminal history size.

```
Router#show terminal
Line 0, Location: "", Type: ""
[output cut]
Modem type is unknown.
Session limit is not set.
Time since activation: 00:21:41
Editing is enabled.
History is enabled, history size is 20.
DNS resolution in show commands is enabled
Full user help is disabled
Allowed input transports are none.
Allowed output transports are pad telnet rlogin lapb-ta mop v120 ssh.
Preferred transport is telnet.
No output characters are padded
No special data dispatching characters
```

The terminal history size command, used from privileged mode, can change the size of the history buffer.

```
Router#terminal history size ?
 <0-256> Size of history buffer
Router#terminal history size 25
```

You verify the change with the show terminal command.

```
Router#show terminal
Line 0, Location: "", Type: ""
[output cut]
Editing is enabled.
History is enabled, history size is 25.
Full user help is disabled
Allowed transports are lat pad v120 telnet mop rlogin
  nasi. Preferred is lat.
No output characters are padded
No special data dispatching characters
Group codes:  0
```

When Do You Use the Cisco Editing Features?

A couple of editing features are used quite often and some not so much, if at all. Understand that Cisco didn't make these up; these are just old Unix commands. However, Ctrl+A is really helpful to negate a command.

For example, if you were to put in a long command and then decide you didn't want to use that command in your configuration after all, or if it didn't work, then you could just press your up arrow key to show the last command entered, press Ctrl+A to move your cursor to the beginning of the line, type **no** and then a space, press Enter—and poof! The command is negated. This doesn't work on every command, but it works on a lot of them.

Gathering Basic Routing Information

The show version command will provide basic configuration for the system hardware as well as the software version and the boot images. Here's an example:

```
Router#show version
Cisco IOS Software, 2800 Software (C2800NM-ADVSECURITYK9-M), Version
   12.4(12), RELEASE SOFTWARE (fc1)
Technical Support: http://www.cisco.com/techsupport
```

```
Copyright (c) 1986-2006 by Cisco Systems, Inc.
Compiled Fri 17-Nov-06 12:02 by prod_rel_team
```

The preceding section of output describes the Cisco IOS running on the router. The following section describes the read-only memory (ROM) used, which is used to boot the router and holds the POST:

```
ROM: System Bootstrap, Version 12.4(13r)T, RELEASE SOFTWARE (fc1)
```

The next section shows how long the router has been running, how it was restarted (if you see a `system restarted by` bus error, that is a very bad thing), the location from which the Cisco IOS was loaded, and the IOS name. Flash is the default, and the "Flash:" before the IOS name shows where the IOS that is currently running was loaded from. The IOS could load from difference sources, such as from a TFTP server.

```
Router uptime is 2 hours, 30 minutes
System returned to ROM by power-on
System restarted at 09:04:07 UTC Sat Aug 25 2007
System image file is "flash:c2800nm-advsecurityk9-mz.124-12.bin"
```

This next section displays the processor, the amount of DRAM and flash memory, and the interfaces the POST found on the router:

```
[some output cut]
Cisco 2811 (revision 53.50) with 249856K/12288K bytes of memory.
Processor board ID FTX1049A1AB
2 FastEthernet interfaces
4 Serial(sync/async) interfaces
1 Virtual Private Network (VPN) Module
DRAM configuration is 64 bits wide with parity enabled.
239K bytes of non-volatile configuration memory.
62720K bytes of ATA CompactFlash (Read/Write)
Configuration register is 0x2102
```

The configuration register value is listed last—it's something I'll cover in Chapter 5.

In addition, the `show interfaces` and `show ip interface brief` commands are very useful in verifying and troubleshooting a router as well as network issues. These commands are covered later in this chapter. Don't miss it!

Router and Switch Administrative Configurations

Even though the following sections aren't critical to making a router or switch *work* on a network, they're still really important; in them, I'm going to lead you through configuring commands that will help you administer your network.

The most popular and most important administrative functions that you can configure on a router and switch are as follows:

- Hostnames
- Banners
- Passwords
- Interface descriptions

Remember, none of these will make your routers or switches work better or faster, but trust me, your life will be a whole lot better if you just take the time to set these configurations on each of your network devices. That's because doing this makes troubleshooting and maintaining your network sooooo much easier—seriously! In this next section, I'll be demonstrating commands on a Cisco router, but these commands are exactly the same on a Cisco switch.

Hostnames

You can set the identity of the router with the hostname command. This is only locally significant, which means that it has no bearing on how the router performs name lookups or how the router works on the internetwork. However, I'll use the hostname in Chapter 10 for authentication purposes when I discuss the WAN protocol PPP.

Here's an example:

```
Router#config t
Enter configuration commands, one per line. End with
   CNTL/Z.
Router(config)#hostname Todd
Todd(config)#hostname Atlanta
Atlanta(config)#hostname Todd
Todd(config)#
```

Even though it's pretty tempting to configure the hostname after your own name, it's definitely a better idea to name the router something pertinent to the location. This is because giving it a hostname that's somehow relevant to where the device actually lives will make finding it a whole lot easier. And it also helps you confirm that you are, indeed, configuring the right device. For this chapter, I'll leave it as *Todd* for now because it's fun.

Banners

A *banner* is more than just a little cool—one very good reason for having a banner is to give any and all who dare attempt to telnet or dial into your internetwork a little security notice. And you can create a banner to give anyone who shows up on the router exactly the information you want them to have.

Make sure you're familiar with these four available banner types: exec process creation banner, incoming terminal line banner, login banner, and message of the day banner (all illustrated in the following code):

```
Todd(config)#banner ?
  LINE            c banner-text c, where 'c' is a delimiting character
  exec            Set EXEC process creation banner
  incoming        Set incoming terminal line banner
  login           Set login banner
  motd            Set Message of the Day banner
  prompt-timeout  Set Message for login authentication timeout
  slip-ppp        Set Message for SLIP/PPP
```

Message of the day (MOTD) is the most extensively used banner. It gives a message to every person dialing into or connecting to the router via Telnet or an auxiliary port, or even through a console port, as shown here:

```
Todd(config)#banner motd ?
LINE c banner-text c, where 'c' is a delimiting character
Todd(config)#banner motd #
Enter TEXT message. End with the character '#'.
$ Acme.com network, then you must disconnect immediately.
#
Todd(config)#^Z
Todd#
00:25:12: %SYS-5-CONFIG_I: Configured from console by
  console
Todd#exit


Router con0 is now available


Press RETURN to get started.


If you are not authorized to be in Acme.com network, then you
must disconnect immediately.
Todd#
```

The preceding MOTD banner essentially tells anyone connecting to the router to get lost if they're not on the guest list! The part to understand is the delimiting character—the thing that's used to tell the router when the message starts and finishes. You can use any character you want for it, but (I hope this is obvious) you can't use the delimiting character in the message itself. Also, once the message is complete, press Enter, then the delimiting character, and then Enter again. It'll still work if you don't do that, but if you have more than one banner, they'll be combined as one message and put on a single line.

For example, you can set a banner on one line, as shown here:

```
Todd(config)#banner motd x Unauthorized access prohibited! x
```

This example will work just fine, but if you add another MOTD banner message, they would end up on a single line.

Here are some details of the other banners I mentioned:

Exec Banner   You can configure a line-activation (exec) banner to be displayed when an EXEC process (such as a line activation or incoming connection to a VTY line) is created. By simply starting a user exec session through a console port, you'll activate the exec banner.

Incoming Banner   You can configure a banner to be displayed on terminals connected to reverse Telnet lines. This banner is useful for providing instructions to users who use reverse Telnet.

Login Banner   You can configure a login banner to be displayed on all connected terminals. This banner is displayed after the MOTD banner but before the login prompts. The login banner can't be disabled on a per-line basis, so to globally disable it, you have to delete it with the no banner login command.

 The login banner is displayed before the login prompts but after the MOTD banner.

Setting Passwords

Five passwords can be used to secure your Cisco routers: console, auxiliary, telnet (VTY), enable password, and enable secret. The enable secret and enable password are used to set the password that's used to secure privileged mode. This will prompt a user for a password when the enable command is used. The other three are used to configure a password when user mode is accessed through the console port, through the auxiliary port, or via Telnet.

Let's take a look at each of these now.

Enable Passwords

You set the enable passwords from global configuration mode like this:

```
Todd(config)#enable ?
  last-resort Define enable action if no TACACS servers
             respond
  password   Assign the privileged level password
  secret     Assign the privileged level secret
  use-tacacs Use TACACS to check enable passwords
```

The following points describe the enable password parameters:

last-resort   This allows you to still enter the router if you set up authentication through a TACACS server and it's not available. But it isn't used if the TACACS server is working.

password   This originally set the enable password on older, pre-10.3 systems, and it is superseded if an enable secret is set.

secret   This is the newer, encrypted password that overrides the enable password if it's set.

use-tacacs   This tells the router to authenticate through a TACACS server. It's convenient if you have anywhere from a dozen to multitudes of routers because, well, would you like to face the fun task of changing the password on all those routers? If you're sane, no, you wouldn't. So instead, just go through the TACACS server and you have to change the password only once—yeah! Now, whenever someone tries to log into privileged mode, they will be forced to authenticate through the TACACS server.

Here's an example of setting the enable passwords:

```
Todd(config)#enable secret todd
Todd(config)#enable password todd
The enable password you have chosen is the same as your
    enable secret. This is not recommended. Re-enter the
    enable password.
```

If you try to set the enable secret and enable passwords the same, the router will give you a nice, polite warning to change the second password. If you don't have older legacy routers, don't even bother to use the enable password—it is outdated and not used anymore, but it could be, so just be aware of the differences between the enable password and the enable secret.

User-mode passwords are assigned by using the `line` command.

```
Todd(config)#line ?
  <0-337>  First Line number
  aux      Auxiliary line
  console  Primary terminal line
  tty      Terminal controller
  vty      Virtual terminal
```

Here are the lines to be concerned with for the exam objectives:

aux   Sets the user-mode password for the auxiliary port. It's usually used for attaching a modem to the router, but it can be used as a console as well.

console   Sets a console user-mode password.

vty   Sets a Telnet password on the router. If this password isn't set, then Telnet can't be used by default.

To configure the user-mode passwords, you configure the password on the line you want and follow it with either the `login` or `no login` command to tell the router to either prompt for or not prompt for authentication. The next sections will provide a line-by-line example of the configuration of each line.

Auxiliary Password

To configure the auxiliary password, go into global configuration mode and type `line aux ?`. You can see here that you only get a choice of 0–0 (that's because there's only one port):

```
Todd#config t
Enter configuration commands, one per line.  End with CNTL/Z.
Todd(config)#line aux ?
  <0-0>  First Line number
Todd(config)#line aux 0
Todd(config-line)#login
% Login disabled on line 1, until 'password' is set
Todd(config-line)#password aux
Todd(config-line)#login
```

It's important to remember the `login` command or the auxiliary port won't prompt for authentication.

Cisco has begun this process of not letting you set the `login` command before a password is set on a line because if you set the `login` command under a line and then don't set a password, the line won't be usable. And it will prompt for a password that doesn't exist. So, this is a good thing—a feature, not a hassle!

 Definitely remember that although Cisco has this "password feature" on its routers starting in its newer IOS (12.2 and newer), it's not in all its IOSs.

Console Password

To set the console password, use the `line console 0` command. But look at what happened when I tried to type `line console ?` from the `(config-line)#` prompt—I received an error. You can still type `line console 0`, and it will accept it, but the help screens just don't work from that prompt. Type `exit` to get back one level, and you'll find that your help screens now work. This is a "feature." Really.

Here's the example:

```
Todd(config-line)#line console ?
% Unrecognized command
Todd(config-line)#exit
Todd(config)#line console ?
  <0-0>  First Line number
```

```
Todd(config-line)#password console
Todd(config-line)#login
```

Since there's only one console port, I can choose only line console 0. You can set all your line passwords to the same password, but for security reasons, I recommend you make them different.

There are a few other important commands to know for the console port.

For one, the `exec-timeout 0 0` command sets the timeout for the console EXEC session to zero, which means to never time out. The default timeout is 10 minutes. (If you're feeling mischievous, try this on people at work: set it to 0 1. That will make the console time out in one second! And to fix it, you have to continually press the down arrow key while changing the timeout time with your free hand!)

`logging synchronous` is a very cool command, and it should be a default command, but it's not. It stops annoying console messages from popping up and disrupting the input you're trying to type. The messages still pop up, but you are returned to your router prompt without your input interrupted. This makes your input messages oh-so-much easier to read.

Here's an example of how to configure both commands:

```
Todd(config-line)#line con 0
Todd(config-line)#exec-timeout ?
  <0-35791>  Timeout in minutes
Todd(config-line)#exec-timeout 0 ?
  <0-2147483>  Timeout in seconds
  <cr>
Todd(config-line)#exec-timeout 0 0
Todd(config-line)#logging synchronous
```

 You can set the console to go from never timing out (0 0) to timing out in 35,791 minutes and 2,147,483 seconds. The default is 10 minutes. I recommend leaving this at the default for security reasons.

Telnet Password

To set the user-mode password for Telnet access into the router, use the `line vty` command. Routers that aren't running the Enterprise edition of the Cisco IOS default to five VTY lines, 0 through 4. But if you have the Enterprise edition, you'll have significantly more. The best way to find out how many lines you have is to use that question mark.

```
Todd(config-line)#line vty 0 ?
% Unrecognized command
Todd(config-line)#exit
Todd(config)#line vty 0 ?
  <1-1180>  Last Line number
  <cr>
```

```
Todd(config)#line vty 0 1180
Todd(config-line)#password telnet
Todd(config-line)#login
```

Remember, you cannot get help from your (config-line)# prompt. You must go back to global config mode in order to use the question mark (?).

So, what will happen if you try to telnet into a router that doesn't have a VTY password set? You'll receive an error stating that the connection is refused because, well, the password isn't set. So, if you telnet into a router and receive the message

```
Todd#telnet SFRouter
Trying SFRouter (10.0.0.1)…Open


Password required, but none set
[Connection to SFRouter closed by foreign host]
Todd#
```

then the remote router (SFRouter in this example) does not have the VTY (Telnet) password set. But you can get around this and tell the router to allow Telnet connections without a password by using the no login command.

```
SFRouter(config-line)#line vty 0 4
SFRouter(config-line)#no login
```

 WARNING

I do not recommend using the no login command to allow Telnet connections without a password unless you are in a testing or classroom environment! In a production network, you should always set your VTY password.

After your routers are configured with an IP address, you can use the Telnet program to configure and check your routers instead of having to use a console cable. You can use the Telnet program by typing **telnet** from any command prompt (DOS or Cisco). Anything Telnet is covered more thoroughly in Chapter 7.

Setting Up Secure Shell (SSH)

Instead of Telnet, you can use Secure Shell, which creates a more secure session than the Telnet application that uses an unencrypted data stream. SSH uses encryption keys to send data so that your username and password are not sent in the clear.

Here are the steps to setting up SSH:

1. Set your hostname.

    ```
    Router(config)#hostname Todd
    ```

2. Set the domain name (both the hostname and domain name are required for the encryption keys to be generated).

    ```
    Todd(config)#ip domain-name Lammle.com
    ```

3. Set the username to allow SSH client access.

    Todd(config)#**username Todd password Lammle**

4. Generate the encryption keys for securing the session.

    ```
    Todd(config)#crypto key generate rsa general-keys modulus ?
      <360-2048>  size of the key modulus [360-2048]
    Todd(config)#crypto key generate rsa general-keys modulus 1024
    The name for the keys will be: Todd.Lammle.com
    % The key modulus size is 1024 bits
    % Generating 1024 bit RSA keys, keys will be non-exportable...[OK]
    *June 24 19:25:30.035: %SSH-5-ENABLED: SSH 1.99 has been enabled
    ```

5. Enable SSH version 2 on the router; although this isn't mandatory, it is highly suggested.

    Todd(config)#ip **ssh version 2**

6. Connect to the VTY lines of the router.

    Todd(config)#**line vty 0 1180**

7. The next command tells the router where the password is stored and you are now using the local database on the router:

    Todd(config-line)#**login local**

8. Last, configure the VTY lines to allow only SSH.

    Todd(config-line)#**transport input ssh**

    Alternately, you can use both SSH and Telnet on the VTY lines with the following:

    Todd(config-line)#**transport input ssh telnet**

    Or you can use any input on the VTY lines with the following:

    Todd(config-line)#**transport input all**

If you do not use the keyword te1net or any at the end of the command string, then only SSH will work on the router. I am not suggesting you use either way, but just understand that SSH is more secure than Telnet.

Encrypting Your Passwords

Because only the enable secret password is encrypted by default, you'll need to manually configure the user-mode and enable passwords for encryption.

Notice that you can see all the passwords except the enable secret when performing a show running-config on a router.

```
Todd#sh running-config
Building configuration...
[output cut]
!
enable secret 5 $1$2R.r$DcRaVoOyBnUJBf7dbG9XE0
enable password todd
!
[output cut]
!
line con 0
 exec-timeout 0 0
 password console
 logging synchronous
 login
line aux 0
 password aux
 login
line vty 0 4

 password telnet
 login
 transport input telnet ssh
line vty 5 15
password telnet
 login
 transport input telnet ssh
line vty 16 1180
 password telnet
 login
!
end
```

To manually encrypt your passwords, use the service password-encryption command. Here's an example of how to do it:

```
Todd#config t
Enter configuration commands, one per line.  End with CNTL/Z.
Todd(config)#service password-encryption
Todd(config)#exit
```

```
Todd#sh run
Building configuration...
[output cut]
!
enable secret 5 $1$2R.r$DcRaVoOyBnUJBf7dbG9XEO
enable password 7 131118160F
!
[output cut]
!
line con 0
 exec-timeout 0 0
 password 7 0605002F5F41051C
 logging synchronous
 login
line aux 0
 password 7 03054E13
 login
line vty 0 4
 access-class 23 in
password 7 01070308550E12
 login
 transport input telnet ssh
line vty 5 15
password 7 01070308550E12
 login
 transport input telnet ssh
line vty 16 1180
 password 7 120D001B1C0E18
 login
!
end


Todd#config t
Todd(config)#no service password-encryption
Todd(config)#^Z
Todd#
```

There you have it! The passwords will now be encrypted. You just encrypt the passwords, perform a show run, and then turn off the command. You can see that the enable
password and the line passwords are all encrypted.

But before I get into showing you all about setting descriptions on your routers, let's talk about encrypting passwords a bit more. As I said, if you set your passwords and then turn on the service password-encryption command, you have to perform a show running-config before you turn off the encryption service or your passwords won't be encrypted. You don't have to turn off the encryption service at all; you'd do that only if your router is running low on processes. And if you turn the service on and leave it on before you set your passwords, then you don't even have to view them to get them encrypted.

The service password-encryption command encrypts all current and future passwords in the plain-text configuration file.

Setting Interface Descriptions

Setting descriptions on an interface is helpful to the administrator and, as with the host-name, only locally significant. The description command is a helpful one because you can, for instance, use it to keep track of circuit numbers.

Here's an example:

```
Todd#config t
Todd(config)#int s0/0/0
Todd(config-if)#description Wan to SF circuit number 6fdda12345678
Todd(config-if)#int fa0/0
Todd(config-if)#description Sales VLAN
Todd(config-if)#^Z
Todd#
```

You can view the description of an interface with either the show running-config command or the show interface command.

```
Todd#sh run
[output cut]
!
interface FastEthernet0/0
 description Sales VLAN
 ip address 10.10.10.1 255.255.255.248
 duplex auto
 speed auto
!
```

```
interface Serial0/0/0
 description Wan to SF circuit number 6fdda 12345678
 no ip address
 shutdown
!
[output cut]
```

```
Todd#sh int f0/0
FastEthernet0/0 is up, line protocol is down
  Hardware is MV96340 Ethernet, address is 001a.2f55.c9e8 (bia 001a.2f55.c9e8)
  Description: Sales VLAN
 [output cut]
```

```
Todd#sh int s0/0/0
Serial0/0/0 is administratively down, line protocol is down
  Hardware is GT96K Serial
  Description: Wan to SF circuit number 6fdda12345678
```

Real World Scenario

description: A Helpful Command

Bob, a senior network administrator at Acme Corporation in San Francisco, has more than 50 WAN links to various branches throughout the United States and Canada. Whenever an interface goes down, Bob spends a lot of time trying to figure out the circuit number as well as the phone number of the provider of the WAN link.

The interface description command would be very helpful to Bob because he can use this command on his LAN links to discern exactly where every router interface is connected. And Bob would benefit tremendously by adding circuit numbers to each and every WAN interface, along with the phone number of the responsible provider.

So, by spending the few hours it would take to add this information to each and every router interface, Bob can save a huge amount of precious time when his WAN links go down—and you know they will!

Doing the *do* Command

Beginning with IOS version 12.3, Cisco has finally added a command to the IOS that allows you to view the configuration and statistics from within configuration mode. (In the examples I gave you in the previous section, all show commands were run from privileged mode.)

In fact, with any IOS, you'd get the following error if you tried to view the configuration from global config:

```
Router(config)#sh run
                 ^
% Invalid input detected at '^' marker.
```

Compare that to the output I get from entering that same command on my router that's running the 12.4 IOS and using the do syntax:

```
Enter configuration commands, one per line.  End with CNTL/Z.
Todd(config)#do show run
Building configuration...


Current configuration : 3276 bytes
!
[output cut]


Todd(config)#do sh int f0/0
FastEthernet0/0 is up, line protocol is down
  Hardware is MV96340 Ethernet, address is 001a.2f55.c9e8 (bia
    001a.2f55.c9e8)
  Description: Sales VLAN
[output cut]
```

So, basically, you can pretty much run any command from any configuration prompt now—cool, huh? Going back to the example of encrypting your passwords, the do command would definitely have gotten the party started sooner—so, my friends, this is a very, very good thing indeed!

Router Interfaces

Interface configuration is one of the most important router configurations because without interfaces, a router is pretty much a completely useless object. Plus, interface configurations must be totally precise to enable communication with other devices. Network layer addresses, media type, bandwidth, and other administrator commands are all used to configure an interface.

Different routers use different methods to choose the interfaces used on them. For instance, the following command shows a Cisco router with 10 serial interfaces, labeled 0 through 9:

```
Router(config)#int serial ?
 <0-9> Serial interface number
```

Now it's time to choose the interface you want to configure. Once you do that, you will be in interface configuration for that specific interface. The following command would be used to choose serial port 5, for example:

```
Router(config)#int serial 5
Router(config)-if)#
```

The old 2522 router I am using in this example has one Ethernet 10BaseT port, and typing **interface ethernet 0** can configure that interface, as shown here:

```
Router(config)#int ethernet ?
 <0-0> Ethernet interface number
Router(config)#int ethernet 0
Router(config-if)#
```

As I showed you earlier, the 2500 router is a fixed-configuration router. This means that when you bought that model, you were stuck with that physical configuration—a huge reason why I don't use them much. I certainly never would use them in a production setting anymore, but for studying for your exam, they can be used quite effectively at a very low cost.

To configure an interface, you always used the interface *type number* sequence, but with the 2600 and 2800 series routers (actually, any ISR router for that matter), there's a physical slot in the router, and there's a port number on the module plugged into that slot. So, on a modular router, the configuration would be interface *type slot/port*, as shown here:

```
Router(config)#int fastethernet ?
 <0-1> FastEthernet interface number
Router(config)#int fastethernet 0
% Incomplete command.
Router(config)#int fastethernet 0?
/
Router(config)#int fastethernet 0/?
 <0-1> FastEthernet interface number
```

Make note of the fact that you can't just type **int fastethernet 0**. You must type the full command: ***type slot/port*** or **int fastethernet 0/0** (or **int fa 0/0**).

For the ISR series, it's basically the same, only you get even more options. For example, the built-in Fast Ethernet interfaces work with the same configuration you used with the 2600 series.

```
Todd(config)#int fastEthernet 0/?
  <0-1>   FastEthernet interface number
Todd(config)#int fastEthernet 0/0
Todd(config-if)#
```

But the rest of the modules are different—they use three numbers instead of two. The first 0 is the router itself, and then you choose the slot and then the port. Here's an example of a serial interface on my 2811:

```
Todd(config)#interface serial ?
  <0-2>   Serial interface number
Todd(config)#interface serial 0/0/?
  <0-1>   Serial interface number
Todd(config)#interface serial 0/0/0
Todd(config-if)#
```

This can look a little dicey, I know, but I promise it's really not that hard! It helps to remember that you should always view a running-config output first so you know what interfaces you have to deal with. Here's my 2801 output:

```
Todd(config-if)#do show run
Building configuration...
[output cut]
!
interface FastEthernet0/0
 no ip address
 shutdown
 duplex auto
 speed auto
!
interface FastEthernet0/1
 no ip address
 shutdown
 duplex auto
 speed auto
!
interface Serial0/0/0
 no ip address
 shutdown
 no fair-queue
!
```

```
interface Serial0/0/1
 no ip address
 shutdown
!
interface Serial0/1/0
 no ip address
 shutdown
!
interface Serial0/2/0
 no ip address
 shutdown
 clock rate 2000000
!
 [output cut]
```

For the sake of brevity, I didn't include my complete running-config, but I've displayed all you need. You can see the two built-in Fast Ethernet interfaces, the two serial interfaces in slot 0 (%/0 and %/1), the serial interface in slot 1 (0/1/0), and the serial interface in slot 2 (0/2/0). Once you see the interfaces like this, it makes it a lot easier for you to understand how the modules are inserted into the router.

Just understand that if you type **interface e0** on a 2500, **interface fastethernet 0/0** on a 2600, or **interface serial 0/1/0** on a 2800, all you're doing is choosing an interface to configure, and basically, they're all configured the same way after that.

I'm going to continue with our router interface discussion in the next sections, and I'll include how to bring up the interface and set an IP address on it.

Bringing Up an Interface

You can disable an interface with the interface command shutdown and enable it with the no shutdown command.

If an interface is shut down, it'll display administratively down when you use the show interfaces command (sh int for short).

```
Todd#sh int f0/1
FastEthernet0/1 is administratively down, line protocol is down
[output cut]
```

Another way to check an interface's status is via the show running-config command. All interfaces are shut down by default. You can bring up the interface with the no shutdown command (no shut for short).

```
Todd#config t
Todd(config)#int f0/1
```

```
Todd(config-if)#no shutdown
Todd(config-if)#
*Feb 28 22:45:08.455: %LINK-3-UPDOWN: Interface FastEthernet0/1,
    changed state to up
Todd(config-if)#do show int f0/1
FastEthernet0/1 is up, line protocol is up
[output cut]
```

Configuring an IP Address on an Interface

Even though you don't have to use IP on your routers, it's most often what people actually do use. To configure IP addresses on an interface, use the ip address command from interface configuration mode.

```
Todd(config)#int f0/1
Todd(config-if)#ip address 172.16.10.2 255.255.255.0
```

Don't forget to enable the interface with the no shutdown command. Remember to look at the command show interface *int* to see whether the interface is administratively shut down or not. show running-config will also give you this information.

 The ip address *address mask* command starts the IP processing on the interface.

If you want to add a second subnet address to an interface, you have to use the secondary parameter. If you type another IP address and press Enter, it will replace the existing primary IP address and mask. This is definitely a most excellent feature of the Cisco IOS.

So, let's try it. To add a secondary IP address, just use the secondary parameter.

```
Todd(config-if)#ip address 172.16.20.2 255.255.255.0 ?
  secondary  Make this IP address a secondary address
  <cr>
Todd(config-if)#ip address 172.16.20.2 255.255.255.0 secondary
Todd(config-if)#^Z
Todd(config-if)#do sh run
Building configuration...
[output cut]

interface FastEthernet0/1
 ip address 172.16.20.2 255.255.255.0 secondary
 ip address 172.16.10.2 255.255.255.0
 duplex auto
 speed auto
!
```

I really don't recommend having multiple IP addresses on an interface because it's ugly and inefficient, but I showed you anyway just in case you someday find yourself dealing with an IT manager who's in love with really bad network design and makes you administer it! And who knows? Maybe someone will ask you about it someday and you'll get to seem really smart because you know this.

Using the Pipe

No, not that pipe. I mean the output modifier. (Although with some of the router configurations I've seen in my career, sometimes I wonder!) This pipe (|) allows you to wade through all the configurations or other long outputs and get straight to your goods fast. Here's an example:

```
Todd#sh run | ?
  append    Append redirected output to URL (URLs supporting append operation
            only)
  begin     Begin with the line that matches
  exclude   Exclude lines that match
  include   Include lines that match
  redirect  Redirect output to URL
  section   Filter a section of output
  tee       Copy output to URL


Todd#sh run | begin interface
interface FastEthernet0/0
 description Sales VLAN
 ip address 10.10.10.1 255.255.255.248
 duplex auto
 speed auto
!
interface FastEthernet0/1
 ip address 172.16.20.2 255.255.255.0 secondary
 ip address 172.16.10.2 255.255.255.0
 duplex auto
 speed auto
!
interface Serial0/0/0
 description Wan to SF circuit number 6fdda 12345678
 no ip address
!
```

Basically, the pipe symbol (output modifier) is what you need to help you get where you want to go light years faster than mucking around in a router's entire configuration. I use it a lot when I am looking at a large routing table to find out whether a certain route is in the routing table. Here's an example:

```
Todd#sh ip route | include 192.168.3.32
R        192.168.3.32 [120/2] via 10.10.10.8, 00:00:25, FastEthernet0/0
Todd#
```

First, you need to know that this routing table had more than 100 entries, so without my trusty pipe, I'd probably still be looking through that output! It's a powerfully efficient tool that saves you major time and effort by quickly finding a line in a configuration—or as the preceding example shows, a single route in a huge routing table.

Give yourself a little time to play around with the pipe command; get the hang of it, and you'll be seriously high on your newfound ability to quickly parse through router output.

Serial Interface Commands

Wait! Before you just jump in and configure a serial interface, you need some key information—like knowing that the interface will usually be attached to a CSU/DSU type of device that provides clocking for the line to the router, as I've shown in Figure 4.4.

FIGURE 4.4   A typical WAN connection

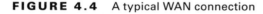

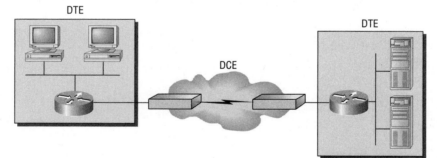

Clocking is typically provided by a DCE network to routers.
In nonproduction environments, a DCE network is not always present.

Here you can see that the serial interface is used to connect to a DCE network via a CSU/DSU that provides the clocking to the router interface. But if you have a back-to-back configuration (for example, one that's used in a lab environment like I've shown you in Figure 4.5), one end—the data communication equipment (DCE) end of the cable—must provide clocking!

By default, Cisco routers' serial interfaces are all data terminal equipment (DTE) devices, which means that you must configure an interface to provide clocking if you need it to act like a DCE device. Again, you would not provide clocking on a production T1 connection, for example, because you would have a CSU/DSU connected to your serial interface, as Figure 4.4 shows.

FIGURE 4.5   Providing clocking on a nonproduction network

Set clock rate if needed.

Todd#config t
Todd(config)#interface serial 0
Todd(config-if)#clock rate 64000

DCE

DTE

DCE side determined by cable.
Add clocking to DCE side only.

Show controllers will show the cable connection type.

You configure a DCE serial interface with the `clock rate` command.

```
Todd#config t
Enter configuration commands, one per line.  End with CNTL/Z.
Todd(config)#int s0/0/0
Todd(config-if)#clock rate ?
       Speed (bits per second)
  1200
  2400
  4800
  9600
  14400
  19200
  28800
  32000
  38400
  48000
  56000
  57600
  64000
  72000
  115200
  125000
```

```
128000
148000
192000
250000
256000
384000
500000
512000
768000
800000
1000000
2000000
4000000
5300000
8000000


<300-8000000>    Choose clockrate from list above
```

```
Todd(config-if)#clock rate 1000000
```

The clock rate command is set in bits per second. Besides looking at the cable end to check for a label of DCE or DTE, you can see whether a router's serial interface has a DCE cable connected with the show controllers *int* command.

```
Todd#sh controllers s0/0/0
Interface Serial0/0/0
Hardware is GT96K
DTE V.35idb at 0x4342FCB0, driver data structure at 0x434373D4
```

Here is an example of an output that shows a DCE connection:

```
Todd#sh controllers s0/2/0
Interface Serial0/2/0
Hardware is GT96K
DCE V.35, clock rate 1000000
```

The next command you need to get acquainted with is the bandwidth command. Every Cisco router ships with a default serial link bandwidth of T1 (1.544Mbps). But this has nothing to do with how data is transferred over a link. The bandwidth value that is configured on the serial interface is used by routing protocols such as EIGRP and OSPF to calculate the best cost (path) to a remote network. So, if you're using RIP routing, the bandwidth setting of a serial link is irrelevant since RIP uses only hop count to determine that.

If you're rereading this part thinking, "Huh—what? Routing protocols? Metrics?"—don't freak! I'm going over all that soon in Chapter 6, "IP Routing."

Here's an example of using the bandwidth command:

```
Todd#config t
Todd(config)#int s0/0/0
Todd(config-if)#bandwidth ?
  <1-10000000>  Bandwidth in kilobits
  inherit        Specify that bandwidth is inherited
  receive        Specify receive-side bandwidth
Todd(config-if)#bandwidth 1000
```

Did you notice that, unlike the clock rate command, the bandwidth command is configured in kilobits per second?

> After going through all these configuration examples regarding the clock rate command, understand that the new ISR routers automatically detect DCE connections and set the clock rate to 2000000. However, you still need to understand the clock rate command for the Cisco objectives, even though the new routers set it for you automatically!

Viewing, Saving, and Erasing Configurations

If you run through setup mode, you'll be asked if you want to use the configuration you just created. If you say yes, then it will copy the configuration running in DRAM (known as the running-config) into NVRAM and name the file startup-config. I hope you will always use the CLI and not setup mode.

You can manually save the file from DRAM (usually just called RAM) to NVRAM by using the copy running-config startup-config command (you can use the shortcut copy run start also).

```
Todd#copy running-config startup-config
Destination filename [startup-config]? [press enter]
Building configuration...
[OK]
Todd#
Building configuration...
```

When you see a question with an answer in [], it means that if you just press Enter, you're choosing the default answer.

You'll take a closer look at how and where to copy files in Chapter 5.

You can view the files by typing **show running-config** or **show startup-config** from privileged mode. The sh run command, which is a shortcut for show running-config, tells you that you are viewing the current configuration.

```
Todd#show running-config
Building configuration...

Current configuration : 3343 bytes
!
version 12.4
[output cut]
```

The sh start command—one of the shortcuts for the show startup-config command—shows you the configuration that will be used the next time the router is reloaded. It also tells you how much NVRAM is being used to store the startup-config file. Here's an example:

```
Todd#show startup-config
Using 1978 out of 245752 bytes
!
version 12.4
[output cut]
```

Deleting the Configuration and Reloading the Router

You can delete the startup-config file by using the erase startup-config command.

```
Todd#erase startup-config
Erasing the nvram filesystem will remove all configuration files!
    Continue? [confirm][enter]
[OK]
Erase of nvram: complete
Todd#
*Feb 28 23:51:21.179: %SYS-7-NV_BLOCK_INIT: Initialized the geometry of nvram
Todd#sh startup-config
startup-config is not present
Todd#reload
```

```
Proceed with reload? [confirm]System configuration has been modified.
   Save? [yes/no]: n
```

If you reload or power down and up the router after using the `erase startup-config` command, you'll be offered setup mode because there's no configuration saved in NVRAM. You can press Ctrl+C to exit setup mode at any time (the `reload` command can be used only from privileged mode).

At this point, you shouldn't use setup mode to configure your router. So, just say **no** to setup mode, because it's there to help people who don't know how to use the Cash-Line Interface, and this no longer applies to you. Be strong—you can do it!

Verifying Your Configuration

Obviously, `show running-config` would be the best way to verify your configuration, and `show startup-config` would be the best way to verify the configuration that'll be used the next time the router is reloaded—right?

Well, once you take a look at the running-config, if all appears well, you can verify your configuration with utilities such as Ping and Telnet. Ping is a program that uses ICMP echo requests and replies. (ICMP is discussed in Chapter 2, "Internet Protocols.") Ping sends a packet to a remote host, and if that host responds, you know that it's alive. But you don't know if it's alive and also *well*—just because you can ping a Microsoft server does not mean you can log in! Even so, Ping is an awesome starting point for troubleshooting an internetwork.

Did you know that you can ping with different protocols? You can, and you can test this by typing **ping ?** at either the router user-mode or privileged-mode prompt.

```
Router#ping ?
  WORD      Ping destination address or hostname
  appletalk Appletalk echo
  clns      CLNS echo
  decnet    DECnet echo
  ip        IP echo
  ipv6      IPv6 echo
  ipx       Novell/IPX echo
  srb       srb echo
  tag       Tag encapsulated IP echo
  <cr>
```

If you want to find a neighbor's Network layer address, either you need to go to the router or switch itself, or you can type **show cdp entry * protocol** to get the Network layer addresses you need for pinging. This is a fantastic Cisco proprietary verification command covered in depth in Chapter 5.

You can also use what's called an *extended* ping to change the default variables, as shown here:

```
Router#ping
Protocol [ip]: [enter]
Target IP address: 1.1.1.1
Repeat count [5]: 100
Datagram size [100]: 1500
Timeout in seconds [2]:
Extended commands [n]: y
Source address or interface: Fastethernet0/0
Type of service [0]:
Set DF bit in IP header? [no]:
Validate reply data? [no]:
Data pattern [0xABCD]:
Loose, Strict, Record, Timestamp, Verbose[none]: verbose
Loose, Strict, Record, Timestamp, Verbose[V]:
Sweep range of sizes [n]:
Type escape sequence to abort.
Sending 100, 1500-byte ICMP Echos to 1.1.1.1, timeout is 2 seconds:
Packet sent with a source address of 10.10.10.1
```

Notice that an extended ping allows you to set the repeat count higher than the default of 5 and the datagram size larger, which raises the maximum transmission unit (MTU) and allows a better testing of throughput. One last important piece I'll pull out of the output is the source interface. You can choose which interface the ping is sourced from. This is helpful in some diagnostic situations.

 Cisco Discovery Protocol (CDP) is covered in Chapter 5.

Traceroute uses ICMP with IP time to live (TTL) timeouts to track the path a packet takes through an internetwork, in contrast to Ping, which just finds the host and responds. And Traceroute can also be used with multiple protocols.

```
Router#traceroute ?
  WORD      Trace route to destination address or hostname
  appletalk AppleTalk Trace
  clns      ISO CLNS Trace
  ip        IP Trace
  ipv6      IPv6 Trace
  ipx       IPX Trace
  <cr>
```

Telnet, FTP, and HTTP are really the best tools because they use IP at the Network layer and TCP at the Transport layer to create a session with a remote host. If you can telnet, ftp, or http into a device, your IP connectivity just has to be good.

```
Router#telnet ?
 WORD IP address or hostname of a remote system
 <cr>
```

From the router prompt, you just type a hostname or IP address and it will assume you want to telnet—you don't need to type the actual command, `telnet`.

In the following sections, I will show you how to verify the interface statistics.

Verifying with the *show interface* Command

Another way to verify your configuration is by typing `show interface` commands, the first of which is `show interface ?`. That will reveal all the available interfaces to verify and configure.

The `show interfaces` command displays the configurable parameters and statistics of all interfaces on a router.

This command is very useful for verifying and troubleshooting router and network issues.

The following output is from my freshly erased and rebooted 2811 router:

```
Router#sh int ?
  Async             Async interface
  BVI               Bridge-Group Virtual Interface
  CDMA-Ix           CDMA Ix interface
  CTunnel           CTunnel interface
  Dialer            Dialer interface
  FastEthernet      FastEthernet IEEE 802.3
  Loopback          Loopback interface
  MFR               Multilink Frame Relay bundle interface
  Multilink         Multilink-group interface
  Null              Null interface
  Port-channel      Ethernet Channel of interfaces
  Serial            Serial
  Tunnel            Tunnel interface
  Vif               PGM Multicast Host interface
  Virtual-PPP       Virtual PPP interface
  Virtual-Template  Virtual Template interface
  Virtual-TokenRing Virtual TokenRing
```

```
  accounting        Show interface accounting
  counters          Show interface counters
  crb               Show interface routing/bridging info
  dampening         Show interface dampening info
  description       Show interface description
  etherchannel      Show interface etherchannel information
  irb               Show interface routing/bridging info
  mac-accounting    Show interface MAC accounting info
  mpls-exp          Show interface MPLS experimental accounting info
  precedence        Show interface precedence accounting info
  pruning           Show interface trunk VTP pruning information
  rate-limit        Show interface rate-limit info
  stats             Show interface packets & octets, in & out, by switching
                    path
  status            Show interface line status
  summary           Show interface summary
  switching         Show interface switching
  switchport        Show interface switchport information
  trunk             Show interface trunk information
  |                 Output modifiers
  <cr>
```

The only "real" physical interfaces are Fast Ethernet, Serial, and Async; the rest are all logical interfaces or commands you can use to verify with.

The next command is show interface fastethernet 0/0. It reveals to you the hardware address, logical address, and encapsulation method as well as statistics on collisions, as shown here:

```
Router#sh int f0/0
FastEthernet0/0 is up, line protocol is up
  Hardware is MV96340 Ethernet, address is 001a.2f55.c9e8 (bia 001a.2f55.c9e8)
  Internet address is 192.168.1.33/27
MTU 1500 bytes, BW 100000 Kbit, DLY 100 usec,
     reliability 255/255, txload 1/255, rxload 1/255
  Encapsulation ARPA, loopback not set
  Keepalive set (10 sec)
  Auto-duplex, Auto Speed, 100BaseTX/FX
  ARP type: ARPA, ARP Timeout 04:00:00
  Last input never, output 00:02:07, output hang never
  Last clearing of "show interface" counters never
  Input queue: 0/75/0/0 (size/max/drops/flushes); Total output drops: 0
  Queueing strategy: fifo
```

```
  Output queue: 0/40 (size/max)
  5 minute input rate 0 bits/sec, 0 packets/sec
  5 minute output rate 0 bits/sec, 0 packets/sec
     0 packets input, 0 bytes
     Received 0 broadcasts, 0 runts, 0 giants, 0 throttles
     0 input errors, 0 CRC, 0 frame, 0 overrun, 0 ignored
     0 watchdog
     0 input packets with dribble condition detected
     16 packets output, 960 bytes, 0 underruns
     0 output errors, 0 collisions, 0 interface resets
     0 babbles, 0 late collision, 0 deferred
     0 lost carrier, 0 no carrier
     0 output buffer failures, 0 output buffers swapped out
Router#
```

As you probably guessed, I'll discuss the important statistics from this output, but first, for fun (this is all fun, right?), I've got to ask you, what subnet is the Fast Ethernet % a member of, and what's the broadcast address and valid host range?

And, my friend, you really have to be able to nail these things NASCAR fast! Just in case you didn't, the address is 192.168.1.33/27. And I've gotta be honest—if you don't know what a /27 is at this point, you'll need a miracle to pass the exam. (A /27 is 255.255.255.224.) The fourth octet is a block size of 32. The subnets are 0, 32, 64, and so on; the Fast Ethernet interface is in the 32 subnet; the broadcast address is 63; and the valid hosts are 33–62.

 If you struggled with any of this, please save yourself from certain doom and get yourself back into Chapter 3, "IP Subnetting, Troubleshooting IP, and Introduction to NAT," now! Read and reread it until you've got it dialed in!

The preceding interface is working and looks to be in good shape. The show interfaces command will show you whether you are receiving errors on the interface; it will show you the maximum transmission unit (MTU), which is the maximum packet size allowed to be transmitted on that interface; bandwidth (BW), which is a value used with routing protocols to calculate route metrics; reliability (255/255 means perfect!); and load (½55 means no load). The last two values can also be used (although rarely) as values in classifying routes by certain routing protocols as well.

Continuing to use the previous output, what is the bandwidth of the interface? Well, other than the easy giveaway of the interface being called a "Fast Ethernet" interface, you can see that the bandwidth is 100000Kbit, which is 100,000,000 (Kbit means to add three zeros), which is 100Mbits per second, or Fast Ethernet. Gigabit would be 1000000Kbits per second.

The most important statistic of the `show interface` command is the output of the line and Data Link protocol status. If the output reveals that Fast Ethernet % is up and the line protocol is up, then the interface is up and running.

```
Router#sh int fa0/0
FastEthernet0/0 is up, line protocol is up
```

The first parameter refers to the Physical layer, and it's up when it receives carrier detect. The second parameter refers to the Data Link layer, and it looks for keepalives from the connecting end. (Keepalives are used between devices to make sure connectivity has not dropped.)

Here's an example of where the problem usually is found—on serial interfaces:

```
Router#sh int s0/0/0
Serial0/0 is up, line protocol is down
```

If you see that the line is up but the protocol is down, as shown here, you're experiencing a clocking (keepalive) or framing problem—possibly an encapsulation mismatch. Check the keepalives on both ends to make sure that they match; that the clock rate is set, if needed; and that the encapsulation type is the same on both ends. The preceding output would be considered a Data Link layer problem.

If you discover that both the line interface and the protocol are down, it's a cable or interface problem. The following output would be considered a Physical layer problem:

```
Router#sh int s0/0/0
Serial0/0 is down, line protocol is down
```

If one end is administratively shut down (as shown next), the remote end would present as down and down.

```
Router#sh int s0/0/0
Serial0/0 is administratively down, line protocol is down
```

To enable the interface, use the command `no shutdown` from interface configuration mode.

The next `show interface serial 0/0/0` command demonstrates the serial line and the MTU—1,500 bytes by default. It also shows the default BW on all Cisco serial links: 1.544Kbps. This is used to determine the bandwidth of the line for routing protocols such as EIGRP and OSPF. Another important configuration to notice is the keepalive, which is 10 seconds by default. Each router sends a keepalive message to its neighbor every 10 seconds, and if both routers aren't configured for the same keepalive time, it won't work.

```
Router#sh int s0/0/0
Serial0/0 is up, line protocol is up
 Hardware is HD64570
```

```
MTU 1500 bytes, BW 1544 Kbit, DLY 20000 usec,
   reliability 255/255, txload 1/255, rxload 1/255
Encapsulation HDLC, loopback not set, keepalive set
 (10 sec)
Last input never, output never, output hang never
Last clearing of "show interface" counters never
Queueing strategy: fifo
Output queue 0/40, 0 drops; input queue 0/75, 0 drops
5 minute input rate 0 bits/sec, 0 packets/sec
5 minute output rate 0 bits/sec, 0 packets/sec
  0 packets input, 0 bytes, 0 no buffer
  Received 0 broadcasts, 0 runts, 0 giants, 0 throttles
  0 input errors, 0 CRC, 0 frame, 0 overrun, 0 ignored,
  0 abort
  0 packets output, 0 bytes, 0 underruns
  0 output errors, 0 collisions, 16 interface resets
  0 output buffer failures, 0 output buffers swapped out
  0 carrier transitions
  DCD=down DSR=down DTR=down RTS=down CTS=down
```

You can clear the counters on the interface by typing the command **clear counters**.

```
Router#clear counters ?
  Async            Async interface
  BVI              Bridge-Group Virtual Interface
  CTunnel          CTunnel interface
  Dialer           Dialer interface
  FastEthernet     FastEthernet IEEE 802.3
  Group-Async      Async Group interface
  Line             Terminal line
  Loopback         Loopback interface
  MFR              Multilink Frame Relay bundle interface
  Multilink        Multilink-group interface
  Null             Null interface
  Serial           Serial
  Tunnel           Tunnel interface
  Vif              PGM Multicast Host interface
  Virtual-Template Virtual Template interface
  Virtual-TokenRing Virtual TokenRing
  <cr>
```

```
Router#clear counters s0/0/0
Clear "show interface" counters on this interface
  [confirm][enter]
Router#
00:17:35: %CLEAR-5-COUNTERS: Clear counter on interface
  Serial0/0/0 by console
Router#
```

Verifying with the *show ip interface* Command

The show ip interface command will provide you with information regarding the layer 3 configurations of a router's interfaces.

```
Router#sh ip interface
FastEthernet0/0 is up, line protocol is up
  Internet address is 1.1.1.1/24
  Broadcast address is 255.255.255.255
  Address determined by setup command
  MTU is 1500 bytes
  Helper address is not set
  Directed broadcast forwarding is disabled
  Outgoing access list is not set
  Inbound  access list is not set
  Proxy ARP is enabled
  Security level is default
  Split horizon is enabled
[output cut]
```

The status of the interface, the IP address and mask, information on whether an access list is set on the interface, and basic IP information are included in this output.

Using the *show ip interface brief* Command

The show ip interface brief command is probably one of the most helpful commands that you can ever use on a Cisco router. This command provides a quick overview of the router's interfaces, including the logical address and status.

```
Router#sh ip int brief
Interface          IP-Address      OK? Method Status     Protocol
FastEthernet0/0    unassigned      YES unset  up         up
FastEthernet0/1    unassigned      YES unset  up         up
Serial0/0/0        unassigned      YES unset  up         down
Serial0/0/1        unassigned      YES unset  administratively down down
Serial0/1/0        unassigned      YES unset  administratively down down
Serial0/2/0        unassigned      YES unset  administratively down down
```

Remember, administratively down means that you need to type no shutdown under the interface. Notice that Serial%/0 is up/down, which means that the Physical layer is good and carrier detect is sensed but no keepalives are being received from the remote end. In a nonproduction network, like the one I am working with, this resulted from the clock rate not being set on the DCE end of the cable.

Verifying with the *show protocols* Command

The show protocols command is a really helpful command you'd use in order to quickly see the status of layers 1 and 2 of each interface as well as the IP addresses used.

Here's a look at one of my production routers:

```
Router#sh protocols
Global values:
  Internet Protocol routing is enabled
Ethernet0/0 is administratively down, line protocol is down
Serial0/0 is up, line protocol is up
  Internet address is 100.30.31.5/24
Serial0/1 is administratively down, line protocol is down
Serial0/2 is up, line protocol is up
  Internet address is 100.50.31.2/24
Loopback0 is up, line protocol is up
  Internet address is 100.20.31.1/24
```

Using the *show controllers* Command

The show controllers command displays information about the physical interface itself. It'll also give you the type of serial cable plugged into a serial port. Usually, this will only be a DTE cable that plugs into a type of data service unit (DSU).

```
Router#sh controllers serial 0/0
HD unit 0, idb = 0x1229E4, driver structure at 0x127E70
buffer size 1524 HD unit 0, V.35 DTE cable
```

```
Router#sh controllers serial 0/1
HD unit 1, idb = 0x12C174, driver structure at 0x131600
buffer size 1524 HD unit 1, V.35 DCE cable
```

Notice that serial % has a DTE cable, whereas the serial 0/1 connection has a DCE cable. Serial 0/1 would have to provide clocking with the clock rate command. Serial % would get its clocking from the DSU.

Let's look at this command again. In Figure 4.6, see the DTE/DCE cable between the two routers? Know that you will not see this in production networks!

FIGURE 4.6   The show controllers command

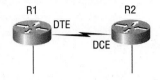

Router R1 has a DTE connection—typically the default for all Cisco routers. Routers R1 and R2 can't communicate. Check out the output of the show controllers s0/0 command here:

```
R1#sh controllers serial 0/0
HD unit 0, idb = 0x1229E4, driver structure at 0x127E70
buffer size 1524 HD unit 0, V.35 DCE cable
```

The show controllers s0/0 command shows that the interface is a V.35 DCE cable. This means that R1 needs to provide clocking of the line to router R2. Basically, the interface has the wrong label on the cable on the R1 router's serial interface. But if you add clocking on the R1 router's serial interface, the network should come right up.

Let's check out another issue, shown in Figure 4.7, that you can solve by using the show controllers command. Again, routers R1 and R2 can't communicate.

FIGURE 4.7   The show controllers command used with the show ip interface command

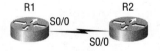

Here's the output of R1's show controllers s0/0 command and show ip interface s0/0:

```
R1#sh controllers s0/0
HD unit 0, idb = 0x1229E4, driver structure at 0x127E70
buffer size 1524 HD unit 0,
DTE V.35 clocks stopped
cpb = 0xE2, eda = 0x4140, cda = 0x4000


R1#sh ip interface s0/0
Serial0/0 is up, line protocol is down
   Internet address is 192.168.10.2/24
   Broadcast address is 255.255.255.255
```

If you use the show controllers command and the show ip interface command, you'll see that router R1 isn't receiving clocking of the line. This network is a nonproduction network, so no CSU/DSU is connected to provide clocking of the line. This means the DCE end of the cable will be providing the clock rate—in this case, the R2 router. The `show ip interface` indicates that the interface is up but the protocol is down, which means that no keepalives are being received from the far end. In this example, the likely culprit is the result of bad cable or no clocking.

Summary

This was a fun chapter! I showed you a lot about the Cisco IOS, and I really hope you gained a lot of insight into the Cisco router world. This chapter started off by explaining the Cisco Internetwork Operating System (IOS) and how you can use the IOS to run and configure Cisco routers. You learned how to bring a router up and what setup mode does. Oh, and by the way, since you can now basically configure Cisco routers after reading this chapter, you should never use setup mode, right?

After I discussed how to connect to a router with a console cable and with a LAN connection, I covered the Cisco help features and how to use the CLI to find commands and command parameters. In addition, I discussed some basic `show` commands to help you verify your configurations.

Administrative functions on a router help you administer your network and verify that you are configuring the correct device. Setting router passwords is one of the most important configurations you can perform on your routers. I showed you the five passwords to set. In addition, I used the hostname, interface description, and banner commands to help you administer your router.

Well, that concludes your introduction to the Cisco IOS. And, as usual, it's super-important for you to have the basics that I went over in this chapter before you move on to the following chapters.

Exam Essentials

Describe the responsibilities of the IOS.   The Cisco router IOS software is responsible for network protocols and providing supporting functions, connecting high-speed traffic between devices, adding security to control access and prevent unauthorized network use, providing scalability for ease of network growth and redundancy, and supplying network reliability for connecting to network resources.

List the options available to connect to a Cisco device for management purposes.   The three options available are the console port, auxiliary port, and Telnet. A Telnet connection is not possible until an IP address has been configured and a Telnet username and password have been configured.

Understand the boot sequence of a router.   When you first bring up a Cisco router, it will run a power-on self-test (POST), and if that passes, it will look for and load the Cisco IOS from flash memory, if a file is present. The IOS then proceeds to load and looks for a valid configuration in NVRAM called the startup-config. If no file is present in NVRAM, the router will go into setup mode.

Describe the use of setup mode.   Setup mode is automatically started if a router boots and no startup-config is in NVRAM. You can also bring up setup mode by typing **setup** from privileged mode. Setup provides a minimum amount of configuration in a prompted format for someone who does not understand how to configure a Cisco router from the command line.

Differentiate user, privileged, and global configuration modes, both visually and from a command capabilities perspective.   User mode, indicated by the Router> prompt, provides a command-line interface with very few available commands by default. User mode does not allow the configuration to be viewed or changed. Privileged mode, indicated by the routername# prompt, allows a user to both view and change the configuration of a router. You can enter privileged mode by typing the command **enable** and entering the enable password or enable secret password, if set. Global configuration mode, indicated by the routername(config)# prompt, allows configuration changes to be made that apply to the entire router (as opposed to a configuration change that might affect only one interface, for example).

Recognize additional prompts available in other modes and describe their use.   Additional modes are reached via the global configuration prompt, routername(config)#, and their prompts include interface, router(config-if)#, for making interface settings; subinterface, router(config-subif)#, used when a physical interface must be logically subdivided; line configuration mode, router(config-line)#, used to set passwords and make other settings to various connection methods; and routing protocol modes for various routing protocols, router(config-router)#, used to enable and configure routing protocols.

Access and utilize editing and help features.   Type a question mark at the end of commands for help in using the commands. Additionally, understand how to filter command help with the same question mark and leading letters of commands of which you are unsure. Use the command history to retrieve commands previously utilized without retyping. Understand the meaning of the caret when an incorrect command is rejected. Finally, identify useful hot key combinations.

Identify the information provided by the show version command.   The show version command will provide basic configuration of the system hardware as well as the software version, the names and sources of configuration files, the configuration register setting, and the names of boot images.

Set the hostname of a router.   The command sequence to set the hostname of a router is as follows:

```
enable
config t
hostname Todd
```

Differentiate the enable password and enable secret password.   Both of these passwords are used to gain access to privileged mode. However, the enable secret password is newer and is always encrypted by default. Also, if you set the enable password and then set the enable secret, only the enable secret will be used.

Describe the configuration and use of banners.   Banners provide information to users accessing the device and can be displayed at various login prompts. They are configured with the banner command and a keyword describing the specific type of banner.

Set the enable secret password on a router.   To set the enable secret password, you use the global config command enable secret. Do not use enable secret password *password*, or you will set your password to *password password*. Here is an example:

```
enable
config t
enable secret todd
```

Set the console password on a router.   To set the console password, use the following sequence:

```
enable
config t
line console 0
password todd
login
```

Set the Telnet password on a router.   To set the Telnet password, the sequence is as follows:

```
enable
config t
line vty 0 4
password todd
login
```

Describe the advantages of using Secure Shell and list its requirements.   Secure Shell (SSH) uses encrypted keys to send data so that usernames and passwords are not sent in the clear. It requires that a hostname and domain name be configured and that encryption keys be generated.

Describe the process of preparing an interface for use.   To use an interface, you must configure it with an IP address and subnet mask in the same subnet of the hosts that will be connecting to the switch that is connected to that interface. It also must be enabled with the no shutdown command. A serial interface that is connected back-to-back with another router serial interface must also be configured with a clock rate on the DCE end of the serial cable.

Understand how to troubleshoot a serial link problem. If you type `show interface serial 0` and see down, line protocol is down, this will be considered a Physical layer problem. If you see it as up, line protocol is down, then you have a Data Link layer problem.

Understand how to verify your router with the `show interfaces` command. If you type `show interfaces`, you can view the statistics for the interfaces on the router, verify whether the interfaces are shut down, and see the IP address of each interface.

Describe how to view, edit, delete, and save a configuration. The `show running-config` command is used to view the current configuration being used by the router. The `show startup-config` command displays the last configuration that was saved and is the one that will be used at next start-up. The `copy running-config startup-config` command is used to save changes made to the running configuration in NVRAM. The `erase startup-config` command deletes the saved configuration and will result in the invocation of the setup menu when the router is rebooted because there will be no configuration present.

Written Lab 4

You can find the answers to the Written Labs in Appendix A.

Write the command or commands and the prompts at which they would be executed for the following questions:

1. What command is used to set a serial interface to provide clocking to another router at 64Kb?

2. If you telnet into a router and get the response connection refused, password not set, what commands would you execute on the destination router to stop receiving this message and not be prompted for a password?

3. If you type **show inter ethernet 0** and notice the port is administratively down, what commands would you execute to enable the interface?

4. If you wanted to delete the configuration stored in NVRAM, what command(s) would you type?

5. If you wanted to set the user-mode password to *todd* for the console port, what command(s) would you type?

6. If you wanted to set the enable secret password to *cisco*, what command(s) would you type?

7. If you wanted to determine whether serial interface 0/2 should provide clocking, what command would you use?

8. What command would you use to see the terminal history size?

9. You want to reinitialize the router and totally replace the running-config with the current startup-config. What command will you use?

10. How would you set the name of a router to *Chicago*?

Hands-on Labs

In this section, you will perform commands on a Cisco router that will help you understand what you learned in this chapter.

You'll need at least one Cisco router—two would be better, three would be outstanding. The hands-on labs in this section are included for use with real Cisco routers. All of these labs work with the Cisco Packet Tracer router simulator. Lastly, for the CCENT, it doesn't matter what series type router you use with these labs (i.e., 2500, 2600, 800, 1800, or 2800).

It is assumed that the router you're going to use has no current configuration present. If necessary, erase any existing configuration with Hands-on Lab 4.1; otherwise, proceed to Hands-on Lab 4.2.

Lab 4.1: Erasing an Existing Configuration

Lab 4.2: Exploring User, Privileged, and Configuration Modes

Lab 4.3: Using the Help and Editing Features

Lab 4.4: Saving a Router Configuration

Lab 4.5: Setting Passwords

Lab 4.6: Setting the Hostname, Descriptions, IP Address, and Clock Rate

Hands-on Lab 4.1: Erasing an Existing Configuration

This lab may require the knowledge of a username and password to enter privileged mode. If the router has a configuration with an unknown username and password for privileged mode, this procedure will not be possible. It is possible to erase a configuration without a privileged mode password, but the exact steps depend on the router model and will not be covered here.

1. Start the router up, and when prompted, press Enter.

2. At the Router> prompt, type **enable**.

3. If prompted, enter the username and press Enter. Then enter the correct password and press Enter.

4. At the privileged mode prompt, type **erase startup-config**.

5. At the privileged mode prompt, type **reload**, and when prompted to save the configuration, type **n** for no.

Hands-on Lab 4.2: Exploring User, Privileged, and Configuration Modes

1. Turn the router on. If you just erased the configuration as in Hands-on Lab 4.1, when prompted to continue with the configuration dialog, enter **n** for no and press Enter. When prompted, press Enter to connect to your router. This will put you into user mode.

2. At the Router> prompt, type a question mark (**?**).

3. Notice the –more– at the bottom of the screen.

4. Press the Enter key to view the commands line by line. Press the spacebar to view the commands a full screen at a time. You can type **q** at any time to quit.

5. Type **enable** or **en** and press Enter. This will put you into privileged mode where you can change and view the router configuration.

6. At the Router# prompt, type a question mark (**?**). Notice how many options are available to you in privileged mode.

7. Type **q** to quit.

8. Type **config** and press Enter.

9. When prompted for a method, press Enter to configure your router using your terminal (which is the default).

10. At the Router(config)# prompt, type a question mark (**?**) and then **q** to quit, or press the spacebar to view the commands.

11. Type **interface e0** or **int e0** (or even **int fa0/0**) and press Enter. This will allow you to configure interface Ethernet 0.

12. At the Router(config-if)# prompt, type a question mark (**?**).

13. Type **int s0 (int s0/0)** or **interface s0** (same as the interface serial 0 command) and press Enter. This will allow you to configure interface serial 0. Notice that you can go from interface to interface easily.

14. Type **encapsulation ?**.

15. Type **exit**. Notice how this brings you back one level.

16. Press Ctrl+Z. Notice how this brings you out of configuration mode and places you back into privileged mode.

17. Type **disable**. This will put you into user mode.

18. Type **exit**, which will log you out of the router.

Hands-on Lab 4.3: Using the Help and Editing Features

1. Log into the router and go to privileged mode by typing **en** or **enable**.

2. Type a question mark (**?**).

3. Type **cl?** and then press Enter. Notice that you can see all the commands that start with *cl*.

4. Type **clock ?** and press Enter.

 NOTE   Notice the difference between steps 3 and 4. Step 3 has you type letters with no space and a question mark, which will give you all the commands that start with *cl*. Step 4 has you type a command, space, and question mark. By doing this, you will see the next available parameter.

5. Set the router's clock by typing **clock ?** and, following the help screens, setting the router's time and date. The following steps walk you through setting the date and time.

6. Type **clock ?**.

7. Type **clock set ?**.

8. Type **clock set 10:30:30 ?**.

9. Type **clock set 10:30:30 14 May ?**.

10. Type **clock set 10:30:30 14 May 2011**.

11. Press Enter.

12. Type **show clock** to see the time and date.

13. From privileged mode, type **show access-list 10**. Don't press Enter.

14. Press Ctrl+A. This takes you to the beginning of the line.

15. Press Ctrl+E. This should take you back to the end of the line.

16. Press Ctrl+A and then Ctrl+F. This should move you forward one character.

17. Press Ctrl+B, which will move you back one character.

18. Press Enter and then press Ctrl+P. This will repeat the last command.

19. Press the up arrow key on your keyboard. This will also repeat the last command.

20. Type **sh history**. This shows you the last 10 commands entered.

21. Type **terminal history size ?**. This changes the history entry size. The ? is the number of allowed lines.

22. Type **show terminal** to gather terminal statistics and history size.

23. Type **terminal no editing**. This turns off advanced editing. Repeat steps 14 through 18 to see that the shortcut editing keys have no effect until you type **terminal editing**.

24. Type **terminal editing** and press Enter to reenable advanced editing.

25. Type **sh run** and then press your Tab key. This will finish typing the command for you.

26. Type **sh start** and then press your Tab key. This will finish typing the command for you.

Hands-on Lab 4.4: Saving a Router Configuration

1. Log into the router, go into privileged mode by typing **en** or **enable**, and then press Enter.

2. To see the configuration stored in NVRAM, type **sh start** and press Tab and Enter, or type **show startup-config** and press Enter. However, if no configuration has been saved, you will get an error message.

3. To save a configuration to NVRAM, which is known as startup-config, you can do one of the following:
   - Type **copy run start** and press Enter.
   - Type **copy running**, press Tab, type **start**, press Tab, and press Enter.
   - Type **copy running-config startup-config** and press Enter.

4. Type **sh start**, press Tab, and then press Enter.

5. Type **sh run**, press Tab, and then press Enter.

6. Type **erase start**, press Tab, and then press Enter. Acknowledge the erasure by pressing Enter.

7. Type **sh start**, press Tab, and then press Enter. You should get an error message.

8. Type **reload** and then press Enter. Acknowledge the reload by pressing Enter. Wait for the router to reload.

9. Say no to entering setup mode, or just press Ctrl+C.

Hands-on Lab 4.5: Setting Passwords

1. Log into the router and go into privileged mode by typing **en** or **enable**.

2. Type **config t** and press Enter.

3. Type **enable ?**.

4. Set your enable secret password by typing **enable secret *password*** (the third word should be your own personalized password) and pressing Enter. Do not add the parameter password after the parameter **secret** (this would make your password the word *password*). An example would be **enable secret todd**.

5. Now let's see what happens when you log all the way out of the router and then log in. Log out by pressing Ctrl+Z and then type **exit** and press Enter. Go to privileged mode. Before you are allowed to enter privileged mode, you will be asked for a password. If you successfully enter the secret password, you can proceed.

6. Remove the secret password. Go to privileged mode, type **config t**, and press Enter. Type **no enable secret** and press Enter. Log out and then log back in again; now you should not be asked for a password.

7. One more password used to enter privileged mode is called the enable password. It is an older, less secure password and is not used if an enable secret password is set. Here is an example of how to set it:

```
config t
enable password todd1
```

8. Notice that the enable secret and enable passwords are different. They cannot be the same.

9. Type **config t** to be at the right level to set your console and auxiliary passwords and then type **line ?**.

10. Notice that the parameters for the line commands are auxiliary, vty, and console. You will set all three.

11. To set the Telnet or VTY password, type **line vty 0 4** and then press Enter. The 0 4 is the range of the five available virtual lines used to connect with Telnet. If you have an enterprise IOS, the number of lines may vary. Use the question mark to determine the last line number available on your router.

12. The next command you need to set for your VTY password is password. Type **password** *password* to set the password. (*password* is your password.)

 NOTE You can use the no login command to disable the user-mode password prompt when using Telnet.

13. One more command is used to set the authentication on or off. Type **login** and press Enter to prompt for a user-mode password when telnetting into the router. You will not be able to telnet into a router if the password is not set.

14. Here is an example of how to set the VTY password: Cisco has begun this process of not letting you set the login command before a password is set on a line because if you set the login command under a line and then don't set a password, the line won't be usable. And it will prompt for a password that doesn't exist. So, this is a good thing—a feature, not a hassle.

```
config t
line vty 0 4
password todd
login
```

15. Set your auxiliary password by first typing **line auxiliary 0** or **line aux 0**.

16. Type **password** *password*.

17. Type*login*.

18. Set your console password by first typing **line console 0** or **line con 0**.

19. Type **password** *password*t.

20. Type *login*. Here is an example of the last two command sequences:

```
config t
line con 0
password todd1
login
line aux 0
password todd
login
```

21. You can add the Exec-timeout 0 0 command to the console 0 line. This will stop the console from timing out and logging you out. The command sequence will now look like this:

```
config t
line con 0
password todd2
login
exec-timeout 0 0
```

22. Set the console prompt to not overwrite the command you're typing with console messages by using the command logging synchronous.

```
config t
line con 0
logging synchronous
```

Hands-on Lab 4.6: Setting the Hostname, Descriptions, IP Address, and Clock Rate

1. Log into the router and go into privileged mode by typing **en** or **enable**. If required, enter a username and password.

2. Set your hostname on your router by using the hostname command. Notice that it is one word. Here is an example of setting your hostname:

```
Router#config t
Router(config)#hostname RouterA
RouterA(config)#
```

Notice that the hostname of the router changed in the prompt as soon as you pressed Enter.

3. Set a banner that the network administrators will see by using the banner command, as shown in the following steps.

4. Type **config t** and then **banner ?**.

5. Notice that you can set at least four different banners. For this lab, you are interested only in the login and message of the day (MOTD) banners.

6. Set your MOTD banner, which will be displayed when a console, auxiliary, or Telnet connection is made to the router, by typing this:

```
config t
banner motd #
This is an motd banner
#
```

7. The preceding example used a # sign as a delimiting character. This tells the router when the message is done. You cannot use the delimiting character in the message itself.

8. You can remove the MOTD banner by typing the following command:

```
config t
no banner motd
```

9. Set the login banner by typing this:

```
config t
banner login #
This is a login banner
#
```

10. The login banner will display immediately after the MOTD but before the user-mode password prompt. Remember that you set your user-mode passwords by setting the console, auxiliary, and VTY line passwords.

11. You can remove the login banner by typing this:

```
config t
no banner login
```

12. You can add an IP address to an interface with the ip address command. You need to get into interface configuration mode first; here is an example of how you do that:

```
config t
int e0 (you can use int Ethernet 0 too)
ip address 1.1.1.1 255.255.0.0
no shutdown
```

Notice that the IP address (1.1.1.1) and subnet mask (255.255.0.0) are configured on one line. The no shutdown (or no shut for short) command is used to enable the interface. All interfaces are shut down by default.

13. You can add identification to an interface by using the description command. This is useful for adding information about the connection. Here is an example:

```
config t
int s0
ip address 1.1.1.2 255.255.0.0
no shut
description Wan link to Miami
```

14. You can add the bandwidth of a serial link as well as the clock rate when simulating a DCE WAN link. Here is an example:

```
config t
int s0
bandwidth 64
clock rate 64000
```

Review Questions

You can find the answers in Appendix B.

The following questions are designed to test your understanding of this chapter's material. For more information on how to get additional questions, please see this book's introduction.

1. You type **show running-config** and get this output:

    ```
    [output cut]
    line console 0
          Exec-timeout 1 44
          Password 7 098C0BQR
          Login
    [output cut]
    ```

    What do the two numbers following the `exec-timeout` command mean?

    A. If no command has been typed in 44 seconds, the console connection will be closed.

    B. If no router activity has been detected in 1 hour and 44 minutes, the console will be locked out.

    C. If no commands have been typed in 1 minute and 44 seconds, the console connection will be closed.

    D. If you're connected to the router by a Telnet connection, input must be detected within 1 minute and 44 seconds or the connection will be closed.

2. Which of the following connection methods available to connect to a router is considered *out-of-band*?

    A. Serial port

    B. VTY port

    C. HTTP port

    D. Aux port

3. Which two of the following commands are required when configuring SSH on your router?

    A. `enable secret` *password*

    B. `exec-timeout 0 0`

    C. `ip domain-name` *name*

    D. `username` *name* `password` *password*

    E. `ip ssh version 2`

4. Which command will show you whether a DTE or a DCE cable is plugged into serial 0?

   A. `sh int s0`

   B. `sh int serial 0`

   C. `show controllers s 0`

   D. `show serial 0 controllers`

5. Which of the following is a correct combination of file type and default location in a Cisco router?

   A. IOS/NVRAM

   B. Startup configuration/flash memory

   C. IOS/flash memory

   D. Running configuration/NVRAM

6. You set the console password, but when you display the configuration, the password doesn't show up; it looks like this:

```
[output cut]
Line console 0
        Exec-timeout 1 44
        Password 7 098C0BQR
        Login
[output cut]
```

What command would configure the password to be stored this way?

   A. `encrypt password`

   B. `service password-encryption`

   C. `service-password-encryption`

   D. `exec-timeout 1 44`

7. Which of the following commands will configure all the default VTY ports on a router on a router with five VTY lines?

   A. `Router#line vty 0 4`

   B. `Router(config)#line vty 0 4`

   C. `Router(config-if)#line console 0`

   D. `Router(config)#line vty all`

8. Which one of the following commands sets the secret password to Cisco?

   A. `enable secret password Cisco`

   B. `enable secret cisco`

   C. `enable secret Cisco`

   D. `enable password Cisco`

9. If you wanted administrators to see a message when logging into the router, which command would you use?

   A. message banner motd

   B. banner message motd

   C. banner motd

   D. message motd

10. Which of the following prompts indicate that the router is currently in privileged mode?

   A. router(config)#

   B. router>

   C. router#

   D. router(config-if)

11. What command do you type to save the configuration stored in RAM to NVRAM?

   A. Router(config)#**copy current to starting**

   B. Router#**copy starting to running**

   C. Router(config)#**copy running-config startup-config**

   D. Router#**copy run startup**

12. You try to telnet into SFRouter from router Corp and receive this message:

Corp#**telnet SFRouter**
Trying SFRouter (10.0.0.1)…Open

Password required, but none set
[Connection to SFRouter closed by foreign host]
Corp#

Which of the following sequences will address this problem correctly?

   A. Corp(config)#line console 0

   Corp (config-line)#password *password*

   Corp (config-line)#login

   B. SFRouter(config)#line console 0

   Corp (config-line)#enable secret *password*

   Corp (config-line)#login

   C. Corp(config)#line vty 0 4

   Corp (config-line)#password *password*

   Corp (config-line)#login

   D. SFRouter(config)#line vty 0 4

   Corp (config-line)#password *password*

   Corp (config-line)#login

13. Which command will delete the contents of NVRAM on a router?

A. `delete NVRAM`

B. `delete startup-config`

C. `erase NVRAM`

D. `erase start`

14. What is the problem with an interface if you type **show interface serial 0** and receive the following message?

`Serial0 is administratively down, line protocol is down`

A. The keepalives are different times.

B. The administrator has the interface shut down.

C. The administrator is pinging from the interface.

D. No cable is attached.

15. Which of the following commands displays the configurable parameters and statistics of all interfaces on a router?

A. `show running-config`

B. `show startup-config`

C. `show interfaces`

D. `show versions`

16. If you delete the contents of NVRAM and reboot the router, what mode will you be in?

A. Privileged mode

B. Global mode

C. Setup mode

D. NVRAM loaded mode

17. You type the following command into the router and receive the following output:

```
Router#show serial 0/0
         ^
% Invalid input detected at '^' marker.
```

Why was this error message displayed?

A. You need to be in privileged mode.

B. You cannot have a space between serial and 0/0.

C. The router does not have a serial0/0 interface.

D. Part of the command is missing.

18. You type **Router#sh ru** and receive a % ambiguous command error. Why did you receive this message?

    A. The command requires additional options or parameters.

    B. There is more than one show command that starts with the letters *ru*.

    C. There is no show command that starts with *ru*.

    D. The command is being executed from the wrong router mode.

19. Which of the following commands will display the current IP addressing and the layer 1 and 2 status of an interface? (Choose two.)

    A. show version

    B. show interfaces

    C. show controllers

    D. show ip interface

    E. show running-config

20. At which layer of the OSI model would you assume the problem is if you type **show interface serial 1** and receive the following message?

```
Serial1 is down, line protocol is down
```

    A. Physical layer

    B. Data Link layer

    C. Network layer

    D. None; it is a router problem.

Chapter

5

Managing a Cisco Internetwork

THE CCENT EXAM OBJECTIVES COVERED IN THIS CHAPTER INCLUDE THE FOLLOWING:

- ✓ Describe the operation of Cisco routers (including: router bootup process, POST, router components)

- ✓ Manage IOS configuration files (including: save, edit, upgrade, restore)

- ✓ Manage Cisco IOS

- ✓ Verify network status and router operation using basic utilities (including: ping, traceroute, telnet, SSH, arp, ipconfig), SHOW & DEBUG commands

Here in Chapter 5, I'll show you how to manage Cisco routers on an internetwork. The Internetwork Operating System (IOS) and configuration files reside in different locations in a Cisco device, so it's really important to understand both where these files are located and how they work.

You'll be learning about the main components of a router, the router boot sequence, and the configuration register, including how to use the configuration register for password recovery. After that, you'll find out how to manage routers by using the copy command with a TFTP host when using the Cisco IOS File System (IFS).

I'll wrap up the chapter with an exploration of the Cisco Discovery Protocol (CDP), and you'll learn how to resolve hostnames and some important Cisco IOS troubleshooting techniques.

 For up-to-the-minute updates for this chapter, please see www.lammle.com/ forum and/or www.sybex.com/go/ccent2e.

The Internal Components of a Cisco Router

To configure and troubleshoot a Cisco internetwork, you need to know the major components of Cisco routers and understand what each one does. Table 5.1 describes the major Cisco router components.

TABLE 5.1   Cisco router components

Component	Description
Bootstrap	Stored in the microcode of the ROM, the bootstrap is used to bring up a router during initialization. It will boot the router and then load the IOS.
POST (power-on self-test)	Stored in the microcode of the ROM, the POST is used to check the basic functionality of the router hardware and determines which interfaces are present.

TABLE 5.1   Cisco router components *(continued)*

Component	Description
ROM monitor	Stored in the microcode of the ROM, the ROM monitor is used for manufacturing, testing, and troubleshooting.
Mini-IOS	Called the RXBOOT or bootloader by Cisco, the mini-IOS is a small IOS in ROM that can be used to bring up an interface and load a Cisco IOS into flash memory. The mini-IOS can also perform a few other maintenance operations.
RAM (random access memory)	Used to hold packet buffers, ARP cache, routing tables, and also the software and data structures that allow the router to function. Running-config is stored in RAM, and most routers expand the IOS from flash into RAM upon boot.
ROM (read-only memory)	Used to start and maintain the router. Holds the POST and the bootstrap program as well as the mini-IOS.
Flash memory	Stores the Cisco IOS by default. Flash memory is not erased when the router is reloaded. It is electronically erasable programmable read-only memory (EEPROM) created by Intel.
NVRAM (nonvolatile RAM)	Used to hold the router and switch configuration. NVRAM is not erased when the router or switch is reloaded and does not store an IOS. The configuration register is stored in NVRAM.
Configuration register	Used to control how the router boots up. This value can be found as the last line of the show version command output and by default is set to 0x2102, which tells the router to load the IOS from flash memory as well as to load the configuration from NVRAM.

The Router Boot Sequence

When a router boots up, it performs a series of steps, called the *boot sequence*, to test the hardware and load the necessary software. The boot sequence consists of the following steps:

1. The router performs a POST.

   The POST tests the hardware to verify that all components of the device are operational and present. For example, the POST checks for the different interfaces on the router. The POST is stored in and run from *read-only memory (ROM)*.

2.   The bootstrap then looks for and loads the Cisco IOS software.

The bootstrap is a program in ROM that is used to execute programs. The bootstrap program is responsible for finding where each IOS program is located and then loading the file. By default, the IOS software is loaded from flash memory in all Cisco routers.

 The default order of an IOS loading from a router is flash, then TFTP server, and then ROM.

3.   The IOS software looks for a valid configuration file stored in NVRAM.

This file is called `startup-config` and is there only if an administrator copies the `running-config` file into NVRAM. (As you already know, the new ISR routers have a small `startup-config` file preloaded.)

4.   If a `startup-config` file is in NVRAM, the router will copy this file and place it in RAM and call the file `running-config`.

The router will use this file to run the router. The router should now be operational. If a `startup-config` file is not in NVRAM, the router will broadcast any interface that detects carrier detect (CD) for a TFTP host looking for a configuration, and when that fails (typically it will fail—most people won't even realize the router has attempted this process), it will start the setup mode configuration process.

Managing Configuration Register

All Cisco routers have a 16-bit software register that's written into NVRAM. By default, the *configuration register* is set to load the Cisco IOS from *flash memory* and to look for and load the `startup-config` file from NVRAM. In the following sections, I will discuss the configuration register settings and how to use these settings to provide password recovery on your routers.

Understanding the Configuration Register Bits

The 16 bits (2 bytes) of the configuration register are read from 15 to 0, from left to right. The default configuration setting on Cisco routers is 0x2102. This means that bits 13, 8, and 1 are on, as shown in Table 5.2. Notice that each set of 4 bits (called a *nibble*) is read in binary with a value of 8, 4, 2, 1.

TABLE 5.2   The configuration register bit numbers

Configuration Register		2					1				0			2	
Bit number	15	14	13	12	11	10	9	8	7	6	5	4	3	2	1	0
Bit value	8	4	2	1	8	4	2	1	8	4	2	1	8	4	2	1
Binary	0	0	1	0	0	0	0	1	0	0	0	0	0	0	1	0

Add the prefix *0x* to the configuration register address. The *0x* means that the digits that follow are in hexadecimal.

Table 5.3 lists the software configuration bit meanings. Notice that bit 6 can be used to ignore the NVRAM contents. This bit is used for password recovery—something I'll go over with you in the section "Recovering Passwords" later in this chapter.

Remember that in hex, the scheme is 0–9 and A–F (A = 10, B = 11, C = 12, D = 13, E = 14, and F = 15). This means that a 210F setting for the configuration register is actually 210(15), or 1111 in binary.

TABLE 5.3   Software configuration meanings

Bit	Hex	Description
0–3	0x0000–0x000F	Boot field (see Table 5.4).
6	0x0040	Ignore NVRAM contents.
7	0x0080	OEM bit enabled.
8	0x101	Break disabled.
10	0x0400	IP broadcast with all zeros.
5, 11–12	0x0800–0x1000	Console line speed.
13	0x2000	Boot default ROM software if network boot fails.
14	0x4000	IP broadcasts do not have net numbers.
15	0x8000	Enable diagnostic messages and ignore NVRAM contents.

The boot field, which consists of bits 0–3 in the configuration register, controls the router boot sequence. Table 5.4 describes the boot field bits.

TABLE 5.4 The boot field (configuration register bits 00–03)

Boot Field	Meaning	Use
00	ROM monitor mode	To boot to ROM monitor mode, set the configuration register to 2100. You must manually boot the router with the b command. The router will show the rommon> prompt.
01	Boot image from ROM	To boot the mini-IOS image stored in ROM, set the configuration register to 2101. The router will show the Router(boot)> prompt.
02–F	Specifies a default boot filename	Any value from 2102 through 210F tells the router to use the boot commands specified in NVRAM.

Checking the Current Configuration Register Value

You can see the current value of the configuration register by using the show version command (sh version or show ver for short), as demonstrated here:

```
Router>sh version
Cisco IOS Software, 2800 Software (C2800NM-ADVSECURITYK9-M), Version
    12.4(12), RELEASE SOFTWARE (fc1)
[output cut]
Configuration register is 0x2102
```

The last information given from this command is the value of the configuration register. In this example, the value is 0x2102—the default setting. The configuration register setting of 0x2102 tells the router to look in NVRAM for the boot sequence.

Notice that the show version command also provides the IOS version, and in the preceding example, it shows the IOS version as 12.4(12).

> The show version command will display system hardware configuration information, software version, and the names of the boot images on a router.

Changing the Configuration Register

You can change the configuration register value to modify how the router boots and runs, as well as perform password recovery. These are the main reasons you would want to change the configuration register:

- To force the system into the ROM monitor mode
- To select a boot source
- To enable or disable the Break function
- To control broadcast addresses
- To set the console terminal baud rate
- To load operating software from ROM
- To enable booting from a Trivial File Transfer Protocol (TFTP) server

 Before you change the configuration register, make sure you know the current configuration register value. Use the show version command to get this information.

You can change the configuration register by using the config-register command. Here's an example. The following commands tell the router to boot a small IOS from ROM and then show the current configuration register value:

```
Router(config)#config-register 0x2101
Router(config)#^Z
Router#sh ver
[output cut]
Configuration register is 0x2102 (will be 0x2101 at next
  reload)
```

Notice that the show version command displays the current configuration register value and also what that value will be when the router reboots. Any change to the configuration register won't take effect until the router is reloaded. The 0x2101 will load the IOS from ROM the next time the router is rebooted. You may see it listed as 0x101—that's basically the same thing, and it can be written either way.

Here is my router after setting the configuration register to 0x2101 and reloading:

```
Router(boot)#sh ver
Cisco IOS Software, 2800 Software (C2800NM-ADVSECURITYK9-M), Version
    12.4(12), RELEASE SOFTWARE (fc1)
[output cut]


ROM: System Bootstrap, Version 12.4(13r)T, RELEASE SOFTWARE (fc1)
```

```
Router uptime is 3 minutes
System returned to ROM by power-on
System image file is "flash:c2800nm-advsecurityk9-mz.124-12.bin"
[output cut]
```

```
Configuration register is 0x2101
```

At this point, if you typed **show flash,** you'd still see the IOS in flash memory ready to go. But I told the router to load from ROM, which is why the hostname shows up with (boot).

```
Router(boot)#sh flash
-#- -length- ---date/time--- path
1      21710744 Jan 2 2007 22:41:14 +00:00 c2800nm-advsecurityk9-mz.124-12.bin
2          1823 Dec 5 2006 14:46:26 +00:00 sdmconfig-2811.cfg
3       4734464 Dec 5 2006 14:47:12 +00:00 sdm.tar
4        833024 Dec 5 2006 14:47:38 +00:00 es.tar
5       1052160 Dec 5 2006 14:48:10 +00:00 common.tar
6          1038 Dec 5 2006 14:48:32 +00:00 home.shtml
7        102400 Dec 5 2006 14:48:54 +00:00 home.tar
8        491213 Dec 5 2006 14:49:22 +00:00 128MB.sdf
9       1684577 Dec 5 2006 14:50:04 +00:00 securedesktop-ios-3.1.1.27-k9.pkg
10       398305 Dec 5 2006 14:50:34 +00:00 sslclient-win-1.1.0.154.pkg
```

```
32989184 bytes available (31027200 bytes used)
```

So, even though I have the full IOS in flash, I changed the default loading of the router's software by changing the configuration register. If you want to set the configuration register back to the default, just type this:

```
Router(boot)#config t
Router(boot)(config)#config-register 0x2102
Router(boot)(config)#^Z
Router(boot)#reload
```

In the next section, I'll show you how to load the router into ROM monitor mode so you can perform password recovery.

Recovering Passwords

If you're locked out of a router because you forgot the password, you can change the configuration register to help you get back on your feet. As I said earlier, bit 6 in the configuration register is used to tell the router whether to use the contents of NVRAM to load a router configuration.

The default configuration register value is 0x2102, meaning that bit 6 is off. With the default setting, the router will look for and load a router configuration stored in NVRAM (startup-config). To recover a password, you need to turn on bit 6. Doing this will tell the router to ignore the NVRAM contents. The configuration register value to turn on bit 6 is 0x2142.

Here are the main steps to password recovery:

1. Boot the router and interrupt the boot sequence by performing a break, which will take the router into ROM monitor mode.

2. Change the configuration register to turn on bit 6 (with the value 0x2142).

3. Reload the router.

4. Enter privileged mode.

5. Copy the `startup-config` file to `running-config`.

6. Change the password.

7. Reset the configuration register to the default value.

8. Save the router configuration.

9. Reload the router (optional).

I'll cover these steps in more detail in the following sections. I'll also show you the commands to restore access to ISR, 2600, and even 2500 series routers. (You can still use 2500s for labs, and you never know when you might need this information!)

As I said, you can enter ROM monitor mode by pressing Ctrl+Break during router bootup. But if the IOS is corrupt or missing, if there's no network connectivity available to find a TFTP host, or if the mini-IOS from ROM doesn't load (meaning the default router fallback failed), the router will enter ROM monitor mode by default.

Interrupting the Router Boot Sequence

Your first step is to boot the router and perform a break. This is usually done by pressing the Ctrl+Break key combination when using HyperTerminal (personally, I use SecureCRT or Putty) while the router first reboots.

After you've performed a break, you should see something like this for a 2600 series router (it is pretty much the same output for the ISR series):

```
System Bootstrap, Version 11.3(2)XA4, RELEASE SOFTWARE (fc1)
Copyright (c) 1999 by cisco Systems, Inc.
TAC:Home:SW:IOS:Specials for info
PC = 0xfff0a530, Vector = 0x500, SP = 0x680127b0
C2600 platform with 32768 Kbytes of main memory
PC = 0xfff0a530, Vector = 0x500, SP = 0x80004374
monitor: command "boot" aborted due to user interrupt
rommon 1 >
```

Notice the line monitor: command "boot" aborted due to user interrupt. At this point, you will be at the rommon 1> prompt, which is called the ROM monitor mode.

Changing the Configuration Register

As I explained earlier, you can change the configuration register from within the IOS by using the config-register command. To turn on bit 6, use the configuration register value 0x2142.

> Remember that if you change the configuration register to 0x2142, the startup-config will be bypassed, and the router will load into setup mode.

Cisco ISR/2600 Series Commands

To change the bit value on a Cisco ISR/2600 series router, you just enter the confreg command at the rommon 1> prompt.

```
rommon 1 >confreg 0x2142
You must reset or power cycle for new config to take effect
rommon 2 >reset
```

Cisco 2500 Series Commands

To change the configuration register on a 2500 series router, type **o** after creating a break sequence on the router. This brings up a menu of configuration register option settings. To change the configuration register, enter the command **o/r**, followed by the new register value. Here's an example of turning on bit 6 on a 2501 router:

```
System Bootstrap, Version 11.0(10c), SOFTWARE
Copyright (c) 1986-1996 by cisco Systems
2500 processor with 14336 Kbytes of main memory
Abort at 0x1098FEC (PC)
>o
Configuration register = 0x2102 at last boot
Bit#    Configuration register option settings:
15      Diagnostic mode disabled
14      IP broadcasts do not have network numbers
13      Boot default ROM software if network boot fails
12-11   Console speed is 9600 baud
10      IP broadcasts with ones
08      Break disabled
07      OEM disabled
06      Ignore configuration disabled
03-00   Boot file is cisco2-2500 (or 'boot system' command)
>o/r 0x2142
```

Notice that the last entry in the router output is 03-00. This tells the router what the IOS boot file is. By default, the router will use the first file found in the flash memory, so if you want to boot a different filename, you can use the `boot system flash:ios_name` command. (I'll show you the `boot system` command in a minute.)

Reloading the Router and Entering Privileged Mode

At this point, you need to reset the router like this:

- From the ISR/2600 series router, type **I** (for initialize) or **reset**.
- From the 2500 series router, type **I**.

The router will reload and ask if you want to use setup mode (because no startup-config is used). Answer no to entering setup mode, press Enter to go into user mode, and then type **enable** to go into privileged mode.

Viewing and Changing the Configuration

Now you're past the point where you would need to enter the user-mode and privileged-mode passwords in a router. Copy the `startup-config` file to the `running-config` file:

```
copy startup-config running-config
```

or use this shortcut:

```
copy start run
```

The configuration is now running in *random access memory (RAM)*, and you're in privileged mode, meaning that you can now view and change the configuration. But you can't view the enable secret setting for the password since it is encrypted. To change the password, do this:

```
config t
enable secret todd
```

Resetting the Configuration Register and Reloading the Router

After you're finished changing passwords, set the configuration register back to the default value with the `config-register` command.

```
config t
config-register 0x2102
```

Finally, save the new configuration with a `copy running-config startup-config` and reload the router with `reload`.

 If you save your configuration and reload the router and it comes up in setup mode, the configuration register setting is probably incorrect.

Boot System Commands

Did you know that you can configure your router to boot another IOS if the flash is corrupted? Well, you can. In fact, you just might want all your routers to boot from a TFTP host each time anyway because that way, you'll never have to upgrade each router individually. This may be a smooth way to go because it allows you to just change one file on a TFTP host to perform an upgrade.

There are some boot commands you can play with that will help you manage the way your router boots the Cisco IOS—but remember, I'm talking about the router's IOS here, *not* the router's configuration!

```
Router>en
Router#config t
Enter configuration commands, one per line.  End with CNTL/Z.
Router(config)#boot ?
  bootstrap  Bootstrap image file
  config     Configuration file
  host       Router-specific config file
  network    Network-wide config file
  system     System image file
```

The boot command truly gives you a wealth of options, but first, I'll show you the typical settings that Cisco recommends. So, let's get started—the boot system command will allow you to tell the router which file to boot from flash memory. Remember that the router, by default, boots the first file found in flash. You can change that with the following commands:

```
Router(config)#boot system ?
  WORD   TFTP filename or URL
  flash  Boot from flash memory
  ftp    Boot from a server via ftp
  mop    Boot from a Decnet MOP server
  rcp    Boot from a server via rcp
  rom    Boot from rom
  tftp   Boot from a tftp server
Router(config)#boot system flash c2800nm-advsecurityk9-mz.124-12.bin
```

The preceding command configures the router to boot the IOS listed in it. This is a helpful command for when you load a new IOS into flash and want to test it or even when you want to totally change which IOS is loading by default.

The next command is considered a fallback routine, but as I said, you can make it a permanent way to have your routers boot from a TFTP host. Personally, I wouldn't necessarily recommend doing this (single point of failure); I'm just showing you that it's possible.

```
Router(config)#boot system tftp ?
  WORD  System image filename
Router(config)#boot system tftp c2800nm-advsecurityk9-mz.124-12.bin ?
  Hostname or A.B.C.D  Address from which to download the file
  <cr>
Router(config)#boot system tftp c2800nm-advsecurityk9-mz.124-12.bin 1.1.1.2
Router(config)#
```

As your last recommended fallback option—the one to go to if the IOS in flash doesn't load and the TFTP host does not produce the IOS—load the mini-IOS from ROM like this:

```
Router(config)#boot system rom
Router(config)#do show run | include boot system
boot system flash c2800nm-advsecurityk9-mz.124-12.bin
boot system tftp c2800nm-advsecurityk9-mz.124-12.bin 1.1.1.2
boot system rom
Router(config)#
```

To sum this up, I now have Cisco's suggested IOS backup routine configured on my router: flash, TFTP host, ROM.

Backing Up and Restoring the Cisco IOS

Before you upgrade or restore a Cisco IOS, you really should copy the existing file to a *TFTP host* as a backup just in case the new image crashes and burns.

And you can use any TFTP host to accomplish this. By default, the flash memory in a router is used to store the Cisco IOS. In the following sections, I'll describe how to check the amount of flash memory, how to copy the Cisco IOS from flash memory to a TFTP host, and how to copy the IOS from a TFTP host to flash memory.

You'll learn how to use the Cisco IFS to manage your IOS files after first learning how to manage them with a TFTP host.

But before you back up an IOS image to a network server on your intranet, you have to do these three things:

- Make sure you can access the network server.
- Ensure that the network server has adequate space for the code image.
- Verify the filenaming and path requirement.

And if you have a laptop or workstation's Ethernet port directly connected to a router's Ethernet interface, as shown in Figure 5.1, you need to verify the following before attempting to copy the image to or from the router:

- TFTP server software must be running on the administrator's workstation.
- The Ethernet connection between the router and the workstation must be made with a crossover cable.
- The workstation must be on the same subnet as the router's Ethernet interface.
- The copy flash tftp command must be supplied with the IP address of the workstation if you are copying from the router flash.
- And if you're copying "into" flash, you need to verify that there's enough room in flash memory to accommodate the file to be copied.

FIGURE 5.1   Copying an IOS from a workstation to a router

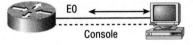

Verifying Flash Memory

Before you attempt to upgrade the Cisco IOS on your router with a new IOS file, it's a good idea to verify that your flash memory has enough room to hold the new image. You verify the amount of flash memory and the file or files being stored in flash memory by using the show flash command (sh flash for short).

```
Router#sh flash
-#- -length- ---date/time--- path
1      21710744 Jan 2 2007 22:41:14 +00:00 c2800nm-advsecurityk9-mz.124-12.bin
[output cut]
32989184 bytes available (31027200 bytes used)
```

The previous router output shows there is 32MB of RAM, and roughly 22MB of the memory is in use.

> **WARNING**   The show flash command will display the amount of memory consumed by the current IOS image as well as tell you if there's enough room available to hold both current and new images. You should know that if there's not enough room for both the old and new images you want to load, the old image will be erased!

You can also see the amount of flash by using the show version command on routers.

```
Router#show version
[output cut]
Cisco 2811 (revision 49.46) with 249856K/12288K bytes of memory.
Processor board ID FTX1049A1AB
2 FastEthernet interfaces
4 Serial(sync/async) interfaces
1 Virtual Private Network (VPN) Module
DRAM configuration is 64 bits wide with parity enabled.
239K bytes of non-volatile configuration memory.
62720K bytes of ATA CompactFlash (Read/Write)
```

The top line provides you with the amount of RAM the router has, and by averaging the two numbers, you'll get around 256MB of RAM. You can see that the amount of flash shows up on the last line of the previous output. By rounding up, you get the amount of flash to 64MB.

Backing Up the Cisco IOS

To back up the Cisco IOS to a TFTP server, you use the copy flash tftp command. It's a straightforward command that requires only the source filename and the IP address of the TFTP server.

The key to success in this backup routine is to make sure you have good, solid connectivity to the TFTP server. Check this by pinging the TFTP device from the router console prompt like this:

```
Router#ping 1.1.1.2
Type escape sequence to abort.
Sending 5, 100-byte ICMP Echos to 1.1.1.2, timeout
  is 2 seconds:
!!!!!
Success rate is 100 percent (5/5), round-trip min/avg/max
  = 4/4/8 ms
```

The *Packet Internet Groper (Ping)* utility is used to test network connectivity, and I use it in some of the examples in this chapter. I'll be talking about it in more detail in the section "Checking and Troubleshooting Network Connectivity" later in the chapter.

After you ping the TFTP server to make sure that IP is working, you can use the copy
flash tftp command to copy the IOS to the TFTP server, as shown next:

```
Router#copy flash tftp
Source filename []?c2800nm-advsecurityk9-mz.124-12.bin
Address or name of remote host []?1.1.1.2
Destination filename [c2800nm-advsecurityk9-mz.124-12.bin]?[enter]
!!!!!!!!!!!!!!!!!!!!!!!!!!!!!!!!!!!!!!!!!!!!!!!!!!!!!!!!!!!!!!!!!!!!!!!!!!!!!!!!
!!!!!
21710744 bytes copied in 60.724 secs (357532 bytes/sec)
Router#
```

Just copy the IOS filename from either the show flash or show version command and
then paste it when prompted for the source filename.

In the preceding example, the contents of flash memory were copied successfully to the
TFTP server. The address of the remote host is the IP address of the TFTP host, and the
source filename is the file in flash memory.

WARNING The copy flash tftp command won't prompt you for the location of any
file or ask you where to put the file. TFTP is just a "grab it and place it" program in this situation. This means that the TFTP server must have a default
directory specified or it won't work!

Restoring or Upgrading the Cisco Router IOS

What happens if you need to restore the Cisco IOS to flash memory to replace an original file that has been damaged or if you want to upgrade the IOS? You can download the
file from a TFTP server to flash memory by using the copy tftp flash command. This
command requires the IP address of the TFTP host and the name of the file you want to
download.

But before you begin, make sure the file you want to place in flash memory is in the
default TFTP directory on your host. When you issue the command, TFTP won't ask you
where the file is, so if the file you want to use isn't in the default directory of the TFTP host,
this just won't work.

```
Router#copy tftp flash
Address or name of remote host []?1.1.1.2
Source filename []?c2800nm-advsecurityk9-mz.124-12.bin
Destination filename [c2800nm-advsecurityk9-mz.124-12.bin]?[enter]
%Warning: There is a file already existing with this name Do you want to over
write? [confirm][enter]
Accessing tftp://1.1.1.2/c2800nm-advsecurityk9-mz.124-12.bin...
```

```
Loading c2800nm-advsecurityk9-mz.124-12.bin from 1.1.1.2 (via
   FastEthernet0/0): !!!!!!!!!!!!!!!!!!!!!!!!!!!!!!!!!!!!!!!!!!!!!!!!!!!!!!!!!!!!!
!!!!!!!!!!!!!!
[OK - 21710744 bytes]


21710744 bytes copied in 82.880 secs (261954 bytes/sec)
Router#
```

In the preceding example, I copied the same file into flash memory, so it asked me if I wanted to overwrite it. Remember that you are "playing" with files in flash memory. If I had just corrupted my file by overwriting it, I won't know until I reboot the router. Be careful with this command! If the file is corrupted, you'll need to do an IOS restore from ROM monitor mode.

If you are loading a new file and you don't have enough room in flash memory to store both the new and existing copies, the router will ask to erase the contents of flash memory before writing the new file into flash memory.

 A Cisco router can become a TFTP server for another router by using an image that's stored in flash memory. The global configuration command is `tftp-server flash:ios_name`.

Using the Cisco IOS File System (Cisco IFS)

Cisco has created a file system called Cisco IFS that allows you to work with files and directories just as you would from a Windows DOS prompt. The commands you use are `dir`, `copy`, `more`, `delete`, `erase` or `format`, `cd` and `pwd`, and `mkdir` and `rmdir`.

Working with IFS gives you the ability to view all files—even those on remote servers. And you definitely want to find out if an image on one of your remote servers is valid before you copy it, right? You also need to know how big it is—size matters here! It's also a really good idea to take a look at the remote server's configuration and make sure it's all good before loading that file on your router.

It's very cool that IFS makes the file system user interface universal—it's not platform specific anymore. You now get to use the same syntax for all your commands on all of your routers, no matter the platform!

Sound too good to be true? Well, it kind of is because you'll find out that support for all commands on each file system and platform just isn't there. But it's really no big deal since various file systems differ in the actions they perform; the commands that aren't relevant to a particular file system are the very ones that aren't supported. Be assured that any file system or platform will fully support all the commands you need to manage it.

Another cool IFS feature is that it cuts down on all those obligatory prompts for a lot of the commands. If you want to enter a command, all you have to do is type all the necessary info straight into the command line—no more jumping through hoops of prompts! So, if you want to copy a file to an FTP server, all you'd do is first indicate where the desired source file is on your router, pinpoint where the destination file is to be on the FTP server, determine the username and password you're going to use when you want to connect to that server, and type it all in on one line—sleek! And for those of you resistant to change, you can still have the router prompt for all the information it needs and enjoy entering a more elegantly minimized version of the command than you did before.

But even in spite of all this, your router might still prompt you—even if you did everything right in your command line. It comes down to how you have the `file prompt` command configured and which command you're trying to use. But no worries—if that happens, the default value will be entered right there in the command, and all you have to do is hit Enter to verify the correct values.

IFS also lets you explore various directories and inventory files in any directory you want. Plus, you can make subdirectories in flash memory or on a card, but you get to do that only if you're working on one of the more recent platforms.

And get this—the new file system interface uses URLs to determine the whereabouts of a file. So, just as they pinpoint places on the Web, URLs now indicate where files are on your Cisco router or even on a remote file server! You just type URLs right into your commands to identify where the file or directory is. It's really that easy—to copy a file from one place to another, you simply enter the `copy source-url destination-url` command—sweet! IFS URLs are a tad different from what you're used to, though, and there's an array of formats to use that vary depending on where, exactly, the file is that you're after.

You're going to use Cisco IFS commands pretty much the same way that you used the copy command in the IOS section earlier:

- For backing up the IOS
- For upgrading the IOS
- For viewing text files

With all that down, let's take a look at the common IFS commands available to you for managing the IOS. I'll get into configuration files soon, but for now I'll get you started with going over the basics used to manage the new Cisco IOS.

dir   Same as with Windows, this command lets you view files in a directory. Type **dir**, hit Enter, and by default you get the contents of the `flash:/` directory output.

copy   This is one popular command, often used to upgrade, restore, or back up an IOS. But as I said, when you use it, it's really important to focus on the details—what you're copying, where it's coming from, and where it's going to land.

more   Same as with Unix, this will take a text file and let you look at it on a card. You can use it to check out your configuration file or your backup configuration file. I'll go over it more when I get into actual configuration.

show file   This command will give you the skinny on a specified file or file system, but it's kind of obscure because people don't use it a lot.

delete   Three guesses—yep, it deletes stuff. But with some types of routers, it doesn't work as well as you'd think. That's because even though it whacks the file, it doesn't always free up the space it was using. To actually get the space back, you have to use something called the squeeze command, too.

erase/format   Use these with care—make sure that when you're copying files, you say no to the dialog that asks you if you want to erase the file system! The type of memory you're using determines whether you can nix the flash drive.

cd/pwd   Same as with Unix and DOS, cd is the command you use to change directories. Use the pwd command to print (show) the working directory.

mkdir/rmdir   Use these commands on certain routers and switches to create and delete directories—the mkdir command for creation and the rmdir command for deletion. Use the cd and pwd commands to change into these directories.

Using the Cisco IFS to Upgrade an IOS

Let's take a look at some of these Cisco IFS commands on my ISR router (1841 series) with a hostname of R1.

I'll start with the pwd command to verify my default directory and then use the dir command to verify the contents of the default directory (flash:/).

```
R1#pwd
flash:
R1#dir
Directory of flash:/
    1  -rw-     13937472   Dec 20 2006 19:58:18 +00:00   c1841-ipbase-
    mz.124-1c.bin
    2  -rw-         1821   Dec 20 2006 20:11:24 +00:00   sdmconfig-18xx.cfg
    3  -rw-      4734464   Dec 20 2006 20:12:00 +00:00   sdm.tar
    4  -rw-       833024   Dec 20 2006 20:12:24 +00:00   es.tar
    5  -rw-      1052160   Dec 20 2006 20:12:50 +00:00   common.tar
    6  -rw-         1038   Dec 20 2006 20:13:10 +00:00   home.shtml
    7  -rw-       102400   Dec 20 2006 20:13:30 +00:00   home.tar
    8  -rw-       491213   Dec 20 2006 20:13:56 +00:00   128MB.sdf
    9  -rw-      1684577   Dec 20 2006 20:14:34 +00:00   securedesktop-
    ios-3.1.1.27-k9.pkg
   10  -rw-       398305   Dec 20 2006 20:15:04 +00:00   sslclient-win-
    1.1.0.154.pkg


32071680 bytes total (8818688 bytes free)
```

What you can see here is that I have the basic IP IOS (c1841-ipbase-mz.124-1c.bin). Looks like I need to upgrade my 1841. You've just got to love how Cisco puts the IOS type in the filename now! You can see the size of the IOS is about 14MB from the previous output, but you can also check the size of the file that's in flash with the show file command (show flash would also work).

```
R1#show file info flash:c1841-ipbase-mz.124-1c.bin
flash:c1841-ipbase-mz.124-1c.bin:
  type is image (elf) []
  file size is 13937472 bytes, run size is 14103140 bytes
  Runnable image, entry point 0x8000F000, run from ram
```

With a file that size, the existing IOS will have to be erased before you can add the new IOS file (c1841-advipservicesk9-mz.124-12.bin), which exceeds 21MB. You'll use the delete command, but remember, you can play with any file in flash memory and nothing serious will happen until you reboot—that is, if you made a mistake. So, obviously, and as I pointed out earlier, you need to be majorly careful here!

```
R1#delete flash:c1841-ipbase-mz.124-1c.bin
Delete filename [c1841-ipbase-mz.124-1c.bin]?[enter]
Delete flash:c1841-ipbase-mz.124-1c.bin? [confirm][enter]
R1#sh flash
-#- -length- ---date/time--- path
1         1821 Dec 20 2006 20:11:24 +00:00 sdmconfig-18xx.cfg
2      4734464 Dec 20 2006 20:12:00 +00:00 sdm.tar
3       833024 Dec 20 2006 20:12:24 +00:00 es.tar
4      1052160 Dec 20 2006 20:12:50 +00:00 common.tar
5         1038 Dec 20 2006 20:13:10 +00:00 home.shtml
6       102400 Dec 20 2006 20:13:30 +00:00 home.tar
7       491213 Dec 20 2006 20:13:56 +00:00 128MB.sdf
8      1684577 Dec 20 2006 20:14:34 +00:00 securedesktop-ios-3.1.1.27-k9.pkg
9       398305 Dec 20 2006 20:15:04 +00:00 sslclient-win-1.1.0.154.pkg
22757376 bytes available (9314304 bytes used)
R1#sh file info flash:c1841-ipbase-mz.124-1c.bin
%Error opening flash:c1841-ipbase-mz.124-1c.bin (File not found)
R1#
```

So, with the preceding commands, I deleted the existing file and then verified the deletion by using both the show flash and show file commands. Let's add the new file with the copy command.

```
R1#copy tftp://1.1.1.2//c1841-advipservicesk9-mz.124-12.bin/ flash:/
    c1841-advipservicesk9-mz.124-12.bin
```

```
Source filename [/c1841-advipservicesk9-mz.124-12.bin/]?[enter]
Destination filename [c1841-advipservicesk9-mz.124-12.bin]?[enter]
Loading /c1841-advipservicesk9-mz.124-12.bin/ from 1.1.1.2 (via
    FastEthernet0/0): !!!!!!!!!!!!!!!!!!!!!!!!!!!!!!!!!!!!!!!!
[output cut]
!!!!!!!!!!!!!!!!!!!!!!!!!!!!!!!!!!!!!!!!!!!!!!!!!!!!!!!!
[OK - 22103052 bytes]
22103052 bytes copied in 72.008 secs (306953 bytes/sec)
R1#sh flash
-#- -length- ---date/time--- path
1         1821 Dec 20 2006 20:11:24 +00:00 sdmconfig-18xx.cfg
2      4734464 Dec 20 2006 20:12:00 +00:00 sdm.tar
3       833024 Dec 20 2006 20:12:24 +00:00 es.tar
4      1052160 Dec 20 2006 20:12:50 +00:00 common.tar
5         1038 Dec 20 2006 20:13:10 +00:00 home.shtml
6       102400 Dec 20 2006 20:13:30 +00:00 home.tar
7       491213 Dec 20 2006 20:13:56 +00:00 128MB.sdf
8      1684577 Dec 20 2006 20:14:34 +00:00 securedesktop-ios-3.1.1.27-k9.pkg
9       398305 Dec 20 2006 20:15:04 +00:00 sslclient-win-1.1.0.154.pkg
10    22103052 Mar 10 2007 19:40:50 +00:00 c1841-advipservicesk9-mz.124-12.bin
651264 bytes available (31420416 bytes used)
R1#
```

You can check the file information as well with the show file command.

```
R1#sh file information flash:c1841-advipservicesk9-mz.124-12.bin
flash:c1841-advipservicesk9-mz.124-12.bin:
  type is image (elf) []
  file size is 22103052 bytes, run size is 22268736 bytes
  Runnable image, entry point 0x8000F000, run from ram
```

Remember that the IOS is expanded into RAM when the router boots, so the new IOS will not run until you reload the router. So, now let's take a look at how to use the Cisco SDM to upgrade a router's IOS.

I really recommend you play with the Cisco IFS commands on a router just to get a good feel for them because, as I've said, they can definitely give you some grief at first!

WARNING   I mention "safer methods" a lot in this chapter. Clearly, I've caused myself some serious pain not being careful enough when working in flash memory! I cannot tell you enough—pay attention when messing around with flash memory!

One of the brilliant features of the ISR routers is that they use the physical flash cards that are accessible from the front or back of any router. You can pull these flash cards out, put them in an appropriate slot in your PC, and the card will show up as a drive. You can then add, change, and delete files. Just put the flash card back in your router and power up—instant upgrade. Nice!

Backing Up and Restoring the Cisco Configuration

Any changes that you make to the router configuration are stored in the running-config file. And if you don't enter a copy run start command after you make a change to running-config, that change will go poof if the router reboots or gets powered down. So, you probably want to make another backup of the configuration information just in case the router or switch completely dies on you. Even if your machine is healthy and happy, it's good to have for reference and documentation reasons.

In the following sections, I'll describe how to copy the configuration of a router to a TFTP server and how to restore that configuration.

Backing Up the Cisco Router Configuration

To copy the router's configuration from a router to a TFTP server, you can use either the copy running-config tftp or the copy startup-config tftp command. Either one will back up the router configuration that's currently running in DRAM or that's stored in NVRAM.

Verifying the Current Configuration

To verify the configuration in DRAM, use the show running-config command (sh run for short) like this:

```
Router#show running-config
Building configuration...


Current configuration : 776 bytes
!
version 12.4
```

The current configuration information indicates that the router is running version 12.4 of the IOS.

Verifying the Stored Configuration

Next, you should check the configuration stored in NVRAM. To see this, use the `show` `startup-config` command (`sh start` for short) like this:

```
Router#show startup-config
Using 776 out of 245752 bytes
!
version 12.4
```

The second line shows you how much room your backup configuration is using. Here, you can see that NVRAM is 245KB (again, memory is easier to see with the `show version` command when you're using an ISR router) and that only 776 bytes of it are used.

If you're not sure that the files are the same and the `running-config` file is what you want to use, then use the `copy running-config startup-config` command. This will help you ensure that both files are in fact the same. I'll go through this with you in the next section.

Copying the Current Configuration to NVRAM

By copying the `running-config` to NVRAM as a backup, as shown in the following output, you're assured that your running-config will always be reloaded if the router gets rebooted. In the new IOS version 12.0, you're prompted for the filename you want to use.

```
Router#copy running-config startup-config
Destination filename [startup-config]?[enter]
Building configuration...
[OK]
Router#
```

The reason the filename prompt appears is that there are now so many options you can use when using the copy command.

```
Router#copy running-config ?
  archive:        Copy to archive: file system
  flash:          Copy to flash: file system
  ftp:            Copy to ftp: file system
  http:           Copy to http: file system
  https:          Copy to https: file system
  ips-sdf         Update (merge with) IPS signature configuration
  null:           Copy to null: file system
  nvram:          Copy to nvram: file system
  rcp:            Copy to rcp: file system
  running-config  Update (merge with) current system configuration
  scp:            Copy to scp: file system
```

```
startup-config   Copy to startup configuration
syslog:          Copy to syslog: file system
system:          Copy to system: file system
tftp:            Copy to tftp: file system
xmodem:          Copy to xmodem: file system
ymodem:          Copy to ymodem: file system
```

I'll go over the copy command again in a minute.

Copying the Configuration to a TFTP Server

Once the file is copied to NVRAM, you can make a second backup to a TFTP server by using the copy running-config tftp command (copy run tftp for short), like this:

```
Router#copy running-config tftp
Address or name of remote host []?1.1.1.2
Destination filename [router-confg]?todd-confg
!!
776 bytes copied in 0.800 secs (970 bytes/sec)
Router#
```

In the preceding example, I named the file todd-confg because I had not set a hostname for the router. If you have a hostname already configured, the command will automatically use the hostname plus the extension -confg as the name of the file.

Restoring the Cisco Router Configuration

If you've changed your router's running-config file and want to restore the configuration to the version in the startup-config file, the easiest way to do this is to use the copy startup-config running-config command (copy start run for short). You can also use the older Cisco command config mem to restore a configuration. Of course, this will work only if you copied running-config into NVRAM before making any changes!

If you did copy the router's configuration to a TFTP server as a second backup, you can restore the configuration using the copy tftp running-config command (copy tftp run for short) or the copy tftp startup-config command (copy tftp start for short), as shown here (the old command that provides this function is config net):

```
Router#copy tftp running-config
Address or name of remote host []?1.1.1.2
Source filename []?todd-confg
Destination filename[running-config]?[enter]
Accessing tftp://1.1.1.2/todd-confg...
```

```
Loading todd-confg from 1.1.1.2 (via FastEthernet0/0): !
[OK - 776 bytes]
776 bytes copied in 9.212 secs (84 bytes/sec)
Router#
*Mar  7 17:53:34.071: %SYS-5-CONFIG_I: Configured from
    tftp://1.1.1.2/todd-confg by console
Router#
```

The configuration file is an ASCII text file, meaning that before you copy the configuration stored on a TFTP server back to a router, you can make changes to the file with any text editor. Last, notice that the command was changed to a URL of `tftp://1.1.1.2/todd-config`. This is the Cisco IOS File System (IFS)—as discussed earlier—and I'll use that to back up and restore the configuration in a minute.

It is important to remember that when you copy or merge a configuration from a TFTP server to a freshly erased and rebooted router's RAM, the interfaces are shut down by default, and you must manually go and enable each interface with the `no shutdown` command.

Erasing the Configuration

To delete the `startup-config` file on a Cisco router, use the command `erase startup-config`, like this:

```
Router#erase startup-config
Erasing the nvram filesystem will remove all configuration files!
    Continue? [confirm][enter]
[OK]
Erase of nvram: complete
*Mar  7 17:56:20.407: %SYS-7-NV_BLOCK_INIT: Initialized the geometry of nvram
Router#reload
System configuration has been modified. Save? [yes/no]:n
Proceed with reload? [confirm][enter]
 *Mar  7 17:56:31.059: %SYS-5-RELOAD: Reload requested by console.
    Reload Reason: Reload Command.
```

This command deletes the contents of NVRAM on the router. If you type **reload** at privileged mode and say no to saving changes, the router will reload and come up into setup mode.

Using the Cisco IOS File System to Manage Your Router's Configuration (Cisco IFS)

Using the old, faithful copy command is still useful, and I recommend it. However, you still need to know about the Cisco IFS. The first thing I'll do is use the show file command to see the contents of NVRAM and RAM.

```
R3#show file information nvram:startup-config
nvram:startup-config:
  type is config
R3#cd nvram:
R3#pwd
nvram:/
R3#dir
Directory of nvram:/

  190  -rw-        830              <no date>  startup-config
  191  --          5              <no date>  private-config
  192  -rw-        830              <no date>  underlying-config
    1  -rw-          0              <no date>  ifIndex-table
196600 bytes total (194689 bytes free)
```

There really are no other commands that will actually show you the contents of NVRAM. However, I am not sure how helpful it is to see them either. Let's look at the contents of RAM.

```
R3#cd system:
R3#pwd
system:/
R3#dir ?
  /all            List all files
  /recursive      List files recursively
  all-filesystems List files on all filesystems
  archive:        Directory or file name
  cns:            Directory or file name
  flash:          Directory or file name
  null:           Directory or file name
  nvram:          Directory or file name
  system:         Directory or file name
```

```
   xmodem:            Directory or file name
   ymodem:            Directory or file name
   <cr>
R3#dir
Directory of system:/

   3  dr-x           0              <no date>  lib
  33  dr-x           0              <no date>  memory
   1  -rw-         750              <no date>  running-config
   2  dr-x           0              <no date>  vfiles
```

Again, not too exciting. Let's use the copy command with the Cisco IFS to copy a file from a TFTP host to RAM. First, let's try the old command config net that hasn't been used for the last 10 years or so to accomplish this same feat.

```
R3#config net
Host or network configuration file [host]?[enter]
This command has been replaced by the command:
        'copy <url> system:/running-config'
Address or name of remote host [255.255.255.255]?
```

Although the output tells you that the old command has been replaced with the new URL command, the old command will still will work. Let's try it with the Cisco IFS. The "URL" is used as is the IP address of the TFTP server, followed by the backup configuration, followed by the destination name:

```
R3#copy tftp://1.1.1.2/todd-confg system://running-config
Destination filename [running-config]?[enter]
Accessing tftp://1.1.1.2/todd-confg...Loading todd-confg from 1.1.1.2
    (via FastEthernet0/0): !
[OK - 776 bytes]
[OK]
776 bytes copied in 13.816 secs (56 bytes/sec)
R3#
*Mar 10 22:12:59.819: %SYS-5-CONFIG_I:
Configured from tftp://1.1.1.2/todd-confg by console
```

I guess I can say that this was easier than using the copy tftp run command—Cisco says it is, so who am I to argue? Maybe it just takes some getting used to.

Using Cisco Discovery Protocol

Cisco Discovery Protocol (CDP) is a proprietary protocol designed by Cisco to help administrators collect information about both locally attached devices. By using CDP, you can gather hardware and protocol information about neighbor devices, which is useful info for troubleshooting and documenting the network.

In the following sections, I will discuss the CDP timer and CDP commands used to verify your network.

Getting CDP Timers and Holdtime Information

The show cdp command (sh cdp for short) gives you information about two CDP global parameters that can be configured on Cisco devices.

- *CDP timer* is how often CDP packets are transmitted out all active interfaces.
- *CDP holdtime* is the amount of time that the device will hold packets received from neighbor devices.

Both Cisco routers and Cisco switches use the same parameters.

The output on the Corp router looks like this:

```
Corp#sh cdp
Global CDP information:
        Sending CDP packets every 60 seconds
        Sending a holdtime value of 180 seconds
        Sending CDPv2 advertisements is  enabled
```

Use the global commands cdp holdtime and cdp timer to configure the CDP holdtime and timer on a router.

```
Corp(config)#cdp ?
  advertise-v2      CDP sends version-2 advertisements
  holdtime          Specify the holdtime (in sec) to be sent in packets
  log               Log messages generated by CDP
  run               Enable CDP
  source-interface  Insert the interface's IP in all CDP packets
  timer             Specify rate (in sec) at which CDP packets are sent
Corp(config)#cdp holdtime ?
  <10-255> Length  of time  (in sec) that receiver must keep this packet
Corp(config)#cdp timer ?
  <5-254>  Rate at which CDP packets are sent (in  sec)
```

You can turn off CDP completely with the `no cdp run` command from the global con-figuration mode of a router. To turn CDP off or on for an interface, use the `no cdp enable` and `cdp enable` commands. Be patient—I'll work through these with you in a second.

Gathering Neighbor Information

The `show cdp neighbor` command (`sh cdp nei` for short) delivers information about directly connected devices. It's important to remember that CDP packets aren't passed through a Cisco switch and that you see only what's directly attached. So, this means that if your router is connected to a switch, you won't see any of the devices hooked up to that switch.

The following output shows the `show cdp neighbor` command used on my Corp 2811 router:

```
Corp#sh cdp neighbor
Capability Codes: R - Router, T - Trans Bridge, B - Source Route Bridge
                  S - Switch, H - Host, I - IGMP, r - Repeater
Device ID    Local Intrfce   Holdtme   Capability  Platform  Port ID
ap           Fas 0/1          165          T I      AIR-AP124 Fas 0
R2           Ser 0/1/0        140         R S I     2801      Ser 0/2/0
R3           Ser 0/0/1        157         R S I     1841      Ser 0/0/1
R1           Ser 0/2/0        154         R S I     1841      Ser 0/0/1
R1           Ser 0/0/0        154         R S I     1841      Ser 0/0/0
Corp#
```

Okay, I am directly connected with a console cable to the Corp router, and the router is directly connected to four devices. I have two connections to the R1 router. The device ID shows the configured hostname of the connected device, the local interface is my interface, and the port ID is the remote devices' directly connected interface. All you get to view are directly connected devices.

Table 5.5 summarizes the information displayed by the `show cdp neighbor` command for each device.

TABLE 5.5   Output of the `show cdp neighbor` command

Field	Description
Device ID	The hostname of the device directly connected.
Local Interface	The port or interface on which you are receiving the CDP packet.

TABLE 5.5   Output of the show cdp neighbor command *(continued)*

Field	Description
Holdtime	The remaining amount of time the router will hold the information before discarding it if no more CDP packets are received.
Capability	The capability of the neighbor, such as the router, switch, or repeater. The capability codes are listed at the top of the command output.
Platform	The type of Cisco device directly connected. In the previous output, a 1240AP, 2801 router, and two 1841 routers are directly connected to the Corp router. Although three 1841s display in the output, there are only two 1841s that the Corp router are connected to; there is just a dual link to one of the devices.
Port ID	The neighbor device's port or interface on which the CDP packets are multicast.

It is imperative that you can look at the output of a show cdp neighbor command and decipher the neighboring device's capability (i.e., router or switch), model number (platform), your port connecting to that device (local interface), and the port of the neighbor connecting to you (port ID).

Another command that will deliver the goods on neighbor information is the show cdp neighbor detail command (show cdp nei de for short). This command can be run on both routers and switches, and it displays detailed information about each device connected to the device you're running the command on. Check out this router output for an example:

```
Corp#sh cdp neighbor detail
-------------
Device ID: ap
Entry address(es): 10.1.1.2
Platform: cisco AIR-AP1242AG-A-K9, Capabilities: Trans-Bridge IGMP
Interface: FastEthernet0/1,  Port ID (outgoing port): FastEthernet0
Holdtime : 122 sec


Version :
Cisco IOS Software, C1240 Software (C1240-K9W7-M), Version 12.3(8)JEA,
    RELEASE SOFTWARE (fc2)
```

Technical Support: http://www.cisco.com/techsupport
Copyright (c) 1986-2006 by Cisco Systems, Inc.
Compiled Wed 23-Aug-06 16:45 by kellythw

advertisement version: 2
Duplex: full
Power drawn: 15.000 Watts

Device ID: R2
Entry address(es):
  IP address: 10.4.4.2
Platform: Cisco 2801, Capabilities: Router Switch IGMP
Interface: Serial0/1/0, Port ID (outgoing port): Serial0/2/0
Holdtime : 135 sec

Version :
Cisco IOS Software, 2801 Software (C2801-ADVENTERPRISEK9-M),
    Experimental Version 12.4(20050525:193634) [jezhao-ani 145]
Copyright (c) 1986-2005 by Cisco Systems, Inc.
Compiled Fri 27-May-05 23:53 by jezhao

advertisement version: 2
VTP Management Domain: ''

Device ID: R3
Entry address(es):
  IP address: 10.5.5.1
Platform: Cisco 1841, Capabilities: Router Switch IGMP
Interface: Serial0/0/1, Port ID (outgoing port): Serial0/0/1
Holdtime : 152 sec

Version :
Cisco IOS Software, 1841 Software (C1841-IPBASE-M), Version 12.4(1c),
    RELEASE SOFTWARE (fc1)
Technical Support: http://www.cisco.com/techsupport
Copyright (c) 1986-2005 by Cisco Systems, Inc.
Compiled Tue 25-Oct-05 17:10 by evmiller

```
advertisement version: 2
VTP Management Domain: ''
-------------
[output cut]
Corp#
```

What are you being shown here? First, you're given the hostname and IP address of all directly connected devices. In addition to the same information displayed by the show cdp neighbor command (see Table 7.5), the show cdp neighbor detail command gives you the IOS version of the neighbor device.

 Remember that you can see the IP address of only directly connected devices.

The show cdp entry * command displays the same information as the show cdp neighbor detail command. Here's an example of the router output using the show cdp entry * command:

```
Corp#sh cdp entry *
-------------
Device ID: ap
Entry address(es):
Platform: cisco AIR-AP1242AG-A-K9, Capabilities: Trans-Bridge IGMP
Interface: FastEthernet0/1,  Port ID (outgoing port): FastEthernet0
Holdtime : 160 sec


Version :
Cisco IOS Software, C1240 Software (C1240-K9W7-M), Version 12.3(8)JEA,
    RELEASE SOFTWARE (fc2)
Technical Support: http://www.cisco.com/techsupport
Copyright (c) 1986-2006 by Cisco Systems, Inc.
Compiled Wed 23-Aug-06 16:45 by kellythw


advertisement version: 2
Duplex: full
Power drawn: 15.000 Watts
-------------
Device ID: R2
Entry address(es):
  IP address: 10.4.4.2
Platform: Cisco 2801,  Capabilities: Router Switch IGMP
 —More—
[output cut]
```

There isn't any difference between the show cdp neighbor detail and show cdp entry * commands. However, the sh cdp entry * command has two options that the show cdp neighbor detail command does not.

```
Corp#sh cdp entry * ?
  protocol  Protocol information
  version   Version information
  |         Output modifiers
  <cr>
Corp#show cdp entry * protocols
Protocol information for ap :
  IP address: 10.1.1.2
Protocol information for R2 :
  IP address: 10.4.4.2
Protocol information for R3 :
  IP address: 10.5.5.1
Protocol information for R1 :
  IP address: 10.3.3.2
Protocol information for R1 :
  IP address: 10.2.2.2
```

The preceding output of the show cdp entry * protocols command can show you just the IP addresses of each directly connected neighbor. The show cdp entry * version command will show you only the IOS version of your directly connected neighbors.

```
Corp#show cdp entry * version
Version information for ap :
  Cisco IOS Software, C1240 Software (C1240-K9W7-M), Version
    12.3(8)JEA, RELEASE SOFTWARE (fc2)
Technical Support: http://www.cisco.com/techsupport
Copyright (c) 1986-2006 by Cisco Systems, Inc.
Compiled Wed 23-Aug-06 16:45 by kellythw


Version information for R2 :
  Cisco IOS Software, 2801 Software (C2801-ADVENTERPRISEK9-M),
    Experimental Version 12.4(20050525:193634) [jezhao-ani 145]
Copyright (c) 1986-2005 by Cisco Systems, Inc.
Compiled Fri 27-May-05 23:53 by jezhao


Version information for R3 :
  Cisco IOS Software, 1841 Software (C1841-IPBASE-M), Version 12.4(1c),
    RELEASE SOFTWARE (fc1)
Technical Support: http://www.cisco.com/techsupport
```

```
Copyright (c) 1986-2005 by Cisco Systems, Inc.
Compiled Tue 25-Oct-05 17:10 by evmiller


 --More--
[output cut]
```

Although the show cdp neighbor detail and show cdp entry commands are very similar, the show cdp entry command allows you to display only one line of output for each directly connected neighbor, whereas the show cdp neighbor detail command does not. Next, let's look at the show cdp traffic command.

Gathering Interface Traffic Information

The show cdp traffic command displays information about interface traffic, including the number of CDP packets sent and received and the errors with CDP.

The following output shows the show cdp traffic command used on the Corp router:

```
Corp#sh cdp traffic
CDP counters :
        Total packets output: 911, Input: 524
        Hdr syntax: 0, Chksum error: 0, Encaps failed: 2
        No memory: 0, Invalid packet: 0, Fragmented: 0
        CDP version 1 advertisements output: 0, Input: 0
        CDP version 2 advertisements output: 911, Input: 524
```

This is not really the most important information you can gather from a router, but it does show how many CDP packets are sent and received on a device.

Gathering Port and Interface Information

The show cdp interface command gives you the CDP status on router interfaces or switch ports.

As I said earlier, you can turn off CDP completely on a router by using the no cdp run command. But remember that you can also turn off CDP on a per-interface basis with the no cdp enable command. You enable a port with the cdp enable command. All ports and interfaces default to cdp enable.

On a router, the show cdp interface command displays information about each interface using CDP, including the encapsulation on the line, the timer, and the holdtime for each interface. Here's an example of this command's output on the ISR router:

```
Corp#sh cdp interface
FastEthernet0/0 is administratively down, line protocol is down
  Encapsulation ARPA
```

```
    Sending CDP packets every 60 seconds
    Holdtime is 180 seconds
FastEthernet0/1 is up, line protocol is up
    Encapsulation ARPA
    Sending CDP packets every 60 seconds
    Holdtime is 180 seconds
Serial0/0/0 is up, line protocol is up
    Encapsulation HDLC
    Sending CDP packets every 60 seconds
    Holdtime is 180 seconds
Serial0/0/1 is up, line protocol is up
    Encapsulation HDLC
    Sending CDP packets every 60 seconds
    Holdtime is 180 seconds
Serial0/1/0 is up, line protocol is up
    Encapsulation HDLC
    Sending CDP packets every 60 seconds
    Holdtime is 180 seconds
Serial0/2/0 is up, line protocol is up
    Encapsulation HDLC
    Sending CDP packets every 60 seconds
    Holdtime is 180 seconds
```

The preceding output is nice because it always tells you the interface's status. To turn off CDP on one interface on a router, use the no cdp enable command from interface configuration mode.

```
Corp#config t
Corp(config)#int s0/0/0
Corp(config-if)#no cdp enable
Corp(config-if)#do show cdp interface
FastEthernet0/0 is administratively down, line protocol is down
    Encapsulation ARPA
    Sending CDP packets every 60 seconds
    Holdtime is 180 seconds
FastEthernet0/1 is up, line protocol is up
    Encapsulation ARPA
    Sending CDP packets every 60 seconds
    Holdtime is 180 seconds
```

```
Serial0/0/1 is up, line protocol is up
  Encapsulation HDLC
  Sending CDP packets every 60 seconds
  Holdtime is 180 seconds
Serial0/1/0 is up, line protocol is up
  Encapsulation HDLC
  Sending CDP packets every 60 seconds
  Holdtime is 180 seconds
Serial0/2/0 is up, line protocol is up
  Encapsulation HDLC
  Sending CDP packets every 60 seconds
  Holdtime is 180 seconds
Corp(config-if)#
```

Notice that serial %/0 isn't listed in the router output. To get that output, you'd have to perform a cdp enable on serial %/0. It would then show up in the output.

```
Corp(config-if)#cdp enable
Corp(config-if)#^Z
Corp#
```

Real World Scenario

CDP Can Save Lives!

Karen has just been hired as a senior network consultant at a large hospital in Dallas, Texas. She is expected to be able to take care of any problem that comes up. No stress here—she only has to worry about people possibly not getting the right health care if the network goes down. Talk about a potential life-or-death situation!

Karen starts her job happily. Soon, of course, the network has some problems. She asks one of the junior administrators for a network map so she can troubleshoot the network. This person tells her that the old senior administrator (who just got fired) had them with him, and now no one can find them—ouch!

Doctors are calling every couple of minutes because they can't get the necessary information they need to take care of their patients. What should she do?

CDP to the rescue! Thank God this hospital has all Cisco routers and switches and that CDP is enabled by default on all Cisco devices. Also, luckily, the disgruntled administrator who just got fired didn't turn off CDP on any devices before he left.

All Karen has to do now is use the show cdp neighbor command to find all the information she needs about each device to help draw out the hospital network and save lives!

The only snag for you nailing this in your own network is if you don't know the passwords of all those devices or you won't be able to telnet between devices. Your only hope then is to somehow find out the access passwords or to perform password recovery on them.

So, use CDP—you never know when you may end up saving someone's life.

This is a true story.

Documenting a Network Topology Using CDP

As the title of this section implies, I'm now going to show you how to document a sample network by using CDP. You'll learn to determine the appropriate router types, interface types, and IP addresses of various interfaces using only CDP commands and the show running-config command. And you can only console into the Lab_A router to document the network. You'll have to assign any remote routers the next IP address in each range. Figure 5.2 is what you'll use to complete the documentation.

FIGURE 5.2   Documenting a network topology using CDP

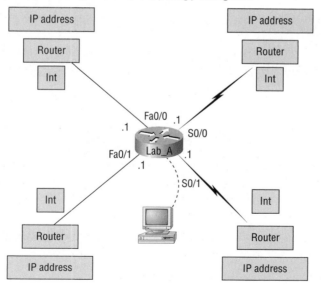

In this output, you can see that you have a router with four interfaces: two FastEthernet and two serial. First, determine the IP addresses of each interface by using the show running-config command.

```
Lab_A#sh running-config
Building configuration...

Current configuration : 960 bytes
!
version 12.2
service timestamps debug uptime
service timestamps log uptime
no service password-encryption
!
hostname Lab_A
!
ip subnet-zero
!
!
interface FastEthernet0/0
 ip address 192.168.21.1 255.255.255.0
 duplex auto
!
interface FastEthernet0/1
 ip address 192.168.18.1 255.255.255.0
 duplex auto
!
interface Serial0/0
ip address 192.168.23.1 255.255.255.0
!
interface Serial0/1
ip address 192.168.28.1 255.255.255.0
!
ip classless
!
line con 0
line aux 0
line vty 0 4
!
end
```

With this step completed, you can now write down the IP addresses of the Lab_A router's four interfaces. Next, you need to determine the type of device on the other end of each of these interfaces. It's easy to do this—just use the show cdp neighbor command.

```
Lab_A#sh cdp neighbor
Capability Codes: R - Router, T - Trans Bridge, B - Source Route Bridge
S - Switch, H - Host, I - IGMP, r - Repeater
Device ID   Local Intrfce   Holdtme   Capability Platform Port ID
Lab_B       Fas 0/0         178           R        2501    E0
Lab_C       Fas 0/1         137           R        2621    Fa0/0
Lab_D       Ser 0/0         178           R        2514    S1
Lab_E       Ser 0/1         137           R        2620    S0/1
Lab_A#
```

You've got a good deal of information now! By using both the show running-config and show cdp neighbor commands, you know about all the IP addresses of the Lab_A router plus the types of routers connected to each of the Lab_A router's links and all the interfaces of the remote routers.

And by using all the information gathered from show running-config and show cdp neighbor, you can now create the topology in Figure 5.3.

FIGURE 5.3   Network topology documented

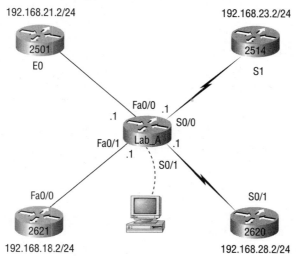

If you needed to, you could've also used the show cdp neighbor detail command to view the neighbor's IP addresses. But since you know the IP addresses of each link on the Lab_A router, you already know what the next available IP address is going to be.

Link Layer Discovery Protocol (LLDP)

Before I move away from CDP, I need to discuss a nonproprietary discovery protocol that provides pretty much the same information as CDP but works in multivendor networks.

The IEEE created a new standardized discovery protocol called 802.1AB for Station and Media Access Control Connectivity Discovery. I'll just call it Link Layer Discovery Protocol (LLDP).

LLDP defines basic discovery capabilities, but it was also enhanced to specifically address the voice application, and this version is called LLDP-MED (Media Endpoint Discovery). LLDP and LLDP-MED are not compatible.

You can find more information here:

`www.cisco.com/en/US/docs/ios/cether/configuration/guide/ce_lldp-med.html`

and here:

`www.cisco.com/en/US/technologies/tk652/tk701/technologies_white_paper0900aecd804cd46d.html`

Using Telnet

Telnet, part of the TCP/IP protocol suite, is a virtual terminal protocol that allows you to make connections to remote devices, gather information, and run programs.

After your routers and switches are configured, you can use the Telnet program to reconfigure and/or check up on them without using a console cable. You run the Telnet program by typing **telnet** from any command prompt (DOS or Cisco). You need to have VTY passwords set on the routers for this to work.

Remember, you can't use CDP to gather information about routers and switches that aren't directly connected to your device. But you can use the Telnet application to connect to your neighbor devices and then run CDP on those remote devices to get information on them.

You can issue the `telnet` command from any router prompt like this:

```
Corp#telnet 10.2.2.2
Trying 10.2.2.2 ... Open


Password required, but none set


[Connection to 10.2.2.2 closed by foreign host]
Corp#
```

As you can see, I didn't set my passwords—how embarrassing! Remember that the VTY ports on a router are configured as login, meaning that you have to either set the VTY passwords or use the no login command. You can review setting passwords in Chapter 4, "Cisco's Internetworking Operating System (IOS)," if needed.

 NOTE If you find you can't telnet into a device, it could be that the password on the remote device hasn't been set. It's also possible that an access control list is filtering the Telnet session.

On a Cisco router, you don't need to use the telnet command; you can just type in an IP address from a command prompt, and the router will assume that you want to telnet to the device. Here's how that looks using just the IP address:

```
Corp#10.2.2.2
Trying 10.2.2.2 ... Open


Password required, but none set


[Connection to 10.2.2.2 closed by foreign host]
Corp#
```

At this point, it would be a great idea to set those VTY passwords on the router I want to telnet into. Here's what I did on the remote router named R1:

```
R1#config t
Enter configuration commands, one per line.  End with CNTL/Z.
R1(config)#line vty 0 ?
  <1-807>  Last Line number
  <cr>
R1(config)#line vty 0 807
R1(config-line)#password telnet
R1(config-line)#login
R1(config-line)#^Z
```

Now let's try this again. Here I'm connecting to the router from the Corp console:

```
Corp#10.2.2.2
Trying 10.2.2.2 ... Open


User Access Verification
```

```
Password:
R1>
```

Remember that the VTY password is the user-mode password, not the enable-mode password. Watch what happens when I try to go into privileged mode after telnetting into router R1:

```
R1>en
% No password set
R1>
```

It is basically saying, "No way!" This is a really good security feature because you don't want anyone telnetting into your device and being able to just type the **enable** command to get into privileged mode. You have to set your enable-mode password or enable secret password to use Telnet to configure remote devices!

 When you telnet into a remote device, you will not see console messages by default. For example, you will not see debugging output. To allow console messages to be sent to your Telnet session, use the **terminal monitor** command.

In the following examples, I am going to show you how to telnet into multiple devices simultaneously and then show you how to use hostnames instead of IP addresses.

Telnetting into Multiple Devices Simultaneously

If you telnet to a router or switch, you can end the connection by typing **exit** at any time. But what if you want to keep your connection to a remote device but still come back to your original router console? To do that, you can press the Ctrl+Shift+6 key combination, release it, and then press X.

Here's an example of connecting to multiple devices from my Corp router console:

```
Corp#10.2.2.2
Trying 10.2.2.2 ... Open


User Access Verification


Password:
R1>Ctrl+Shift+6
Corp#
```

In this example, I telnetted to the R1 router and then typed the password to enter user mode. I next pressed Ctrl+Shift+6 and then X (but you can't see any of that because it doesn't show on the screen output). Notice that my command prompt is now back at the Corp router.

Let's run through some verification commands.

Checking Telnet Connections

To see the connections made from your router to a remote device, use the `show sessions` command.

```
Corp#sh sessions
Conn Host            Address          Byte  Idle Conn Name
   1 10.2.2.2        10.2.2.2          0     0 10.2.2.2
*  2 10.1.1.2        10.1.1.2          0     0 10.1.1.2
Corp#
```

See that asterisk (*) next to connection 2? It means that session 2 was your last session. You can return to your last session by pressing Enter twice. You can also return to any session by typing the number of the connection and pressing Enter.

Checking Telnet Users

You can list all active consoles and VTY ports in use on your router with the `show users` command.

```
Corp#sh users
     Line      User      Host(s)          Idle       Location
*  0 con 0               10.1.1.2         00:00:01
                         10.2.2.2         00:01:06
```

In the command's output, con represents the local console. In this example, the console session is connected to two remote IP addresses or, in other words, two devices. In the next example, I typed sh users on the ap device that the Corp router had telnetted into and is connected to via line 1:

```
Corp#sh sessions
Conn Host            Address          Byte  Idle Conn Name
   1 10.1.1.2        10.1.1.2          0     0 10.1.1.2
*  2 10.2.2.2        10.2.2.2          0     0 10.2.2.2
Corp#1
[Resuming connection 1 to 10.1.1.2 ... ]
ap>sh users
     Line      User      Host(s)          Idle       Location
```

```
*  1 vty 0                idle              00:00:00 10.1.1.1
ap>
```

This output shows that the console is active and that VTY router line 1 is being used. The asterisk represents the current terminal session from which the show user command was entered.

Closing Telnet Sessions

You can end Telnet sessions a few different ways—typing exit or disconnect is probably the easiest and quickest.

To end a session from a remote device, use the exit command.

```
ap>exit
[Connection to 10.1.1.2 closed by foreign host]
Corp#
```

To end a session from a local device, use the disconnect command.

```
Corp#sh session
Conn Host                Address            Byte  Idle Conn Name
  *2 10.2.2.2             10.2.2.2              0     0 10.2.2.2
Corp#disconnect ?
  <2-2>  The number of an active network connection
  qdm    Disconnect QDM web-based clients
  ssh    Disconnect an active SSH connection
Corp#disconnect 2
Closing connection to 10.2.2.2 [confirm][enter]
Corp#
```

In this example, I used session number 2 because that was the connection to the R1 router that I wanted to end. As I showed, you can use the show sessions command to see the connection number.

Resolving Hostnames

If you want to use a hostname rather than an IP address to connect to a remote device, the device you are using to make the connection must be able to translate the hostname to an IP address.

There are two ways to resolve hostnames to IP addresses: building a host table on each router or building a Domain Name System (DNS) server, which is similar to a dynamic host table (assuming dynamic DNS).

Building a Host Table

A host table provides name resolution only on the router that it was built upon. The command to build a host table on a router is as follows:

```
ip host host_name [tcp_port_number] ip_address
```

The default is TCP port number 23, but you can create a session using Telnet with a different TCP port number if you want. You can also assign up to eight IP addresses to a hostname.

Here's an example of configuring a host table on the Corp router with two entries to resolve the names for the R1 router and the ap device:

```
Corp#config t
Corp(config)#ip host R1 ?
  <0-65535>   Default telnet port number
  A.B.C.D     Host IP address
  additional  Append addresses
  mx          Configure a MX record
  ns          Configure an NS record
  srv         Configure a SRV record
Corp(config)#ip host R1 10.2.2.2 ?
  A.B.C.D  Host IP address
  <cr>
Corp(config)#ip host R1 10.2.2.2
Corp(config)#ip host ap 10.1.1.2
```

Notice in the preceding router configuration that I can just keep adding IP addresses to reference a host, one after another, up to eight IP addresses. And to see the newly built host table, just use the show hosts command.

```
Corp(config)#do show hosts
Default domain is not set
Name/address lookup uses domain service
Name servers are 255.255.255.255


Codes: UN - unknown, EX - expired, OK - OK, ?? - revalidate
       temp - temporary, perm - permanent
       NA - Not Applicable None - Not defined
Host                     Port  Flags      Age Type  Address(es)
ap                       None  (perm, OK)  0  IP    10.1.1.2
R1                       None  (perm, OK)  0  IP    10.2.2.2
Corp(config)#^Z
Corp#
```

You can see the two hostnames plus their associated IP addresses in the preceding router output. The perm in the Flags column means that the entry is manually configured. If it said temp, it would be an entry that was resolved by DNS.

> The show hosts command provides information on temporary DNS entries and permanent name-to-address mappings created using the ip host command.

To verify that the host table resolves names, try typing the hostnames at a router prompt. Remember that if you don't specify the command, the router assumes you want to telnet.

In the following example, I'll use the hostnames to telnet into the remote devices and press Ctrl+Shift+6 and then X to return to the main console of the Corp router.

```
Corp#r1
Trying R1 (10.2.2.2)... Open


User Access Verification


Password:
R1>Ctrl+Shift+6
Corp#ap
Trying ap (10.1.1.2)... Open


User Access Verification


Password:
ap>Ctrl+Shift+6
Corp#
```

I successfully used entries in the host table to create a session to two devices by using the names to telnet into both devices. Names in the host table are not case sensitive.

Notice that the entries in the following show sessions output now display the hostnames and IP addresses instead of just the IP addresses:

```
Corp#sh sessions
Conn Host            Address          Byte  Idle Conn Name
   1 r1              10.2.2.2            0     1 r1
*  2 ap              10.1.1.2            0     0 ap
Corp#
```

If you want to remove a hostname from the table, just use the `no ip host` command like this:

```
Corp(config)#no ip host R1
```

The problem with the host table method is that you would need to create a host table on each router to be able to resolve names. And if you have a whole bunch of routers and want to resolve names, using DNS is a much better choice!

Using DNS to Resolve Names

If you have a lot of devices and don't want to create a host table in each device, you can use a DNS server to resolve hostnames.

Any time a Cisco device receives a command it doesn't understand, it will try to resolve it through DNS by default. Watch what happens when I type the special command `todd` at a Cisco router prompt:

```
Corp#todd
Translating "todd"...domain server (255.255.255.255)
Translating "todd"...domain server (255.255.255.255)
Translating "todd"...domain server (255.255.255.255)
% Unknown command or computer name, or unable to find
  computer address
Corp#
```

It doesn't know my name or what command I am trying to type, so it tries to resolve this through DNS. This is really annoying for two reasons: first, because it doesn't know my name <grin>, and second, because I need to hang out and wait for the name lookup to time out. You can get around this and prevent a time-consuming DNS lookup by using the `no ip domain-lookup` command on your router from global configuration mode.

If you have a DNS server on your network, you need to add a few commands to make DNS name resolution work.

- The first command is `ip domain-lookup`, which is turned on by default. It needs to be entered only if you previously turned it off (with the `no ip domain-lookup` command). The command can be used without the hyphen as well (`ip domain lookup`).

- The second command is `ip name-server`. This sets the IP address of the DNS server. You can enter the IP addresses of up to six servers.

- The last command is `ip domain-name`. Although this command is optional, it really should be set. It appends the domain name to the hostname you type in. Since DNS uses a fully qualified domain name (FQDN) system, you must have a second-level DNS name, in the form `domain.com`.

Here's an example of using these three commands:

```
Corp#config t
Corp(config)#ip domain-lookup
Corp(config)#ip name-server ?
  A.B.C.D  Domain server IP address (maximum of 6)
Corp(config)#ip name-server 192.168.0.70
Corp(config)#ip domain-name lammle.com
Corp(config)#^Z
Corp#
```

After the DNS configurations are set, you can test the DNS server by using a hostname to ping or telnet a device like this:

```
Corp#ping R1
Translating "R1"...domain server (192.168.0.70) [OK]
Type escape sequence to abort.
Sending 5, 100-byte ICMP Echos to 10.2.2.2, timeout is
  2 seconds:
!!!!!
Success rate is 100 percent (5/5), round-trip min/avg/max
  = 28/31/32 ms
```

Notice that the router uses the DNS server to resolve the name.

After a name is resolved using DNS, use the show hosts command to see that the device cached this information in the host table.

```
Corp#sh hosts
Default domain is lammle.com
Name/address lookup uses domain service
Name servers are 192.168.0.70
Host              Flags      Age Type  Address(es)
R1                (temp, OK)  0   IP    10.2.2.2
ap                (perm, OK)  0   IP    10.1.1.2
Corp#
```

The entry that was resolved is shown as temp, but the ap device is still perm, meaning that it's a static entry. Notice that the hostname is a full domain name. If I hadn't used the ip domain-name lammle.com command, I would have needed to type in ping r1.lammle.com, which is a pain.

⊕ **Real World Scenario**

Should You Use a Host Table or a DNS Server?

Karen has finally finished drawing out her network by using CDP, and the doctors are much happier. However, Karen is having a difficult time administering the network because she has to look at the network drawing to find an IP address every time she needs to telnet to a remote router.

Karen was thinking about putting host tables on each router, but with literally hundreds of routers, this is a daunting task.

Most networks have a DNS server now anyway, so adding 100 or so hostnames into it would be an easy way to go—certainly easier than adding these hostnames to each and every router! She can just add the three commands on each router, and blammo—she's resolving names.

Using a DNS server makes it easy to update any old entries too—remember, even one little change, and off she goes to each and every router to manually update its table if she's using static host tables.

Keep in mind that this has nothing to do with name resolution on the network and nothing to do with what a host on the network is trying to accomplish. This is used only when you're trying to resolve names from the router console.

Checking and Troubleshooting Network Connectivity

You can use the ping and traceroute commands to test connectivity to remote devices, and both of them can be used with many protocols, not just IP. But don't forget that the show ip route command is a good troubleshooting command for verifying your routing table, and the show interfaces command will show you the status of each interface.

I'm not going to get into the show interfaces commands here because I've already been over that in Chapter 4. But I am going to go over both the debug command and the show processes command you may need to troubleshoot a router.

Using the *ping* Command

So far, you've seen many examples of pinging devices to test IP connectivity and name resolution using the DNS server. To see all the different protocols that you can use with the Ping program, type **ping ?**.

```
Corp#ping ?
  WORD  Ping destination address or hostname
  clns  CLNS echo
  ip    IP echo
  srb   srb echo
  tag   Tag encapsulated IP echo
  <cr>
```

The ping output displays the minimum, average, and maximum times it takes for a ping packet to find a specified system and return. Here's an example:

```
Corp#ping R1
Translating "R1"...domain server (192.168.0.70)[OK]
Type escape sequence to abort.
Sending 5, 100-byte ICMP Echos to 10.2.2.2, timeout
  is 2 seconds:
!!!!!
Success rate is 100 percent (5/5), round-trip min/avg/max
  = 1/2/4 ms
Corp#
```

You can see that the DNS server was used to resolve the name, and the device was pinged in a minimum of 1 ms (milliseconds), an average of 2 ms, and up to 4 ms.

The ping command can be used in user and privileged modes but not in configuration mode.

Using the *traceroute* Command

Traceroute (the traceroute command, or trace for short) shows the path a packet takes to get to a remote device. It uses time to live (TTL) timeouts and ICMP error messages to outline the path a packet takes through an internetwork to arrive at remote host.

Trace (the trace command), which can be used from either user mode or privileged mode, allows you to figure out which router in the path to an unreachable network host should be examined more closely for the cause of the network's failure.

To see the protocols that you can use with the traceroute command, type **traceroute ?**.

```
Corp#traceroute ?
  WORD       Trace route to destination address or hostname
  appletalk  AppleTalk Trace
  clns       ISO CLNS Trace
  ip         IP Trace
  ipv6       IPv6 Trace
  ipx        IPX Trace
  <cr>
```

The traceroute command shows the hop or hops that a packet traverses on its way to a remote device. Here's an example:

```
Corp#traceroute r1


Type escape sequence to abort.
Tracing the route to R1 (10.2.2.2)


  1 R1 (10.2.2.2) 4 msec *  0 msec
Corp#
```

You can see that the packet went to only one hop to find the destination.

 Do not get confused! You can't use the tracert command—it's a Windows command. For a router, use the traceroute command!

Here's an example of using tracert from a Windows DOS prompt (notice the command tracert!):

```
C:\>tracert www.whitehouse.gov


Tracing route to a1289.g.akamai.net [69.8.201.107]
over a maximum of 30 hops:


  1    *         *         *       Request timed out.
  2    53 ms     61 ms     53 ms   hlrn-dsl-gw15-207.hlrn.qwest.net
       [207.225.112.207]
  3    53 ms     55 ms     54 ms   hlrn-agw1.inet.qwest.net [71.217.188.113]
  4    54 ms     53 ms     54 ms   hlr-core-01.inet.qwest.net [205.171.253.97]
```

```
5     54 ms     53 ms     54 ms   apa-cntr-01.inet.qwest.net [205.171.253.26]
6     54 ms     53 ms     53 ms   63.150.160.34
7     54 ms     54 ms     53 ms   www.whitehouse.gov [69.8.201.107]
```

```
Trace complete.
```

Okay, let's move on now and talk about how to troubleshoot your network using the debug command.

Debugging

Debug is a troubleshooting command that's available from the privileged exec mode of Cisco IOS. It's used to display information about various router operations and the related traffic generated or received by the router, plus any error messages.

It's a useful and informative tool, but you really need to understand some important facts about its use. Debug is regarded as a very high-overhead task because it can consume a huge amount of resources and the router is forced to process-switch the packets being debugged. So, you don't just use debug as a monitoring tool—it's meant to be used for a short period of time and only as a troubleshooting tool. By using it, you can really find out some truly significant facts about both working and faulty software and/or hardware components.

Because debugging output takes priority over other network traffic and because the debug all command generates more output than any other debug command, it can severely diminish the router's performance—even render it unusable. So, in virtually all cases, it's best to use more-specific debug commands.

As you can see from the following output, you can't enable debugging from user mode, only privileged mode:

```
Corp>debug ?
% Unrecognized command
Corp>en
Corp#debug ?
  aaa                   AAA Authentication, Authorization and Accounting
  access-expression     Boolean access expression
  adjacency             adjacency
  all                   Enable all debugging
[output cut]
```

If you have the freedom to pretty much take out a router and you really want to have some fun with debugging, use the debug all command.

```
Corp#debug all
```

```
This may severely impact network performance. Continue? (yes/[no]):yes
```

```
All possible debugging has been turned on
```

```
2d20h: SNMP: HC Timer 824AE5CC fired
2d20h: SNMP: HC Timer 824AE5CC rearmed, delay = 20000
2d20h: Serial0/0: HDLC myseq 4, mineseen 0, yourseen 0, line down
2d20h:
2d20h: Rudpv1 Sent: Pkts 0,   Data Bytes 0,   Data Pkts 0
2d20h: Rudpv1 Rcvd: Pkts 0,   Data Bytes 0,   Data Pkts 0
2d20h: Rudpv1 Discarded: 0,   Retransmitted 0
2d20h:
2d20h: RIP-TIMER: periodic timer expired
2d20h: Serial0/0: HDLC myseq 5, mineseen 0, yourseen 0, line down
2d20h: Serial0/0: attempting to restart
2d20h: PowerQUICC(0/0): DCD is up.
2d20h: is_up: 0 state: 4 sub state: 1 line: 0
2d20h:
2d20h: Rudpv1 Sent: Pkts 0,   Data Bytes 0,   Data Pkts 0
2d20h: Rudpv1 Rcvd: Pkts 0,   Data Bytes 0,   Data Pkts 0
2d20h: Rudpv1 Discarded: 0,   Retransmitted 0
2d20h: un all
All possible debugging has been turned off
Corp#
```

To disable debugging on a router, just use the command no in front of the debug command.

```
Corp#no debug all
```

But I typically just use the undebug all command since it is so easy when using the shortcut.

```
Corp#un all
```

Remember that instead of using the debug all command, it's almost always better to use specific commands—and only for short periods of time. Here's an example of deploying debug ip rip that will show you RIP updates being sent and received on a router:

```
Corp#debug ip rip
RIP protocol debugging is on
Corp#
1w4d: RIP: sending v2 update to 224.0.0.9 via Serial0/0 (192.168.12.1)
1w4d: RIP: build update entries
1w4d:    10.10.10.0/24 via 0.0.0.0, metric 2, tag 0
1w4d:    171.16.125.0/24 via 0.0.0.0, metric 3, tag 0
1w4d:    172.16.12.0/24 via 0.0.0.0, metric 1, tag 0
1w4d:    172.16.125.0/24 via 0.0.0.0, metric 3, tag 0
1w4d: RIP: sending v2 update to 224.0.0.9 via Serial0/2 (172.16.12.1)
```

```
1w4d: RIP: build update entries
1w4d:    192.168.12.0/24 via 0.0.0.0, metric 1, tag 0
1w4d:    192.168.22.0/24 via 0.0.0.0, metric 2, tag 0
1w4d: RIP: received v2 update from 192.168.12.2 on Serial0/0
1w4d:    192.168.22.0/24 via 0.0.0.0 in 1 hops
Corp#un all
```

I'm sure you can see that the debug command is one powerful command. And because of this, I'm also sure you realize that before you use any of the debugging commands, you should make sure you check the utilization of your router. This is important because in most cases, you don't want to negatively impact the device's ability to process the packets through on your internetwork. You can determine a specific router's utilization information by using the show processes command.

> Remember, when you telnet into a remote device, you will not see console messages by default! For example, you will not see debugging output. To allow console messages to be sent to your Telnet session, use the terminal monitor command.

Using the *show processes* Command

As mentioned in the previous section, you've really got to be careful when using the debug command on your devices. If your router's CPU utilization is consistently at 50 percent or more, it's probably not a good idea to type in the debug all command unless you want to see what a router looks like when it crashes!

So, what other approaches can you use? Well, the show processes (or show processes cpu) is a good tool for determining a given router's CPU utilization. Plus, it'll give you a list of active processes along with their corresponding process ID, priority, scheduler test (status), CPU time used, number of times invoked, and so on. Lots of great stuff! Plus, this command is super handy when you want to evaluate your router's performance and CPU utilization—for instance, when you find yourself otherwise tempted to reach for the debug command.

Okay, what do you see in the following output? The first line shows the CPU utilization output for the last five seconds, one minute, and five minutes. The output provides 2%/0% in front of the CPU utilization for the last five seconds. The first number equals the total utilization, and the second one indicates the utilization because of interrupt routines.

```
Corp#sh processes
CPU utilization for five seconds: 2%/0%; one minute: 0%; five minutes: 0%
 PID QTy PC Runtime (ms)    Invoked   uSecs    Stacks TTY Process
   1 Cwe 8034470C    0         1       0 5804/6000   0 Chunk Manager
   2 Csp 80369A88    4       1856      2 2616/3000 0 Load Meter
```

```
3 M*            0     112      14    800010656/12000  0 Exec
5 Lst 8034FD9C  268246        52101 5148 5768/6000    0 Check heaps
6 Cwe 80355E5C  20            3     6666 5704/6000     0 Pool Manager
7 Mst 802AC3C4  0             2        0 5580/6000     0 Timers
[output cut]
```

So, basically, the output from the show processes command shows that the router is happily able to process debugging commands without being overloaded.

Summary

In this chapter, you learned how Cisco routers are configured and how to manage those configurations.

This chapter covered the internal components of a router, which included ROM, RAM, NVRAM, and flash.

In addition, I covered what happens when a router boots and which files are loaded. The configuration register tells the router how to boot and where to find files, and you learned how to change and verify the configuration register settings for password recovery purposes.

Next, you learned how to back up and restore a Cisco IOS image as well as how to back up and restore the configuration of a Cisco router. I showed you how to manage these files using the CLI and IFS.

Then you learned how to use CDP and Telnet to gather information about remote devices. Finally, the chapter covered how to resolve hostnames and use the ping and trace commands to test network connectivity as well as how to use the debug and show processes commands.

Exam Essentials

Define the Cisco router components.   Describe the functions of the bootstrap, POST, ROM monitor, mini-IOS, RAM, ROM, flash memory, NVRAM, and the configuration register.

Identify the steps in the router boot sequence.   The steps in the boot sequence are POST, loading the IOS, and copying the startup configuration from NVRAM to RAM.

Understand configuration register commands and settings.   The 0x2102 setting is the default on all Cisco routers and tells the router to look in NVRAM for the boot sequence. 0x2101 tells the router to boot from ROM, and 0x2142 tells the router to not load the startup-config in NVRAM to provide password recovery.

Perform password recovery.   The steps in the password recovery process are interrupt the router boot sequence, change the configuration register, reload the router and enter privileged mode, change/set the password, save the new configuration, reset the configuration register, and reload the router.

Back up an IOS image.   By using the privileged-mode command copy flash tftp, you can back up a file from flash memory to a TFTP (network) server.

Restore or upgrade an IOS image.   By using the privileged-mode command copy tftp flash, you can restore or upgrade a file from a TFTP (network) server to flash memory.

Describe best practices to prepare to back up an IOS image to a network server.   Make sure that you can access the network server, ensure that the network server has adequate space for the code image, and verify the filenaming and path requirement.

Save the configuration of a router.   There are a couple of ways to do this, but the most common, as well as most tested, method is copy running-config startup-config.

Erase the configuration of a router.   Type the privileged-mode command erase startup-config and reload the router.

Understand and use Cisco IFS file system management commands.   The commands to use are dir, copy, more, delete, erase or format, cd and pwd, and mkdir and rmdir.

Describe the value of CDP.   Cisco Discovery Protocol can be used to help you document as well as troubleshoot your network.

List the information provided by the output of the show cdp neighbor command.   The show cdp neighbor command provides the following information: device ID, local interface, holdtime, capability, platform, and port ID (remote interface).

Understand how to establish a Telnet session with multiple routers simultaneously.   If you telnet to a router or switch, you can end the connection by typing **exit** at any time. However, if you want to keep your connection to a remote device but still come back to your original router console, you can press the Ctrl+Shift+6 key combination, release it, and then press X.

Identify current Telnet sessions.   The command show sessions will provide you with information about all the currently active sessions your router has with other routers.

Build a static host table on a router.   By using the global configuration command ip host *host_name ip_address*, you can build a static host table on your router. You can apply multiple IP addresses against the same host entry.

Verify the host table on a router.   You can verify the host table with the show hosts command.

Describe the function of the ping command.   Packet Internet Groper (Ping) uses ICMP echo request and ICMP echo replies to verify an active IP address on a network.

Ping a valid host ID from the correct prompt.   You can ping an IP address from a router's user mode or privileged mode but not from configuration mode. You must ping a valid address, such as 1.1.1.1.

Written Lab 5

You can find the answers in Appendix A.

In this section, you'll complete the following labs to make sure you have the information and concepts contained within them fully dialed in:

Lab 5.1: IOS Management

Lab 5.2: Router Memory

(The answers to the written labs can be found in Appendix A.)

Written Lab 5.1

Write the answers to the following questions:

1. What is the command to copy a Cisco IOS to a TFTP server?
2. What is the command to copy a Cisco startup-config file to a TFTP server?
3. What is the command to copy the startup-config file to DRAM?
4. What is an older command that you can use to copy the startup-config file to DRAM?
5. What command can you use to see the neighbor router's IP address from your router prompt?
6. What command can you use to see the hostname, local interface, platform, and remote port of a neighbor router?

7. What command is used to suspend a telnet session rather than disconnect it?

8. What command will show you your active Telnet connections to neighbor and remote devices?

9. What command can you use to upgrade a Cisco IOS?

10. What command can you use to merge a backup configuration with the configuration in RAM?

Written Lab 5.2

Identify the location in a router where each of the following files is stored by default.

1. Cisco IOS

2. Bootstrap

3. Startup configuration

4. POST routine

5. Running configuration

6. ARP cache

7. Mini-IOS

8. ROM monitor

9. Routing tables

10. Packet buffers

Hands-on Labs

To complete the labs in this section, you need at least one router (three would be best) and at least one PC running as a TFTP server. TFTP server software must be installed and running on the PC. For this lab, it is also assumed that your PC and the router(s) are connected together with a switch or hub and that all interfaces (PC NIC and router interfaces) are in the same subnet. You can alternately connect the PC directly to the router or connect the routers directly to one another (use a crossover cable in that case). Remember that the labs listed here were created for use with real routers but can easily be used with Cisco's Packet Tracer program.

Here is a list of the labs in this chapter:

Lab 5.1: Backing Up Your Router IOS

Lab 5.2: Upgrading or Restoring Your Router IOS

Lab 5.3: Backing Up the Router Configuration

Lab 5.4: Using the Cisco Discovery Protocol (CDP)

Hands-on Lab 5.1: Backing Up Your Router IOS

1. Log into your router, and go into privileged mode by typing **en** or **enable**.

2. Make sure you can connect to the TFTP server that is on your network by pinging the IP address from the router console.

3. Type **show flash** to see the contents of flash memory.

4. Type **show version** at the router privileged-mode prompt to get the name of the IOS currently running on the router. If there is only one file in flash memory, the show flash and show version commands show the same file. Remember that the show version command shows you the file that is currently running, and the show flash command shows you all of the files in flash memory.

5. Once you know you have good Ethernet connectivity to the TFTP server and you also know the IOS filename, back up your IOS by typing **copy flash tftp**. This command tells the router to copy a specified file from flash memory (this is where the IOS is stored by default) to a TFTP server.

6. Enter the IP address of the TFTP server and the source IOS filename. The file is now copied and stored in the TFTP server's default directory.

Hands-on Lab 5.2: Upgrading or Restoring Your Router IOS

1. Log into your router, and go into privileged mode by typing **en** or **enable**.

2. Make sure you can connect to the TFTP server by pinging the IP address of the server from the router console.

3. Once you know you have good Ethernet connectivity to the TFTP server, issue the **copy tftp flash** command.

4. Confirm that the router will not function during the restore or upgrade by following the prompts provided on the router console. It is possible this prompt may not occur.

5. Enter the IP address of the TFTP server.

6. Enter the name of the IOS filename you want to restore or upgrade.

7. Confirm that you understand that the contents of flash memory will be erased if there is not enough room in flash to store the new image.

8. Watch in amazement as your IOS is deleted out of flash memory and your new IOS is copied to flash memory.

If the file that was in flash memory is deleted but the new version wasn't copied to flash memory, the router will boot from ROM monitor mode. You'll need to figure out why the copy operation did not take place.

Hands-on Lab 5.3: Backing Up the Router Configuration

1. Log into your router, and go into privileged mode by typing **en** or **enable**.
2. Ping the TFTP server to make sure you have IP connectivity.
3. From RouterB, type **copy run tftp**.
4. When prompted, type the IP address of the TFTP server (for example, **172.16.30.2**), and press Enter.
5. By default, the router will prompt you for a filename. The hostname of the router is followed by the suffix -confg (yes, I spelled that correctly). You can use any name you want.

   ```
   Name of configuration file to write [RouterB-confg]?
   ```

   Press Enter to accept the default name.

   ```
   Write file RouterB-confg on host 172.16.30.2? [confirm]
   ```

   Press Enter to confirm.

Hands-on Lab 5.4: Using the Cisco Discovery Protocol (CDP)

1. Log into your router, and go into privileged mode by typing **en** or **enable**.
2. From the router, type **sh cdp**, and press Enter. You should see that CDP packets are being sent out to all active interfaces every 60 seconds and the holdtime is 180 seconds (these are the defaults).
3. To change the CDP update frequency to 90 seconds, type **cdp timer 90** in global configuration mode.

   ```
   RouterC#config t
   Enter configuration commands, one per line.  End with
     CNTL/Z.
   RouterC(config)#cdp timer ?
     <5-900>  Rate at which CDP packets are sent (in sec)
   RouterC(config)#cdp timer 90
   ```

4. Verify that your CDP timer frequency has changed by using the command **show cdp** in privileged mode.

```
RouterC#sh cdp
Global CDP information:
Sending CDP packets every 90 seconds
Sending a holdtime value of 180 seconds
```

5. Now use CDP to gather information about neighbor routers. You can get the list of available commands by typing **sh cdp ?**.

```
RouterC#sh cdp ?
  entry     Information for specific neighbor entry
  interface CDP interface status and configuration
  neighbors CDP neighbor entries
  traffic   CDP statistics
  <cr>
```

6. Type **sh cdp int** to see the interface information plus the default encapsulation used by the interface. It also shows the CDP timer information.

7. Type **sh cdp entry** * to see complete CDP information received from all devices.

8. Type **show cdp neighbor** to gather information about all connected neighbors. (You should know the specific information output by this command.)

9. Type **show cdp neighbor detail**. Notice that it produces the same output as show cdp entry *.

Hands-on Lab 5.5: Using Telnet

1. Log into your router, and go into privileged mode by typing **en** or **enable**.

2. From RouterA, telnet into your remote router (RouterB) by typing **telnet** *ip_address* from the command prompt. Type **exit** to disconnect.

3. Now type in RouterB's IP address from RouterA's command prompt. Notice that the router automatically tries to telnet to the IP address you specified. You can use the telnet command or just type in the IP address.

4. From RouterB, press Ctrl+Shift+6 and then X to return to RouterA's command prompt. Now telnet into your third router, RouterC. Press Ctrl+Shift+6 and then X to return to RouterA.

5. From RouterA, type **show sessions**. Notice your two sessions. You can press the number displayed to the left of the session and press Enter twice to return to that session. The asterisk shows the default session. You can press Enter twice to return to that session.

6. Go to the session for your RouterB. Type **show users**. This shows the console connection and the remote connection. You can use the **disconnect** command to clear the session or just type **exit** from the prompt to close your session with RouterB.

7. Go to the RouterC's console port by typing **show sessions RouterA** and using the connection number to return to RouterC. Type **show user**, and notice the connection to your first router, RouterA.

8. Type **clear line *line_number*** to disconnect the Telnet session.

Hands-on Lab 5.6: Resolving Hostnames

1. Log into your router, and go into privileged mode by typing **en** or **enable**.

2. From RouterA, type **todd**, and press Enter at the command prompt. Notice the error you receive and the delay. The router is trying to resolve the hostname to an IP address by looking for a DNS server. You can turn this feature off by using the **no ip domain-lookup** command from global configuration mode.

3. To build a host table, you use the **ip host** command. From RouterA, add a host table entry for RouterB and RouterC by entering the following commands:

```
ip host routerb ip_address
ip host routerc ip_address
```

Here is an example:

```
ip host routerb 172.16.20.2
ip host routerc 172.16.40.2
```

4. Test your host table by typing **ping routerb** from the privileged mode prompt (not the config prompt).

```
RouterA#ping routerb
Type escape sequence to abort.
Sending 5, 100-byte ICMP Echos to 172.16.20.2, timeout
  is 2 seconds:
!!!!!
Success rate is 100 percent (5/5), round-trip
  min/avg/max = 4/4/4 ms
```

5. Test your host table by typing **ping routerc**.

```
RouterA#ping routerc
Type escape sequence to abort.
Sending 5, 100-byte ICMP Echos to 172.16.40.2, timeout
```

```
   is 2 seconds:
!!!!!
Success rate is 100 percent (5/5), round-trip
   min/avg/max = 4/6/8 ms
```

6. Telnet to RouterB, and keep your session to RouterB open to RouterA by pressing Ctrl+Shift+6 and then X.

7. Telnet to RouterC by typing **routerc** at the command prompt.

8. Return to RouterA, and keep the session to RouterC open by pressing Ctrl+Shift+6, then X.

9. View the host table by typing **show hosts** and pressing Enter.

```
Default domain is not set
Name/address lookup uses domain service
Name servers are 255.255.255.255
Host               Flags        Age Type   Address(es)
routerb            (perm, OK)   0   IP     172.16.20.2
routerc            (perm, OK)   0   IP     172.16.40.2
```

Review Questions

You can find the answers in Appendix B.

 The following questions are designed to test your understanding of this chapter's material. For more information on how to get additional questions, please see this book's introduction.

1. What is the command `confreg 0x2142` used for?

   A. It is used to restart the router.

   B. It is used to bypass the configuration in NVRAM.

   C. It is used to enter ROM monitor mode.

   D. It is used to view the lost password.

2. Which command will copy the IOS to a backup host on your network?

   A. `transfer IOS to 172.16.10.1`

   B. `copy run start`

   C. `copy tftp flash`

   D. `copy start tftp`

   E. `copy flash tftp`

3. You are troubleshooting a connectivity problem in your corporate network and want to isolate the problem. You suspect that a router on the route to an unreachable network is at fault. What IOS user exec command should you issue?

   A. `Router>ping`

   B. `Router>trace`

   C. `Router>show ip route`

   D. `Router>show interface`

   E. `Router>show cdp neighbor`

4. You copy a configuration from a network host to a router's RAM. The configuration looks correct, yet it is not working at all. What could the problem be?

   A. You copied the wrong configuration into RAM.

   B. You copied the configuration into flash memory instead.

   C. The copy did not override the `shutdown` command in running-config.

   D. The IOS became corrupted after the `copy` command was initiated.

5. A network administrator wants to upgrade the IOS of a router without removing the image currently installed. What command will display the amount of memory consumed by the current IOS image and indicate whether there is enough room available to hold both the current and new images?

   A. `show version`

   B. `show flash`

   C. `show memory`

   D. `show buffers`

   E. `show running-config`

6. The corporate office sends you a new router to connect, but upon connecting the console cable, you see that there is already a configuration on the router. What should be done before a new configuration is entered in the router?

   A. RAM should be erased and the router restarted.

   B. Flash should be erased and the router restarted.

   C. NVRAM should be erased and the router restarted.

   D. The new configuration should be entered and saved.

7. Which command loads a new version of the Cisco IOS into a router?

   A. `copy flash ftp`

   B. `copy ftp flash`

   C. `copy flash tftp`

   D. `copy tftp flash`

8. Which command will show you the IOS version running on your router?

   A. `sh IOS`

   B. `sh flash`

   C. `sh version`

   D. `sh running-config`

9. What should the configuration register value be after you successfully complete the password recovery procedure and return the router to normal operation?

   A. 0x2100

   B. 0x2101

   C. 0x2102

   D. 0x2142

10. You save the configuration on a router with the `copy running-config startup-config` command and reboot the router. The router, however, comes up with a blank configuration. What can the problem be?

   A. You didn't boot the router with the correct command.

   B. NVRAM is corrupted.

   C. The configuration register setting is incorrect.

   D. The newly upgraded IOS is not compatible with the hardware of the router.

   E. The configuration you save is not compatible with the hardware.

11. If you want to have more than one Telnet session open at the same time, what keystroke combination would you use?

   A. Tab+spacebar

   B. Ctrl+X and then 6

   C. Ctrl+Shift+X and then 6

   D. Ctrl+Shift+6 and then X

12. You are unsuccessful in telnetting into a remote device, but you could telnet to the router earlier. What could the problem be? (Choose two.)

   A. IP addresses are incorrect.

   B. Access control list is filtering Telnet.

   C. There is a defective serial cable.

   D. The VTY password has been removed.

13. What information is displayed by the `show hosts` command? (Choose two.)

   A. Temporary DNS entries

   B. The names of the routers created using the `hostname` command

   C. The IP addresses of workstations allowed to access the router

   D. Permanent name-to-address mappings created using the `ip host` command

   E. The length of time a host has been connected to the router via Telnet

14. Which *three* commands can be used to check LAN connectivity problems on a router?

   A. `show interfaces`

   B. `show ip route`

   C. `tracert`

   D. `ping`

   E. `dns lookups`

15. You telnet to a router and make your necessary changes; now you want to end the Telnet session. What command do you type in?

A. `close`

B. `disable`

C. `disconnect`

D. `exit`

16. You telnet into a remote device and type `debug ip rip`, but no output from the `debug` command is seen. What could the problem be?

A. You must type the `show ip rip` command first.

B. IP addressing on the network is incorrect.

C. You must use the `terminal monitor` command.

D. Debug output is sent only to the console.

17. Which command displays the configuration register setting?

A. `show ip route`

B. `show boot version`

C. `show version`

D. `show flash`

18. You need to gather the IP address of a remote switch that is located in Hawaii. What can you do to find the address?

A. Fly to Hawaii, console into the switch, and then relax and have a drink with an umbrella in it.

B. Issue the `show ip route` command on the router connected to the switch.

C. Issue the `show cdp neighbor` command on the router connected to the switch.

D. Issue the `show ip arp` command on the router connected to the switch.

E. Issue the `show cdp neighbor detail` command on the router connected to the switch.

19. You have your laptop directly connected into a router's Ethernet port. Which of the following are among the requirements for the `copy flash tftp` command to be successful? (Choose three.)

A. TFTP server software must be running on the router.

B. TFTP server software must be running on your laptop.

C. The Ethernet cable connecting the laptop directly into the router's Ethernet port must be a straight-through cable.

D. The laptop must be on the same subnet as the router's Ethernet interface.

E. The `copy flash tftp` command must be supplied the IP address of the laptop.

F. There must be enough room in the flash memory of the router to accommodate the file to be copied.

20. The configuration register setting of 0x2102 provides what instructions to a router?

    A. Tells the router to boot into ROM monitor mode

    B. Provides password recovery

    C. Tells the router to look in NVRAM for the boot sequence

    D. Boots the IOS from a TFTP server

    E. Boots an IOS image stored in ROM

Chapter

6

IP Routing

THE CCENT EXAM OBJECTIVES COVERED IN THIS CHAPTER INCLUDE THE FOLLOWING:

- ✓ Describe basic routing concepts (including: packet forwarding, router lookup process)

- ✓ Configure, verify, and troubleshoot RIPv2

- ✓ Perform and verify routing configuration tasks for a static or default route given specific routing requirements

- ✓ Interpret network diagrams

- ✓ Determine the path between two hosts across a network

- ✓ Describe the components required for network and Internet communications

In this chapter, I'll discuss the IP routing process. This is an important subject to understand since it pertains to all routers and configurations that use IP. IP routing is the process of moving packets from one network to another network using routers. And as before, by routers I mean Cisco routers, of course!

But before you read this chapter, you must understand the difference between a routing protocol and a routed protocol. A *routing protocol* is used by routers to dynamically find all the networks in the internetwork and to ensure that all routers have the same routing table. Basically, a routing protocol determines the path of a packet through an internetwork. Examples of routing protocols are RIP, RIPv2, EIGRP, and OSPF.

Once all routers know about all networks, a *routed protocol* can be used to send user data (packets) through the established enterprise. Routed protocols are assigned to an interface and determine the method of packet delivery. Examples of routed protocols are IP and IPv6.

I'm pretty sure that I don't have to tell you that this is definitely important stuff to know. You most likely understand that from what I've said so far. IP routing is basically what Cisco routers do, and they do it very well. Again, this chapter is dealing with truly fundamental material—these are things you must know if you want to understand the objectives covered in this book!

In this chapter, I'll show you how to configure and verify IP routing with Cisco routers. I'll be covering the following:

- Routing basics
- The IP routing process
- Static routing
- Default routing
- Dynamic routing

But the first thing I really have to do is really nail down the basics of how packets actually move through an internetwork, so let's get started!

For up-to-the minute updates for this chapter, please see www.lammle.com/forum and/or www.sybex.com/go/ccent2e.

Routing Basics

Once you create an internetwork by connecting your WANs and LANs to a router, you'll need to configure logical network addresses, such as IP addresses, on all hosts on the internetwork so that they can communicate across that internetwork.

The term *routing* describes the process of taking a packet from one device and sending it through the network to another device on a different network. Routers don't really care about hosts—they care only about networks and the best path to each network. The logical network address of the destination host is used to get packets to a network through a routed network, and then the hardware address of the host is used to deliver the packet from a router to the correct destination host.

If your network has no routers, then it should be apparent that you are not routing. Routers route traffic to all the networks in your internetwork. To be able to route packets, a router must know, at a minimum, the following:

- Destination address

- Neighbor routers from which it can learn about remote networks

- Possible routes to all remote networks

- The best route to each remote network

- How to maintain and verify routing information

The router learns about remote networks from neighbor routers or from an administrator. The router then builds a routing table (a map of the internetwork) that describes how to find the remote networks. If a network is directly connected, then the router already knows how to get to it.

If a network isn't directly connected to the router, the router must use one of two ways to learn how to get to the remote network: static routing, meaning that someone must hand-type all network locations into the routing table, or something called dynamic routing.

In *dynamic routing*, a routing protocol on one router communicates with the same routing protocol running on neighbor routers. The routers then update each other about all the networks they know about and place this information into the routing table. If a change occurs in the network, the dynamic routing protocols automatically inform all routers about the event. If *static routing* is used, the administrator is responsible for updating all changes by hand into all routers. Typically, in a large network, a combination of both dynamic and static routing is used.

Before jumping into the IP routing process, let's take a look at a very simple example that demonstrates how a router uses the routing table to route packets out of an interface. I'll be going into a more detailed study of the process in the next section, but what I am showing now is called the *longest match rule*, which means that IP will look through a routing table for the longest match compared to the destination address of a packet. Let's take a look.

Figure 6.1 shows a simple two-router network. Lab_A has one serial interface and three LAN interfaces. Looking at Figure 6.1, can you see which interface Lab_A will use to forward an IP datagram to a host with an IP address of 10.10.10.10?

FIGURE 6.1   A simple routing example

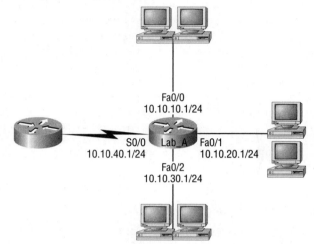

By using the command show ip route, you can see the routing table (map of the internetwork) that Lab_A uses to make forwarding decisions.

```
Lab_A#sh ip route
[output cut]
Gateway of last resort is not set
C    10.10.10.0/24 is directly connected, FastEthernet0/0
C    10.10.20.0/24 is directly connected, FastEthernet0/1
C    10.10.30.0/24 is directly connected, FastEthernet0/2
C    10.10.40.0/24 is directly connected, Serial 0/0
```

The C in the routing table output means that the networks listed are "directly connected," and until you add a routing protocol—something like RIPv2, EIGRP, and so on—to the routers in the internetwork (or use static routes), you'll have only directly connected networks in the routing table.

So, let's get back to the original question. By looking at the figure and the output of the routing table, can you tell what IP will do with a received packet that has a destination IP address of 10.10.10.10? The router will packet-switch the packet to interface FastEthernet 0/0, and this interface will frame the packet and then send it out on the network segment. To reiterate on the longest match rule, IP would look for 10.10.10.10 in this example, and if that is not found in the table, then IP would search for 10.10.10.0, then 10.10.0.0, and so on, until a route is found.

Because we can, let's do another example. Based on the output of the next routing table, which interface will a packet with a destination address of 10.10.10.14 be forwarded from?

```
Lab_A#sh ip route
[output cut]
Gateway of last resort is not set
C       10.10.10.16/28 is directly connected, FastEthernet0/0
C       10.10.10.8/29 is directly connected, FastEthernet0/1
C       10.10.10.4/30 is directly connected, FastEthernet0/2
C       10.10.10.0/30 is directly connected, Serial 0/0
```

First, you can see that the network is subnetted and each interface has a different mask. And I have to tell you—you just can't answer this question if you can't subnet! 10.10.10.14 would be a host in the 10.10.10.8/29 subnet connected to the FastEthernet0/1 interface. Don't freak out if you don't get it. Just go back and reread Chapter 3, "IP Subnetting, Troubleshooting IP, and Introduction to NAT," if you're struggling, and this should make perfect sense to you afterward.

For everyone who's ready to move on, let's get into this process in more detail.

The IP Routing Process

The IP routing process is fairly simple and doesn't change, regardless of the size of your network. For an example, I'll use Figure 6.2 to describe step-by-step what happens when Host_A wants to communicate with Host_B on a different network.

FIGURE 6.2   IP routing example using two hosts and one router

In this example, a user on Host_A pings Host_B's IP address. Routing doesn't get simpler than this, but it still involves a lot of steps. Let's work through them.

1. Internet Control Message Protocol (ICMP) creates an echo request payload (which is just the alphabet in the data field).

2. ICMP hands that payload to Internet Protocol (IP), which then creates a packet.

At a minimum, this packet contains an IP source address, an IP destination address, and a Protocol field with 01h. (Remember that Cisco likes to use *0x* in front of hex characters, so this could look like 0x01.) That tells the receiving host to whom it should hand the payload when the destination is reached—in this example, ICMP.

3. Once the packet is created, IP determines whether the destination IP address is on the local network or a remote one.

   Since IP determines that this is a remote request, the packet needs to be sent to the default gateway so it can be routed to the remote network.

4. The Registry in Windows is parsed to find the configured default gateway.

5. The default gateway of host 172.16.10.2 (Host_A) is configured to 172.16.10.1.

   For this packet to be sent to the default gateway, the hardware address of the router's interface Ethernet 0 (configured with the IP address of 172.16.10.1) must be known. Why? So, the packet can be handed down to the Data Link layer, framed, and sent to the router's interface that's connected to the 172.16.10.0 network. Because hosts communicate only via hardware addresses on the local LAN, it's important to recognize that for Host_A to communicate to Host_B, it has to send packets to the Media Access Control (MAC) address of the default gateway on the local network.

 MAC addresses are always local on the LAN and never go through and past a router.

6. Next, the Address Resolution Protocol (ARP) cache of the host is checked to see whether the IP address of the default gateway has already been resolved to a hardware address.

   - If it has, the packet is then free to be handed to the Data Link layer for framing. (The hardware destination address is also handed down with that packet.) To view the ARP cache on your host, use the following command:

   ```
   C:\>arp -a
   Interface: 172.16.10.2 -- 0x3
     Internet Address      Physical Address      Type
     172.16.10.1           00-15-05-06-31-b0     dynamic
   ```

   - If the hardware address isn't already in the ARP cache of the host, an ARP broadcast is sent out onto the local network to search for the hardware address of 172.16.10.1. The router responds to the request and provides the hardware address of Ethernet 0, and the host caches this address.

7. Once the packet and destination hardware address are handed to the Data Link layer, the LAN driver is used to provide media access via the type of LAN being used (in this example, Ethernet).

A frame is then generated, encapsulating the packet with control information. Within that frame are the hardware destination and source addresses plus, in this case, an Ether-Type field that describes the Network layer protocol that handed the packet to the Data Link layer—in this instance, IP. At the end of the frame is something called a Frame Check Sequence (FCS) field that houses the result of the cyclic redundancy check (CRC). The frame would look something like what I've detailed in Figure 6.3. It contains Host_A's hardware (MAC) address and the destination hardware address of the default gateway. It does not include the remote host's MAC address—remember that!

FIGURE 6.3   Frame used from Host_A to the Lab_A router when Host_B is pinged

Destination MAC (router's E0 MAC address)	Source MAC (Host_A MAC address)	Ether-Type field	Packet	FCS (CRC)

8. Once the frame is completed, it's handed down to the Physical layer to be put on the physical medium (in this example, twisted-pair wire) one bit at a time.

9. Every device in the collision domain receives these bits and builds the frame. They each run a CRC and check the answer in the FCS field. If the answers don't match, the frame is discarded.

   ▪ If the CRC matches, then the hardware destination address is checked to see whether it matches too (which, in this example, is the router's interface Ethernet 0).

   ▪ If it's a match, then the Ether-Type field is checked to find the protocol used at the Network layer.

10. The packet is pulled from the frame, and what is left of the frame is discarded. The packet is handed to the protocol listed in the Ether-Type field—it's given to IP.

11. IP receives the packet and checks the IP destination address. Since the packet's destination address doesn't match any of the addresses configured on the receiving router itself, the router will look up the destination IP network address in its routing table.

12. The routing table must have an entry for the network 172.16.20.0 or the packet will be discarded immediately and an ICMP message will be sent back to the originating device with a destination network unreachable message.

13. If the router does find an entry for the destination network in its table, the packet is switched to the exit interface—in this example, interface Ethernet 1.

   The following output displays the Lab_A router's routing table. The C means "directly connected." No routing protocols are needed in this network since all networks (all two of them) are directly connected.

```
Lab_A>sh ip route
Codes:C - connected,S - static,I - IGRP,R - RIP,M - mobile,B -
[output cut]
Gateway of last resort is not set
```

```
       172.16.0.0/24 is subnetted, 2 subnets
C          172.16.10.0 is directly connected, Ethernet0
C          172.16.20.0 is directly connected, Ethernet1
```

14. The router packet-switches the packet to the Ethernet 1 buffer.

15. The Ethernet 1 buffer needs to know the hardware address of the destination host and first checks the ARP cache.

    ▪ If the hardware address of Host_B has already been resolved and is in the router's ARP cache, then the packet and the hardware address are handed down to the Data Link layer to be framed. Let's take a look at the ARP cache on the Lab_A router by using the show ip arp command.

    ```
    Lab_A#sh ip arp
    Protocol  Address      Age(min) Hardware Addr   Type   Interface
    Internet  172.16.20.1   -         00d0.58ad.05f4  ARPA   Ethernet1
    Internet  172.16.20.2   3         0030.9492.a5dd  ARPA   Ethernet1
    Internet  172.16.10.1   -         00d0.58ad.06aa  ARPA   Ethernet0
    Internet  172.16.10.2   12        0030.9492.a4ac  ARPA   Ethernet0
    ```

    The dash (-) means that this is the physical interface on the router. From the previous output, you can see that the router knows the 172.16.10.2 (Host_A) and 172.16.20.2 (Host_B) hardware addresses. Cisco routers will keep an entry in the ARP table for four hours.

    If the hardware address has not already been resolved, the router will send an ARP request out E1 looking for the hardware address of 172.16.20.2. Host_B responds with its hardware address, and the packet and destination hardware addresses are both sent to the Data Link layer for framing.

16. The Data Link layer creates a frame with the destination and source hardware address, Ether-Type field, and FCS field at the end. The frame is handed to the Physical layer to be sent out on the physical medium one bit at a time.

17. Host_B receives the frame and immediately runs a CRC. If the result matches what's in the FCS field, the hardware destination address is then checked. If the host finds a match, the Ether-Type field is then checked to determine the protocol that the packet should be handed to at the Network layer—IP in this example.

18. At the Network layer, IP receives the packet and runs a CRC on the IP header. If that passes, IP then checks the destination address. Since there's finally a match made, the Protocol field is checked to find out to whom the payload should be given.

19. The payload is handed to ICMP, which understands that this is an echo request. ICMP responds to this by immediately discarding the packet and generating a new payload as an echo reply.

20. A packet is then created including the source and destination addresses, Protocol field, and payload. The destination device is now Host_A.

21. IP then checks to see whether the destination IP address is a device on the local LAN or on a remote network. Since the destination device is on a remote network, the packet needs to be sent to the default gateway.

22. The default gateway IP address is found in the Registry of the Windows device, and the ARP cache is checked to see whether the hardware address has already been resolved from an IP address.

23. Once the hardware address of the default gateway is found, the packet and destination hardware addresses are handed down to the Data Link layer for framing.

24. The Data Link layer frames the packet of information and includes the following in the header:

   - The destination and source hardware addresses
   - The Ether-Type field with 0x0800 (IP) in it
   - The FCS field with the CRC result in tow

25. The frame is now handed down to the Physical layer to be sent out over the network medium one bit at a time.

26. The router's Ethernet 1 interface receives the bits and builds a frame. The CRC is run, and the FCS field is checked to make sure the answers match.

27. Once the CRC is found to be okay, the hardware destination address is checked. Since the router's interface is a match, the packet is pulled from the frame, and the Ether-Type field is checked to see what protocol at the Network layer the packet should be delivered to.

28. The protocol is determined to be IP, so it gets the packet. IP runs a CRC check on the IP header first and then checks the destination IP address.

IP does not run a complete CRC as the Data Link layer does—it only checks the header for errors.

Since the IP destination address doesn't match any of the router's interfaces, the routing table is checked to see whether it has a route to 172.16.10.0. If it doesn't have a route over to the destination network, the packet will be discarded immediately.

This is the source point of confusion for a lot of administrators—when a ping fails, most people think the packet never reached the destination host. But as you see here, that's not *always* the case. All it takes is for just one of the remote routers to be lacking a route back to the originating host's network and—*poof!*—the packet is dropped on the *return trip*, not on its way to the host.

Just a quick note to mention that when (if) the packet is lost on the way back to the originating host, you will typically see a request timed out message because it is an unknown error.

If the error occurs because of a known issue, such as if a route is not in the routing table on the way to the destination device, you will see a destination unreachable message. This should help you determine whether the problem occurred on the way to the destination or on the way back.

29. In this case, the router does know how to get to network 172.16.10.0—the exit interface is Ethernet 0—so the packet is switched to interface Ethernet 0.

30. The router checks the ARP cache to determine whether the hardware address for 172.16.10.2 has already been resolved.

31. Since the hardware address to 172.16.10.2 is already cached from the originating trip to Host_B, the hardware address and packet are handed to the Data Link layer.

32. The Data Link layer builds a frame with the destination hardware address and source hardware address and then puts IP in the Ether-Type field. A CRC is run on the frame, and the result is placed in the FCS field.

33. The frame is then handed to the Physical layer to be sent out onto the local network one bit at a time.

34. The destination host receives the frame, runs a CRC, checks the destination hardware address, and looks in the Ether-Type field to find out whom to hand the packet to.

35. IP is the designated receiver, and after the packet is handed to IP at the Network layer, it checks the Protocol field for further direction. IP finds instructions to give the payload to ICMP, and ICMP determines the packet to be an ICMP echo reply.

36. ICMP acknowledges that it has received the reply by sending an exclamation point (!) to the user interface. ICMP then attempts to send four more echo requests to the destination host.

You've just experienced Todd's 36 easy steps to understanding IP routing. The key point to understand here is that if you had a much larger network, the process would be the *same*. In a really big internetwork, the packet just goes through more hops before it finds the destination host.

It's super-important to remember that when Host_A sends a packet to Host_B, the destination hardware address used is the default gateway's Ethernet interface. Why? Because frames can't be placed on remote networks—only local networks. So, packets destined for remote networks must go through the default gateway.

Let's take a look at Host_A's ARP cache now.

```
C:\ >arp -a
Interface: 172.16.10.2 -- 0x3
  Internet Address        Physical Address        Type
  172.16.10.1             00-15-05-06-31-b0       dynamic
  172.16.20.1             00-15-05-06-31-b0       dynamic
```

Did you notice that the hardware (MAC) address that Host_A uses to get to Host_B is the Lab_A E0 interface? Hardware addresses are *always* local, and they never pass a router's interface. Understanding this process is as important as air to you, so carve this into your memory!

Testing Your IP Routing Understanding

I really want to make sure you understand IP routing because it's super-important. So, I'm going to use this section to test your understanding of the IP routing process by having you look at a couple of figures and answer some very basic IP routing questions.

Figure 6.4 shows a LAN connected to RouterA, which is, in turn, connected via a WAN link to RouterB. RouterB has a LAN connected with an HTTP server attached.

FIGURE 6.4   IP routing example 1

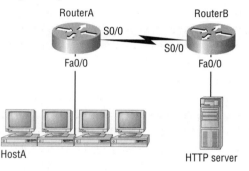

The critical information you need to glean from this figure is exactly how IP routing will occur in this example. Okay—you can cheat a bit. I'll give you the answer, but then you should go back over the figure and see whether you can answer example 2 without looking at my answers.

1.   The destination MAC address of a frame, from HostA, will be the MAC address of the Fa0/0 interface of the RouterA router.

2.   The destination IP address of a packet will be the IP address of the network interface card (NIC) of the HTTP server.

3.   The destination port number in the segment header will have a value of 80.

That example was a pretty simple one, and it was also very to the point. One thing to remember is that if multiple hosts are communicating to the server using HTTP, they must all use a different source port number. That is how the server keeps the data separated at the Transport layer.

Let's mix it up a little and add another internetworking device into the network and then see whether you can find the answers. Figure 6.5 shows a network with only one router but two switches.

FIGURE 6.5 IP routing example 2

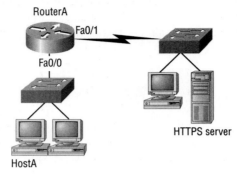

What you want to understand about the IP routing process here is what happens when HostA sends data to the HTTPS server.

1. The destination MAC address of a frame, from HostA, will be the MAC address of the Fa0/0 interface of the RouterA router.

2. The destination IP address of a packet will be the IP address of the network interface card (NIC) of the HTTPS server.

3. The destination port number in the segment header will have a value of 443.

Notice that the switches weren't used as either a default gateway or another destination. That's because switches have nothing to do with routing. I wonder how many of you chose the switch as the default gateway (destination) MAC address for HostA? If you did, don't feel bad—just take another look with that fact in mind. It's very important to remember that the destination MAC address will always be the router's interface—if your packets are destined for outside the LAN, as they were in these last two examples.

Before I move into some of the more advanced aspects of IP routing, I'll discuss ICMP in more detail, as well as how ICMP is used in an internetwork. Take a look at the network shown in Figure 6.6. Ask yourself, "What will happen if the LAN interface of Lab_C is down and Host A pings Host B?"

FIGURE 6.6 ICMP error example

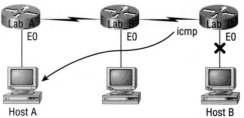

Lab_C will use ICMP to inform Host A that Host B can't be reached, and it will do this by sending an ICMP destination unreachable message. The point of this figure is to help you visualize how ICMP data is routed via IP back to the originating station.

Let's look at another problem. Here's the output of a corporate router's routing table:

```
Corp#sh ip route
[output cut]
R     192.168.215.0 [120/2] via 192.168.20.2, 00:00:23, Serial0/0
R     192.168.115.0 [120/1] via 192.168.20.2, 00:00:23, Serial0/0
R     192.168.30.0 [120/1] via 192.168.20.2, 00:00:23, Serial0/0
C     192.168.20.0 is directly connected, Serial0/0
C     192.168.214.0 is directly connected, FastEthernet0/0
```

What do you see here? If I were to tell you that the corporate router received an IP packet with a source IP address of 192.168.214.20 and a destination address of 192.168.22.3, what do you think the Corp router will do with this packet?

If you said, "The packet came in on the FastEthernet 0/0 interface, but since the routing table doesn't show a route to network 192.168.22.0 (or a default route), the router will discard the packet and send an ICMP destination unreachable message back out interface FastEthernet 0/0," you're a genius! The reason it does this is because that's the source LAN where the packet originated from.

Now, let's check out another figure and talk about the frames and packets in detail. Really, I'm not exactly chatting about anything new; I'm just making sure that you totally, completely, fully understand basic IP routing. That's because this book, and the exam objectives it's geared toward, are all about IP routing, which means you need to be all over this stuff! I'll use Figure 6.7 for the next few questions.

FIGURE 6.7   Basic IP routing using MAC and IP addresses

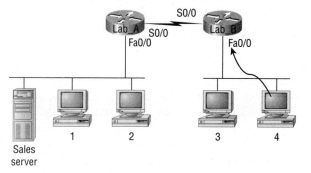

Referring to Figure 6.7, here's a list of all the questions you need the answers to emblazoned in your brain:

1. In order to begin communicating with the Sales server, Host 4 sends out an ARP request. How will the devices exhibited in the topology respond to this request?

2. Host 4 has received an ARP reply. Host 4 will now build a packet and then place this packet in the frame. What information will be placed in the header of the packet that leaves Host 4 if Host 4 is going to communicate to the Sales server?

3. At last, the Lab_A router has received the packet and will send it out Fa0/0 onto the LAN toward the server. What will the frame have in the header as the source and destination addresses?

4. Host 4 is displaying two web documents from the Sales server in two browser windows at the same time. How did the data find its way to the correct browser windows?

I probably should write the following in a teensy font and put them upside down in another part of the book so it would be really hard for you to cheat and peek, but since it's actually you who's going to lose out if you peek, here are your answers:

1. To begin communicating with the server, Host 4 determines that this is a remote request and sends out an ARP request for the default gateway hardware address. The Lab_B router will respond with the MAC address of the Fa0/0 interface, and Host 4 will send all frames to the MAC address of the Lab_B Fa0/0 interface when sending packets to the Sales server.

2. Host 4 has received an ARP reply. Host 4 will now build a packet and then place this packet in the frame. What information will be placed in the header of the packet that leaves Host 4 if Host 4 is going to communicate to the Sales server? Since I'm now talking about packets, not frames, the source address will be the IP address of Host 4, and the destination address will be the IP address of the Sales server.

3. Finally, the Lab_A router has received the packet and will send it out Fa0/0 onto the LAN toward the server. What will the frame have in the header as the source and destination addresses? The source MAC address will be the Lab_A router's Fa0/0 interface, and the destination MAC address will be the Sales server's MAC address. (All MAC addresses must be local on the LAN.)

4. Host 4 is displaying two web documents from the Sales server in two different browser windows at the same time. How did the data find its way to the correct browser windows? TCP port numbers are used to direct the data to the correct application window.

Great! But you're not quite done yet. I've got a few more questions for you before you actually get to configure routing in a real network. Ready? Figure 6.8 shows a basic network, and Host 4 needs to get email. Which address will be placed in the destination address field of the frame when it leaves Host 4?

FIGURE 6.8   Testing basic routing knowledge

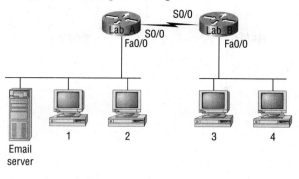

The answer is that Host 4 will use the destination MAC address of the Fa0/0 interface of the Lab_B router—which I'm so sure you knew, right? Look at Figure 6.8 again: Host 4 needs to communicate with Host 1. Which OSI layer 3 source address will be placed in the packet header when it reaches Host 1?

I hope you know this. At layer 3, the source IP address will be Host 4, and the destination address in the packet will be the IP address of Host 1. Of course, the destination MAC address from Host 4 will always be the Fa0/0 address of the Lab_B router if the destination is remote, right? And since there is more than one router, you'll need a routing protocol that communicates between both of them so that traffic can be forwarded in the right direction to reach the network in which Host 1 is attached.

Okay—one more question, and you're on your way to being an IP routing genius! Again, look at Figure 6.8; Host 4 is transferring a file to the email server connected to the Lab_A router. What would be the layer 2 destination address leaving Host 4? Yes, I've asked this question more than once. But not this one: what will be the source MAC address when the frame is received at the email server?

Ideally, you answered that the layer 2 destination address leaving Host 4 will be the MAC address of the Fa0/0 interface of the Lab_B router and that the source layer 2 address that the email server will receive will be the Fa0/0 interface of the Lab_A router.

If you did, you're all set to get the skinny on how IP routing is handled in a larger network.

Configuring IP Routing

It's time to get serious and configure a real network! Figure 6.9 shows four routers: Corp, Remote1, Remote2, and Remote3. Remember that, by default, these routers know only about networks that are directly connected to them. I'll continue to use this figure and network throughout the rest of the chapters in this book.

FIGURE 6.9 Configuring IP routing

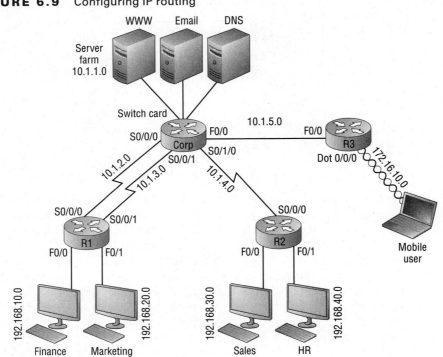

As you might guess, I've got quite a nice collection of routers for us to play with. The Corp router is a 2811 with four serial interfaces and a switch module, and remote routers 1 and 2 are 1841 routers. Remote 3 is another 2811 with a wireless interface card. I'm simply going to call the remote routers R1, R2, and R3. (Understand that you can still perform most of the commands I use in this book with older routers or with a router simulator.)

The first step for this project is to correctly configure each router with an IP address on each interface. Table 6.1 shows the IP address scheme I'm going to use to configure the network. After I go over how the network is configured, I'll cover how to configure IP routing. Each network in the table has a 24-bit subnet mask (255.255.255.0), which makes the interesting (subnet) octet the third one.

TABLE 6.1   Network addressing for the IP network

Router	Network Address	Interface	Address
CORP			
Corp	10.1.1.0	Vlan1 (switch card)	10.1.1.1
Corp	10.1.2.0	S0/0/0	10.1.2.1
Corp	10.1.3.0	S0/0/1(DCE)	10.1.3.1
Corp	10.1.4.0	S0/1/0	10.1.4.1
Corp	10.1.5.0	F0/0	10.1.5.1
R1			
R1	10.1.2.0	S0/0/0 (DCE)	10.1.2.2
R1	10.1.3.0	S0/0/1	10.1.3.2
R1	192.168.10.0	F0/0	192.168.10.1
R1	192.168.20.0	F0/1	192.168.20.1
R2			
R2	10.1.4.0	S0/0/0 (DCE)	10.1.4.2
R2	192.168.30.0	F0/0	192.168.30.1
R2	192.168.40.0	F0/1	192.168.40.1
R3			
R3	10.1.5.0	F0/0	10.1.5.2
R3	172.16.10.0	Dot11Radio0/0/0	172.16.10.1

The router configuration is really a pretty straightforward process since you just need to add IP addresses to your interfaces and then perform a `no shutdown` on those same interfaces. It gets a tad more complex later, but for right now, let's configure the IP addresses in the network.

Corp Configuration

I need to configure five interfaces to configure the Corp router. And configuring the host-names of each router will make identification much easier. While I'm at it, why not set the interface descriptions, banner, and router passwords too? It's a really good idea to make a habit of configuring these commands on every router.

To get started, I performed an `erase startup-config` on the router and reloaded, so I'll start in setup mode. I choose no to entering setup mode, which will get me straight to the username prompt of the console. I'm going to configure all my routers this same way.

I need to mention one small issue before I configure the Corp router, and that is the switch card configuration. The IP address is configured on a logical interface on a switch, not a physical interface, and that interface by default is named vlan 1. Also, unlike with standalone switches, the interfaces on my switch card installed in the router are not enabled by default, so you'll see that I enable the ports I am using in this lab.

Here's how I did all that:

```
-- System Configuration Dialog --


Would you like to enter the initial configuration dialog? [yes/no]: n


Press RETURN to get started!
Router>en
Router#config t
Enter configuration commands, one per line.  End with CNTL/Z.
Router(config)#hostname Corp
Corp(config)#enable secret todd
Corp(config)#interface vlan 1
Corp(config-if)#description Switch Card to Core Network
Corp(config-if)#ip address 10.1.1.1 255.255.255.0
Corp(config-if)#no shutdown
Corp(config-if)#int f1/0
Corp(config-if)#description Switch Port connection to WWW Server
Corp(config-if)#no shutdown
Corp(config-if)#int f1/1
Corp(config-if)#description Switch port connection to Email Server
Corp(config-if)#no shut
Corp(config-if)#int f1/2
Corp(config-if)#description Switch port connection to DNS Server
Corp(config-if)#no shut
Corp(config-if)#int s0/0/0
```

```
Corp(config-if)#description 1st Connection to R1
Corp(config-if)#ip address 10.1.2.1 255.255.255.0
Corp(config-if)#no shut
Corp(config-if)#int s0/0/1
Corp(config-if)#description 2nd Connection to R1
Corp(config-if)#ip address 10.1.3.1 255.255.255.0
Corp(config-if)#no shut
Corp(config-if)#int s0/1/0
Corp(config-if)#description Connection to R2
Corp(config-if)#ip address 10.1.4.1 255.255.255.0
Corp(config-if)#no shut
Corp(config-if)#int fa0/0
Corp(config-if)# description Connection to R3
Corp(config-if)# ip address 10.1.5.1 255.255.255.0
Corp(config-if)#no shut
Corp(config-if)#line con 0
Corp(config-line)#password console
Corp(config-line)#login
Corp(config-line)#logging synchronous
Corp(config-line)#exec-timeout 0 0
Corp(config-line)#line aux 0
Corp(config-line)#password aux
Corp(config-line)#login
Corp(config-line)#exit
Corp(config)#line vty 0 ?
  <1-15>  Last Line number
  <cr>
Corp(config)#line vty 0 15
Corp(config-line)#password telnet
Corp(config-line)#login
Corp(config-line)#exit
Corp(config)#no ip domain lookup
Corp(config)#banner motd # This is my Corp 2811 ISR Router #
Corp(config-if)#^Z
Corp#copy running-config startup-config
Destination filename [startup-config]?[enter]
Building configuration...
[OK]
Corp#
```

If you have a hard time understanding this configuration process, refer to Chapter 4, "Cisco's Internetworking Operating System (IOS)."

To view the IP routing tables created on a Cisco router, use the command show ip route. The command output is as follows:

```
Corp#sh ip route
Codes: C - connected, S - static, R - RIP, M - mobile, B - BGP
       D - EIGRP, EX - EIGRP external, O - OSPF, IA - OSPF inter area
       N1 - OSPF NSSA external type 1, N2 - OSPF NSSA external type 2
       E1 - OSPF external type 1, E2 - OSPF external type 2
       i - IS-IS, su - IS-IS summary, L1 - IS-IS level-1, L2 - IS-IS
    level-2, ia - IS-IS inter area, * - candidate default, U - per-user
    static route, o - ODR, P - periodic downloaded static route


Gateway of last resort is not set


     10.0.0.0/24 is subnetted, 1 subnets
C        10.1.1.0 is directly connected, Vlan1
Corp#
```

It's important to remember that only configured, directly connected networks are going to show up in the routing table. So, why is it that I see only the Vlan1 interface in the routing table? No worries—that's just because you won't see the serial interfaces come up until the other side of the links are operational. As soon as I configure the R1, R2, and R3 routers, all those interfaces should pop right up.

But did you notice the C on the left side of the output of the routing table? When you see that there, it means that the network is directly connected. The codes for each type of connection are listed at the top of the show ip route command, along with their descriptions.

In the interest of brevity, the codes will be cut in the rest of this chapter.

R1 Configuration

Now I'm ready to configure the next router—R1. To make that happen correctly, keep in mind that I have four interfaces to deal with: serial 0/0/0, serial 0/0/1, FastEthernet 0/0, and FastEthernet 0/1. So, let's make sure I don't forget to add the hostname, passwords, interface descriptions, and banner to the router configuration. As I did with the Corp router, I erased the configuration and reloaded.

Here's the configuration I used:

```
R1#erase start
% Incomplete command.
R1#erase startup-config
Erasing the nvram filesystem will remove all configuration files!
   Continue? [confirm][enter]
[OK]
Erase of nvram: complete
R1#reload
Proceed with reload? [confirm][enter]
[output cut]
%Error opening tftp://255.255.255.255/network-confg (Timed out)
%Error opening tftp://255.255.255.255/cisconet.cfg (Timed out)


        -- System Configuration Dialog --


Would you like to enter the initial configuration dialog? [yes/no]: n
```

Before moving on, I really want to discuss the preceding output with you. First, notice that the new 12.4 ISR routers will no longer take the command erase start. The router has only one command after erase that starts with *s*, as shown here:

```
Router#erase s?
startup-config
```

I know, you'd think that the IOS would continue to accept the command, but nope—sorry! The second thing I want to point out is that the output tells you the router is looking for a TFTP host to see whether it can download a configuration. When that fails, it goes straight into setup mode. This gives you a great picture of the Cisco router default boot sequence I talked about in Chapter 5, "Managing a Cisco Internetwork."

Okay, let's get back to configuring the router.

```
Press RETURN to get started!
Router>en
Router#config t
Router(config)#hostname R1
R1(config)#enable secret todd
R1(config)#int s0/0/0
R1(config-if)#ip address 10.1.2.2 255.255.255.0
R1(config-if)#Description 1st Connection to Corp Router
R1(config-if)#no shut
```

```
R1(config-if)#int s0/0/1
R1(config-if)#ip address 10.1.3.2 255.255.255.0
R1(config-if)#no shut
R1(config-if)#description 2nd connection to Corp Router
R1(config-if)#int f0/0
R1(config-if)#ip address 192.168.10.1 255.255.255.0
R1(config-if)#description Connection to Finance PC
R1(config-if)#no shut
R1(config-if)#int f0/1
R1(config-if)#ip address 192.168.20.1 255.255.255.0
R1(config-if)#description Connection to Marketing PC
R1(config-if)#no shut
R1(config-if)#line con 0
R1(config-line)#password console
R1(config-line)#login
R1(config-line)#logging synchronous
R1(config-line)#exec-timeout 0 0
R1(config-line)#line aux 0
R1(config-line)#password aux
R1(config-line)#login
R1(config-line)#exit
R1(config)#line vty 0 ?
  <1-807>  Last Line number
  <cr>
R1(config)#line vty 0 807
R1(config-line)#password telnet
R1(config-line)#login
R1(config-line)#banner motd # This is my R1 Router #
R1(config)#no ip domain-lookup
R1(config)#exit
R1#copy run start
Destination filename [startup-config]?[enter]
Building configuration...
[OK]
R1#
```

Let's take a look at the configuration of the interfaces.

```
R1#sh run | begin interface
interface FastEthernet0/0
 description Connection to Finance PC
```

```
 ip address 192.168.10.1 255.255.255.0
 duplex auto
 speed auto
!
interface FastEthernet0/1
 description Connection to Marketing PC
 ip address 192.168.20.1 255.255.255.0
 duplex auto
 speed auto
!
interface Serial0/0/0
 description 1st Connection to Corp Router
 ip address 10.1.2.2 255.255.255.0
!
interface Serial0/0/1
 description 2nd connection to Corp Router
 ip address 10.1.3.2 255.255.255.0
!
```

The show ip route command displays the following:

```
R1#show ip route
     10.0.0.0/24 is subnetted, 4 subnets
C       10.1.3.0 is directly connected, Serial0/0/1
C       10.1.2.0 is directly connected, Serial0/0/0
C       192.168.20.0 is directly connected, FastEthernet0/1
C       192.168.10.0 is directly connected, FastEthernet0/0
R1#
```

Notice that router R1 knows how to get to networks 10.1.3.0, 10.1.2.0, 192.168.20.0, and 192.168.10.0. I can now ping to the Corp router from R1.

```
R1#10.1.2.1

Type escape sequence to abort.
Sending 5, 100-byte ICMP Echos to 10.1.2.1, timeout is 2 seconds:
!!!!!
Success rate is 100 percent (5/5), round-trip min/avg/max = 1/2/4 ms
R1#
```

Now let's go back to the Corp router and look at the routing table.

```
Corp#sh ip route
[output cut]
```

```
        10.0.0.0/24 is subnetted, 4 subnets
C         10.1.3.0 is directly connected, Serial0/0/1
C         10.1.2.0 is directly connected, Serial0/0/0
C         10.1.1.0 is directly connected, Vlan1
Corp#
```

The R1 serial interface 0/0/0 and 0/0/1 are DCE connections, which means a clock rate needs to be set on the interface. Remember that you don't need to use the clock rate command in production. Even though this is very true, it's still imperative that you know how/when you can use it and that you understand it really well when studying for your CCNA exam!

You can see the clocking with the show controllers command.

```
R1#sh controllers s0/0/1
Interface Serial0/0/1
Hardware is GT96K
DCE V.35, clock rate 2000000
```

One last thing before I get into configuring the other remote routers: did you notice the clock rate is 2000000 under the serial interfaces of the R1 router? That's important because if you think back to when I was configuring the R1 router, you'll recall that I didn't set the clock rate. The reason I didn't is because ISR routers will autodetect a DCE-type cable and automatically configure the clock rate—a really sweet feature!

Since the serial links are showing up, you can now see three networks in the Corp routing table. And once I configure R2 and R3, you'll see two more networks in the routing table of the Corp router. The Corp router can't see either the 192.168.10.0 or 192.168.20.0 network because I don't have any routing configured yet—routers see only directly connected networks by default.

R2 Configuration

To configure R2, I'm going to do pretty much the same thing I did with the other two routers. There are three interfaces (serial 0/0/0, FastEthernet 0/0, and FastEthernet 0/1) to deal with, and again, I'll be sure to add the hostname, passwords, interface descriptions, and a banner to the router configuration.

```
Router>en
Router#config t
Router(config)#hostname R2
R2(config)#enable secret todd
R2(config)#int s0/0/0
R2(config-if)#ip address 10.1.4.2 255.255.255.0
R2(config-if)#description Connection to Corp Router
R2(config-if)#no shut
R2(config-if)#int f0/0
```

```
R2(config-if)#ip address 192.168.30.1 255.255.255.0
R2(config-if)#description Connection to Sales PC
R2(config-if)#no shut
R2(config-if)#int f0/1
R2(config-if)#ip address 192.168.40.1 255.255.255.0
R2(config-if)#description Connection to HR PC
R2(config-if)#no shut
R2(config-if)#line con 0
R2(config-line)#password console
R2(config-line)#login
R2(config-line)#logging sync
R2(config-line)#exec-timeout 0 0
R2(config-line)#line aux 0
R2(config-line)#password aux
R2(config-line)#login
R2(config-line)#exit
R2(config)#line vty 0 ?
  <1-807>  Last Line number
  <cr>
R2(config)#line vty 0 807
R2(config-line)#password telnet
R2(config-line)#login
R2(config-line)#exit
R2(config)#banner motd # This is my R2 Router #
R2(config)#no ip domain-lookup
R2(config)#^Z
R2#copy run start
Destination filename [startup-config]?[enter]
Building configuration...
[OK]
R2#
```

Nice—everything was pretty straightforward. The output of the following show ip route command displays the directly connected networks of 192.168.30.0, and 192.168.40.0 and 10.1.4.0, as you can see here:

```
R2#sh ip route
     10.0.0.0/24 is subnetted, 3 subnets
C       192.168.30.0 is directly connected, FastEthernet0/0
C       192.168.40.0 is directly connected, FastEthernet0/1
C       10.1.4.0 is directly connected, Serial0/0/0
R2#
```

The Corp, R1, and R2 routers now have all their directly connected links up. But I still need to configure the R3 router.

R3 Configuration

To configure R3, I'm going to do pretty much the same thing I did with the other routers. However, there are only two interfaces (FastEthernet 0/0 and Dot11Radio0/0/0) to deal with, and again, I'll be sure to add the hostname, passwords, interface descriptions, and a banner to the router configuration.

```
Router>en
Router#config t
Router(config)#hostname R3
R3(config)#enable secret todd
R3(config)#int f0/0
R3(config-if)#ip address 10.1.5.2 255.255.255.0
R3(config-if)#description Connection to Corp Router
R3(config-if)#no shut
R3(config-if)#int dot11radio0/0/0
R3(config-if)#ip address 172.16.10.1 255.255.255.0
R3(config-if)#description WLAN for Mobile User
R3(config-if)#no shut
R3(config-if)#ssid ADMIN
R3(config-if-ssid)#guest-mode
R3(config-if-ssid)#authentication open
R3(config-if-ssid)#infrastructure-ssid
R3(config-if-ssid)#exit
R3(config-line)#line con 0
R3(config-line)#password console
R3(config-line)#login
R3(config-line)#logging sync
R3(config-line)#exec-timeout 0 0
R3(config-line)#line aux 0
R3(config-line)#password aux
R3(config-line)#login
R3(config-line)#exit
R3(config)#line vty 0 ?
  <1-807>  Last Line number
  <cr>
```

```
R3(config)#line vty 0 807
R3(config-line)#password telnet
R3(config-line)#login
R3(config-line)#exit
R3(config)#banner motd # This is my R3 Router #
R3(config)#no ip domain-lookup
R3(config)#^Z
R3#copy run start
Destination filename [startup-config]?[enter]
Building configuration...
[OK]
R3#
```

Nice—everything again was pretty straightforward...except for that wireless interface. It's true, the wireless interface is really just another interface on a router, and it looks just like that in the routing table as well. But, to bring up the wireless interface, more configurations are needed than for a simple FastEthernet interface. So, check out the following output, and then I'll tell you about the special configuration needs for this wireless interface:

```
R3(config-if)#int dot11radio0/0/0
R3(config-if)#ip address 172.16.10.1 255.255.255.0
R3(config-if)# description WLAN for Mobile User
R3(config-if)#no shut
R3(config-if)#ssid ADMIN
R3(config-if-ssid)#guest-mode
R3(config-if-ssid)#authentication open
R3(config-if-ssid)#infrastructure-ssid
```

So, what you see here is that everything is pretty commonplace until you get to the SSID configuration. This is the Service Set Identifier that creates a wireless network that hosts can connect to. Unlike access points, the interface on the R3 router is actually a routed interface, which is the reason the IP address is placed under the physical interface—typically, if this was an access point only and not a router, the IP address would be placed under the Bridge-Group Virtual Interface (BVI), which is a logical management interface.

That guest-mode line means that the interface will broadcast the SSID so wireless hosts will understand that they can connect to this interface. Authentication open means just that...no authentication. (Even so, you still have to type that command in at a minimum to make the wireless interface work.) Last, the infrastructure-ssid indicates that this interface can be used to communicate to other access points, or other devices on the infrastructure, to the actual wired network itself.

Configuring DHCP on the Router

But wait, I'm not done yet—I still need to configure the DHCP pool for the wireless clients connecting to the Dot11Radio0/0/0 interface, so let's do that now.

```
R3#config t
R3(config)#ip dhcp pool Admin
R3(dhcp-config)#network 172.16.10.0 255.255.255.0
R3(dhcp-config)#default-router 172.16.10.1
R3(dhcp-config)#dns-server 172.16.10.2
R3(dhcp-config)#exit
R3(config)#ip dhcp excluded-address 172.16.10.1 172.16.10.10
R3(config)#
```

Creating DHCP pools on a router is actually a pretty simple process, and this would be the same configuration for any router you need to add a DHCP pool to. To create the DHCP server on a router, follow these steps:

1. Just create the pool name.

2. Add the network/subnet and the default gateway.

3. Exclude any addresses you don't want handed out (like the default gateway address).

4. You'd usually add a DNS server as well.

Don't forget to add your exclusions, which are addresses you don't want the DHCP server handing out as valid host IPs. These exclusions are configured from global config mode, not within the DHCP pool config. Notice, also, that you can exclude a range of addresses on one line—very convenient. In the preceding example, I excluded 172.16.10.1 through 172.16.10.10 from being assigned by the DHCP server as valid IP address to DHCP clients. You can verify the DHCP pool with the show ip dhcp binding command.

```
R3#sh ip dhcp binding
IP address         Client-ID/           Lease expiration      Type
                   Hardware address
172.16.10.11       0001.96AB.8538          --                 Automatic
R3#
```

And of course, you can verify the client with the ipconfig command on the Mobile User laptop.

```
PC>ipconfig /all

Physical Address................: 0001.96AB.8538
IP Address......................: 172.16.10.11
Subnet Mask.....................: 255.255.255.0
Default Gateway.................: 172.16.10.1
DNS Servers.....................: 172.16.10.2
```

Now that I did a basic WLAN configuration, the mobile user is connected to the wireless network. The user just can't get anywhere else yet in the internetwork! Let's fix that.

Wireless networks will be discussed in detail in Chapter 8, "Wireless Technologies."

Configuring IP Routing in the Network

The network is good to go—right? After all, it's been correctly configured with IP addressing, administrative functions, and even clocking (automatically on the ISR routers). But how does a router send packets to remote networks when the only way it can send them is by looking at the routing table to find out how to get to the remote networks? The configured routers have information only about directly connected networks in each routing table. And what happens when a router receives a packet for a network that isn't listed in the routing table? It doesn't send a broadcast looking for the remote network—the router just discards it. Period.

So, I'm not exactly ready to rock after all. But no worries—there are several ways to configure the routing tables to include all the networks in our little internetwork so that packets will be forwarded. And what's best for one network isn't necessarily what's best for another. Understanding the different types of routing will really help you come up with the best solution for your specific environment and business requirements.

You'll learn about the following types of routing in the following sections:

- Static routing
- Default routing
- Dynamic routing

I'll start off by describing and implementing static routing on the network because if you can implement static routing *and* make it work, it means you have a solid understanding of the internetwork. Let's get started.

Static Routing

Static routing occurs when you manually add routes in each router's routing table. There are pros and cons to static routing, but that's true for all routing processes.

Static routing has the following benefits:

- There is no overhead on the router CPU, which means you could possibly buy a cheaper router than you would use if you were using dynamic routing.
- There is no bandwidth usage between routers, which means you could possibly save money on WAN links.
- It adds security because the administrator can choose to allow routing access to certain networks only.

Static routing has the following disadvantages:

■   The administrator must really understand the internetwork and how each router is connected in order to configure routes correctly.

■   If a network is added to the internetwork, the administrator has to add a route to it on all routers—by hand.

■   It's not feasible in large networks because maintaining it would be a full-time job in itself.

That said, here's the command syntax you use to add a static route to a routing table:

```
ip route [destination_network] [mask] [next-hop_address or
    exitinterface] [administrative_distance] [permanent]
```

This list describes each command in the string:

ip route   The command used to create the static route.

destination_network   The network you're placing in the routing table.

mask   The subnet mask being used on the network.

next-hop_address   The address of the next-hop router that will receive the packet and forward it to the remote network. This is the IP address of a router interface that's on a directly connected network. You must be able to ping the router interface before you can successfully add the route. If you type in the wrong next-hop address or the interface to that router is down, the static route will show up in the router's configuration but not in the routing table.

exitinterface   Used in place of the next-hop address if you want and shows up as a directly connected route.

administrative_distance   By default, static routes have an administrative distance of 1 (or even 0 if you use an exit interface instead of a next-hop address). You can change the default value by adding an administrative weight at the end of the command. I'll talk a lot more about this subject later in the "Dynamic Routing" section.

permanent   If the interface is shut down or the router can't communicate to the next-hop router, the route will automatically be discarded from the routing table by default. Choosing the permanent option keeps the entry in the routing table no matter what happens.

Before diving into configuring static routes, take a look at a sample static route and see what you can find out about it.

```
Router(config)#ip route 172.16.3.0 255.255.255.0 192.168.2.4
```

■   The ip route command tells you simply that it is a static route.

■   172.16.3.0 is the remote network you want to send packets to.

- 255.255.255.0 is the mask of the remote network.
- 192.168.2.4 is the next hop, or router, you will send packets to.

However, suppose the static route looked like this:

```
Router(config)#ip route 172.16.3.0 255.255.255.0 192.168.2.4 150
```

The 150 at the end changes the default administrative distance (AD) of 1 to 150. No worries—I'll talk much more about AD when I get into dynamic routing. For now, just remember that the AD is the trustworthiness of a route, where 0 is best and 255 is worst.

One more example, and then I'll start configuring.

```
Router(config)#ip route 172.16.3.0 255.255.255.0 s0/0/0
```

Instead of using a next-hop address, you can use an exit interface that will make the route show up as a directly connected network. Functionally, the next hop and exit interface work exactly the same.

To help you understand how static routes work, I'll demonstrate the configuration on the internetwork shown previously in Figure 6.9. I have shown this internetwork again here, in Figure 6.10, to save you from having to go back many pages to view the same figure when needed.

FIGURE 6.10   The example internetwork

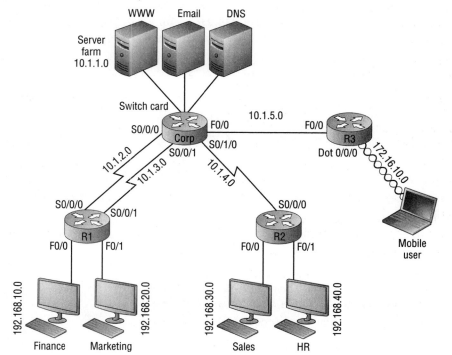

Corp

Each routing table automatically includes directly connected networks. To be able to route to all indirectly connected networks within the internetwork, the routing table must include information that describes where these other networks are located and how to get to them.

The Corp router is connected to five networks. For the Corp router to be able to route to all networks, the following networks have to be configured into its routing table:

- 192.168.10.0
- 192.168.20.0
- 192.168.30.0
- 192.168.40.0
- 172.16.10.0

The following router output shows the static routes on the Corp router and the routing table after the configuration. For the Corp router to find the remote networks, I had to place an entry into the routing table describing the remote network, the remote mask, and where to send the packets. I am going to add a *150* at the end of each line to raise the administrative distance. (When I get to dynamic routing, you'll see why I did it this way.)

```
Corp(config)#ip route 192.168.10.0 255.255.255.0 10.1.2.2 150
Corp(config)#ip route 192.168.20.0 255.255.255.0 10.1.3.2 150
Corp(config)#ip route 192.168.30.0 255.255.255.0 10.1.4.2 150
Corp(config)#ip route 192.168.40.0 255.255.255.0 10.1.4.2 150
Corp(config)#ip route 172.16.10.0 255.255.255.0 10.1.5.2 150
Corp(config)#do show run | begin ip route
ip route 192.168.10.0 255.255.255.0 10.1.2.2 150
ip route 192.168.20.0 255.255.255.0 10.1.3.2 150
ip route 192.168.30.0 255.255.255.0 10.1.4.2 150
ip route 192.168.40.0 255.255.255.0 10.1.4.2 150
ip route 172.16.10.0 255.255.255.0 10.1.5.2 150
```

For networks 192.168.10.0 and 192.168.20.0, I used a different path for each network, although I could have used just one. After the router is configured, you can type **show ip route** to see the static routes.

```
Corp(config)#do show ip route
10.0.0.0/24 is subnetted, 5 subnets
C       10.1.1.0 is directly connected, Vlan1
C       10.1.2.0 is directly connected, Serial0/0/0
C       10.1.3.0 is directly connected, Serial0/0/1
C       10.1.4.0 is directly connected, Serial0/1/0
C       10.1.5.0 is directly connected, FastEthernet0/0
```

```
         172.16.0.0/24 is subnetted, 1 subnets
S           172.16.10.0 [150/0] via 10.1.5.2
S        192.168.10.0/24 [150/0] via 10.1.2.2
S        192.168.20.0/24 [150/0] via 10.1.3.2
S        192.168.30.0/24 [150/0] via 10.1.4.2
S        192.168.40.0/24 [150/0] via 10.1.4.2
```

The Corp router is configured to route and know about all routes to all networks.

I want you to understand that if the routes don't appear in the routing table, it's because the router can't communicate with the next-hop address you've configured. You can use the permanent parameter to keep the route in the routing table even if the next-hop device can't be contacted.

The S in the preceding routing table entries means that the route is a static entry. The [150/0] is the administrative distance and metric (something I'll cover later) to the remote network. Here, the next-hop interface is 0, indicating that it's a directly connected static route.

Okay—I'm good. The Corp router now has all the information it needs to communicate with the other remote networks. But keep in mind that if the R1, R2, and R3 routers aren't configured with all the same information, the packets will simply be discarded. I'll need to fix this by configuring static routes.

Don't stress about the 150 at the end of the static route configuration. I promise I will discuss the topic really soon in this chapter, not a later one! Be assured that you don't need to worry about it at this point.

R1

The R1 router is directly connected to the networks 10.1.2.0, 10.1.3.0, 192.168.10.0, and 192.168.20.0, so I have to configure the following static routes on the R1 router:

- 10.1.1.0
- 10.1.4.0
- 10.1.5.0
- 192.168.30.0
- 192.168.40.0
- 172.16.10.0

Here's the configuration for the R1 router. Remember, you'll never create a static route to any network you're directly connected to, and you can use the next hop of either 10.1.2.1 or 10.1.3.1 since you have two links between the Corp and R1 router. I'll change between next hops so all data doesn't go down one link. It really doesn't matter which link I use at this point. Let's check out the commands.

```
R1(config)#ip route 10.1.1.0 255.255.255.0 10.1.2.1 150
R1(config)#ip route 10.1.4.0 255.255.255.0 10.1.3.1 150
R1(config)#ip route 10.1.5.0 255.255.255.0 10.1.2.1 150
R1(config)#ip route 192.168.30.0 255.255.255.0 10.1.3.1 150
R1(config)#ip route 192.168.40.0 255.255.255.0 10.1.2.1 150
R1(config)#ip route 172.16.10.0 255.255.255.0 10.1.3.1 150
R1(config)#do show run | begin ip route
ip route 10.1.1.0 255.255.255.0 10.1.2.1 150
ip route 10.1.4.0 255.255.255.0 10.1.3.1 150
ip route 10.1.5.0 255.255.255.0 10.1.2.1 150
ip route 192.168.30.0 255.255.255.0 10.1.3.1 150
ip route 192.168.40.0 255.255.255.0 10.1.2.1 150
ip route 172.16.10.0 255.255.255.0 10.1.3.1 150
```

By looking at the routing table, you can see that the R1 router now understands how to find each network.

```
R1(config)#do show ip route
      10.0.0.0/24 is subnetted, 5 subnets
S        10.1.1.0 [150/0] via 10.1.2.1
C        10.1.2.0 is directly connected, Serial0/0/0
C        10.1.3.0 is directly connected, Serial0/0/1
S        10.1.4.0 [150/0] via 10.1.3.1
S        10.1.5.0 [150/0] via 10.1.2.1
     172.16.0.0/24 is subnetted, 1 subnets
S        172.16.10.0 [150/0] via 10.1.3.1
C    192.168.10.0/24 is directly connected, FastEthernet0/0
C    192.168.20.0/24 is directly connected, FastEthernet0/1
S    192.168.30.0/24 [150/0] via 10.1.3.1
S    192.168.40.0/24 [150/0] via 10.1.2.1
```

The R1 router now has a complete routing table. As soon as the other routers in the internetwork have all the networks in their routing table, R1 will be able to communicate with all remote networks.

R2

The R2 router is directly connected to three networks 10.1.4.0, 192.168.30.0, and 192.168.40.0, so these are the routes that need to be added:

- 10.1.1.0
- 10.1.2.0

- 10.1.3.0
- 10.1.5.0
- 192.168.10.0
- 192.168.20.0
- 172.16.10.0

Here's the configuration for the R2 router:

```
R2(config)#ip route 10.1.1.0 255.255.255.0 10.1.4.1 150
R2(config)#ip route 10.1.2.0 255.255.255.0 10.1.4.1 150
R2(config)#ip route 10.1.3.0 255.255.255.0 10.1.4.1 150
R2(config)#ip route 10.1.5.0 255.255.255.0 10.1.4.1 150
R2(config)#ip route 192.168.10.0 255.255.255.0 10.1.4.1 150
R2(config)#ip route 192.168.20.0 255.255.255.0 10.1.4.1 150
R2(config)#ip route 172.16.10.0 255.255.255.0 10.1.4.1 150
R2(config)#do show run | begin ip route
ip route 10.1.1.0 255.255.255.0 10.1.4.1 150
ip route 10.1.2.0 255.255.255.0 10.1.4.1 150
ip route 10.1.3.0 255.255.255.0 10.1.4.1 150
ip route 10.1.5.0 255.255.255.0 10.1.4.1 150
ip route 192.168.10.0 255.255.255.0 10.1.4.1 150
ip route 192.168.20.0 255.255.255.0 10.1.4.1 150
ip route 172.16.10.0 255.255.255.0 10.1.4.1 150
```

The following output shows the routing table on the R2 router:

```
R2(config)#do show ip route
      10.0.0.0/24 is subnetted, 5 subnets
S        10.1.1.0 [150/0] via 10.1.4.1
S        10.1.2.0 [150/0] via 10.1.4.1
S        10.1.3.0 [150/0] via 10.1.4.1
C        10.1.4.0 is directly connected, Serial0/0/0
S        10.1.5.0 [150/0] via 10.1.4.1
      172.16.0.0/24 is subnetted, 1 subnets
S        172.16.10.0 [150/0] via 10.1.4.1
S     192.168.10.0/24 [150/0] via 10.1.4.1
S     192.168.20.0/24 [150/0] via 10.1.4.1
C     192.168.30.0/24 is directly connected, FastEthernet0/0
C     192.168.40.0/24 is directly connected, FastEthernet0/1
```

R2 now shows all 10 networks in the internetwork, so it too can now communicate with all routers and networks (that are configured so far).

R3

The R3 router is directly connected to networks 10.1.5.0 and 172.16.10.0, but I need to add all these routes, eight in total:

- 10.1.1.0
- 10.1.2.0
- 10.1.3.0
- 10.1.4.0
- 192.168.10.0
- 192.168.20.0
- 192.168.30.0
- 192.168.40.0

Here's the configuration for the R3 router; however, I am going to use the exit interface instead of the next hop address for this router:

```
R3#show run | begin ip route
R3(config)#ip route 10.1.1.0 255.255.255.0 fastethernet 0/0 150
R3(config)#ip route 10.1.2.0 255.255.255.0 fastethernet 0/0 150
R3(config)#ip route 10.1.3.0 255.255.255.0 fastethernet 0/0 150
R3(config)#ip route 10.1.4.0 255.255.255.0 fastethernet 0/0 150
R3(config)#ip route 192.168.10.0 255.255.255.0 fastethernet 0/0 150
R3(config)#ip route 192.168.20.0 255.255.255.0 fastethernet 0/0 150
R3(config)#ip route 192.168.30.0 255.255.255.0 fastethernet 0/0 150
R3(config)#ip route 192.168.40.0 255.255.255.0 fastethernet 0/0 150
R3#show ip route
      10.0.0.0/24 is subnetted, 5 subnets
S        10.1.1.0 is directly connected, FastEthernet0/0
S        10.1.2.0 is directly connected, FastEthernet0/0
S        10.1.3.0 is directly connected, FastEthernet0/0
S        10.1.4.0 is directly connected, FastEthernet0/0
C        10.1.5.0 is directly connected, FastEthernet0/0
      172.16.0.0/24 is subnetted, 1 subnets
C        172.16.10.0 is directly connected, Dot11Radio0/0/0
S     192.168.10.0/24 is directly connected, FastEthernet0/0
S     192.168.20.0/24 is directly connected, FastEthernet0/0
S     192.168.30.0/24 is directly connected, FastEthernet0/0
S     192.168.40.0/24 is directly connected, FastEthernet0/0
R3#
```

Looking at the show ip route command output, you can see that the static routes are listed as directly connected. Strange? Not really, because I used the exit interface instead of the next-hop address, and functionally, there's no difference between them, only how they display in the routing table. However, now that I showed you what using an exit interface displays in the routing table instead of using a next hop with static routing, let me show you an easier way for the R3 router.

Default Routing

Although I don't fully explain default routing for another couple pages, I feel it would be advantageous to configure default routing at this time to help you understand when you'd typically consider configuring it. The R2 and R3 routers, which I have connected to the Corp router, are considered stub routers. A stub indicates that the networks in this design have only one way out to reach all other networks. I'll show you the configuration, verify the network in the next section, and then discuss default routing in detail. Here's the configuration I could have done on the R3 router instead of typing in eight static routes because of its stub status:

```
R3(config)#no ip route 10.1.1.0 255.255.255.0 FastEthernet0/0 150
R3(config)#no ip route 10.1.2.0 255.255.255.0 FastEthernet0/0 150
R3(config)#no ip route 10.1.3.0 255.255.255.0 FastEthernet0/0 150
R3(config)#no ip route 10.1.4.0 255.255.255.0 FastEthernet0/0 150
R3(config)#no ip route 192.168.10.0 255.255.255.0 FastEthernet0/0 150
R3(config)#no ip route 192.168.20.0 255.255.255.0 FastEthernet0/0 150
R3(config)#no ip route 192.168.30.0 255.255.255.0 FastEthernet0/0 150
R3(config)#no ip route 192.168.40.0 255.255.255.0 FastEthernet0/0 150
R3(config)#ip route 0.0.0.0 0.0.0.0 10.1.5.1
R3(config)#ip classless
R3(config)#do show ip route
      10.0.0.0/24 is subnetted, 1 subnets
C        10.1.5.0 is directly connected, Vlan1
172.16.0.0/24 is subnetted, 1 subnets
C        172.16.10.0 is directly connected, Dot11Radio0
S*    0.0.0.0/0 [1/0] via 10.1.5.1
```

Okay—once I removed all the initial static routes I configured, this seems a lot easier than typing eight static routes, doesn't it? And it is, but there's a catch—you can't do things like this on all routers, only on stub routers. I could've used default routing on the R2 as well since that router is considered a stub, and I didn't add the 150 to this default route even though I easily could have. I didn't do that because it's really simple to just remove the route if you need to when I get to dynamic routing later.

So, I've done it! All the routers have the correct routing table, so all routers and hosts should be able to communicate without a hitch—for now. But if you add even one more network or another router to the internetwork, you'll have to update each and every router's routing tables by hand—yikes! This isn't a problem at all if you have a small network, but it's obviously extremely time-consuming if you're dealing with a large internetwork!

Verifying Your Configuration

I'm not done yet—once all the routers' routing tables are configured, they need to be verified. The best way to do this, besides using the show ip route command, is with the Ping program. I'll start by pinging from the R3 router to the R1 router.

Here's the output:

```
R3#ping 10.1.2.2
Type escape sequence to abort.
Sending 5, 100-byte ICMP Echos to 10.1.2.2, timeout is 2 seconds:
!!!!!
Success rate is 100 percent (5/5), round-trip min/avg/max = 1/2/4 ms
```

From router R3, a ping to the WWW, Email, and DNS servers on the Corp backbone would be a good test as well. Here's the router output:

```
R3#ping 10.1.1.1
Type escape sequence to abort.
Sending 5, 100-byte ICMP Echos to 10.1.1.1, timeout is 2 seconds:
!!!!!
Success rate is 100 percent (5/5), round-trip min/avg/max = 1/2/5 ms


R3#ping 10.1.1.2
Type escape sequence to abort.
Sending 5, 100-byte ICMP Echos to 10.1.1.2, timeout is 2 seconds:
!!!!!
Success rate is 100 percent (5/5), round-trip min/avg/max = 4/7/10 ms


R3# ping 10.1.1.3
Type escape sequence to abort.
Sending 5, 100-byte ICMP Echos to 10.1.1.3, timeout is 2 seconds:
!!!!!
Success rate is 100 percent (5/5), round-trip min/avg/max = 5/7/10 ms


R3#ping 10.1.1.4
Type escape sequence to abort.
Sending 5, 100-byte ICMP Echos to 10.1.1.4, timeout is 2 seconds:
!!!!!
Success rate is 100 percent (5/5), round-trip min/avg/max = 3/5/10 ms
```

Also, I can trace from the Mobile User wireless host to the Finance host connected to the R2 router to see the hops the packet takes to get to the Finance host, but first I have to make sure the Mobile User host received a DHCP server address from the R3 router.

PC>**ipconfig**

```
IP Address......................: 172.16.10.2
Subnet Mask.....................: 255.255.255.0
Default Gateway.................: 172.16.10.1
```

PC>**ping 192.168.10.2**
```
Pinging 192.168.10.2 with 32 bytes of data:
Reply from 192.168.10.2: bytes=32 time=17ms TTL=125
Reply from 192.168.10.2: bytes=32 time=21ms TTL=125
Reply from 192.168.10.2: bytes=32 time=19ms TTL=125
Reply from 192.168.10.2: bytes=32 time=17ms TTL=125
```

```
Ping statistics for 192.168.10.2:
    Packets: Sent = 4, Received = 4, Lost = 0 (0% loss),
Approximate round trip times in milli-seconds:
    Minimum = 17ms, Maximum = 21ms, Average = 18ms
```

PC>**tracert 192.168.10.2**
```
Tracing route to 192.168.10.2 over a maximum of 30 hops:
```

```
1    15 ms      11 ms      14 ms      172.16.10.1
2    13 ms      13 ms      8 ms       10.1.5.1
3    12 ms      14 ms      15 ms      10.1.2.2
4    16 ms      14 ms      15 ms      192.168.10.2
Trace complete.
```

Notice I used a tracert command because I am on a Windows host. Remember, tracert is not a valid Cisco command; you must use the command traceroute from a router prompt.

Okay, since I can communicate from end to end and to each host without a problem, the static and default route configurations have been a success!

Default Routing

We use *default routing* to send packets with a remote destination network not in the routing table to the next-hop router. You should use default routing only on stub networks—those with only one exit path out of the network, although there are exceptions to this statement, and default routing is configured on a case-by-case basis when a network is designed. This is a rule of thumb to keep in mind.

If you tried to put a default route on a router that isn't a stub, it is possible that packets wouldn't be forwarded to the correct networks because they have more than one interface routing to other routers. You can easily create loops with default routing, so be careful!

To configure a default route, you use wildcards in both the network address and mask of a static route (as I demonstrated in the R3 configuration). In fact, you can just think of a default route as a static route that uses wildcards instead of network and mask information.

By using a default route, you can just create one static route entry instead. This sure is easier than typing in all those routes!

```
R3(config)#ip route 0.0.0.0 0.0.0.0 10.1.5.1
R3(config)#ip classless
R3(config)#do show ip route
Gateway of last resort is 10.1.5.1 to network 0.0.0.0
     10.0.0.0/24 is subnetted, 1 subnets
C       10.1.5.0 is directly connected, FastEthernet0/0
     172.16.0.0/24 is subnetted, 1 subnets
C       172.16.10.0 is directly connected, Dot11Radio0/0/0
S*   0.0.0.0/0 [1/0] via 10.1.5.1
```

If you look at the routing table, you'll see only the two directly connected networks plus an S*, which indicates that this entry is a candidate for a default route. So, instead of configuring eight static routes on R3, I could also have completed the default route command another way.

```
R3(config)#ip route 0.0.0.0 0.0.0.0 Fa0/0
```

What this is telling you is that if you don't have an entry for a packet with a destination IP in the routing table, just forward it out Fa0/0. You can choose the IP address of the next-hop router or the exit interface—either way, it will work the same. Remember, I used the exit interface configuration with the R3 static route configs, which showed as directly connected in the router table. However, when I configured the default route on R3, I used the next-hop functionally; there is no difference.

Notice also on the first line in the routing table that the gateway of last resort is now set. Even so, there's one more command you must be aware of when using default routes: the `ip classless` command.

All Cisco routers are *classful* routers, meaning they expect a default subnet mask on each interface of the router. When a router receives a packet for a destination subnet that's not in the routing table, it will drop the packet by default. If you're using default routing, you must use the `ip classless` command because it is possible that no remote subnets will be in the routing table. Why? Because a configured default route will be ignored for subnets that are members of the same classful network as the other routes in the router's routing table, and this command basically says, "Hey, IP! Before you discard that packet, check to see whether a gateway of last resort is set!"

Since I have version 12.4 of the IOS on my routers, the `ip classless` command is on by default, and it doesn't even show in the configuration. If you're using default routing and this command isn't in your configuration, you will need to add it if you have subnetted networks on your routers. The command is shown here:

```
R3(config)#ip classless
```

There's another command you can use to help you in your internetwork if you have configured a gateway of last resort—the `ip default-network` command. I'll use this in a configuration example at the end of the chapter. Figure 6.11 shows a network that needs to have a gateway of last resort statement configured.

FIGURE 6.11   Configuring a gateway of last resort

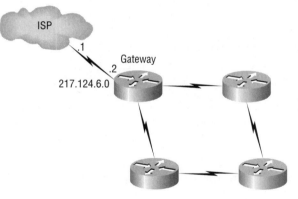

Here are three commands (all providing a default route solution) for adding a gateway of last resort on the router to the ISP:

```
Gateway(config)#ip route 0.0.0.0 0.0.0.0 217.124.6.1
```

```
Gateway(config)#ip route 0.0.0.0 0.0.0.0 s0/0
```

```
Gateway(config)#ip default-network 217.124.6.0
```

The first two are the same command; one just uses the next hop and the other the exit interface. You will find no difference in this configuration, as I've already discussed. However, if you set them both for some reason, the exit interface would be used. Do you know why? Directly connected routes have an administrative distance of 0, but in this example, you'd see absolutely no functional difference between the two commands.

The `ip default-network` command would advertise the default route you configured on your border router when you configure an IGP (like RIPv2) on the router. This is so other routers in your internetwork will receive this route as a default route automatically. Again, I'll configure this in the network at the end of the chapter, so now you have something pretty exciting to look forward to!

But what happens if you misconfigured a default route? Let's take a look at the output of a `show ip route` command and compare that to the network in Figure 6.12 to see whether you can find a problem.

```
Router#sh ip route
[output cut]
Gateway of last resort is 172.19.22.2 to network 0.0.0.0


C       172.17.22.0 is directly connected, FastEthernet0/0
C       172.18.22.0  is directly connected, Serial0/0
S*      0.0.0.0/0 [1/0] via 172.19.22.2
```

FIGURE 6.12 Misconfigured default route

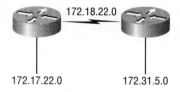

Find anything? You can see by looking at the figure and the directly connected routes in the routing table that the WAN link is on network 172.18.22.0 and that the default route is forwarding all packets to the 172.19.22.2 next-hop address. This is just bad—it will never work, so the problem is a misconfigured static (default) route. The default route should have been set to 172.18.22.2 or the exit interface.

One last thing before moving on to dynamic routing. If you have the routing table output as shown in the following lines, what happens if the router receives a packet from 10.1.6.100 destined for host 10.1.8.5?

```
Router#sh ip route
[output cut]
Gateway of last resort is 10.1.5.5 to network 0.0.0.0
```

```
R      10.1.3.0 [120/1] via 101.2.2, 00:00:00, Serial 0/0
C      10.1.2.0  is directly connected, Serial0/0
C      10.1.5.0  is directly connected, Serial0/1
C      10.1.6.0  is directly connected, Fastethernet0/0
R*     0.0.0.0/0 [120/0] via 10.1.5.5, 00:00:00 Serial 0/1
```

This is a tad different from what I've shown you up until now because the default route is listed as R*, which means it's a RIP-injected route. This is because someone configured the ip default-network command on a remote router as well as configuring RIP, causing RIP to advertise this route through the internetwork as a default route. Since the destination address is 10.1.8.5 and there is no route to network 10.1.8.0, the router would use the default route and send the packet out serial 0/1.

Dynamic Routing

Dynamic routing is when protocols are used to find networks and update routing tables on routers. True, this is easier than using static or default routing, but it'll cost you in terms of router CPU processing and bandwidth on the network links. A routing protocol defines the set of rules used by a router when it communicates routing information between neighboring routers.

The routing protocol I'm going to talk about in this chapter is Routing Information Protocol (RIP) versions 1 and 2.

Two types of routing protocols are used in internetworks: interior gateway protocols (IGPs) and exterior gateway protocols (EGPs). IGPs are used to exchange routing information with routers in the same autonomous system (AS). An AS is a collection of networks under a common administrative domain, which basically means that all routers sharing the same routing table information are in the same AS. EGPs are used to communicate between ASs. An example of an EGP is Border Gateway Protocol (BGP), which is beyond the scope of this book.

Since routing protocols are so essential to dynamic routing, I'll give you the basic information you need to know about them next. Later in this chapter, I'll focus on configuration.

Routing Protocol Basics

There are some important things you should know about routing protocols before getting deeper into RIP. Specifically, you need to understand administrative distances, the three different kinds of routing protocols, and routing loops. I will cover each of these in more detail in the following sections.

Administrative Distances

The *administrative distance (AD)* is used to rate the trustworthiness of routing information received on a router from a neighbor router. An administrative distance is an integer from 0 to 255, where 0 is the most trusted and 255 means no traffic will be passed via this route.

If a router receives two updates listing the same remote network, the first thing the router checks is the AD. If one of the advertised routes has a lower AD than the other, then the route with the lowest AD will be placed in the routing table.

If both advertised routes to the same network have the same AD, then routing protocol metrics (such as *hop count* or bandwidth of the lines) will be used to find the best path to the remote network. The advertised route with the lowest metric will be placed in the routing table. But if both advertised routes have the same AD as well as the same metrics, then the routing protocol will load balance to the remote network (which means that it sends packets down each link).

Table 6.2 shows the default administrative distances that a Cisco router uses to decide which route to take to a remote network.

TABLE 6.2   Default administrative distances

Route Source	Default AD
Connected interface	0
Static route	1
EIGRP	90
IGRP	100
OSPF	110
RIP	120
External EIGRP	170
Unknown	255 (This route will never be used.)

If a network is directly connected, the router will always use the interface connected to the network. If you configure a static route, the router will then believe that route over any other learned routes. You can change the administrative distance of static routes, but by default, they have an AD of 1. In the previous static route configuration, the AD of each route is set at 150. This lets you configure routing protocols without having to remove the static routes. They'll be used as backup routes in case the routing protocol experiences a failure of some type.

For example, if you have a static route, a RIP advertised route, and an EIGRP-advertised route listing the same network, then by default, the router will always use the static route unless you change the AD of the static route—which I did.

Routing Protocols

There are three classes of routing protocols.

Distance Vector   The *distance-vector protocols* in use today find the best path to a remote network by judging distance. For example, in the case of RIP routing, each time a packet goes through a router, that's called a *hop*. The route with the least number of hops to the network is determined to be the best route. The vector indicates the direction to the remote network. RIPv2 is a distance-vector routing protocol. RIPv2 periodically sends the entire routing table to directly connected neighbors.

Link state   In *link-state protocols*, also called *shortest-path-first protocols*, the routers each create three separate tables. One of these tables keeps track of directly attached neighbors, one determines the topology of the entire internetwork, and one is used as the routing table. Link-state routers know more about the internetwork than routers running a distance-vector routing protocol. OSPF is an IP routing protocol that is completely link state. Link-state protocols send updates containing the state of their own links to all other directly connected routers on the network, which is then propagated to their neighbors.

Hybrid   *Hybrid protocols* use aspects of both distance vector and link state—for example, EIGRP. However, Cisco mostly calls EIGRP an Advanced Distance Vector routing protocol.

There's no set way of defining routing protocols for use with every business. This is something you really have to do on a case-by-case basis. If you understand how the different routing protocols work, you can make good, solid decisions that truly meet the individual needs of any business.

Distance-Vector Routing Protocols

The distance-vector routing algorithm passes complete routing table contents to neighboring routers, which then combine the received routing table entries with their own routing tables to complete the router's routing table. This is called *routing by rumor* because a router receiving an update from a neighbor router believes the information about remote networks without actually finding out for itself.

It's possible to have a network that has multiple links to the same remote network, and if that's the case and if the routes were learned from different routing protocols, the administrative distance of each received update is checked first. If the AD is the same (which typically means the routes came from the same routing protocol), the protocol will have to use metrics to determine the best path to use to that remote network.

RIP uses only hop count to determine the best path to a network. If RIP finds more than one route with the same hop count to the same remote network, it will automatically perform round-robin load balancing. RIP can perform load balancing for up to sixteen equal-cost links (four by default).

However, a problem with this type of routing metric arises when the two routes to a remote network have different bandwidths but the same hop count. Figure 6.13, for example, shows two links to remote network 172.16.10.0.

FIGURE 6.13   Pinhole congestion

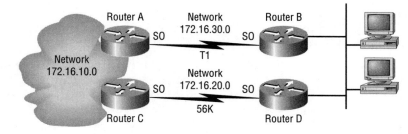

Since network 172.16.30.0 is a T1 link with a bandwidth of 1.544Mbps and network 172.16.20.0 is a 56K link, you'd want the router to choose the T1 over the 56K link, right? But because hop count is the only metric used with RIP routing, the two links would be seen as being of equal cost. This little snag is called *pinhole congestion*.

It's important to understand what a distance-vector routing protocol does when it starts up. In Figure 6.14, the four routers start off with only their directly connected networks in their routing tables. After a distance-vector routing protocol is started on each router, the routing tables are updated with all route information gathered from neighbor routers.

FIGURE 6.14   The internetwork with distance-vector routing

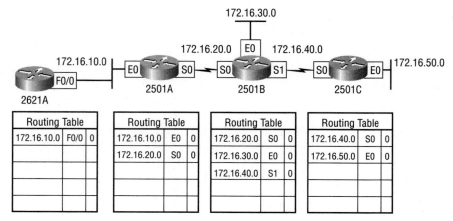

As shown in Figure 6.14, each router has only the directly connected networks in each routing table. Each router sends its complete routing table out to each active interface. The routing table of each router includes the network number, exit interface, and hop count to the network.

In Figure 6.15, the routing tables are complete because they include information about all the networks in the internetwork. They are considered *converged*. When the routers are converging, it is possible that no data will be passed. That's why fast convergence time is a serious plus. In fact, that's one of the problems with RIP—its slow convergence time.

FIGURE 6.15   Converged routing tables

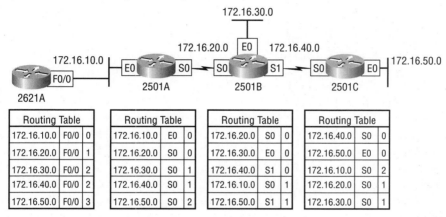

The routing table in each router keeps information regarding the remote network number, the interface to which the router will send packets to reach that network, and the hop count or metric to the network.

Routing Loops

Distance-vector routing protocols keep track of any changes to the internetwork by broadcasting periodic routing updates out all active interfaces. This broadcast includes the complete routing table. This works just fine, but it's expensive in terms of CPU processing and link bandwidth. And if a network outage happens, real problems can occur. Plus, the slow convergence of distance-vector routing protocols can result in inconsistent routing tables and routing loops.

Routing loops can occur because every router isn't updated simultaneously, or even close to it. Here's an example—let's say that the interface to Network 5 in Figure 6.16 fails. All routers know about Network 5 from RouterE. RouterA, in its tables, has a path to Network 5 through RouterB.

FIGURE 6.16   Routing loop example

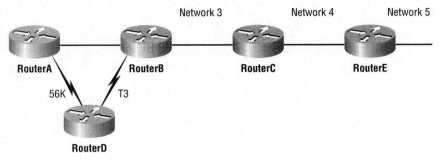

When Network 5 fails, RouterE tells RouterC. This causes RouterC to stop routing to Network 5 through RouterE. But routers A, B, and D don't know about Network 5 yet, so they keep sending out update information. RouterC will eventually send out its update and cause B to stop routing to Network 5, but routers A and D are still not updated. To them, it appears that Network 5 is still available through RouterB with a metric of 3.

The problem occurs when RouterA sends out its regular 30-second "Hello, I'm still here—these are the links I know about" message, which includes the ability to reach Network 5, and now routers B and D receive the wonderful news that Network 5 can be reached from RouterA, so routers B and D then send out the information that Network 5 is available. Any packet destined for Network 5 will go to RouterA, to RouterB, and then back to RouterA. This is a routing loop—how do you stop it?

Maximum Hop Count

The routing loop problem just described can create an issue called *counting to infinity*, and it's caused by gossip (broadcasts) and wrong information being communicated and propagated throughout the internetwork. Without some form of intervention, the hop count increases indefinitely each time a packet passes through a router.

One way of solving this problem is to define a *maximum hop count*. RIP permits a hop count of up to 15, so anything that requires 16 hops is deemed unreachable. In other words, after a loop of 15 hops, Network 5 will be considered down. Thus, the maximum hop count will control how long it takes for a routing table entry to become invalid or questionable.

Split Horizon

Another solution to the routing loop problem is called *split horizon*. This reduces incorrect routing information and routing overhead in a distance-vector network by enforcing the rule that routing information cannot be sent back in the direction from which it was received.

In other words, the routing protocol differentiates which interface a network route was learned on, and once this is determined, it won't advertise the route back out that same interface. This would have prevented RouterA from sending the update information it received from RouterB back to RouterB.

Route Poisoning

Another way to avoid problems caused by inconsistent updates and stop network loops is *route poisoning*. For example, when Network 5 goes down, RouterE initiates route poisoning by advertising Network 5 with a hop count of 16, or unreachable (sometimes referred to as *infinite*).

This poisoning of the route to Network 5 keeps RouterC from being susceptible to incorrect updates about the route to Network 5. When RouterC receives a route poisoning from RouterE, it sends an update, called a *poison reverse*, back to RouterE. This ensures that all routers on the segment have received the poisoned route information.

Holddowns

A *holddown* prevents regular update messages from reinstating a route that is going up and down (called *flapping*). Typically, this happens on a serial link that's losing connectivity and then coming back up. If there wasn't a way to stabilize this, the network would never converge, and that one flapping interface could bring the entire network down!

Holddowns prevent routes from changing too rapidly by allowing time for either the downed route to come back up or the network to stabilize somewhat before changing to the next best route. These also tell routers to restrict, for a specific time period, changes that might affect recently removed routes. This prevents inoperative routes from being prematurely restored to other routers' tables.

Routing Information Protocol

Routing Information Protocol (RIP) is a true distance-vector routing protocol. RIP sends the complete routing table out to all active interfaces every 30 seconds. RIP only uses hop count to determine the best way to a remote network, but it has a maximum allowable hop count of 15 by default, meaning that 16 is deemed unreachable. RIP works well in small networks, but it's inefficient on large networks with slow WAN links or on networks with a large number of routers installed.

RIP version 1 uses only *classful routing*, which means that all devices in the network must use the same subnet mask. This is because RIP version 1 doesn't send updates with subnet mask information in tow. RIP version 2 provides something called *prefix routing* and does send subnet mask information with the route updates. This is called *classless routing*.

In the following sections, I will first discuss the RIP timers that are used to try to keep the network stable, and then the RIP configuration.

RIP Timers

RIP uses four different kinds of timers to regulate its performance.

Route Update Timer   Sets the interval (typically 30 seconds) between periodic routing updates in which the router sends a complete copy of its routing table out to all neighbors.

Route Invalid Timer   Determines the length of time that must elapse (180 seconds) before a router determines that a route has become invalid. It will come to this conclusion if it hasn't heard any updates about a particular route for that period. When that happens, the router will send out updates to all its neighbors letting them know that the route is invalid.

Holddown Timer   This sets the amount of time during which routing information is suppressed. Routes will enter into the holddown state when an update packet is received that indicated the route is unreachable. This continues either *until* an update packet is received with a better metric, until the original route comes back up, or until the holddown timer expires. The default is 180 seconds.

Route Flush Timer   Sets the time between a route becoming invalid and its removal from the routing table (240 seconds). Before it's removed from the table, the router notifies its neighbors of that route's impending demise. The value of the route invalid timer must be less than that of the route flush timer. This gives the router enough time to tell its neighbors about the invalid route before the local routing table is updated.

Configuring RIP Routing

To configure RIP routing, just turn on the protocol with the `router rip` command and tell the RIP routing protocol which networks to advertise. That's it. Let's configure the example five-router internetwork (refer to Figure 6.10) with RIP routing.

Corp

RIP has an administrative distance of 120. Static routes have an administrative distance of 1 by default, and since I currently have static routes configured, the routing tables won't be populated with RIP information. However, because I added the 150 to the end of each static route, I'm good to go.

You can add the RIP routing protocol by using the `router rip` command and the `network` command. The `network` command tells the routing protocol which classful network to advertise. By doing this process, you activate the RIP routing process on the interfaces whose addressing falls within the specified classful networks configured with the network command under the RIP routing process.

Look at the Corp router configuration and see how easy this is.

```
Corp#config t
Corp(config)#router rip
Corp(config-router)#network 10.0.0.0
```

That's it. Typically just two or three commands, and you're done—sure makes your job a lot easier than when using static routes, doesn't it? However, keep in mind the extra router CPU processing and bandwidth that you're consuming.

Notice I didn't type in subnets, only the classful network address (all subnet bits and host bits off!). It is the job of the routing protocol to find the subnets and populate the routing tables. Since you have no router buddies running RIP, you won't see any RIP routes in the routing table yet.

> Remember that RIP uses the classful address when configuring the network address. Because of this, all subnet masks of any particular classful network must be the same on all devices in the network (this is called *classful routing*). To clarify this, let's say you're using a Class B network address of 172.16.0.0/24 with subnets 172.16.10.0, 172.16.20.0, and 172.16.30.0. You would only type in the classful network address of 172.16.0.0 and let RIP find the subnets and place them in the routing table.

R1

Let's configure the R1 router, which is connected to three networks, and you need to configure all directly connected classful network (not subnets).

```
R1#config t
R1(config)#router rip
R1(config-router)#network 10.0.0.0
R1(config-router)#network 192.168.10.0
R1(config-router)#network 192.168.20.0
R1(config-router)#do show ip route


      10.0.0.0/24 is subnetted, 5 subnets
R        10.1.1.0 [120/1] via 10.1.2.1, 00:00:15, Serial0/0/0
                  [120/1] via 10.1.3.1, 00:00:15, Serial0/0/1
C        10.1.2.0 is directly connected, Serial0/0/0
C        10.1.3.0 is directly connected, Serial0/0/1
R        10.1.4.0 [120/1] via 10.1.2.1, 00:00:15, Serial0/0/0
                  [120/1] via 10.1.3.1, 00:00:15, Serial0/0/1
R        10.1.5.0 [120/1] via 10.1.2.1, 00:00:15, Serial0/0/0
                  [120/1] via 10.1.3.1, 00:00:15, Serial0/0/1
      172.16.0.0/24 is subnetted, 1 subnets
S        172.16.10.0 [150/0] via 10.1.3.1
C     192.168.10.0/24 is directly connected, FastEthernet0/0
C     192.168.20.0/24 is directly connected, FastEthernet0/1
```

```
S     192.168.30.0/24 [150/0] via 10.1.3.1
S     192.168.40.0/24 [150/0] via 10.1.2.1
R1(config-router)#
```

That was pretty straightforward. Let's talk about this routing table. Since I have one RIP buddy out there that I am exchanging routing tables with, you can see the RIP networks coming from the Corp router. (All the other routes still show up as static.) RIP also found both connections to the Corp router and will load balance between them for each network that is advertised as a RIP injected route since the hop count is being advertised as 1 to each network. Luckily, they are all the same bandwidth or I'd have pinhole congestion!

R2

Let's configure the R2 router with RIP.

```
R2#config t
R2(config)#router rip
R2(config-router)#network 10.0.0.0
R2(config-router)#network 192.168.30.0
R2(config-router)#network 192.168.40.0
R2(config-router)#do show ip route
     10.0.0.0/24 is subnetted, 5 subnets
R       10.1.1.0 [120/1] via 10.1.4.1, 00:00:17, Serial0/0/0
R       10.1.2.0 [120/1] via 10.1.4.1, 00:00:17, Serial0/0/0
R       10.1.3.0 [120/1] via 10.1.4.1, 00:00:17, Serial0/0/0
C       10.1.4.0 is directly connected, Serial0/0/0
R       10.1.5.0 [120/1] via 10.1.4.1, 00:00:17, Serial0/0/0
     172.16.0.0/24 is subnetted, 1 subnets
S       172.16.10.0 [150/0] via 10.1.4.1
R     192.168.10.0/24 [120/2] via 10.1.4.1, 00:00:17, Serial0/0/0
R     192.168.20.0/24 [120/2] via 10.1.4.1, 00:00:17, Serial0/0/0
C     192.168.30.0/24 is directly connected, FastEthernet0/0
C     192.168.40.0/24 is directly connected, FastEthernet0/1
R2(config-router)#
```

The routing table is growing Rs as I add RIP buddies! You can still see that all routes are in the routing table; only one is still a static route—just one more router to go.

R3

Let's configure the R3 router with RIP—here is the last router's RIP configuration:

```
R3#config t
R3(config)#router rip
R3(config-router)#network 10.0.0.0
R3(config-router)#network 172.16.0.0
```

```
R3(config-router)#do sh ip route
     10.0.0.0/24 is subnetted, 5 subnets
R       10.1.1.0 [120/1] via 10.1.5.1, 00:00:15, FastEthernet0/0
R       10.1.2.0 [120/1] via 10.1.5.1, 00:00:15, FastEthernet0/0
R       10.1.3.0 [120/1] via 10.1.5.1, 00:00:15, FastEthernet0/0
R       10.1.4.0 [120/1] via 10.1.5.1, 00:00:15, FastEthernet0/0
C       10.1.5.0 is directly connected, FastEthernet0/0
     172.16.0.0/24 is subnetted, 1 subnets
C       172.16.10.0 is directly connected, Dot11Radio0/0/0
R    192.168.10.0/24 [120/2] via 10.1.5.1, 00:00:15, FastEthernet0/0
R    192.168.20.0/24 [120/2] via 10.1.5.1, 00:00:15, FastEthernet0/0
R    192.168.30.0/24 [120/2] via 10.1.5.1, 00:00:15, FastEthernet0/0
R    192.168.40.0/24 [120/2] via 10.1.5.1, 00:00:15, FastEthernet0/0
R3#
```

Finally, all routes showing in the routing table are RIP injected routes. Notice that since I am configuring classful network statements that the WLAN network is 172.16.0.0, not 172.16.10.0!

It's also to important to remember administrative distances and why I needed to either remove the static routes before I added RIP routing or set them higher than 120 as I did.

By default, directly connected routes have an administrative distance of 0, static routes have an administrative distance of 1, and RIP has an administrative distance of 120. I call RIP the "gossip protocol" because it reminds me of junior-high school, where if you hear a rumor (advertised route), it just has to be true without exception. And that pretty much sums up how RIP behaves on an internetwork—rumor mill as protocol!

Verifying the RIP Routing Tables

Each routing table should now have all directly connected routes as well as RIP-injected routes received from neighboring routers. Now you can go back to the Corp router and check it out.

This output shows you the contents of the Corp routing table:

```
     10.0.0.0/24 is subnetted, 5 subnets
C       10.1.1.0 is directly connected, Vlan1
C       10.1.2.0 is directly connected, Serial0/0/0
C       10.1.3.0 is directly connected, Serial0/0/1
C       10.1.4.0 is directly connected, Serial0/1/0
C       10.1.5.0 is directly connected, FastEthernet0/0
     172.16.0.0/16 is variably subnetted, 2 subnets, 2 masks
R       172.16.0.0/16 [120/1] via 10.1.5.2, 00:00:19, FastEthernet0/0
S       172.16.10.0/24 [150/0] via 10.1.5.2
R    192.168.10.0/24 [120/1] via 10.1.2.2, 00:00:19, Serial0/0/0
                      [120/1] via 10.1.3.2, 00:00:19, Serial0/0/1
```

```
R     192.168.20.0/24 [120/1] via 10.1.2.2, 00:00:19, Serial0/0/0
                       [120/1] via 10.1.3.2, 00:00:19, Serial0/0/1
R     192.168.30.0/24 [120/1] via 10.1.4.2, 00:00:19, Serial0/1/0
R     192.168.40.0/24 [120/1] via 10.1.4.2, 00:00:19, Serial0/1/0
Corp#
```

This output shows you basically the same routing table has the same entries that it had when I was using static routes—except for that R. The R means that the networks were added dynamically using the RIP routing protocol. The [120/1] is the administrative distance of the route (120) along with the number of hops to that remote network (1). From the Corp router, all networks are one hop away. There is one odd entry in this table, and you may have notice this: the 172.16.10.0 network is listed twice, once as a /16 and once as a /24. One route is listed as a static route, and one is listed as a RIP injected route. This route should not be in the table twice, especially since the static route even has [150/0], which is a high administrative distance.

Let's take a look at R2's routing table as well.

```
      10.0.0.0/24 is subnetted, 5 subnets
R        10.1.1.0 [120/1] via 10.1.4.1, 00:00:21, Serial0/0/0
R        10.1.2.0 [120/1] via 10.1.4.1, 00:00:21, Serial0/0/0
R        10.1.3.0 [120/1] via 10.1.4.1, 00:00:21, Serial0/0/0
C        10.1.4.0 is directly connected, Serial0/0/0
R        10.1.5.0 [120/1] via 10.1.4.1, 00:00:21, Serial0/0/0
      172.16.0.0/16 is variably subnetted, 2 subnets, 2 masks
R        172.16.0.0/16 [120/2] via 10.1.4.1, 00:00:21, Serial0/0/0
S        172.16.10.0/24 [150/0] via 10.1.4.1
R     192.168.10.0/24 [120/2] via 10.1.4.1, 00:00:21, Serial0/0/0
R     192.168.20.0/24 [120/2] via 10.1.4.1, 00:00:21, Serial0/0/0
C     192.168.30.0/24 is directly connected, FastEthernet0/0
C     192.168.40.0/24 is directly connected, FastEthernet0/1
R2#
```

Notice the same issue. RIPv1 doesn't work with discontiguous networks, and that is what this is. Keep this thought in mind, and I'll tell you why this is happening later in this chapter and what must be done to fix it.

So, while yes, it's true that RIP has worked in my little internetwork, it's not the solution for every enterprise. That's because this technique has a maximum hop count of only 15 (16 is deemed unreachable). Plus, it performs full routing-table updates every 30 seconds, which would bring a larger internetwork to a painful crawl pretty quick!

There's one more thing I want to show you about RIP routing tables and the parameters used to advertise remote networks. Notice, using as an example a different router on a different network for a second, that the following routing table shows [120/15] in the 10.1.3.0 network metric. This means that the administrative distance is 120, the default for

RIP, but the hop count is 15. Remember that each time a router sends out an update to a neighbor router, it increments the hop count by one for each route.

```
Router#sh ip route
     10.0.0.0/24 is subnetted, 12 subnets
C       10.1.11.0 is directly connected, FastEthernet0/1
C       10.1.10.0 is directly connected, FastEthernet0/0
R       10.1.9.0 [120/2] via 10.1.5.1, 00:00:15, Serial0/0/1
R       10.1.8.0 [120/2] via 10.1.5.1, 00:00:15, Serial0/0/1
R       10.1.12.0 [120/1] via 10.1.11.2, 00:00:00, FastEthernet0/1
R       10.1.3.0 [120/15] via 10.1.5.1, 00:00:15, Serial0/0/1
R       10.1.2.0 [120/1] via 10.1.5.1, 00:00:15, Serial0/0/1
R       10.1.1.0 [120/1] via 10.1.5.1, 00:00:15, Serial0/0/1
R       10.1.7.0 [120/2] via 10.1.5.1, 00:00:15, Serial0/0/1
R       10.1.6.0 [120/2] via 10.1.5.1, 00:00:15, Serial0/0/1
C       10.1.5.0 is directly connected, Serial0/0/1
R       10.1.4.0 [120/1] via 10.1.5.1, 00:00:15, Serial0/0/1
```

So, this [120/15] is really bad because the next router that receives the table from router R3 will just discard the route to network 10.1.3.0 since the hop count would then be 16, which is invalid.

 If a router receives a routing update that contains a higher-cost path to a network that's already in its routing table, the update will be ignored.

Configuring RIP Routing Example 2

Before moving onto learning more about RIP configurations, let's take a look at Figure 6.17. In this example, I first will show how to find and implement the subnets and then add the RIP configuration to the router.

FIGURE 6.17   RIP routing example 2

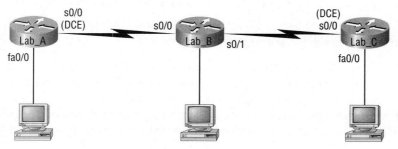

For this configuration, consider that the Lab_B and Lab_C routers are already configured and I just need to configure the Lab_A router. I will use the network ID of 192.168.164.0/28. The s0/0 interface of Lab_A will use the last available IP address in the eighth subnet, and the fa0/0 will use the last available IP address in the second subnet. Do not consider the zero subnet valid.

Before starting, you do know that /28 is a 255.255.255.240 mask, right? And that I have a block size of 16 in the fourth octet? It is very important that you know this, and if you need another review of Chapters 3 and 4, that's okay! Reviewing subnetting will never hurt you.

Since I have a block size of 16, the subnets are 16 (remember I am not starting at zero for this example), 32, 48, 64, 80, 96, 112, 128, 144, and so on. The eighth subnet (which I will use for the s0/0 interface) is subnet 128. The valid host range for the 128 subnet is 129 through 142, and 143 is the broadcast address of the 128 subnet. The second subnet (which I will use for the fa0/0 interface) is the 32 subnet. The valid hosts are 33 through 46, and 47 is the broadcast address of the 32 subnet.

So, here is what the configuration on the Lab_A router will look like:

```
Lab_A(config)#interface s0/0
Lab_A(config-if)#ip address 192.168.164.142 255.255.255.240
Lab_A(config-if)#no shutdown
Lab_A(config-if)#interface fa0/0
Lab_A(config-if)#ip address 192.168.164.46 255.255.255.240
Lab_A(config-if)#no shutdown
Lab_A(config-if)#router rip
Lab_A(config-router)#network 192.168.164.0
Lab_A(config-router)#^Z
Lab_A#
```

Finding the subnets and configuring the last valid host should be pretty straightforward. If not, head back to Chapter 3. However, what I really want you to notice is that although I added two subnets to the Lab_A router, I had only one network statement under RIP. Sometimes it is hard to remember that you configure only the classful network statement, which means you turn all host bits off.

This was the real purpose of this second RIP configuration example—to remind you of classful network addressing. And it never hurts to practice subnetting, right?

Holding Down RIP Propagations

You probably don't want your RIP network advertised everywhere on your LAN and WAN. There's not a whole lot to be gained by advertising your RIP network to the Internet, now, is there?

There are a few different ways to stop unwanted RIP updates from propagating across your LANs and WANs, and the easiest one is through the passive-interface command.

This command prevents RIP update broadcasts from being sent out a specified interface, yet that same interface can still receive RIP updates.

Here's an example of how to configure a `passive-interface` on a router using the CLI:

```
Lab_A#config t
Lab_A(config)#router rip
Lab_A(config-router)#network 192.168.10.0
Lab_A(config-router)#passive-interface serial 0/0
```

This command will stop RIP updates from being propagated out serial interface 0/0, but serial interface 0/0 can still receive RIP updates.

RIP Version 2

Let's spend a couple of minutes discussing RIP version 2 (RIPv2). But first, remember the little routing table mystery of two routes to the same network in the Corp and R2 routing table? Well, the answer lies within this section, and I'll also advertise the default route on R3 to the other routers in the internetwork.

🌐 Real World Scenario

Should You Really Use RIP in an Internetwork?

You have been hired as a consultant to install a couple of Cisco routers into a growing network. They have a couple of old Unix routers that they want to keep in the network. These routers do not support any routing protocol except RIP. I guess this means you just have to run RIP on the entire network.

Well, yes and no. You can run RIP on a router connecting that old network, but you certainly don't need to run RIP throughout the whole internetwork!

You can do what is called *redistribution*, which is basically translating from one type of routing protocol to another. This means you can support those old routers using RIP but use Enhanced IGRP, for example, on the rest of your network.

This will stop RIP routes from being sent all over the internetwork and eating up all that precious bandwidth.

RIP version 2 is mostly the same as RIP version 1. Both RIPv1 and RIPv2 are distance-vector protocols, which means that each router running RIP sends its complete routing table out all active interfaces at periodic time intervals. Also, the timers and loop-avoidance schemes are the same in both RIP versions (i.e., holddown timers and split horizon rule).

Both RIPv1 and RIPv2 are configured using classful addressing (but RIPv2 is considered classless because subnet information is sent with each route update), and both have the same administrative distance (120).

But there are some important differences that make RIPv2 more scalable than RIPv1. And I have to add a word of advice here before we move on: I'm definitely not advocating using RIP of either version in your network. But since RIP is an open standard, you can use it with any brand of router. You can also use OSPF, but that is beyond the scope of the CCENT objectives, since OSPF is an open standard as well. RIP just requires too much bandwidth, making it pretty intensive to use in your network. Why go there when you have other, more elegant options?

Table 6.3 discusses the differences between RIPv1 and RIPv2.

TABLE 6.3   RIPv1 vs. RIPv2

RIPv1	RIPv2
Distance vector	Distance vector
Maximum hop count of 15	Maximum hop count of 15
Classful	Classless
Broadcast based	Uses multicast 224.0.0.9
No support for VLSM	Supports VLSM networks
No authentication	Allows for MD5 authentication
No support for discontiguous networks	Supports discontiguous networks

RIPv2, unlike RIPv1, is a classless routing protocol (even though it is configured as classful, like RIPv1), which means that it sends subnet mask information along with the route updates. By sending the subnet mask information with the updates, RIPv2 can support variable-length subnet masks (VLSMs), as well as the summarization of network boundaries, which cause more harm than good at times in the current network designs. In addition, RIPv2 can support discontiguous networking.

What's a *discontiguous* network? I mentioned this term a few times in this chapter, and it's now time to get to the answer! It's one internetwork that has two or more subnetworks of a classful network connected by different classful networks. Sounds complicated, but it's not. Let's take a look. Figure 6.18 displays a typical discontiguous network.

FIGURE 6.18   A discontiguous network

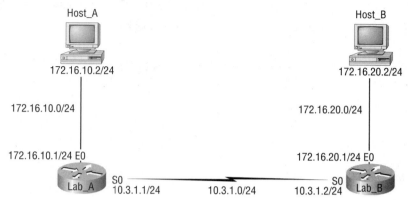

The subnets 172.16.10.0 and 172.16.20.0 are connected with a 10.3.1.0 network. By default, for the purpose of route advertising, each router thinks it has the only 172.16.0.0 classful network.

It's important to understand that discontiguous networks just won't work with RIPv1 or Cisco's old IGRP at all. And they don't work by default on RIPv2 or EIGRP either, but discontiguous networks do work on OSPF networks by default because OSPF does not autosummarize like EIGRP. Ah-ha! So, that must be the answer I've been looking for. RIP, RIPv2, and EIGRP autosummarize classful boundaries by default! But no worries—there are ways to make this work; it just doesn't work by default.

Configuring your routing protocol to work with discontiguous networks is very simple if you are running RIPv2 or EIGRP; you just use the command no auto-summary under the routing protocol configuration, and the routing protocol will advertise subnets and stop autosummarizing. Let's enable RIPv2 now.

Configuring RIPv2 is pretty straightforward. Here's an example:

```
Lab_C(config)#router rip
Lab_C(config-router)#network 192.168.40.0
Lab_C(config-router)#network 192.168.50.0
Lab_C(config-router)#version 2
Lab_C(config-router)#no auto-summary
```

That's it; just add the command version 2 under the (config-router)# prompt, and you are now running RIPv2. I recommend that when configuring RIPv2 (or EIGRP for that matter), always use the no auto-summary command in order to advertise subnets. This would stop any problems from occurring in your routing if you had a discontiguous network design.

I am going to go through the RIP verification commands and then configure RIPv2 on the internetwork.

RIPv2 is classless and supports VLSM and discontiguous networks.

Verifying Your Configurations

It's important to verify your configurations once you've completed them, or at least once you *think* you've completed them. The following list includes the commands you can use to verify the routed and routing protocols configured on your Cisco routers:

- show ip route
- show ip protocols
- debug ip rip

The first command was covered in the previous section—I'll go over the others in the sections that follow.

The *show ip protocols* Command

The show ip protocols command shows you the routing protocols that are configured on your router. Looking at the following output, you can see that RIP is running on the router and the timers that RIP uses:

```
Corp#sh ip protocols
Routing Protocol is "rip"
Sending updates every 30 seconds, next due in 23 seconds
Invalid after 180 seconds, hold down 180, flushed after 240
Outgoing update filter list for all interfaces is not set
Incoming update filter list for all interfaces is not set
Redistributing: rip
Default version control: send version 1, receive any version
  Interface          Send  Recv  Triggered RIP  Key-chain
  Vlan1               1     2 1
  FastEthernet0/0     1     2 1
  Serial0/0/0         1     2 1
  Serial0/0/1         1     2 1
  Serial0/1/0         1     2 1
Automatic network summarization is in effect
Maximum path: 4
Routing for Networks:
      10.0.0.0
```

```
Passive Interface(s):
Routing Information Sources:
       Gateway          Distance      Last Update
       10.1.5.2             120       00:00:28
       10.1.2.2             120       00:00:21
       10.1.3.2             120       00:00:21
       10.1.4.2             120       00:00:12
Distance: (default is 120)
```

Notice in this output that RIP is sending updates every 30 seconds, which is the default. The other timers used in distance vector are also shown.

Notice further down that RIP is routing for the directly connected interfaces f0/0, S0/0/0, s0/0/1, and s0/1/0. The send and receive versions are listed to the right of the interfaces—RIPv1 and v2. This is an important troubleshooting section. If the interface you need is not listed in this section, you did not type in the correct network statements, and this information can be found under the heading Routing for Networks.

Under the Gateway heading, the neighbors it found and the last entry is the default AD for RIP (120).

Troubleshooting with the *show ip protocols* Command

Let's use a sample router and use the show ip protocols command to see what you can determine about routing by looking at this output from a router on another network:

```
Router#sh ip protocols
Routing Protocol is "rip"
  Sending updates every 30 seconds, next due in 6 seconds
  Invalid after 180 seconds, hold down 180, flushed afteR340
  Outgoing update filter list for all interfaces is
  Incoming update filter list for all interfaces is
  Redistributing: rip
  Default version control: send version 1, receive any version
    Interface        Send  Recv   Key-chain
    Serial0/0         1     1 2
    Serial0/1         1     1 2
  Routing for Networks:
    10.0.0.0
  Routing Information Sources:
    Gateway          Distance     Last Update
    10.168.11.14        120       00:00:21
  Distance: (default is 120)
```

Let's also look at the show ip interface brief command from the same router and see what you find out.

```
Router#sh ip interface brief
Interface       IP-Address      OK?     Method Status
FastEthernet0/0 192.168.18.1    YES     manual up
Serial0/0       10.168.11.17    YES     manual up
FastEthernet0/1 unassigned      YES     NRAM   Administratively down
Serial0/1       192.168.11.21   YES     manual up
```

Under the show ip protocols output, you can see that I'm using RIP routing for network 10.0.0.0, which means the configuration would look like this:

```
Router(config)#router rip
Router(config-router)#network 10.0.0.0
```

Also, only serial 0/0 and serial 0/1 are participating in the RIP network. And last, the neighbor router is 10.168.11.14.

From the output of the show ip interface brief command, you can see that only serial 0/0 is in the 10.0.0.0 network. This means that the router will send and receive routing updates only with the 10.0.0.0 network and not advertise the 192.168.0.0 networks out any interface. To fix this, you would need to add the 192.168.11.0 and 192.168.18.0 networks under the router rip global command.

The *debug ip rip* Command

The debug ip rip command directs routing updates as they are sent and received on the router to the console session. If you are telnetted into the router, you'll need to use the terminal monitor command to be able to receive the output from the debug commands.

You can see in this output that RIP is both sending and receiving (the metric is the hop count):

```
R3#debug ip rip
RIP protocol debugging is on
RIP: received v1 update from 10.1.5.1 on FastEthernet0/0
       10.1.1.0 in 1 hops
       10.1.2.0 in 1 hops
       10.1.3.0 in 1 hops
       10.1.4.0 in 1 hops
       192.168.10.0 in 2 hops
       192.168.20.0 in 2 hops
       192.168.30.0 in 2 hops
       192.168.40.0 in 2 hops
```

```
RIP: sending  v1 update to 255.255.255.255 via Dot11Radio0/0/0(172.16.10.1)
RIP: build update entries
      network 10.0.0.0 metric 1
      network 192.168.10.0 metric 3
      network 192.168.20.0 metric 3
      network 192.168.30.0 metric 3
      network 192.168.40.0 metric 3


RIP: sending  v1 update to 255.255.255.255 via FastEthernet0/0 (10.1.5.2)
RIP: build update entries
      network 172.16.0.0 metric 1)
```

Let's talk about the output for a minute. First, R3 received all the routes that the Corp router has, and RIP is sending v1 packets to 255.255.255.255—an "all-hands" broadcast—out interface Dot11Radio0/0/0/0 via 172.16.10.1. This is where RIPv2 will come in handy. Why? Because RIPv2 doesn't send broadcasts; it used the multicast 224.0.0.9. So, even though the RIP packets could be transmitted onto a network with no routers, all hosts would just ignore them, making RIPv2 a bit of an improvement over RIPv1.

Okay—now check out the fact that RIP is sending advertisements for all networks out Dot11Radio0/0/0/0, yet the last advertisement out FastEthernet 0/0 on R3 is only advertising 172.16.0.0. Why? If you answered the split horizon rule, you nailed it! The R3 router in this example will not advertise all those networks received from a neighbor router back to the same router.

> **WARNING** If the metric of a route shows 16, this is a route poison, and the network being advertised is unreachable.

Troubleshooting with the *debug ip rip* Command

Now let's use the debug ip rip command to both discover a problem and figure out how RIP was configured on a router from a different sample network.

```
07:12:58: RIP: sending v1 update to 255.255.255.255 via
   FastEthernet0/0 (172.16.1.1)
07:12:58:   network 10.0.0.0, metric 1
07:12:58:   network 192.168.1.0, metric 2
07:12:58: RIP: sending v1 update to 255.255.255.255 via
   Serial0/0 (10.0.8.1)
07:12:58:   network 172.16.0.0, metric 1
07:12:58: RIP: Received v1 update from 10.0.15.2 n Serial0/0
07:12:58:   192.168.1.0 in one hop
07:12:58:   192.168.168.0 in 16 hops (inaccessible)
```

You can see from the updates that I'm sending out information about networks 10.0.0.0, 192.168.1.0, and 172.16.0.0. But both the 10.0.0.0 network and the 172.16.0.0 network are being advertised with a hop count (metric) of 1, meaning that these networks are directly connected. The 192.168.1.0 is being advertised as a metric of 2, which means that it is not directly connected.

For this to be happening, the configuration would have to look like this:

```
Router(config)#router rip
Router(config-router)#network 10.0.0.0
Router(config-router)#network 172.16.0.0
```

And there's something else you can find out by looking at this: there are at least two routers participating in the RIP network because I'm sending out two interfaces and receiving RIP updates on one interface (if I'm receiving updates, there must be another router on that interface). Also, notice that the network 192.168.168.0 is being advertised as 16 hops away. RIP has a maximum hop count of 15, so 16 is considered unreachable, making this network inaccessible. So, what will happen if you try to ping to a host on network 192.168.168.0? You just will not be successful, that's what! But if you try any pings to network 10.0.0.0, you should be successful.

I have one more output I want to show you—see whether you can find the problem. Both a debug ip rip and a show ip route output are shown from the sample router.

```
07:12:56: RIP: received v1 update from 172.16.100.2 on Serial0/0
07:12:56:        172.16.10.0 in 1 hops
07:12:56:        172.16.20.0 in 1 hops
07:12:56:        172.16.30.0 in 1 hops


Router#sh ip route
[output cut]
Gateway of last resort is not set


     172.16.0.0/24 is subnetted, 8 subnets
C    172.16.150.0 is directly connected, FastEthernet0/0
C    172.16.220.0 is directly connected, Loopback2
R    172.16.210.0 is directly connected, Loopback1
R    172.16.200.0 is directly connected, Loopback0
R    172.16.30.0 [120/2] via 172.16.100.2, 00:00:04, Serial0/0
S    172.16.20.0 [120/2] via 172.16.150.15
R    172.16.10.0 [120/2] via 172.16.100.2, 00:00:04, Serial0/0
R    172.16.100.0 [120/2] is directly connected, Serial0/0
```

Looking at the two outputs, can you tell why users can't access 172.16.20.0?

The debug output shows that network 172.16.20.0 is one hop away and being received on serial0/0 from 172.16.100.2. By viewing the show ip route output, you can see that packets with a destination of 172.16.20.0 are being sent to 172.16.150.15 because of a static route entry. The output also shows that 172.16.150.0 is directly connected to FastEthernet 0/0 and network 172.16.20.0 is really out serial 0/0, so packets with a destination of 172.16.20.0 are being sent out the wrong interface because of a misconfigured static route.

Enabling RIPv2 on the Internetwork

Before moving on to Chapter 7 and discussing Layer 2 switching, I want to enable RIPv2 on the routers. It'll take only a second. Here are my configurations:

```
Corp#config t
Corp(config)#router rip
Corp(config-router)#version 2
Corp(config-router)#^Z
```

```
R1#config t
R1(config)#router rip
R1(config-router)#version 2
R1(config-router)#^Z
```

```
R2#config t
Enter configuration commands, one per line.  End with CNTL/Z.
R2(config)#router rip
R2(config-router)#version 2
R2(config-router)#^Z
```

```
R3#config t
R3#(config)#router rip
R3#(config-router)#version 2
R3#(config-router)#^Z
```

This was probably the easiest configuration in the book so far. Let's see whether you can find a difference in the routing tables. Here's the Corp router's routing table now:

```
     10.0.0.0/24 is subnetted, 5 subnets
C        10.1.1.0 is directly connected, Vlan1
C        10.1.2.0 is directly connected, Serial0/0/0
C        10.1.3.0 is directly connected, Serial0/0/1
C        10.1.4.0 is directly connected, Serial0/1/0
C        10.1.5.0 is directly connected, FastEthernet0/0
```

```
       172.16.0.0/16 is variably subnetted, 2 subnets, 2 masks
R        172.16.0.0/16 [120/1] via 10.1.5.2, 00:00:18, FastEthernet0/0
S        172.16.10.0/24 [150/0] via 10.1.5.2
R     192.168.10.0/24 [120/1] via 10.1.2.2, 00:00:04, Serial0/0/0
                       [120/1] via 10.1.3.2, 00:00:04, Serial0/0/1
R     192.168.20.0/24 [120/1] via 10.1.2.2, 00:00:04, Serial0/0/0
                       [120/1] via 10.1.3.2, 00:00:04, Serial0/0/1
R     192.168.30.0/24 [120/1] via 10.1.4.2, 00:00:06, Serial0/1/0
R     192.168.40.0/24 [120/1] via 10.1.4.2, 00:00:06, Serial0/1/0
Corp#
```

Well—looks the same to me, and it still didn't fix my double entry for the 172.16.0.0 network. I'm going to turn on debugging and see whether that shows anything new.

```
Corp#debug ip rip
RIP protocol debugging is on
Corp#RIP: sending  v2 update to 224.0.0.9 via Vlan1 (10.1.1.1)


RIP: build update entries
        10.1.2.0/24 via 0.0.0.0, metric 1, tag 0
        10.1.3.0/24 via 0.0.0.0, metric 1, tag 0
        10.1.4.0/24 via 0.0.0.0, metric 1, tag 0
        10.1.5.0/24 via 0.0.0.0, metric 1, tag 0
        172.16.0.0/16 via 0.0.0.0, metric 2, tag 0
        192.168.10.0/24 via 0.0.0.0, metric 2, tag 0
        192.168.20.0/24 via 0.0.0.0, metric 2, tag 0
        192.168.30.0/24 via 0.0.0.0, metric 2, tag 0
        192.168.40.0/24 via 0.0.0.0, metric 2, tag 0


RIP: sending  v2 update to 224.0.0.9 via FastEthernet0/0 (10.1.5.1)
[output cut]
```

Bingo! Look at that! The networks are still being advertised every 30 seconds, but they're now sending the advertisements as v2 and as a multicast address of 224.0.0.9. Let's take a look at the show ip protocols output.

```
Corp#sh ip protocols
Routing Protocol is "rip"
Sending updates every 30 seconds, next due in 20 seconds
Invalid after 180 seconds, hold down 180, flushed after 240
Outgoing update filter list for all interfaces is not set
```

```
Incoming update filter list for all interfaces is not set
Redistributing: rip
Default version control: send version 2, receive 2
  Interface              Send  Recv  Triggered RIP  Key-chain
  Vlan1                   2     2
  FastEthernet0/0         2     2
  Serial0/0/0             2     2
  Serial0/0/1             2     2
  Serial0/1/0             2     2
Automatic network summarization is in effect
Maximum path: 4
Routing for Networks:
      10.0.0.0
Passive Interface(s):
Routing Information Sources:
      Gateway        Distance      Last Update
      10.1.5.2          120        00:00:09
      10.1.2.2          120        00:00:20
      10.1.3.2          120        00:00:20
      10.1.4.2          120        00:00:23
Distance: (default is 120)
```

I am now sending and receiving RIPv2. Nice when things work out well, huh? However, I never did fix that double entry for the 172.16.0.0 network in the Corp and R2 routing tables, even though I could have done so using RIPv2. I want to save that solution for EIGRP. But the answer for the problem was previously shown in Table 6.3, and the solution was discussed following Figure 6.13 if you just can't wait!

Advertising a Default Route Using RIP

I want to show you how to advertise a way out of your autonomous system. Imagine that you were to look at the network diagram and that instead of having the wireless network connected to R3, you could use a serial interface and configure the little internetwork to the Internet from R3.

If you do add an Internet connection to R3, all routers in the AS need to know where to send packets that are destined for networks on the Internet, or they'll just drop the packets if they get a packet with a remote request. One solution would be to put a default route on every router and funnel the information to R3, which in turn would have a default route to the ISP. Most people do this type of configuration in small to medium-sized networks.

However, since I am running RIPv2 on all routers including R3, I'll just add a default route on R3 to the ISP, as I would normally, but then add another command to advertise my network to the other routers in the AS as the default route.

Here is an example of my new R3 configuration:

```
R3(config)#interface s0/0
R3(config-if)#ip address 172.16.10.5 255.255.255.252
R3(config-if)#exit
R3(config)#ip route 0.0.0.0 0.0.0.0 s0/0
R3(config)#ip default-network 172.16.0.0
```

Now, let's see what the Corp and R2 routers' routing tables see.

```
Corp#
10.0.0.0/24 is subnetted, 5 subnets
C       10.1.1.0 is directly connected, Vlan1
C       10.1.2.0 is directly connected, Serial0/0/0
C       10.1.3.0 is directly connected, Serial0/0/1
C       10.1.4.0 is directly connected, Serial0/1/0
C       10.1.5.0 is directly connected, FastEthernet0/0
    172.16.0.0/16 is variably subnetted, 2 subnets, 2 masks
R       172.16.0.0/16 [120/1] via 10.1.5.2, 00:00:16, FastEthernet0/0
S       172.16.10.0/24 [150/0] via 10.1.5.2
R     192.168.10.0/24 [120/1] via 10.1.2.2, 00:00:16, Serial0/0/0
                       [120/1] via 10.1.3.2, 00:00:16, Serial0/0/1
R     192.168.20.0/24 [120/1] via 10.1.2.2, 00:00:16, Serial0/0/0
                       [120/1] via 10.1.3.2, 00:00:16, Serial0/0/1
R     192.168.30.0/24 [120/1] via 10.1.4.2, 00:00:02, Serial0/1/0
R     192.168.40.0/24 [120/1] via 10.1.4.2, 00:00:02, Serial0/1/0
R*    0.0.0.0/0 [120/1] via 10.1.5.2, 00:00:16, FastEthernet0/0
Corp#
```

Nice—look at the last entry: R3 is advertising to the Corp router that "Hey, I am the way to the Internet!" or "I am the way out of the AS!" Let's see whether R2 can see this same entry.

```
R2#
 10.0.0.0/24 is subnetted, 5 subnets
R       10.1.1.0 [120/1] via 10.1.4.1, 00:00:29, Serial0/0/0
R       10.1.2.0 [120/1] via 10.1.4.1, 00:00:29, Serial0/0/0
R       10.1.3.0 [120/1] via 10.1.4.1, 00:00:29, Serial0/0/0
C       10.1.4.0 is directly connected, Serial0/0/0
R       10.1.5.0 [120/1] via 10.1.4.1, 00:00:29, Serial0/0/0
```

```
       172.16.0.0/16 is variably subnetted, 2 subnets, 2 masks
R        172.16.0.0/16 [120/2] via 10.1.4.1, 00:00:29, Serial0/0/0
S        172.16.10.0/24 [150/0] via 10.1.4.1
R      192.168.10.0/24 [120/2] via 10.1.4.1, 00:00:29, Serial0/0/0
R      192.168.20.0/24 [120/2] via 10.1.4.1, 00:00:29, Serial0/0/0
C      192.168.30.0/24 is directly connected, FastEthernet0/0
C      192.168.40.0/24 is directly connected, FastEthernet0/1
R*     0.0.0.0/0 [120/2] via 10.1.4.1, 00:00:29, Serial0/0/0
R2#
```

R2 is seeing it as well, so the `ip default-network` command is working and advertising with RIP, and in addition, I verified that R1 is receiving the default route as well. This command would work with either RIP or RIPv2.

You're ready now to move on to the next chapter!

Summary

This chapter covered IP routing in detail. It's extremely important that you really understand the basics I covered in this chapter because everything that's done on a Cisco router typically will have some type of IP routing configured and running.

You learned in this chapter how IP routing uses frames to transport packets between routers and to the destination host. From there, I showed how to configure static routing on my routers and discussed the administrative distance used by IP to determine the best route to a destination network. If you have a stub network, you can configure default routing, which sets the gateway of last resort on a router.

I then discussed dynamic routing in detail, specifically RIP and how it works on an internetwork (not well). I finished by verifying RIP and then adding RIPv2 to my little internetwork and also advertising a default route throughout the AS.

Exam Essentials

Describe the basic IP routing process.   You need to remember that the frame changes at each hop but that the packet is never changed or manipulated in any way until it reaches the destination device (the TTL field in the IP header is decremented for each hop, but that's it!).

List the information required by a router to successfully route packets.   To be able to route packets, a router must know, at a minimum, the destination address, the location of neighboring routers through which it can reach remote networks, possible routes to all remote networks, the best route to each remote network, and how to maintain and verify routing information.

Describe how MAC addresses are used during the routing process.   A MAC (hardware) address will be used only on a LAN. It will never pass a router's interface. A frame uses MAC (hardware) addresses to send a packet on a LAN. The frame will take the packet to either a host on the LAN or a router's interface (if the packet is destined for a remote network). As packets move from one router to another, the MAC addresses used will change, but normally the original source and destination IP addresses within the packet will not.

View and interpret the routing table of a router.   Use the show ip route command to view the routing table. Each route will be will be listed along with the source of the routing information. A C to the left of the route will indicate directly connected routes, and other letters next to the route can also indicate a particular routing protocol that provided the information, such as, for example, R for RIP.

Differentiate the three types of routing.   The three types of routing are static (in which routes are manually configured at the CLI), dynamic (in which the routers share routing information via a routing protocol), and default routing (in which a special route is configured for all traffic without a more specific destination network found in the table).

Compare and contrast static and dynamic routing.   Static routing creates no routing update traffic and creates less overhead on the router and network links, but it must be configured manually and does not have the ability to react to link outages. Dynamic routing creates routing update traffic and uses more overhead on the router and network links, but it can both react to link outages and choose the best route when multiple routes exist to the same network.

Configure static routes at the CLI.   The command syntax to add a route is ip route [destination_network] [mask] [next-hop_address or exitinterface] [administrative_distance] [permanent].

Create a default route.   To add a default route, use the command syntax ip route 0.0.0.0 0.0.0.0 *ip-address* or *exit interface type and number.*

Understand administrative distance and its role in the selection of the best route. Administrative distance (AD) is used to rate the trustworthiness of routing information received on a router from a neighbor router. Administrative distance is an integer from 0 to 255, where 0 is the most trusted and 255 means no traffic will be passed via this route. All routing protocols are assigned a default AD, but it can be changed at the CLI.

Differentiate distance-vector, link-state, and hybrid routing protocols.   Distance-vector routing protocols make routing decisions based on hop count (think RIP), while link-state routing protocols are able to consider multiple factors such as bandwidth available and delay when selecting the best route. Hybrid (Advanced Distance Vector) routing protocols exhibit characteristics of both types.

List mechanisms used to prevent routing loops in the network.   Maximum hop count, split horizon, route poisoning, and holddown counters all play roles in preventing routing loops.

Describe the counters used in the operation of RIP.   The route update timer is the interval between routing updates, the route invalid timer determines the length of time that must elapse (180 seconds) before a router determines that a route has become invalid, the hold-down timer sets the amount of time during which routing information is suppressed (when a link is lost), and the route flush timer sets the time between a route becoming invalid and its removal from the routing table (240 seconds).

Configure RIP routing.   To configure RIP routing, first you must be in global configuration mode, and then you type the command `router rip`. Then you add all directly connected networks, making sure to use the classful address.

Identify commands used to verify RIP routing.   The `show ip route` command will provide you with the contents of the routing table. An R on the left side of the table indicates a RIP-found route. The `debug ip rip` command will show you RIP updates being sent and received on your router. If you see a route with a metric of 16, that route is considered down.

Describe the differences between RIPv1 and RIPv2.   RIPv1 sends broadcasts every 30 seconds and has an AD of 120. RIPv2 sends multicasts (224.0.0.9) every 30 seconds and also has an AD of 120. RIPv2 sends subnet mask information with the route updates, which allows it to support classless networking and discontiguous networks. RIPv2 also supports authentication between routers, and RIPv1 does not.

Written Lab 6

Write the answers to the following questions:

1. At the appropriate command prompt, create a static route to network 172.16.10.0/24 with a next-hop gateway of 172.16.20.1 and an administrative distance of 150.

2. When a PC sends a packet to another PC in a remote network, what destination IP address and MAC address will be in the frame that it sends to its default gateway?

3. At the appropriate command prompt, create a default route to 172.16.40.1.

4. If you are using default routing in a classless environment, what command must also be used?

5. On which type of network is a default route most beneficial?

6. At the appropriate command prompt, display the routing table on your router.

7. When creating a static or default route, you don't have to use the next-hop IP address; you can use the _____.

8. True/False: To reach a destination host, you must know the MAC address of the remote host.

9. True/False: To reach a destination host, you must know the IP address of the remote host.

10. At the appropriate command prompt, execute the command required on a DCE serial interface that is not required on a DTE serial interface.

11. At the appropriate command prompt(s), enable RIP routing on the interface with the IP address 10.0.0.1/24.

12. At the appropriate command prompt(s), prevent a router from propagating RIP information out serial 1.

13. What routing loop prevention mechanism sends out a maximum hop count as soon as a link fails?

14. What routing loop prevention mechanism suppresses the resending of routing information to an interface through which it was received?

15. At the appropriate command prompt, display RIP routing updates as they are sent and received on the router to the console session.

(The answers to Written Lab 6 can be found in Appendix A.)

Hands-on Labs

In the following hands-on labs, you will configure a network with three routers. These exercises assume all the same setup requirements as the labs found in earlier chapters.

This chapter includes the following labs:

Lab 6.1: Creating Static Routes

Lab 6.2: Configuring RIP Routing

The internetwork shown in the following graphic will be used to configure all routers.

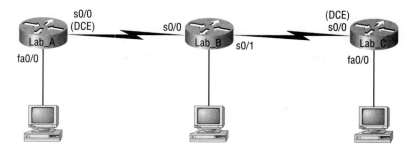

Table 6.4 shows the IP addresses for each router (each interface uses a /24 mask).

TABLE 6.4   IP addresses

Router	Interface	IP Address
Lab_A	F0/0	172.16.10.1
Lab_A	S0/0	172.16.20.1
Lab_B	S0/0	172.16.20.2
Lab_B	S0/1	172.16.30.1
Lab_C	S0/0	172.16.30.2
Lab_C	Fa0/0	172.16.40.1

These labs were written without using the LAN interface on the Lab_B router. You can choose to add that LAN into the labs if necessary.

Hands-on Lab 6.1: Creating Static Routes

In this lab, you will create a static route in all three routers so that the routers see all networks. Verify with the Ping program when complete.

1. The Lab_A router is connected to two networks, 172.16.10.0 and 172.16.20.0. You need to add routes to networks 172.16.30.0 and 172.16.40.0. Use the following commands to add the static routes:

```
Lab_A#config t
Lab_A(config)#ip route 172.16.30.0 255.255.255.0
   172.16.20.2
Lab_A(config)#ip route 172.16.40.0 255.255.255.0
   172.16.20.2
```

2. Save the current configuration for the Lab_A router by going to the privileged mode, typing **copy run start**, and pressing Enter.

3. On the Lab_B router, you have direct connections to networks 172.16.20.0 and 172.16.30.0. You need to add routes to networks 172.16.10.0 and 172.16.40.0. Use the following commands to add the static routes:

```
Lab_B#config t
Lab_B(config)#ip route 172.16.10.0 255.255.255.0
  172.16.20.1
Lab_B(config)#ip route 172.16.40.0 255.255.255.0
  172.16.30.2
```

4. Save the current configuration for router Lab_B by going to the enabled mode, typing **copy run start**, and pressing Enter.

5. On router Lab_C, create a static route to networks 172.16.10.0 and 172.16.20.0, which are not directly connected. Create static routes so that router Lab_C can see all networks, using the commands shown here:

```
Lab_C#config t
Lab_C(config)#ip route 172.16.10.0 255.255.255.0
  172.16.30.1
Lab_C(config)#ip route 172.16.20.0 255.255.255.0
  172.16.30.1
```

6. Save the current configuration for router Lab_C by going to the enable mode, typing **copy run start**, and pressing Enter.

7. Check your routing tables to make sure all four networks show up by executing the **show ip route** command.

8. Now ping from each router to your hosts and from each router to each router. If it is set up correctly, it will work.

Hands-on Lab 6.2: Configuring RIP Routing

In this lab, you will use the dynamic routing protocol RIP instead of static routing.

1. Remove any static routes or default routes configured on your routers by using the no ip route command. For example, here is how you would remove the static routes on the Lab_A router:

```
Lab_A#config t
Lab_A(config)#no ip route 172.16.30.0 255.255.255.0
  172.16.20.2
Lab_A(config)#no ip route 172.16.40.0 255.255.255.0
  172.16.20.2
```

Do the same thing for routers Lab_B and Lab_C. Verify that only your directly connected networks are in the routing tables.

2. After your static and default routes are clear, go into configuration mode on router Lab_A by typing **config t**.

3. Tell your router to use RIP routing by typing **router rip** and pressing Enter, as shown here:

```
config t
router rip
```

4. Add the network number for the networks you want to advertise.

Since router Lab_A has two interfaces that are in two different networks, you must enter a network statement using the network ID of the network in which each interface resides. Alternately, you could use a summarization of these networks and use a single statement, minimizing the size of the routing table. Since the two networks are 172.16.10.0/24 and 172.16.20.0/24, the network summarization 172.16.0.0 would include both subnets. Do this by typing **network 172.16.0.0** and pressing Enter.

5. Press Ctrl+Z to get out of configuration mode.

6. The interfaces on Lab_B and Lab_C are in the 172.16.20.0/24 and 172.16.30.0/24 networks; therefore, the same summarized network statement will work there as well. Type the same commands, as shown here:

```
Config t
Router rip
network 172.16.0.0
```

7. Verify that RIP is running at each router by typing the following commands at each router:

```
show ip protocols
```

This should indicate to you that RIP is present on the router.

```
show ip route
```

(This should have routes present with an *R* to the left of them.)

```
show running-config or show run
```

(This should indicate that RIP is present and the networks are being advertised.)

8. Save your configurations by typing **copy run start** or **copy running-config startup-config** and pressing Enter at each router.

9. Verify the network by pinging all remote networks and hosts.

Review Questions

You can find the answers in Appendix B.

 The following questions are designed to test your understanding of this chapter's material. For more information on how to get additional questions, please see this book's introduction.

1. The Acme Company uses a router named Gateway to connect to its ISP. The address of the ISP router is 206.143.5.2. Which commands could be configured on the Gateway router to allow Internet access to the entire network? (Choose two.)

   A. Gateway(config)#**ip route 0.0.0.0 0.0.0.0 206.143.5.2**

   B. Gateway(config)#**router rip**
      Gateway(config-router)#**network 206.143.5.0**

   C. Gateway(config)#**router rip**
      Gateway(config-router)#**network 206.143.5.0 default**

   D. Gateway(config)#**ip route 206.143.5.0 255.255.255.0 default**

   E. Gateway(config)#**ip default-network 206.143.5.0**

2. What command will prevent RIP routing updates from exiting an interface but will still allow the interface to receive RIP route updates?

   A. Router(config-if)#**no routing**

   B. Router(config-if)#**passive-interface**

   C. Router(config-router)#**passive-interface s0**

   D. Router(config-router)#**no routing updates**

3. Which of the following statements are true regarding the command ip route 172.16.4.0 255.255.255.0 192.168.4.2? (Choose two.)

   A. The command is used to establish a static route.

   B. The default administrative distance is used.

   C. The command is used to configure the default route.

   D. The subnet mask for the source address is 255.255.255.0.

   E. The command is used to establish a stub network.

4. What destination addresses will be used by HostA to send data to the HTTPS server as shown in the following network? (Choose two.)

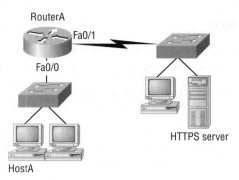

A. The IP address of the switch

B. The MAC address of the remote switch

C. The IP address of the HTTPS server

D. The MAC address of the HTTPS server

E. The IP address of RouterA's Fa0/0 interface

F. The MAC address of RouterA's Fa0/0 interface

5. Which of the following is true regarding the following output? (Choose two.)

```
04:06:16: RIP: received v1 update from 192.168.40.2 on Serial0/1
04:06:16:       192.168.50.0 in 16 hops (inaccessible)
04:06:40: RIP: sending v1 update to 255.255.255.255 via
    FastEthernet0/0 (192.168.30.1)
04:06:40: RIP: build update entries
04:06:40:        network 192.168.20.0 metric 1
04:06:40:        network 192.168.40.0 metric 1
04:06:40:        network 192.168.50.0 metric 16
04:06:40: RIP: sending v1 update to 255.255.255.255 via Serial0/1
    (192.168.40.1)
```

A. There are three interfaces on the router participating in this update.

B. A ping to 192.168.50.1 will be successful.

C. There are at least two routers exchanging information.

D. A ping to 192.168.40.2 will be successful.

6. Which of the following is the best description of the operation of split horizon?

A. Information about a route should not be sent back in the direction from which the original update came.

B. It splits the traffic when you have a large bus (horizon) physical network.

C. It holds the regular updates from broadcasting to a downed link.

D. It prevents regular update messages from reinstating a route that has gone down.

7. Which of the following would be true if HostA is trying to communicate to HostB and the LAN interface of RouterC goes down, as shown in the following graphic? (Choose two.)

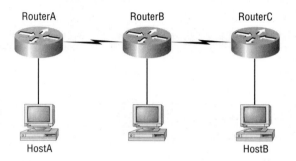

A. RouterC will use an ICMP to inform HostA that HostB cannot be reached.

B. RouterC will use ICMP to inform RouterB that HostB cannot be reached.

C. RouterC will use ICMP to inform HostA, RouterA, and RouterB that HostB cannot be reached.

D. RouterC will send a destination unreachable message type.

E. RouterC will send a router selection message type.

F. RouterC will send a source quench message type.

8. Which statement is true regarding classless routing protocols? (Choose two.)

A. The use of discontiguous networks is not allowed.

B. The use of variable-length subnet masks is permitted.

C. RIPv1 is a classless routing protocol.

D. IGRP supports classless routing within the same autonomous system.

E. RIPv2 supports classless routing.

9. Which *two* of the following are true regarding the distance-vector and link-state routing protocols?

    A. Link state sends its complete routing table out all active interfaces at periodic time intervals.

    B. Distance vector sends its complete routing table out all active interfaces at periodic time intervals.

    C. Link state sends updates containing the state of its own links to all routers in the internetwork.

    D. Distance vector sends updates containing the state of its own links to all routers in the internetwork.

10. Which command displays RIP routing updates?

    A. `show ip route`

    B. `debug ip rip`

    C. `show protocols`

    D. `debug ip route`

11. What does RIPv2 use to prevent routing loops? (Choose two.)

    A. CIDR

    B. Split horizon

    C. Authentication

    D. Classless masking

    E. Holddown timers

12. A network administrator views the output from the `show ip route` command. A remote router advertises a network with both RIPv2 and EIGRP. However, only the EIGRP route appears in the routing table. Why is the RIP route to this network not used in the routing table?

    A. EIGRP has a faster update timer.

    B. EIGRP has a lower administrative distance.

    C. RIP has a higher metric value for that route.

    D. The EIGRP route has fewer hops.

    E. The RIP path has a routing loop.

13. You type **`debug ip rip`** on your router console and see that 172.16.10.0 is being advertised to you with a metric of 16. What does this mean?

    A. The route is 16 hops away.

    B. The route has a delay of 16 microseconds.

    C. The route is inaccessible.

    D. The route is queued at 16 messages a second.

14. What metric does RIPv2 use to find the best path to a remote network?

  A. Hop count

  B. MTU

  C. Cumulative interface delay

  D. Load

  E. Path bandwidth value

15. The Corporate router receives an IP packet with a source IP address of 192.168.214.20 and a destination address of 192.168.22.3. Looking at the output from the Corporate router, what will the router do with this packet?

```
Corp#sh ip route
[output cut]
R    192.168.215.0 [120/2] via 192.168.20.2, 00:00:23, Serial0/0
R    192.168.115.0 [120/1] via 192.168.20.2, 00:00:23, Serial0/0
R    192.168.30.0 [120/1] via 192.168.20.2, 00:00:23, Serial0/0
C    192.168.20.0 is directly connected, Serial0/0
C    192.168.214.0 is directly connected, FastEthernet0/0
```

  A. The packet will be discarded.

  B. The packet will be routed out the S0/0 interface.

  C. The router will broadcast looking for the destination.

  D. The packet will be routed out the Fa0/0 interface.

16. If your routing table has a static, a RIP, and an EIGRP route to the same network, which route will be used to route packets by default?

  A. Any available route.

  B. RIP route.

  C. Static route.

  D. EIGRP route.

  E. They will all load balance.

17. You have the following routing table. Which of the following networks will not be placed in the neighbor routing table?

```
R    192.168.30.0/24 [120/1] via 192.168.40.1, 00:00:12, Serial0
C    192.168.40.0/24 is directly connected, Serial0
     172.16.0.0/24 is subnetted, 1 subnets
C       172.16.30.0 is directly connected, Loopback0
R    192.168.20.0/24 [120/1] via 192.168.40.1, 00:00:12, Serial0
R    10.0.0.0/8 [120/15] via 192.168.40.1, 00:00:07, Serial0
C    192.168.50.0/24 is directly connected, Ethernet0
```

A. 172.16.30.0.

B. 192.168.30.0.

C. 10.0.0.0.

D. All of them will be placed in the neighbor routing table.

18. Two connected routers are configured only with RIP routing. What will be the result when a router receives a routing update that contains a higher-cost path to a network already in its routing table?

A. The updated information will be added to the existing routing table.

B. The update will be ignored, and no further action will occur.

C. The updated information will replace the existing routing table entry.

D. The existing routing table entry will be deleted from the routing table, and all routers will exchange routing updates to reach convergence.

19. Which of the following is true about route poisoning?

A. It sends back the protocol received from a router as a poison pill, which stops the regular updates.

B. It is information received from a router that can't be sent back to the originating router.

C. It prevents regular update messages from reinstating a route that has just come up.

D. It describes when a router sets the metric for a downed link to infinity.

20. Which of the following is true regarding RIPv2?

A. It has a lower administrative distance than RIPv1.

B. It converges faster than RIPv1.

C. It has the same timers as RIPv1.

D. It is harder to configure than RIPv1.

Chapter

7

Layer 2 Switching

THE CCENT EXAM OBJECTIVES COVERED IN THIS CHAPTER INCLUDE THE FOLLOWING:

✓ **Implement a small switched network**

- Explain network segmentation and basic traffic management concepts

- Explain the operation of Cisco switches and basic switching concepts

- Perform, save, and verify initial switch configuration tasks including remote access management

- Verify network status and switch operation using basic utilities (including: ping, traceroute, telnet, SSH, arp, ipconfig), SHOW & DEBUG commands

- Implement and verify basic security for a switch (port security, deactivate ports)

- Identify, prescribe, and resolve common switched network media issues, configuration issues, autonegotiation, and switch hardware failures

When folks at Cisco discuss switching, they're talking about layer 2 switching unless they say otherwise. Layer 2 switching is the process of using the hardware address of devices on a LAN to segment a network. Since you've got the basic ideas down, I'm now going to focus on the particulars of layer 2 switching and nail down how it works.

You know that switching breaks large collision domains into smaller ones and that a collision domain is a network segment with two or more devices sharing the same bandwidth. A hub network is a typical example of this type of technology. But since each port on a switch is actually its own collision domain, you can make a much better Ethernet LAN network just by replacing your hubs with switches!

Switches truly have changed the way networks are designed and implemented. If a pure switched design is properly implemented, it absolutely will result in a clean, cost-effective, and resilient internetwork. In this chapter, I'll survey and compare how networks were designed before and after switching technologies were introduced.

For up-to-the minute updates for this chapter, please see www.lammle.com/ forum and/or www.sybex.com/go/ccent2e.

Before Layer 2 Switching

Let's go back in time a bit and take a look at the condition of networks before switches and how switches have helped segment the corporate LAN. Before LAN switching, the typical network design looked like the network in Figure 7.1.

The design in Figure 7.1 was called a *collapsed backbone* because all hosts needed to go to the corporate backbone to reach any network services—both LAN and mainframe.

Going back even further, before networks like the one shown in Figure 7.1 had physical segmentation devices such as routers and hubs, there was the mainframe network. This network included the mainframe (IBM, Honeywell, Sperry, DEC, etc.), controllers, and dumb terminals that connected into the controller. Any remote sites were connected to the mainframe with bridges.

FIGURE 7.1   Before switching

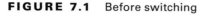
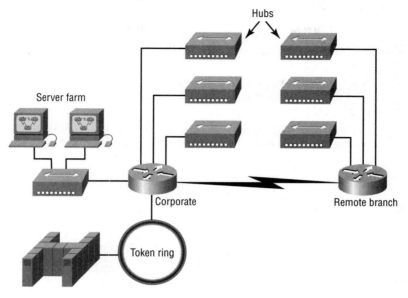

And then the PC began its rise to stardom, and the mainframe was connected to the Ethernet or to a Token Ring LAN where the servers were installed. These servers were usually OS/2 or LAN Manager because this was "pre-NT." Each floor of a building ran either coax or twisted-pair wiring to the corporate backbone and was then connected to a router. PCs ran an emulating software program that allowed them to connect to the mainframe services, giving those PCs the ability to access services from the mainframe and LAN simultaneously. Eventually the PC became robust enough to allow application developers to port applications more effectively than they could ever before—an advance that markedly reduced networking prices and enabled businesses to grow at a much faster rate.

When Novell became more popular in the late 1980s and early 1990s, OS/2 and LAN Manager servers were by and large replaced with NetWare servers. This made the Ethernet network even more popular, because that's what Novell 3.x servers used to communicate with client-server software.

So, that's the story about how the network in Figure 7.1 came into being. There was only one problem—the corporate backbone grew and grew, and as it grew, network services became slower. A big reason for this was that, at the same time this huge burst in growth was taking place, LAN services needed even faster service, and the network was becoming totally saturated. Everyone was dumping the Macs and dumb terminals used for the mainframe service in favor of those slick new PCs so they could more easily connect to the corporate backbone and network services.

All this was taking place before the Internet's momentous popularity, so everyone in the company needed to access the corporate network's services. Why? Because without the Internet, all network services were internal—exclusive to the company network. This created a screaming need to segment that one humongous and plodding corporate network, connected with sluggish old routers. At first, Cisco just created faster routers (no doubt about that), but more segmentation was needed, especially on the Ethernet LANs. The invention of Fast Ethernet was a very good and helpful thing, too, but it didn't address that network segmentation need at all.

But devices called bridges did, and they were first used in the network to break up collision domains. Bridges were sorely limited by the amount of ports and other network services they could provide, and that's when layer 2 switches came to the rescue. These switches saved the day by breaking up collision domains on each and every port—like a bridge—and switches could provide hundreds of ports! This early, switched LAN looked like the network pictured in Figure 7.2.

FIGURE 7.2   The first switched LAN

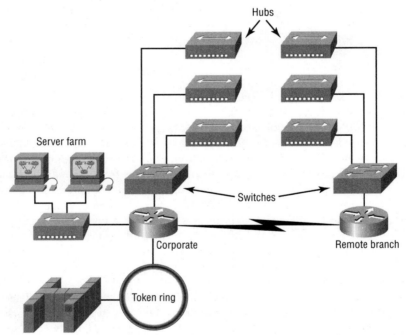

Each hub was placed into a switch port, an innovation that vastly improved the network. Now, instead of each building being crammed into the same collision domain, each hub became its own separate collision domain. But there was a catch—switch ports were still very new and hence unbelievably expensive. Because of that, simply adding a switch into each floor of the building just wasn't going to happen—at least not yet. Thanks to whomever you choose to thank for these things, the price has dropped dramatically, so now having every one of your users plugged into a switch port is both good and feasible.

So, there it is—if you're going to create a network design and implement it, including switching services is a must. A typical contemporary network design would look something like Figure 7.3, a complete switched network design and implementation.

FIGURE 7.3   The typical switched network design

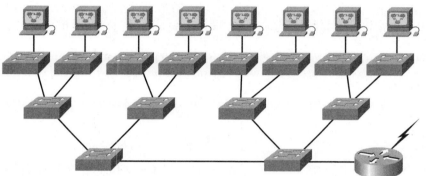

"But I still see a router in there," you say! Yes, it's not a mirage—there *is* a router in there. But its job has changed. Instead of performing physical segmentation, it now creates and handles logical segmentation. Those logical segments are called VLANs, and if you'd like to know more about them, pick up my *CCNA: Cisco Certified Network Associate Study Guide, Seventh Edition* (Sybex, 2011).

Switching Services

Unlike bridges, which use software to create and manage a filter table, switches use application-specific integrated circuits (ASICs) to build and maintain their filter tables. But it's still okay to think of a layer 2 switch as a multiport bridge because their basic reason for being is the same: to break up collision domains.

Layer 2 switches and bridges are faster than routers because they don't take up time looking at the Network layer header information. Instead, they look at the frame's hardware addresses before deciding to either forward, flood, or drop the frame.

Switches create private, dedicated collision domains and provide independent bandwidth on each port, unlike hubs. Cisco calls this *microsegmentation*.

Layer 2 switching provides the following:

- Hardware-based bridging (ASIC)
- Wire speed
- Low latency
- Low cost

What makes layer 2 switching so efficient is that no modification to the data packet takes place. The device only reads the frame encapsulating the packet, which makes the switching process considerably faster and less error-prone than routing processes are.

And if you use layer 2 switching for both workgroup connectivity and network segmentation (breaking up collision domains), you can create a flatter network design with more network segments than you can with traditional routed networks.

Plus, layer 2 switching increases bandwidth for each user because, again, each connection (interface) into the switch is its own collision domain. This feature makes it possible for you to connect multiple devices to each interface.

In the following sections, I will dive deeper into the layer 2 switching technology.

Limitations of Layer 2 Switching

Since we commonly stick layer 2 switching into the same category as bridged networks, we also tend to think it has the same hang-ups and issues that bridged networks do. Keep in mind that bridges are good and helpful things if you design the network correctly, keeping their features as well as their limitations in mind. And to design well with bridges, these are the two most important considerations:

- You absolutely must break up the collision domains correctly.
- The right way to create a functional bridged network is to make sure that its users spend 80 percent of their time on the local segment.

Bridged networks break up collision domains, but remember, that a network is still one large broadcast domain. Neither layer 2 switches nor bridges break up broadcast domains by default—something that not only limits your network's size and growth potential but also can reduce its overall performance.

Layer 2 switches break up collision domains on each port, but these switches can also be configured to break up broadcast domains by configuring ports on a switch into separate bridge groups, called *virtual LANs* (VLANs). VLANs are outside the ICND1 objectives and are covered in my *CCNA: Cisco Certified Network Associate Study Guide, Seventh Edition* (Sybex, 2011). You just remember that switches create microsegmentation (meaning each port is a collision domain) but are one large broadcast domain by default. VLANs help you break up broadcast domains in a layer 2 switched network.

Broadcasts and multicasts, along with the slow convergence time of spanning trees (loop avoidance protocol), can give you some major grief as your network grows. These are the big reasons layer 2 switches and bridges cannot completely replace routers (layer 3 devices) in the internetwork.

Bridging vs. LAN Switching

It's true—layer 2 switches really are pretty much just bridges that give you a lot more ports, but you should always keep in mind these important differences:

- Bridges are software based, while switches are hardware based because they use ASIC chips to help make filtering decisions.
- A switch can be viewed as a multiport bridge.
- There can be only one spanning-tree instance per bridge, while switches can have many.
- Switches have a higher number of ports than most bridges.
- Both bridges and switches forward layer 2 broadcasts.
- Bridges and switches learn MAC addresses by examining the source address of each frame received.
- Both bridges and switches make forwarding decisions based on layer 2 addresses.

Now, it's time to take a look at what the three main purposes are that a LAN switch provides to your networks.

Three Switch Functions at Layer 2

There are three distinct functions of layer 2 switching (you need to remember these!): *address learning*, *forward/filter decisions*, and *loop avoidance*.

Address Learning   Layer 2 switches and bridges remember the source hardware address of each frame received on an interface, and they enter this information into a MAC database called a *forward/filter table*.

Forward/Filter Decisions   When a frame is received on an interface, the switch looks at the destination hardware address and finds the exit interface in the MAC database. The frame is only forwarded out the specified destination port.

Loop Avoidance   If multiple connections between switches are created for redundancy purposes, network loops can occur. Spanning Tree Protocol (STP) is used to stop network loops while still permitting redundancy. STP is covered extensively in my *CCNA: Cisco Certified Network Associate Study Guide, Seventh Edition* (Sybex, 2011), and it is not an ICND1 objective.

I'm going to talk about address learning and forward/filtering decisions in detail in the next sections, which are very large ICND1 objectives.

Address Learning

When a switch is first powered on, the MAC forward/filter table is empty, as shown in Figure 7.4.

FIGURE 7.4   Empty forward/filter table on a switch

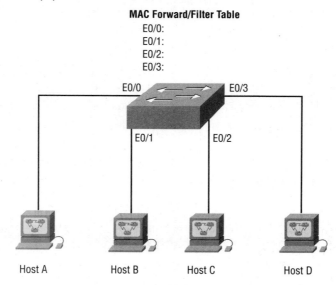

When a device transmits and an interface receives a frame, the switch places the frame's source address in the MAC forward/filter table, allowing it to remember which interface the sending device is located on. The switch then has no choice but to flood the network with this frame out of every port except the source port because it has no idea where the destination device is actually located.

If a device answers this flooded frame and sends a frame back, then the switch will take the source address from that frame and place that MAC address in its database as well, associating this address with the interface that received the frame. Since the switch now has both of the relevant MAC addresses in its filtering table, the two devices can make a point-to-point connection. The switch doesn't need to flood the frame as it did the first time because now the frames can and will be forwarded only between the two devices. This is exactly the thing that makes layer 2 switches better than hubs. In a hub network, all frames are forwarded out all ports every time—no matter what. Figure 7.5 shows the processes involved in building a MAC database.

FIGURE 7.5   How switches learn hosts' locations

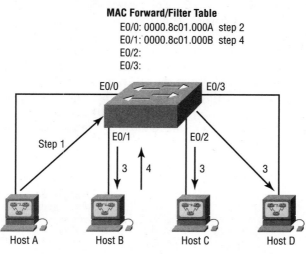

In this figure, you can see four hosts attached to a switch. When the switch is powered on, it has nothing in its MAC address forward/filter table, just as in Figure 7.4. But when the hosts start communicating, the switch places the source hardware address of each frame in the table along with the port that the frame's address corresponds to.

Let me give you an example of how a forward/filter table is populated.

1. Host A sends a frame to Host B. Host A's MAC address is 0000.8c01.000A; Host B's MAC address is 0000.8c01.000B.

2. The switch receives the frame on the E0/0 interface and places the source address in the MAC address table.

3. Since the destination address is not in the MAC database, the frame is forwarded out all interfaces—except the source port.

4. Host B receives the frame and responds to Host A. The switch receives this frame on interface E0/1 and places the source hardware address in the MAC database.

5. Host A and Host B can now make a point-to-point connection, and only the two devices will receive the frames. Hosts C and D will not see the frames, nor are their MAC addresses found in the database because they haven't yet sent a frame to the switch.

If Host A and Host B don't communicate to the switch again within a certain amount of time, the switch will flush their entries from the database to keep it as current as possible.

Forward/Filter Decisions

When a frame arrives at a switch interface, the destination hardware address is compared to the forward/filter MAC database. If the destination hardware address is known and listed in the database, the frame is sent out only the correct exit interface. The switch doesn't transmit the frame out any interface except for the destination interface. This preserves bandwidth on the other network segments and is called *frame filtering*.

But if the destination hardware address is not listed in the MAC database, then the frame is flooded out all active interfaces except the interface the frame was received on. If a device answers the flooded frame, the MAC database is updated with the device's location (interface).

If a host or server sends a broadcast on the LAN, the switch will flood the frame out all active ports except the source port by default. Remember, the switch creates smaller collision domains, but it's still one large broadcast domain by default.

In Figure 7.6, Host A sends a data frame to Host D. What will the switch do when it receives the frame from Host A?

FIGURE 7.6   Forward/filter table

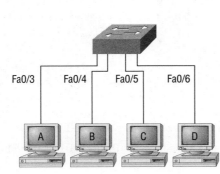

```
Switch#sh mac address-table
Vlan    Mac Address        Ports
----    -----------        -----
   1    0005.dccb.d74b     Fa0/4
   1    000a.f467.9e80     Fa0/5
   1    000a.f467.9e8b     Fa0/6
```

Since Host A's MAC address is not in the forward/filter table, the switch will add the source address and port to the MAC address table and then forward the frame to Host D. If Host D's MAC address was not in the forward/filter table, the switch would have flooded the frame out all ports except for port Fa0/3.

Now let's take a look at the output of a show mac address-table command from another switch.

```
Switch#sh mac address-table
Vlan    Mac Address      Type       Ports
--      ------           ----       ---
   1    0005.dccb.d74b   DYNAMIC    Fa0/1
   1    000a.f467.9e80   DYNAMIC    Fa0/3
   1    000a.f467.9e8b   DYNAMIC    Fa0/4
   1    000a.f467.9e8c   DYNAMIC    Fa0/3
   1    0010.7b7f.c2b0   DYNAMIC    Fa0/3
   1    0030.80dc.460b   DYNAMIC    Fa0/3
   1    0030.9492.a5dd   DYNAMIC    Fa0/1
   1    00d0.58ad.05f4   DYNAMIC    Fa0/1
```

Suppose the preceding switch received a frame with the following MAC addresses:

Source MAC: **0005.dccb.d74b**

Destination MAC: **000a.f467.9e8c**

How will the switch handle this frame? Answer: the destination MAC address will be found in the MAC address table, and the frame will be forwarded out Fa0/3 only. *Remember* that if the destination MAC address is not found in the forward/filter table, it will forward the frame out all ports of the switch looking for the destination device. Now that you can see the MAC address table and how switches add hosts addresses to the forward filter table, how can you secure unauthorized users from just plugging a hub or access point into an open switch port?

Port Security

Okay—So just how do you stop someone from simply plugging a host into one of your switch ports—or, worse, adding a hub, switch, or access point into the Ethernet jack in their office? By default, MAC addresses will just dynamically appear in your MAC forward/filter database. You can stop them in their tracks by using port security, which prevents unauthorized hosts from accessing the LAN.

Here are your options:

```
Switch#config t
Switch(config)#int f0/1
Switch(config-if)#switchport port-security ?
    aging          Port-security aging commands
    mac-address    Secure mac address
    maximum        Max secure addresses
    violation      Security violation mode
    <cr>
```

You can see clearly in the preceding output that the `switchport port-security` command can be used with four options. Personally, I like the `port-security` command because it allows me to easily control users on my network. You can use the `switchport port-security mac-address` *mac-address* command to assign individual MAC addresses to each switch port, but if you choose to go there, you'd better have a lot of time on your hands!

If you want to set up a switch port to allow only one host per port and to shut down the port if this rule is violated, use the following commands:

```
Switch#config t
Switch(config)#int f0/1
Switch(config-if)#switchport port-security maximum 1
Switch(config-if)#switchport port-security violation shutdown
```

These commands are probably the most popular because they prevent users from connecting to a switch or access point that's in their office. The `maximum` setting of 1 means only one MAC address can be used on that port; if the user tries to add another host on that segment, the switch port will shut down. If that happens, you'd have to manually go into the switch and enable the port with a no shutdown command.

Probably one of my favorite commands is the sticky command. Not only does it perform a cool function, but it's got a cool name! You can find this command under the mac-address command.

```
Switch(config-if)#switchport port-security mac-address sticky
Switch(config-if)#switchport port-security maximum 2
Switch(config-if)#switchport port-security violation shutdown
```

Basically, what this does is provide static MAC address security without having to type in everyone's MAC address on the network. As I said—cool!

In the preceding example, the first two MAC addresses into the port "stick" as static addresses and will stay that way for however long you set the aging command for. Why did I set it to 2? Well, I needed one for the PC/data and one for telephony/phone.

> More detail regarding port security can be found in Chapter 9, "Security."

Cisco Catalyst Switches

Just as I did with the routers configured in Chapter 6, "IP Routing," I'll use a figure and set up the switches as examples in this chapter. Figure 7.7 shows the switched network I'll be working on.

I'm going to use a new 3560, a 2960, and a 3550 switch. But before I actually get into configuring one of the Catalyst switches, I have to fill you in regarding the bootup process of these switches, just as I did with the routers in Chapter 4, "Cisco's Internetworking Operating System (IOS)."

Figure 7.8 shows the detail of a typical Cisco Catalyst switch, and I need to tell you about the different interfaces and features of this product.

The first thing I want you to know is that the console port for a Catalyst switch is typically located on the back of the switch. But on a smaller switch like the 3560 shown in the figure, the console is right in the front to make it easier to use. (The eight-port 2960 looks exactly the same as the 3560.) When you power on a Cisco switch, the power-on self-test (POST) is run to verify the hardware of the device. If the POST completes successfully, the system LED turns green; if the POST fails, it will turn amber. And seeing the amber glow is a very bad thing—typically fatal. So, you may just want to keep a spare switch around, especially in case it happens to be a production switch that's croaked!

The bottom button is used to show you which ports are providing *Power over Ethernet* (PoE). You can see this by pressing the Mode button, which will enable the lights on the ports providing PoE. This is a very nice feature of these switches. It allows me to power my access point and phone by just connecting them into the switch with an Ethernet cable! Sweet.

FIGURE 7.7   The switched network

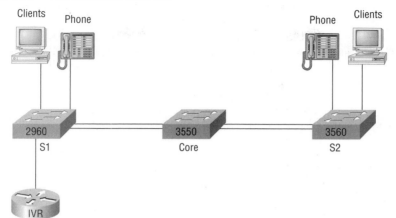

FIGURE 7.8   A Cisco Catalyst switch

Now if I connect the switches to each other, as shown in Figure 7.7, remember that first I'll need a crossover cable between the switches. My 2960 and 3560 switches autodetect the connection type, so I was able to use straight-through cables. But a 2950 or 3550 switch won't autodetect the cable type. Different switches have different needs and abilities, so just keep this in mind when connecting various switches, but always remember that the CCENT and CCNA exams never consider autodetect mechanisms as an option, so you'd always opt for a crossover cable between switches.

When you first connect the switch ports to each other, the link lights are amber and then turn green indicating normal operation. This is spanning-tree converging, and this process takes around 50 seconds with no extensions enabled. But if you connect into a switch port and the switch port LED is alternating green and amber, this means the port is experiencing errors. If this happens, check the host NIC card or the cabling.

If you connect a host or router to a switch and the ports on the switch are not turning amber or green, you will want to ensure that the cables running from the host and the router to the switch are straight-through cables, make sure the switch is powered up, and then, last, reseat all the cables to verify physical connection.

S1

Let's start the configuration by connecting into each switch and setting the administrative functions. I'll also assign an IP address to each switch, but this isn't really necessary to make the network function. The only reason I'm going to do that is so I can manage/administer it. Let's use a simple IP scheme like 192.168.10.16/28. This mask should be familiar to you! Check out the following output:

```
Switch>en
Switch#config t
Enter configuration commands, one per line. End with CNTL/Z.
Switch(config)#hostname S1
S1(config)#enable secret todd
S1(config)#int f0/1
S1(config-if)#description 1st Connection to Core Switch
S1(config-if)#int f0/2
S1(config-if)#description 2nd Connection to Core Switch
S1(config-if)#int f0/3
S1(config-if)#description Connection to HostA
S1(config-if)#int f0/4
S1(config-if)#description Connection to PhoneA
S1(config-if)#int f0/8
S1(config-if)#description Connection to IVR
S1(config-if)#line console 0
S1(config-line)#password console
S1(config-line)#login
S1(config-line)#exit
S1(config)#line vty 0 ?
  <1-15>  Last Line number
  <cr>
S1(config)#line vty 0 15
S1(config-line)#password telnet
S1(config-line)#login
S1(config-line)#int vlan 1
S1(config-if)#ip address 192.168.10.17 255.255.255.240
S1(config-if)#no shut
S1(config-if)#exit
S1(config)#banner motd # This is the S1 switch #
S1(config)#exit
```

```
S1#copy run start
Destination filename [startup-config]? [enter]
Building configuration...
[OK]
S1#
```

The first thing to notice about this is that there's no IP address configured on the switch's interfaces. Since all ports on a switch are enabled by default, there's not so much to configure. The IP address is configured under a logical interface, called a *management interface* or *native VLAN*. You would typically use the default VLAN 1 interface to manage a switched network just as I'm doing here. The rest of the configuration is basically the same as the process you go through for router configuration. Remember, no IP addresses on switch interfaces, no routing protocols, and so on. You're performing layer 2 switching at this point, not routing! Also, note that there is no aux port on Cisco switches.

S2

Here is the S2 configuration:

```
Switch#config t
Switch(config)#hostname S2
S2(config)#enable secret todd
S2(config)#int fa0/1
2(config-if)#description 1st Connection to Core
S2(config-if)#int fa0/2
S2(config-if)#description 2nd Connection to Core
S2(config-if)#int fa0/3
S2(config-if)#description Connection to HostB
S2(config-if)#int fa0/4
S2(config-if)#description Connection to PhoneB
S2(config-if)#line con 0
S2(config-line)#password console
S2(config-line)#login
S2(config-line)#exit
S2(config)#line vty 0 ?
  <1-15>  Last Line number
  <cr>
S2(config)#line vty 0 15
S2(config-line)#password telnet
```

```
S2(config-line)#login
S2(config-line)#int vlan 1
S2(config-if)#ip address 192.168.10.18 255.255.255.240
S2(config-if)#no shut
S2(config-if)#exit
S2(config)#banner motd # This is my S2 Switch #
S2(config)#exit
S2#copy run start
Destination filename [startup-config]?[enter]
Building configuration...
[OK]
S2#
```

You should now be able to ping from S2 to S1. Let's try it.

```
S2#ping 192.168.10.17


Type escape sequence to abort.
Sending 5, 100-byte ICMP Echos to 192.168.10.17, timeout is 2 seconds:
.!!!!
Success rate is 80 percent (4/5), round-trip min/avg/max = 1/1/1 ms
S2#
```

I have two questions for you: how can I ping through the core switch if I haven't configured it yet, and why did I get only four pings to work instead of five? (The first period [.] is a timeout; the exclamation point [!] is a success.)

Both are good questions. Here's why: first, you don't need the switch configured to make it work. All ports are enabled by default, so by just turning it on you should be able to communicate between hosts. Second, the first ping didn't work because of the time that ARP takes to resolve the IP address to a hardware MAC address.

Core

Here is the Core switch configuration:

```
Switch>en
Switch#config t
Switch(config)#hostname Core
Core(config)#enable secret todd
Core(config)#int f0/5
Core(config-if)#description 1st Connection to S2
Core(config-if)#int fa0/5
```

```
Core(config-if)#description 2nd Connection to S2
Core(config-if)#int f0/7
Core(config-if)#desc 1st Connection to S1
Core(config-if)#int f0/8
Core(config-if)#desc 2nd Connection to S1
Core(config-if)#line con 0
Core(config-line)#password console
Core(config-line)#login
Core(config-line)#line vty 0 15
Core(config-line)#password telnet
Core(config-line)#login
Core(config-line)#int vlan 1
Core(config-if)#ip address 192.168.10.19 255.255.255.240
Core(config-if)#no shut
Core(config-if)#exit
Core(config)#banner motd # This is the Core Switch #
Core(config)#exit
Core#copy run start
Destination filename [startup-config]?[enter]
Building configuration...
[OK]
Core#
```

Now let's ping to S1 and S2 from the Core switch and see what happens.

```
Core#ping 192.168.10.17
Type escape sequence to abort.
Sending 5, 100-byte ICMP Echos to 192.168.10.17, timeout is 2 seconds:
.!!!!
Success rate is 80 percent (4/5), round-trip min/avg/max = 1/1/1 ms
Core#ping 192.168.10.18
Type escape sequence to abort.
Sending 5, 100-byte ICMP Echos to 192.168.10.18, timeout is 2 seconds:
.!!!!
Success rate is 80 percent (4/5), round-trip min/avg/max = 1/1/1 ms
Core#sh ip arp
Protocol  Address           Age (min)  Hardware Addr   Type    Interface
Internet  192.168.10.18          0     001a.e2ce.ff40  ARPA    Vlan1
Internet  192.168.10.19          -     000d.29bd.4b80  ARPA    Vlan1
Internet  192.168.10.17          0     001b.2b55.7540  ARPA    Vlan1
Core#
```

Now, you can easily verify the switch configurations with the commands `show running-config`, `show ip interface brief`, and so on, but you need to know about one more command, even though you don't need it in the current example network because you don't have a router involved. It's the `ip default-gateway` command. If you want to manage your switches from outside your LAN or VLAN, you need to set a default gateway on the switches, just as you would with a host. You do this from global config. You do not set the default gateway for the switch under the VLAN 1 interface but from global configuration mode. Here's an example where I introduce the router with an IP address using the last IP address in my subnet range:

```
Core#config t
Core(config)#ip default-gateway 192.168.10.30
Core(config)#exit
Core#
```

 It's imperative that you remember how to set a default gateway on a switch and from which prompt you set it!

Summary

In this chapter, I talked about the differences between switches and bridges and how they both work at layer 2 and create a MAC address forward/filter table in order to make decisions on whether to forward or flood a frame.

Most importantly in this chapter is the fundamental understanding of how a switch handles a frame. I covered in detail what the switch will do when a frame is received and the destination hardware address is not in the MAC address table, as well as when a broadcast or multicast frame is received: all are flooded out all ports except for the port that it was received on.

Finally, I covered detailed configuration of Cisco's Catalyst switches, including verifying the configuration and, most importantly, how to manage the switch from remote networks.

Exam Essentials

Remember the three switch functions.   Address learning, forward/filter decisions, and loop avoidance are the functions of a switch.

Remember the command show mac address-table.   The command show mac address-table will show you the forward/filter table used on the LAN switch.

Remember how to configure a switch to be managed from outside the LAN.   To configure a switch to be managed from outside its LAN or VLAN, you must set the default gateway of the switch. The command, from global config mode, is ip default-gateway *ip_address*.

Remember how a switch handles a frame that has a destination address not found in the forward/filter table.   If a switch receives a frame with a destination address that is not in the forward/filter (MAC table), it will forward the frame out all ports except the port it was received on.

Remember how a switch handles a frame that is a broadcast or multicast.   If a switch receives a frame that is a broadcast or multicast, it will forward the frame out all ports except the port it was received on.

Written Lab 7

Write the answers to the following questions:

1.   What command will show you the forward/filter table?

2.   If a destination MAC address is not in the forward/filter table, what will the switch do with the frame?

3.   What are the three switch functions at layer 2?

4.   If a frame is received on a switch port and the source MAC address is not in the forward/filter table, what will the switch do?

5.   What is used at layer 2 to prevent switching loops?

6.   If a switch receives a frame and it is a broadcast, what will the switch do to the frame?

7.   How can you stop unauthorized hosts from connecting to your switch?

8.   Switches break up _____ domains.

9.   When a switch boots, the system light turns amber. When it passes the POST test, the light turns green. What does it typically mean if the light stays amber?

10.   When a switch port light alternates between amber and green, what does this mean?

(The answers to Written Lab 7 can be found in Appendix A.)

Review Questions

You can find the answers in Appendix B.

 The following questions are designed to test your understanding of this chapter's material. For more information on how to get additional questions, please see this book's introduction.

1. Which *three* of the following statements about switch microsegmentations are correct?

    A. Microsegmentation increases bandwidth availability.

    B. Implementing a bridge creates microsegmentation.

    C. Microsegmentation uses half-duplex operation.

    D. Microsegmentation eliminates collisions.

    E. Each device on a network segment is connected directly to a switch port.

    F. Microsegmentation limits the number of segments on a network.

2. What command will display the forward/filter table?

    A. show mac filter

    B. show run

    C. show mac address-table

    D. show mac filter-table

3. What is the result of segmenting a network with a bridge (switch)? (Choose two options.)

    A. It increases the number of collision domains.

    B. It decreases the number of collision domains.

    C. It increases the number of broadcast domains.

    D. It decreases the number of broadcast domains.

    E. It makes smaller collision domains.

    F. It makes larger collision domains.

4. Why would a network administrator configure port security on a switch?

    A. To prevent unauthorized Telnet access to a switch port

    B. To limit the number of layer 2 broadcasts on a particular switch port

    C. To prevent unauthorized hosts from accessing the LAN

    D. To block unauthorized access to the switch management interfaces over common TCP ports

5. An Ethernet cable is attached to a PC NIC and then attached to a switch port. The PC power is turned on, and the switch port link LED turns green. The link light indicates what *two* conditions?

    A. Layer 2 communication has been established between the PC and switch.

    B. The PC has received a DHCP address.

    C. Traffic is being sent from the switch to the PC.

    D. If flashing, the green LED indicates port speed of 100Mbps.

    E. The layer 1 media is functioning between the PC and switch.

    F. The switch port is functioning as a half-duplex connection.

6. What are the *three* distinct functions of layer 2 switching that increase available bandwidth on the network?

    A. Address learning

    B. Routing

    C. Forwarding and filtering

    D. Creating network loops

    E. Loop avoidance

    F. IP addressing

7. Your switch has a port status LED that is alternating between green and amber. What could this indicate?

    A. The port is experiencing errors.

    B. The port is shut down.

    C. The port is in STP blocking mode.

    D. Nothing; this is normal.

8. Which of the following statements is true?

    A. A switch creates a single collision domain and a single broadcast domain. A router creates a single collision domain.

    B. A switch creates separate collision domains but one broadcast domain. A router provides a separate broadcast domain for each interface.

    C. A switch creates a single collision domain and separate broadcast domains. A router provides a separate broadcast domain as well.

    D. A switch creates separate collision domains and separate broadcast domains. A router provides separate collision domains.

9. You need to configure a Catalyst switch so it can be managed remotely. Which of the following would you use to accomplish this task?

    A. `Switch(config)#int fa0/1`

    B. `Switch(config-if)#ip address 192.168.10.252 255.255.255.0`

    C. `Switch(config-if)#no shut`

    D. `Switch(config-if)#ip gateway 192.168.10.254 255.255.255.0`

    E. `Switch(config)#ip default-gateway 192.168.10.254`

    F. `Switch(config)#ip default-network 192.168.10.254`

10. What does a switch do when a frame is received on an interface and the destination hardware address is unknown or not in the filter table?

    A. Forwards the switch to the first available link

    B. Drops the frame

    C. Floods the frame out all ports looking for the device

    D. Floods the frame out all ports except the port the frame was received on

11. If a switch receives a frame and the source MAC address is not in the MAC address table but the destination address is, what will the switch do with the frame?

    A. Discard it and send an error message back to the originating host.

    B. Flood the network with the frame.

    C. Add the source address and port to the MAC address table and forward the frame out the destination port.

    D. Add the destination to the MAC address table and then forward the frame.

12. You connect a router into a switch port, and the port is not turning orange or green. What steps would you take to troubleshoot this problem? (Choose three.)

    A. Make sure the Ethernet encapsulations match between the router and switch.

    B. Ensure that the cable from the router to the switch is a straight-through cable.

    C. Make sure the cable is plugged into a trunk port on the switch.

    D. Reboot all the devices.

    E. Ensure that the switch has power.

    F. Reseat all the cables.

13. Which *two* characteristics apply to layer 2 switches?

    A. Increases the number of collision domains

    B. Decreases the number of collision domains

    C. Implements VLAN

    D. Decreases the number of broadcast domains

    E. Uses the IP address to make decisions for forwarding data packets

14. Which command was used to produce the following output:

Vlan	Mac Address	Type	Ports
--	------	----	---
1	0005.dccb.d74b	DYNAMIC	Fa0/1
1	000a.f467.9e80	DYNAMIC	Fa0/3
1	000a.f467.9e8b	DYNAMIC	Fa0/4
1	000a.f467.9e8c	DYNAMIC	Fa0/3
1	0010.7b7f.c2b0	DYNAMIC	Fa0/3
1	0030.80dc.460b	DYNAMIC	Fa0/3

   A. show vlan

   B. show ip route

   C. show mac address-table

   D. show mac address-filter

15. What are *two* advantages of layer 2 Ethernet switches over hubs?

   A. They decrease the number of collision domains.

   B. They filter frames based on MAC addresses.

   C. They allow simultaneous frame transmissions.

   D. They increase the size of broadcast domains.

16. Why does the switch in the following illustration have two MAC addresses assigned to the Fast Ethernet 0/1 port in the switch address table?

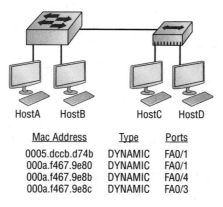

Mac Address	Type	Ports
0005.dccb.d74b	DYNAMIC	FA0/1
000a.f467.9e80	DYNAMIC	FA0/1
000a.f467.9e8b	DYNAMIC	FA0/4
000a.f467.9e8c	DYNAMIC	FA0/3

   A. Data from HostC and HostD has been received by the switch port Fast Ethernet 0/1.

   B. Data from two of the devices connected to the switch has been forwarded out to HostD.

   C. HostC and HostD had their NICs replaced.

   D. HostC and HostD are on different VLANs.

17. Layer 2 switching provides which of the following? (Choose four.)

 A. Hardware-based bridging (ASIC)

 B. Wire speed

 C. Low latency

 D. Low cost

 E. Routing

 F. WAN services

18. You type **show mac address-table** and receive the following output:

```
Switch#sh mac address-table
Vlan    Mac Address       Type       Ports
--      ------            ----       ---
  1     0005.dccb.d74b    DYNAMIC    Fa0/1
  1     000a.f467.9e80    DYNAMIC    Fa0/3
  1     000a.f467.9e8b    DYNAMIC    Fa0/4
  1     000a.f467.9e8c    DYNAMIC    Fa0/3
  1     0010.7b7f.c2b0    DYNAMIC    Fa0/3
  1     0030.80dc.460b    DYNAMIC    Fa0/3
```

Suppose the previous switch received a frame with the following MAC addresses:

▪ Source MAC: **0005.dccb.d74b**

▪ Destination MAC: **000a.f467.9e8c**

What will it do?

 A. It will discard the frame.

 B. It will forward the frame out port Fa0/3 only.

 C. It will forward it out Fa0/1 only.

 D. It will send it out all ports except Fa0/1.

19. You need to allow one host to be permitted to attach dynamically to each switch interface. Which *two* of the following commands must you configure on your catalyst switch to meet this policy?

 A. Switch(config-if)#ip access-group 10

 B. Switch(config-if)#switchport port-security maximum 1

 C. Switch(config)#access-list 10 permit ip host 1

 D. Switch(config-if)#switchport port-security violation shutdown

 E. Switch(config)#mac-address-table secure

20. The system LED is amber on a Cisco switch. What does this mean?

    A. The system is malfunctioning.

    B. The system is not powered up.

    C. The system is powered up and operational.

    D. The system has excessive collisions.

Chapter

8

Wireless Technologies

THE CCENT EXAM OBJECTIVES COVERED IN THIS CHAPTER INCLUDE THE FOLLOWING:

✓ **Explain and select the appropriate administrative tasks required for a WLAN**

- Describe standards associated with wireless media (including: IEEE WI-FI Alliance, ITU/FCC)

- Identify and describe the purpose of the components in a small wireless network (including: SSID, BSS, ESS)

- Identify the basic parameters to configure on a wireless network to ensure that devices connect to the correct access point

- Compare and contrast wireless security features and capabilities of WPA security (including: open, WEP, WPA-1/2)

- Identify common issues with implementing wireless networks

If you want to understand the basic wireless LANs or WLANs that are most commonly used today, just think 10BaseT Ethernet with hubs. What this means is that our WLANs typically run half-duplex communication—everyone is sharing the same bandwidth, and only one user is communicating at a time. This isn't necessarily bad; it's just not good enough. Because most people rely upon wireless networks today, it's critical that they evolve faster than greased lightning to keep up with our rapidly escalating needs. The good news is that this is actually happening; Cisco has reacted by coming up with an answer called the Cisco Unified Wireless Solution that works with all types of wireless connections. And it works securely, too!

This chapter will introduce you to wireless technologies in general by covering basic wireless LAN technologies and committees as well as the wireless security in use today, from no security to good security.

For up-to-the-minute updates on the topics covered in this chapter, please see www.lammle.com/forum and/or www.sybex.com/go/ccent2e.

Introducing Wireless Technology

Transmitting a signal using the typical 802.11 specifications works a lot like it does with a basic Ethernet hub: they're both two-way forms of communication, and they both use the same frequency to both transmit and receive, often referred to as *half-duplex* and mentioned in the introduction to this chapter. Wireless LANs (WLANs) use radio frequencies (RFs) that are radiated into the air from an antenna that creates radio waves. These waves can be absorbed, refracted, or reflected by walls, water, and metal surfaces, resulting in low signal strength. So, because of this innate vulnerability to surrounding environmental factors, it's pretty apparent that wireless will never offer the same robustness as a wired network can, but that still doesn't mean you're not going to run wireless. Believe me, you definitely will!

You can increase the transmitting power and gain a greater transmitting distance, but doing so can create some nasty distortion, so it has to be done carefully. By using higher frequencies, you can attain higher data rates, but this is, unfortunately, at the cost of decreased transmitting distances. And if you use lower frequencies, you get to transmit greater distances but at lower data rates. This should make it pretty clear to you that understanding all the various types of WLANs you can implement is imperative to creating the WLAN solution that best meets the specific requirements of the unique situation you're dealing with.

Also important to note is that the 802.11 specifications were developed so there would be no licensing required in most countries—to ensure the user the freedom to install and operate without any licensing or operating fees. This means that any manufacturer can create products and sell them at a local computer store or wherever. It also means you should all be able to get your computers to communicate wirelessly without configuring much.

Various agencies have been around for a very long time to help govern the use of wireless devices, frequencies, standards, and how the frequency spectrums are used. Table 8.1 shows the current agencies that help create, maintain, and even enforce wireless standards worldwide.

TABLE 8.1　Wireless agencies and standards

Agency	Purpose	Website
Institute of Electrical and Electronics Engineers (IEEE)	Creates and maintains operational standards	www.ieee.org
Federal Communications Commission (FCC)	Regulates the use of wireless devices in the United States	www.fcc.gov
European Telecommunications Standards Institute (ETSI)	Chartered to produce common standards in Europe	www.etsi.org
Wi-Fi Alliance	Promotes and tests for WLAN interoperability	www.wi-fi.com
WLAN Association (WLANA)	Educates and raises consumer awareness regarding WLANs	www.wlana.org

Because WLANs transmit over radio frequencies, they're regulated by the same types of laws used to govern things like AM/FM radios. It's the FCC that regulates the use of wireless LAN devices, and the IEEE takes it from there and creates standards based on what frequencies the FCC releases for public use.

The FCC has released three unlicensed bands for public use: 900MHz, 2.4GHz, and 5GHz. The 900MHz and 2.4GHz bands are referred to as the Industrial, Scientific, and Medical (ISM) bands, and the 5GHz band is known as the Unlicensed National Information

Infrastructure (UNII) band. Figure 8.1 shows where the unlicensed bands sit within the RF spectrum.

FIGURE 8.1   Unlicensed frequencies

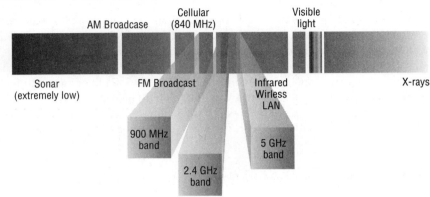

It follows that if you opt to deploy wireless in a range outside of the three public bands shown in Figure 8.1, you need to get a specific license from the FCC to do so. Once the FCC opened the three frequency ranges for public use, many manufacturers were able to start offering myriad products that flooded the market, with 802.11b/g being the most widely used wireless network found today.

The Wi-Fi Alliance grants certification for interoperability among 802.11 products offered by various vendors. This certification provides a sort of comfort zone for users purchasing the many types of products, although in my personal experience, it's just a whole lot easier if you buy all your access points from the same manufacturer. So, when the Wi-Fi logo appears on a wireless access point or client adapter, it signifies the following:

- The Wi-Fi Alliance has tested this device and determined that it meets IEEE WLAN standards.
- The Wi-Fi Alliance has verified that the device can interoperate with other devices using the same standards.

In the current U.S. wireless LAN market, there are several accepted operational standards and drafts created and maintained by the IEEE. Let's take a look at these standards and then talk about how the most commonly used standards work.

The 802.11 Standards

Taking off from what you learned in Chapter 1, "Internetworking," wireless networking has its own 802 standards group—remember, Ethernet's committee is 802.3. Wireless starts with 802.11, and there are various other up-and-coming standard groups as well, like

802.16 and 802.20. And there's no doubt that cellular networks will become huge players in our wireless future. But for now, we're going to concentrate on the 802.11 standards committee and subcommittees.

IEEE 802.11 was the first, original standardized WLAN, operating at 1Mbps and 2Mbps. It runs in the 2.4GHz radio frequency and was ratified in 1997 even though we didn't see many products pop up until around 1999 when 802.11b was introduced. All the committees listed in Table 8.2 created amendments to the original 802.11 standard except for 802.11F and 802.11T, both of which created stand-alone documents.

TABLE 8.2   802.11 Committees and subcommittees

Committee	Purpose
IEEE 802.11a	54Mbps, 5GHz standard
IEEE 802.11b	Enhancements to 802.11 to support 5.5Mbps and 11Mbps
IEEE 802.11c	Bridge operation procedures; included in the IEEE 802.1D standard
IEEE 802.11d	International roaming extensions
IEEE 802.11e	Quality of service
IEEE 802.11f	Inter-Access Point Protocol
IEEE 802.11g	54Mbps, 2.4GHz standard (backward compatible with 802.11b)
IEEE 802.11h	Dynamic Frequency Selection (DFS) and Transmit Power Control (TPC) at 5GHz; adds more non-overlapping channels for 802.11a
IEEE 802.11i	Enhanced security
IEEE 802.11j	Extensions for Japan and U.S. public safety
IEEE 802.11k	Radio resource measurement enhancements
IEEE 802.11m	Maintenance of the standard; odds and ends
IEEE 802.11n	Higher throughput improvements using multiple-input, multiple-output (MIMO) antennas
IEEE 802.11p	Wireless Access for the Vehicular Environment (WAVE)
IEEE 802.11r	Fast roaming

TABLE 8.2   802.11 Committees and subcommittees   *(continued)*

Committee	Purpose
IEEE 802.11s	Extended Service Set (ESS) Mesh Networking
IEEE 802.11t	Wireless Performance Prediction (WPP)
IEEE 802.11u	Internetworking with non-802 networks (cellular, for example)
IEEE 802.11v	Wireless network management
IEEE 802.11w	Protected management frames
IEEE 802.11y	3650–3700MHz operation in the United States

Okay, now let's discuss some important specifics of the most popular 802.11 WLANs.

2.4GHz (802.11b)

First on the menu is the 802.11b standard. It was the most widely deployed wireless standard, and it operates in the 2.4GHz unlicensed radio band that delivers a maximum data rate of 11Mbps. The 802.11b standard has been widely adopted by both vendors and customers who found that its 11Mbps data rate worked pretty well for most applications. But now that 802.11b has a big brother (802.11g), no one goes out and just buys an 802.11b card or access point anymore because why, for example, would you buy a 10Mbps Ethernet card when you can score a 10/100 Ethernet card for the same price?

An interesting thing about all Cisco 802.11 WLAN products is that they have the ability to data-rate-shift while moving. This allows the person operating at 11Mbps to shift to 5.5Mbps, to 2Mbps, and finally still communicate farthest from the access point at 1Mbps. And furthermore, this rate shifting happens without losing the connection and with no interaction from the user. Rate shifting also occurs on a transmission-by-transmission basis. This is important because it means that the access point can support multiple clients at varying speeds depending upon the location of each client.

 Cordless phones and microwave ovens can cause interference in the 2.4GHz range. Also, keep your access points away from devices that contain metal.

The problem with 802.11b lies in how the Data Link layer is dealt with. To solve problems in the RF spectrum and compensate for the half-duplex nature of wireless communication, a type of Ethernet collision detection was created called Carrier Sense Multiple Access with Collision Avoidance (CSMA/CA). Check this out in Figure 8.2.

FIGURE 8.2  802.11b CSMA/CA

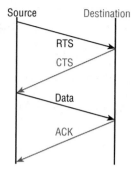

CSMA/CA is sometimes referred to as a request to send, clear to send (RTS/CTS) because of the way it requires hosts to communicate to the access point (AP). For every packet sent, an RTS/CTS and acknowledgment must be received, which doesn't exactly meet present-day networking demands efficiently!

2.4GHz (802.11g)

The 802.11g standard was ratified in June 2003 and is backward compatible to 802.11b. The 802.11g standard delivers the same 54Mbps maximum data rate as 802.11a but runs in the 2.4GHz range—the same as 802.11b.

Because 802.11b/g operates in the same 2.4GHz unlicensed band, migrating to 802.11g is an affordable choice for organizations with existing 802.11b wireless infrastructures. Just keep in mind that 802.11b products can't be "software upgraded" to 802.11g. This limitation is because 802.11g radios use a different chipset to deliver the higher data rate.

But still, much like Ethernet and Fast Ethernet, 802.11g products can be commingled with 802.11b products in the same network. Yet, for example, completely unlike Ethernet, if you have four users running 802.11g cards and one user starts using an 802.11b card, everyone connected to the same access point is then forced to run the 802.11b's encoding and modulation method—an ugly fact that really makes throughput suffer. So, to optimize performance, it's recommended that you disable the 802.11b-only mode on all your access points.

To explain this further, 802.11b uses a modulation technique called Direct Sequence Spread Spectrum (DSSS) that's just not as robust as the Orthogonal Frequency Division Multiplexing (OFDM) modulation used by both 802.11g and 802.11a. 802.11g clients using OFDM enjoy much better performance at the same ranges as 802.11b clients do, but—and remember this—when 802.11g clients are operating at the 802.11b rates (11Mbps, 5.5Mbps, 2Mbps, and 1Mbps), they're actually using the same modulation 802.11b does.

Figure 8.3 shows the 14 different channels (each 22MHz wide) that the FCC released in the 2.4GHz range.

FIGURE 8.3 ISM 2.4GHz channels

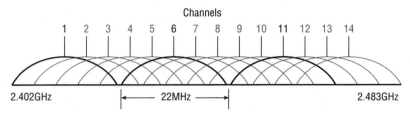

In the United States, only 11 channels are configurable, with channels 1, 6, and 11 being non-overlapping when using three APs in the same area. This allows you to have three access points in the same area without experiencing interference.

5GHz (802.11a)

The IEEE ratified the 802.11a standard in 1999, but the first 802.11a products didn't begin appearing on the market until late 2001. And, boy, could these hot new commodities seriously set you back! The 802.11a standard delivers a maximum data rate of 54Mbps with up to 28 non-overlapping frequency channels—a whopping 23 of them are available in the United States. Figure 8.4 shows the UNII bands.

FIGURE 8.4 UNII 5GHz band has 12 non-overlapping channels (U.S.).

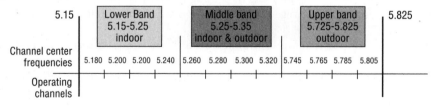

Another 802.11a/g benefit when operating in the 5GHz radio band is that it's immune to interference from devices that operate in the 2.4GHz band, such as microwave ovens, cordless phones, and Bluetooth devices. As you probably guessed, 802.11a isn't backward compatible with 802.11b because they operate at different frequencies, so you don't get to just "upgrade" pieces and parts of your network and expect everything to sing in perfect harmony. But no worries—there are plenty of dual-radio devices that will work in both types of networks. Oh, and another definite plus for 802.11a is that it can

work in the same physical environment without having to take measures to avoid interference from 802.11b users.

Like 802.11b/g radios, all 802.11a products also have the ability to data-rate-shift while moving. The difference is that 802.11a products allow someone moving at 54Mbps to shift to 48Mbps, 36Mbps, 24Mbps, 18Mbps, 12Mbps, and 9Mbps, and finally still communicate farthest from the AP way down at 6Mbps.

Comparing 802.11

Before I move on to Cisco-specific products, take a look at Table 8.3, which lists the characteristics of 802.11a, b, and g.

TABLE 8.3: 802.11 comparison

	802.11b	802.11g	802.11a/h
Frequency	2.4GHz	2.4GHz	5GHz
Scope of use	Most common		
Available Speeds	1, 2, 5.5, and 11Mbps	6, 9, 12, 18, 24, 36, 48, and 54Mbps	6, 9, 12, 18, 24, 36, 48, and 54Mbps
Maximum data rate	Up to 11Mpbs	Up to 54Mbps*	Up to 54Mbps
Modulations	DSSS	DSSS/OFDM	OFDM
Channel	3 non-overlapping channels	3 non-overlapping channels	Up to 23 non-overlapping channels
Density	About 25 users per cell**	About 20 users per cell	About 15 users per cell
	Distance limited by Multipath	Throughput degraded by 802.11b clients	Lower market penetrations

* Runs Direct Sequence Spread Spectrum when also running 802.11b at speeds of 11Mbps and slower.

** This happens to be Cisco's rule of thumb. Know that the actual amount of users per cell varies based on many factors.

All good, but there's one more IEEE 802.11 standard I want to cover that you'll use to get even higher speeds at greater distances.

🌐 **Real World Scenario**

You Won't Use 802.11b in *My* Network!

By now you should get the idea that you really shouldn't be using IEEE 802.11b clients or APs in your wireless networks, and since most laptops and other wireless devices all run a/b/g, you should be able to disable the 802.11b capabilities on your APs.

A few years back when I was installing a wireless network at a client, I disabled all the 802.11b capabilities on all access points. The next day a woman working in sales came up to me and said her wireless laptop stopped working. She had an older laptop with an external PCMIA wireless card, so I pretty much figured out the problem right away. Once I pulled the card out, I showed her that it was old and defective and that she needed to get a new wireless card. (It really wasn't defective, but it was defective in my network!) The next day she came back with a new wireless card in hand. Since it is impossible these days to buy an 802.11b card, except maybe a used one from eBay, I wasn't worried that the card was a "b-only" card. However, after looking at the card, sure enough, it was a new 802.11b card. I was stunned! Where would she get a new 802.11b card? She said that CompUSA was going out of business and she found this new card for only four bucks in a clearance bin! Perfect.

2.4GHz/5GHz (802.11n)

802.11n builds on previous 802.11 standards by adding *MIMO*, which uses multiple transmitters and receiver antennas to increase data throughput and range. 802.11n can allow up to eight antennas, but most of today's APs use only four to six. This setup permits considerably higher data rates than 802.11a/b/g does.

The following three vital items are combined in 802.11n to enhance performance:

- At the Physical layer, the way a signal is sent is changed, enabling reflections and interferences to become an advantage instead of a source of degradation.
- Two 20MHz-wide channels are combined to increase throughput.
- At the MAC layer, a different way of managing packet transmission is used.

It's important to know that 802.11n isn't truly compatible with 802.11b, 802.11g, or even 802.11a, but it is designed to be backward compatible with them. How 802.11n achieves backward compatibility is by changing the way frames are sent so they can be understood by 802.11a/b/g.

Here's a list of some of the primary components of 802.11n that together sum up why people claim 802.11n is more reliable and predictable:

40MHz Channels   802.11g and 802.11a use 20MHz channels and employ tones on the sides of each channel that are not used in order to protect the main carrier. This means that 11Mbps go unused and are basically wasted. 802.11n aggregates two carriers to double the speed from 54Mbps to more than 108. Add those wasted 11Mbps rescued from the side tones, and you get a grand total of 119Mbps!

MAC Efficiency   802.11 protocols require acknowledgment of each and every frame. 802.11n can pass many packets before an acknowledgment is required, which saves you a huge amount of overhead. This is called *block acknowledgment*.

Multiple-Input Multiple-Output   Several frames are sent by several antennae over several paths and are then recombined by another set of antennae to optimize throughput and multipath resistance. This is called *spatial multiplexing*.

Now that you've nailed down the a/b/g/n networks, it's time to move on and get into some detail about how wireless frames are actually sent, about frame shapes and speeds, and about the management frame used to discover and connect to the wireless network.

Basic Service Sets

With a range of products that support IEEE 802.11a/b/g/n technologies, Cisco really does offer a pretty complete and impressive line of indoor and outdoor wireless LAN solutions. These products include access points, wireless controllers, wireless LAN client adapters, security and management servers, wireless management devices, wireless integrated switches and routers, and even antennas and accessories. Did I say impressive or what?

Since about the year 2000, a lot of corporations have relied upon simple-to-manage access points (autonomous) as their main wireless networks and connected them into an infrastructure (wired network), which allowed users to roam within their complete network.

Let's discuss service sets in a little more detail.

There are typically three types of wireless networks that you can create with wireless networks:

- Ad hoc (IBSS)
- Basic service set (BSS)
- Extended service set (ESS)

Ad hoc, or independent basic service set, is just a term for connecting two or three wireless hosts together without an AP. This is helpful for home, or very, very small office transfers of data. Ad hoc would not typically be used in today's corporate networks.

BSS and ESS networks define what is called a Service Set ID (SSID) that's used to advertise your wireless network so hosts can connect to the access point. An example of a BSS is one access point at home with one SSID. You can have multiple SSIDs configured on an access point for security reasons; typically this will be found in a corporate environment.

For example, you can designate that one SSID is open access for a public hot spot, while another SSID can use WEP or WPA2 for the employees that work at this public hot spot. The SSID name is broadcast by default from the AP so the clients can find the AP and connect to the wireless network, and of course you can turn this SSID broadcast feature off for security reasons.

BSS/IBSS

A BSS involves only a single access point. You create a BSS by bringing up an AP and creating a name for the service set ID. Users can then connect to and use this SSID to access the wireless network, which may provide connectivity to wired resources. When hosts communicate with each other, they must go through the AP.

When the AP connects to a wired network, it then becomes known as a basic service set. Keep in mind that if you have a BSS/IBSS, users won't be able to maintain network connectivity when roaming from AP to AP because each AP is configured with a different SSID name.

BSS wireless networks are also really helpful if you happen to have a couple of hosts that need to establish wireless communication directly between just them, for example, a home network. You can also make this happen through the ad hoc network I already mentioned, but if you have an AP between the hosts, it's just called a BSS.

Figure 8.5 shows a basic service set using one SSID and not connecting to an infrastructure.

FIGURE 8.5   Basic service set

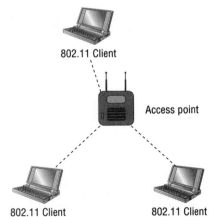

802.11 Client

Access point

802.11 Client   802.11 Client

If the AP connected to a wired network, this would now be called an Infrastructure BSS (IBSS).

ESS

Mobile wireless clients can roam from AP to AP within the same network if you set all your access points to the same Service Set ID. Doing this creates an extended service set. Figure 8.6 shows four APs configured with the same SSID in an office, thereby creating the ESS network.

FIGURE 8.6   Extended service set

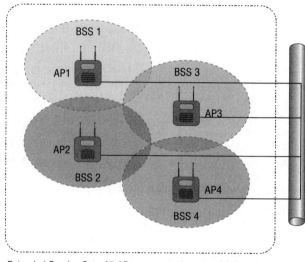

Extended Service Set: All APs are set to the same SSID and connect to an Infrastructure.

   For users to be able to roam throughout the wireless network—from AP to AP without losing their connection to the network—all APs cells must overlap by at least 10 percent or more, and the channels on each AP shouldn't be set the same, either. And remember, in an 802.11b/g network, there are only three non-overlapping channels (1, 6, and 11) if you have access points in the same area, so design is super important here!

Wireless Security

By default, wireless security is nonexistent on access points and clients. The original 802.11 committee just didn't imagine that wireless hosts would one day outnumber bounded media hosts, but that's truly where we're headed. Also, and unfortunately, just as with the IPv4 routed protocol, engineers and scientists didn't add security standards that are robust enough to work in a corporate environment. So, we're left with proprietary solution add-ons to aid us in our quest to create a secure wireless network. And no—I'm not just sitting here bashing the standards committees. The security problems we're experiencing were also created by the U.S. government because of export issues with its own security standards. Our world is a complicated place, so it follows that our security solutions are going to be as well.

A good place to start is by discussing the standard basic security that was added into the original 802.11 standards and why those standards are way too flimsy and incomplete to enable you to create a secure wireless network relevant to today's challenges.

Open Access

All Wi-Fi Certified wireless LAN products are shipped in "open-access" mode, with their security features turned off. While open access or no security may be appropriate and acceptable for public hot spots such as coffee shops, college campuses, and maybe airports, it's definitely not an option for an enterprise organization, and likely not even adequate for your private home network.

Security needs to be enabled on wireless devices during their installation in enterprise environments. It may come as quite a shock, but some companies actually don't enable any WLAN security features. Obviously, the companies that do this are exposing their networks to tremendous risk!

The reason that the products are shipped with open access is so that any person who knows absolutely nothing about computers can just buy an access point, plug it into their cable or DSL modem, and *voilà*—they're up and running. It's marketing, plain and simple, and simplicity sells.

SSIDs, WEP, and MAC Address Authentication

What the original designers of 802.11 did to create basic security was include the use of Service Set Identifiers, open or shared-key authentication, static Wired Equivalency Protocol (WEP), and optional Media Access Control (MAC) authentication. It sounds like a lot, but none of these really offers any type of serious security solution—although they may be close to adequate for use on a common home network. But I'll go over them anyway.

An SSID is a common network name for the devices in a WLAN system and hosts the services an AP can provide. Disabling SSID broadcasts (called *beaconing*) prevents access by any client device that doesn't have the SSID configured on the host. The thing is, by default, an access point broadcasts its SSID in its beacon many times a second. And even if SSID broadcasting is turned off, a bad guy can discover the SSID by monitoring the network and just waiting for a client response to the access point. Why? Because, believe it or not, that information, as regulated in the original 802.11 specifications, must be sent in the clear—how secure!

If an AP does have SSID broadcasting disabled, the client needs to set the SSID value of the AP on the client software in order to connect to the AP.

Two types of authentication were specified by the IEEE 802.11 committee: open authentication and shared-key authentication. Open authentication involves little more than supplying the correct SSID—but it's the most common method in use today. With shared-key authentication, the access point sends the client device a challenge-text packet that the client must then encrypt with the correct Wired Equivalency Protocol key and return to the access point. Without the correct key, authentication fails, and the client won't be allowed to associate with the access point. But shared-key authentication is still not considered secure, because all an intruder has to do to get around this is detect both the clear-text challenge and the same challenge encrypted with a WEP key and then decipher the WEP key. Surprise—shared key isn't used in today's WLANs because of clear-text challenge.

With open authentication, even if a client can complete authentication and associate with an access point, the use of WEP prevents the client from sending and receiving data from the access point unless the client has the correct WEP key. A WEP key is composed of either 40 bits or 128 bits. In its basic form, the key is usually statically defined by the network administrator on the access point and all clients that communicate with that access point. When static WEP keys are used, a network administrator must perform the time-consuming task of entering the same keys on every device in the WLAN. Obviously, we now have fixes for this because this would be administratively impossible in today's huge corporate wireless networks!

Last, client MAC addresses can be statically typed into each access point, and any of them that try to connect without that MAC addresses in the filter table would be denied access. Sounds good, but of course all MAC layer information must be sent in the clear—anyone equipped with a free wireless sniffer can just read the client packets sent to the access point and spoof their MAC address.

WEP can actually work if administered correctly. But basic static WEP keys are no longer a viable option in today's corporate networks without some of the proprietary fixes that run on top of it. So, let's talk about some of these now.

WPA or WPA 2 Pre-Shared Key

Now we're getting somewhere. Although this is another form of basic security that's really just an add-on to the specifications, WPA or WPA2 Pre-Shared Key (PSK) is a better form of wireless security than any other basic wireless security method mentioned so far. I did say basic.

Wi-Fi Protected Access (WPA) is a standard developed in 2003 by the Wi-Fi Alliance, formerly known as WECA. WPA provides a standard for authentication and encryption of WLANs that's intended to solve known security problems. The standard takes into account the well-publicized AirSnort and man-in-the-middle WLAN attacks. Of course, now I'll show how to use WPA2 to help you with today's security issues.

The PSK verifies users via a password or identifying code (also called a *passphrase*) on both the client machine and the access point. A client gains access to the network only if its password matches the access point's password. The PSK also provides keying material that TKIP (WPA) or CCMP AES uses to generate an encryption key for each packet of transmitted data. While more secure than static WEP, PSK still has a lot in common with static WEP in that the PSK is stored on the client station and can be compromised if the client station is lost or stolen even though finding this key isn't all that easy to do.

It's a definite recommendation to use a strong PSK passphrase that includes a mixture of letters, numbers, and nonalphanumeric characters. However, it is possible to specify with WPA the use of dynamic encryption keys that change each time a client establishes a connection.

The benefit of WPA over static WEP is that WPA can change dynamically while the system is used.

WPA is a step toward the IEEE 802.11i standard and uses many of the same components, with the exception of encryption—802.11i (WPA2) uses AES-CCMP encryption. The IEEE 802.11i standard replaced Wired Equivalent Privacy with a specific mode of the Advanced Encryption Standard (AES) known as the Counter Mode Cipher Block Chaining-Message Authentication Code (CBC-MAC) Protocol (CCMP). This allows AES-CCMP to provide both data confidentiality (encryption) and data integrity.

WPA's mechanisms are designed to be implementable by current hardware vendors, meaning that users should be able to implement WPA on their systems with only a firmware/software modification.

The IEEE 802.11i standard has been sanctioned by WPA and is termed *WPA version 2*.

Summary

Like rock 'n' roll, wireless technologies are here to stay, and for those of us who have come to depend on wireless technologies, it's actually pretty hard to imagine a world without wireless networks—what did we do before cell phones?

So, I began this chapter by exploring the essentials and fundamentals of how wireless networks function.

Springing off that foundation, I then introduced you to the basics of wireless RF and the IEEE standards. I discussed 802.11 from its inception through its evolution to current and near future standards and talked about the subcommittees that create them.

All of this led into a discussion of wireless security—or, rather, nonsecurity for the most part.

Exam Essentials

Understand the IEEE 802.11a specification.   802.11a runs in the 5GHz spectrum, and if you use the 802.11h extensions, you have 23 non-overlapping channels. 802.11a can run up to 54Mbps, but only if you are less than 50 feet from an access point.

Understand the IEEE 802.11b specification.   IEEE 802.11b runs in the 2.4GHz range and has three non-overlapping channels. It can handle long distances, but with a maximum data rate of up to 11Mpbs.

Understand the IEEE 802.11g specification.   IEEE 802.11g is 802.11b's big brother and runs in the same 2.4GHz range, but it has a higher data rate of 54Mbps if you are less than 100 feet from an access point.

Understand the basic service set configurations.   There are various types of wireless network defined by the 802.11 standards: ad hoc, meaning two or more hosts connected directly together (wirelessly, of course); BSS, when two or more hosts communicate wirelessly but through an AP; and ESS, a wireless network that consists of at least two APs that are configured with the same SSID and connected together via an Ethernet network.

Written Lab 8

Write the answers to the following questions:

1. What is the maximum data rate of IEEE 802.11b?
2. What is the maximum data rate of IEEE 802.11g?
3. What is the maximum data rate of IEEE 802.11a?
4. What is the frequency range of IEEE 802.11b?
5. What is the frequency range of IEEE 802.11g?
6. What is the frequency range of IEEE 802.11a?
7. Which spread spectrum technology does the 802.11b standard define?
8. How many non-overlapping channels does 802.11b/g provide?
9. Which IEEE standard has been sanctioned by WPA and is called WPA2?
10. The IEEE 802.11a basic standard has how many non-overlapping channels?

   (The answers to Written Lab 8 can be found in Appendix A.)

Review Questions

You can find the answers in Appendix B.

 The following questions are designed to test your understanding of this chapter's material. For more information on how to get additional questions, please see this book's introduction.

1. Which *two* statements best describe the wireless security standard that is defined by WPA?

   A. It specifies the use of a static encryption key that must be changed frequently to enhance security.

   B. It requires the use of an open authentication method.

   C. It specifies the use of dynamic encryption keys that change each time a client establishes a connection.

   D. It requires that all access points and wireless devices always require the same encryption key.

   E. It includes authentication by PSK.

2. What is the frequency range of the IEEE 802.11b standard?

   A. 2.4Gbps

   B. 5Gbps

   C. 2.4GHz

   D. 5GHz

3. What is the frequency range of the IEEE 802.11a standard?

   A. 2.4Gbps

   B. 5Gbps

   C. 2.4GHz

   D. 5GHz

4. What is the frequency range of the IEEE 802.11g standard?

   A. 2.4Gbps

   B. 5Gbps

   C. 2.4GHz

   D. 5GHz

5. Which spread spectrum technology does the 802.11b standard define for operation?

   A. Infrared

   B. DSSS

   C. FHSS

   D. DSSS and FHSS

6. How many non-overlapping channels are available with 802.11g?

    A. 3

    B. 12

    C. 23

    D. 40

7. How many non-overlapping channels are available with 802.11b?

    A. 3

    B. 12

    C. 23

    D. 40

8. Which *two* statements about wireless networks are accurate?

    A. Instead of cables, wireless communication uses RFs or infrared waves to transmit data.

    B. To receive the signals for the access point, a computer needs to have a wireless adapter card or wireless NIC.

    C. For wireless LANs, a key component is a router, which propagates signal distribution.

    D. Wireless networks are not very common, and generally only large corporations use them.

9. What is the maximum data rate for the 802.11b standard?

    A. 6Mbps

    B. 11Mbps

    C. 22Mbps

    D. 54Mbps

10. Refer to Figure 8.7. What *two* factors can be determined from the WLAN diagram?

FIGURE 8.7 WLAN diagram

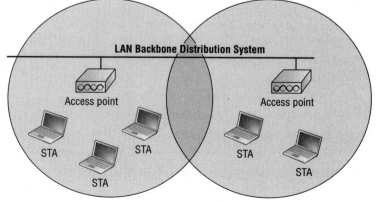

    A. The area of overlap of the two cells represents a basic service set (BSS).

    B. The network diagram represents an extended service set (ESS).

    C. Access points in each cell must be configured to use channel 1.

    D. The area of overlap must be less that 10 percent of the area to ensure connectivity.

    E. The two APs should be configured to operate on different channels.

11. What are the data rates for the 802.11b standard? (Choose four.)

    A. 1Mbps

    B. 11Mbps

    C. 2Mbps

    D. 5.5Mbps

    E. 6Mbps

    F. 54Mbps

12. Which *two* statements are true concerning wireless standards?

    A. Three standards exist: 802.11a/b, 802.11g, and 802.11w.

    B. 802.11 divides the 2.4GHz into 14 channels.

    C. 802.11b is superior to 802.11a because of its support for data rates up to 54Mbps.

    D. 802.11b is intended to compensate for the half-duplex nature of wireless communication.

    E. 802.11g is not as widely accepted because of production costs.

13. When the Wi-Fi logo appears on a wireless access point or client adapter, it signifies which *two* of these?

    A. The Wi-Fi alliance has tested this device and determined that is meets IEEE WLAN standards.

    B. The IEEE certifies that the device is in compliance with its wireless fidelity requirements.

    C. The access point or client adapter has been manufactured by the Wireless Fidelity company.

    D. The Wi-Fi Alliance has verified that the device can interoperate with other devices using the same standards.

    E. The manufacturer of the equipment has paid the Wi-Fi Alliance to market its products.

14. What is one reason that WPA encryption is preferred over WEP?

    A. A WPA key is longer and requires more special characters than the WEP key.

    B. The access point and the client are manually configured with different WPA key values.

    C. WPA key values remain the same until the current configuration is changed.

    D. The values of WPA keys can change dynamically while the system is used.

15. Which additional configuration step is necessary to connect to an AP that has SSID broadcasting disabled?

   A. Set the SSID value in the client software to public.

   B. Configure open authentication on the AP and the client.

   C. Set the SSID value on the client to the SSID configured on the AP.

   D. Configure MAC address filtering to permit the client to connect to the AP.

16. Which encryption type does WPA2 use?

   A. AES-CCMP

   B. PPK via IV

   C. PSK

   D. TKIP/MIC

17. Three access points have been installed and configured to cover a small office. What term defines the wireless topology?

   A. BSS

   B. IBSS

   C. ESS

   D. SSID

18. You want your mobile users to roam throughout your office. You have two access points. How should you configure them? (Choose three.)

   A. The APs should be configured in the same channel.

   B. The APs should be configured in different channels.

   C. You should connect only one mobile user to an Ethernet connection.

   D. You should connect both to an Ethernet connection.

   E. By setting both of the APs to the same SSID, you will create a BSS.

   F. By setting both of the APs to the same SSID, you will create an ESS.

19. You are connecting your access point, and it is connected to a wired network with more than one other access point on your network. What does *extended service set ID* mean?

   A. That you have more than one access point and they are in the same SSID connected by a distribution system

   B. That you have more than one access point and they are in separate SSIDs connected by a distribution system

   C. That you have multiple access points, but they are placed physically in different buildings

   D. That you have multiple access points, but one is a repeater access point

20. A single 802.11g access point has been installed in the center of a square office. Users are complaining about slow performance. What could be the possible problems with the wireless network? (Choose three.)

   A. Mismatched TKI encryption

   B. Null SSID

   C. Cordless phones

   D. Mismatched SSID

   E. Metal file cabinets

   F. Antenna type or direction

Chapter

9

Security

THE CCENT EXAM TOPICS COVERED IN THIS CHAPTER INCLUDE THE FOLLOWING:

✓ **Identify security threats to a network and describe general methods to mitigate those threats**

- Explain today's increasing network security threats and the need to implement a comprehensive security policy to mitigate the threats

- Explain general methods to mitigate common security threats to network devices, hosts, and applications

- Describe the functions of common security appliances and applications

- Describe security recommended practices including initial steps to secure network devices

If you're a sys admin, my guess is that shielding sensitive, critical data, as well as your network's resources, from every possible evil exploit is a top priority of yours. Right? Good to know you're on the right page—Cisco has some really effective security solutions that will arm you with the tools you need to make this happen.

This chapter will cover both router and switch security. You'll learn how to configure and use Secure Shell (SSH) instead of Telnet to configure your routers in-band (meaning, through the network).

I'll start by providing you with an introduction to security, as well as the most common attacks on networks. Next, I'll give you the information you need to protect your routers and switches with passwords, SSH, and banners as well as implement port security on a switch (yes, some of this is a refresher from other chapters). Finally, I'll introduce you to virtual private networks (VPNs).

For up-to-the minute updates for this chapter, please see www.lammle.com/forum and/or www.sybex.com/go/ccent2e.

Introduction to Security

You see this a lot—typically, in medium to large enterprise networks, the various strategies for security are based on some recipe of internal and perimeter routers plus firewall devices. Internal routers provide additional security to the network by screening traffic to various parts of the protected corporate network, and they do this using *access lists*.

Access lists are beyond the scope of this book, but they're covered in *CCNA: Cisco Certified Network Associate Study Guide, Seventh Edition* (Sybex, 2011).

Figure 9.1 shows where each of these types of devices is found.

FIGURE 9.1   A typical secured network

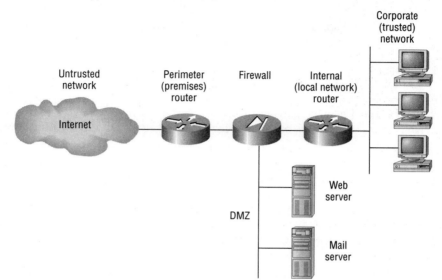

To protect network device configuration files from outside network security threats, use a firewall, as shown in Figure 9.1, to restrict access from the outside to the network devices, and use SSH instead of Telnet to access device configurations.

Figure 9.1 uses the terms *trusted network* and *untrusted network*. You can see where they are found in a typical secured network as well as the demilitarized zone (DMZ), which use global (real) Internet addresses or private addresses, depending on how you configure your firewall. However, this is typically where you'll find the HTTP, DNS, email, and other Internet-type corporate servers.

Instead of having routers, you can use *virtual local area networks* (VLANs) with switches on the inside trusted network. Multilayer switches containing their own security features can sometimes replace internal (LAN) routers to provide higher performance in VLAN architectures.

Let's discuss the security threats a typical secured internetwork faces; then I'll provide some ways of protecting the Cisco router and switch.

Recognizing Security Threats

Yes, it's true: security attacks vary considerably in their complexity and threat level. You see, it all comes down to planning—or, rather, lack thereof. Basically, the vital tool that the Internet has become today was absolutely unforeseen by those who brought it into being. This is a big reason why security is now such an issue; most IP implementations are innately insecure. No worries, though, because Cisco has a few tricks up its sleeve to help you with this.

WUI

Security attacks sometimes happen because of *witless user ignorance* (WUI). Knowing this term isn't an exam objective, but WUI causes security attacks more than you'd think!

The following are common trouble spots in the type of enterprise network shown in Figure 9.1:

Wireless LANs (WLANs)   Any user that can connect to the WLAN can access the devices in the trusted network. People from outside the building may even be able to gain access if the WLAN access points are left unsecured. Use the highest security you can afford on your WLANs.

Mobile Devices   When a mobile user connects their laptop at home or at another remote location, the laptop may become infected with a virus or a Trojan horse. When the user returns to the office and connects to the trusted network, the infection may spread. It is critical that all PCs and laptops are running the latest virus scanning software.

Employees   I am sure this is no shock to you, but some employees may be disgruntled workers. This may be the worst security problem a company can have. The employees are inside the trusted network and have access to many, if not all, devices and servers. It is important to grant each employee the minimum access they need.

Remember, attacks from inside the network remain as high a threat as those from outside. Prepare your network security plan accordingly.

Common Attack Profiles

This section covers the most common attacks used on today's networks.

Application-Layer Attacks   These attacks commonly zero in on well-known holes in the software that's typically found running on servers. Favorite targets include FTP, sendmail, and HTTP. Because the permission levels granted to these accounts are most often "privileged," bad guys simply access and exploit the machine that's running one of the applications I just mentioned.

Autorooters   You can think of these as a kind of hacker automaton. Bad guys use something called a *rootkit* to probe, scan, and then capture data on a strategically positioned computer that's poised to give them "eyes" into entire systems—automatically!

Back Doors   These are simply paths leading into a computer or network. Through simple invasions, or via more elaborate Trojan horse code, bad guys can use their implanted inroads into a specific host or even a network whenever they want—until you detect and stop them, that is!

Denial-of-Service (DoS) and Distributed Denial-of-Service (DDoS) Attacks   These are bad—pretty tough to get rid of, too! But even hackers don't respect other hackers who execute them because, though nasty, they're really easy to accomplish. (This means that some 10-year-old could actually bring you to your knees, and that is just wrong!) Basically, a DoS attack is a flood of packets requesting a TCP connection to server. And there are several different flavors.

TCP SYN Flood   TCP SYN flood attacks begin with a client-initiated, seemingly run-of-the-mill, TCP connection that sends a SYN message to a server. The server predictably responds by sending a SYN-ACK message back to the client machine, which then establishes the connection by returning an ACK message. That sounds fine, but it's actually during this process—when the connection is only halfway open—that the victim machine is flooded with a deluge of half-open connections and pretty much becomes paralyzed.

"Ping of Death" Attacks   You probably know that TCP/IP's maximum packet size is 65,536 octets. It's okay if you didn't know that—just understand that this attack is executed by simply pinging with oversized packets, causing a device to keep rebooting incessantly, freeze up, or just totally crash.

Tribe Flood Network (TFN) and Tribe Flood Network 2000 (TFN2K)   These nasty little numbers are more complex in that they initiate synchronized DoS attacks from multiple sources and can target multiple devices. This is achieved, in part, by something known as *IP spoofing*, which I'll be describing soon.

Stacheldraht   This attack is actually a *mélange* of methods, and it translates from the German term for barbed wire. It basically incorporates TFN and adds a dash of encryption. It all begins with a huge invasion at the root level, followed up with a DoS attack finale.

IP Spoofing   This is pretty much what it sounds like it is—a bad guy from within or outside of your network masquerades as a trusted host machine by doing one of two things.

- Presenting with an IP address that's inside your network's scope of trusted addresses
- Using an approved, trusted external IP address

Because the hacker's true identity is veiled behind the spoofed address, this is often just the beginning of your problems.

Keystroke Loggers   This is a software program that is actually kinda cool, depending on which side of the program you are on. The keystroke logger keeps track of all keystrokes a person types on a keyboard. Some loggers actually can email the information to the attacker.

Man-in-the-Middle Attacks   Interception! But it's not a football; it's a bunch of your network's packets—your precious data! A common guilty party could be someone working for your very own ISP using a tool known as a *sniffer* (discussed later) and augmenting it with routing and transport protocols.

Network Reconnaissance   Before breaking into a network, hackers often gather all the information they can about it, because the more they know about the network, the better they can compromise it. They accomplish their objectives through methods such as port scans, DNS queries, and ping sweeps.

Packet Sniffers   This is the tool I mentioned earlier, but I didn't tell you what it is, and it may come as a surprise that it's actually software. Here's how it works:

1. A network adapter card is set to promiscuous mode (meaning it reads every frame that is on the LAN or WLAN even if the frame is destined for another device on the network) so it will send all packets snagged from the network's physical layer through to a special application to be viewed and sorted out.

2. A packet sniffer nicks some highly valuable, sensitive data including, but not limited to, passwords and usernames, making them prized among identity thieves.

Password Attacks   These come in many flavors, and even though they can be achieved via more sophisticated types of attacks like IP spoofing, packet sniffing, and Trojan horses, their sole purpose is to—surprise—discover user passwords so the thief can pretend they're a valid user and then access that user's privileges and resources.

Brute-Force Attack   This is another user or software-oriented attack that employs a program running on a targeted network to try to log in to some type of shared network resource like a server. For the hacker, it's ideal if the accessed accounts have a lot of privileges because then the bad guys can form back doors to use for gaining access later and bypass the need for passwords entirely. Basically, a brute-force attack is guessing the password, but the software today can use the full dictionary very quickly!

Port Redirection Attacks   This approach requires a host machine that the hacker has broken into and uses to get wonky traffic (that normally wouldn't be allowed passage) through a firewall by using various ports (as described in Chapter 2, "Internet Protocols").

Trojan Horse Attacks and Viruses   These two are actually pretty similar—both Trojan horses and viruses infect user machines with malicious code and mess it up with varying degrees of paralysis, destruction, and even death! But they do have their differences— viruses are really just nasty programs attached to command.com, which just happens to be the main interpreter for all Windows systems. Viruses then run amok, deleting files and infecting any flavor files they find on the now-diseased machine. The difference between a virus and a Trojan horse is that Trojans are actually complete applications encased inside code that makes them appear to be a completely different entity—say, a simple, innocent game—not the ugly implements of destruction they truly are!

Trust Exploitation Attacks   These attacks happen when someone exploits a trust relationship inside your network. For example, a company's perimeter network connection usually shelters important things such as SMTP, DNS, and HTTP servers, making the servers really vulnerable because they're all on the same segment.

To be honest, I'm not going to go into detail on how to mitigate each and every one of the security threats I just talked about, not only because that would be outside the scope of this book but also because the methods I am going to teach you will truly protect you from being attacked in general. You will learn enough tricks to make all but the most determined bad guys give up on you and search for easier prey. Basically, think of this as a chapter on how to practice "safe networking."

Mitigating Security Threats

To mitigate security threats, you need to create a comprehensive network security plan. This plan will include how to mitigate numerous kinds of security threats.

- Hardware threats

- Environmental threats

- Electrical threats

- Maintenance threats

- Reconnaissance attacks

- Access attacks

- Password attacks

- Anti-x

Cisco's Adaptive Security Appliance (ASA) helps you provide an overall, in-depth, security design for your network with a variety of tools that can prevent a lot of the security problems I've listed in this chapter. Since a lot of the individual tool names start with *anti*, Cisco uses the term *anti-x* to refer to the whole class of security tools that prevent these problems, including antivirus, antispyware, antispam, and so on.

There are a couple of other security appliances that can be used to help prevent the more sophisticated kinds of attacks. These tools are known as *intrusion detection systems* (IDSs) and *intrusion prevention systems* (IPSs). They help prevent threats by watching for trends, particular patterns, and other factors.

IDS   An intrusion detection system is used to detect several types of malicious behaviors that can compromise the security and trust of a computer system. This includes network attacks against vulnerable services, data-driven attacks on applications, host-based attacks such as privilege escalation, unauthorized logins and access to sensitive files, and malware (viruses, Trojan horses, and worms). It is important to remember that intrusion detection systems do not stop any type of attack but instead log them and can send alerts to management stations.

IPS   An intrusion prevention system is a computer security device that monitors network and/or system activities for malicious or unwanted behavior and can react, in real time, to block or prevent those activities. Network-based IPS, for example, will operate in-line to monitor all network traffic for malicious code or attacks. When an attack is detected, it can drop the offending packets while still allowing all other traffic to pass.

Password and hardware attacks are the most important to know for the CCENT exam, and that is what I'll cover in the next section.

Mitigating Password, Router, and Switch Attacks

This section discusses the basics of mitigating password and basic router and switch security attacks.

Here's how to mitigate password attacks:

- Do not allow users to use the same password on multiple systems.

- Disable accounts after a certain number of unsuccessful login attempts.

- Do not use clear-text passwords; for example, use SSH instead of Telnet, and use the enable secret password instead of the clear-text enable password.

- Use strong passwords, such as !@gL0bAlN8t rather than globalnet.

- Passwords should expire on periodic time intervals, set by the administrator, forcing the users to change passwords.

To mitigate router and switch security attacks, apply the principles I just outlined for mitigating password attacks.

First, mitigate any hardware attacks on your router and switches by physically securing network equipment from potential access by unauthorized individuals. Lock your equipment in a computer room, inside locked racks. Then configure SSH, encrypted passwords, and banners. Here is an example of how this is done (I already covered these commands in Chapter 4, "Cisco's Internetworking Operating System (IOS)" and Chapter 7, "Layer 2 Switching," but a refresher never hurt anyone):

```
Router#config t
Router(config)#hostname R1
R1(config)#enable secret cisco
R1(config)#username Todd password Lammle
R1(config)#ip domain name lammle.com
R1(config)#ip http secure-server
R1(config)#service password-encryption
R1(config)#line con 0
R1(config-line)#password console
R1(config-line)#login
R1(config-line)#line aux 0
R1(config-line)#password aux
R1(config-line)#login
```

```
R1(config-line)#exit
R1(config)#line vty 0 ?
 <1-807>  Last Line number
 <cr>
R1(config)#line vty 0 807
R1(config-line)#password SSHonly
R1(config-line)#login local
R1(config-line)#transport input ssh
R1(config-line)#exit
R1(config)#banner motd # Authorized Access Only! Please enter
your username and password. #
R1(config)#exit
R1#copy run start
Destination filename [startup-config]?[enter]
Building configuration...
[OK]
R1#
```

The preceding commands work on both a router and a switch. It is important to remember how to configure your router to allow Secure Shell instead of the insecure telnet protocol (`transport input ssh`).

> Remember that the `service password-encryption` command will encrypt all current and future passwords in the plain-text configuration file.

Now, let's add port security on a switch to enable even more security.

Switch Port Security

You can stop someone from simply plugging a host into one of your switch ports—or worse, adding a hub, switch, or access point into the Ethernet jack in their office—by using port security, which prevents unauthorized hosts from accessing the LAN.

Here are your options:

```
Switch#config t
Switch(config)#int f0/1
Switch(config-if)#switchport port-security ?
  aging           Port-security aging commands
  mac-address     Secure mac address
  maximum         Max secure addresses
  violation       Security violation mode
  <cr>
```

You can see clearly in the preceding output that the `switchport port-security` command can be used with four options. Personally, I like the `port-security` command because it allows me to easily control users on my network. You can use the `switchport port-security mac-address mac-address` command to assign individual MAC addresses to each switch port.

Before I get into more details about the options, you need to understand some simple basics. First, you configure a switch port with port security after you set the port mode to access. Once you make sure the port (or ports) is an access port, then you can configure the options. However, this does not enable port security; you still have to enable this separately, as shown in the following configurations. Here is how I always start my port security configurations:

```
Switch(config)#int f0/1
Switch(config-if)#switchport mode access
Switch(config-if)#switchport port-security
```

This both sets the mode to access and enables port security. Please remember that setting the port security options on a switch port does not enable port security on the port; you must type that in manually! Now let's go through those options.

If you want to set up a switch port to allow only one host per port and to shut down the port if this rule is violated, use the following commands:

```
Switch#config t
Switch(config)#int f0/1
Switch(config-if)#switchport mode access
Switch(config-if)#swithport port-security
Switch(config-if)#switchport port-security maximum 1
Switch(config-if)#switchport port-security violation shutdown
```

These commands are probably the most popular (and most restrictive) because they prevent users from connecting a switch or access point to your network without authorization. The `maximum` setting of 1 means only one MAC address can be used on that port; if the user tries to add another host on that segment, the switch port will shut down. If that happens, you'd have to manually go into the switch and enable the port with a `no shutdown` command.

MAC Address Security

You can add a static MAC address on a switch port to provide security, but that seems like a lot of administrative work to add every user's MAC address into the switch configuration! Probably one of my favorite commands is the `sticky` command. You can find this command under the `mac-address` command:

```
Switch(config-if)#switchport port-security mac-address sticky
Switch(config-if)#switchport port-security maximum 2
Switch(config-if)#switchport port-security violation shutdown
```

Basically, what this does is provide static MAC address security without having to type in everyone's MAC address on the network.

In the preceding example, the first two MAC addresses into the port "stick" as static addresses and will stay that way for however long you set the aging command for. Why did I set it to 2? Well, I wanted one for the PC/data and one for telephony/phone.

To verify port security on a Catalyst switch, use the command show port-security. Here's an example:

```
Switch#show port-security
Secure Port  MaxSecureAddr  CurrentAddr  SecurityViolation Security Action
             (Count)        (Count)      (Count)
-----------------------------------------------
    Fa0/1        2              1            0         Shutdown
-----------------------------------------------
Total Addresses in System (excluding one mac per port)    : 0
Max Addresses limit in System (excluding one mac per port) : 1024
Switch#
```

You can even get more granular information with the following command:

```
Switch#show port-security interface fastEthernet 0/1
Port Security              : Enabled
Port Status                : Secure-up
Violation Mode             : Shutdown
Aging Time                 : 0 mins
Aging Type                 : Absolute
SecureStatic Address Aging : Disabled
Maximum MAC Addresses      : 2
Total MAC Addresses        : 1
Configured MAC Addresses   : 0
Sticky MAC Addresses       : 1
Last Source Address        : 001a.2f52.3bf8
Security Violation Count   : 0
Switch#
```

Notice that the first line in the output shows that port security is enabled! If you didn't type in switchport port-security but only set the options, then the output of the first line would show Disabled.

Now here is where the coolest part of the sticky command comes into play. When a MAC address "sticks" to the interface, it is actually placed in running-config. This allows you to save the MAC address (with a copy running-config startup-config command) and basically have static MAC address mappings for each port—with a lot less administration!

```
Switch#sh run | begin interface
interface FastEthernet0/1
switchport mode access
switchport port-security
switchport port-security mac-address sticky
switchport port-security mac-address sticky 001a.2f52.3bf8
!
```

Securing Unused Ports

Last, you need to secure unused ports on your switch because they can create a security hole. You don't want anyone connecting a host or another switch into your switches and adding devices to the network, right? Shut down any unused ports to disable the interfaces:

```
Switch(config-if)#shutdown
```

And remember, you can use the range command to configure multiple ports at the same time:

```
Switch(config)#interface range f0/1 - 12
Switch(config-if)#shutdown
```

Virtual Private Networks

I'd be pretty willing to bet you've heard the term *VPN* more than once. Maybe you even know what one is, but just in case, a *virtual private network (VPN)* allows the creation of private networks across untrusted networks, enabling privacy and tunneling of non-TCP/IP protocols. Figure 9.2 shows the typical VPN network in use today.

VPNs are used daily to give remote users and disjointed networks connectivity over a public medium like the Internet instead of using more expensive permanent means. For example, instead of shelling out for a point-to-point connection between two sites (which is pretty secure in itself), you can use a less-expensive Internet connection to each site and then run a VPN tunnel between the sites. These are the benefits of a VPN for a typical small to large business:

- Cost
- Security
- Scalability

FIGURE 9.2   A typical VPN network

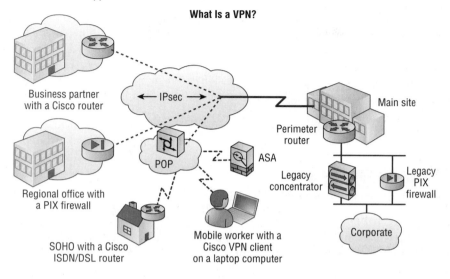

Virtual: Information within a private network is transported over a public network.
Private: The traffic is encrypted to keep the data confidential.

There are three different categories of VPNs, based upon the role they play in a business.

Remote Access VPNs   *Remote access VPNs* allow remote users like telecommuters to securely access the corporate network wherever and whenever they need.

Site-to-Site VPNs   *Site-to-site VPNs*, or intranet VPNs, allow a company to connect its remote sites to the corporate backbone securely over a public medium like the Internet instead of requiring more expensive WAN connections such as MPLS or Frame Relay. You would install a Cisco Adaptive Security Appliance at a branch office to enable and mange an IPsec site-to-site VPN.

Extranet VPNs   *Extranet VPNs* allow an organization's suppliers, partners, and customers to be connected to the corporate network in a limited way for business-to-business (B2B) communications.

A typical branch office would use a Cisco Adaptive Security Appliance to connect VPN tunnels to the corporate network across the public internet.

IPsec

There's more than one way to bring a VPN into being. The first approach uses IPsec to create authentication and encryption services between endpoints on an IP network. The IPsec protocol suite is an open standard protocol framework that is commonly used in VPNs to provide secure end-to-end connections.

The second way is done via tunneling protocols, allowing you to establish a tunnel between endpoints on a network. The tunnel itself is a means for data or protocols to be encapsulated inside another protocol—clean!

However, what I want to discuss in this section of this chapter is the IPsec security services that are provided to a VPN. Here are the most common services and protocols used for these services:

- Confidentiality (encryption)

- Data integrity (verify data wasn't altered)

- Authentication (certify the source)

Confidentiality/Encryption   When confidentiality is required, the Encapsulating Security Payload (ESP) IPsec security protocol should be used. ESP encrypts the payload of the IP packet and is unencrypted at the other end of the tunnel.

Data Integrity   HMAC-SHA-1 and RSA are two data integrity algorithms that are commonly used in VPN solutions. HMAC-SHA-1 provides hashing of the data to verify the data was not altered along the way, and RSA provides encrypted key exchange between two peers so that each host has the key to unencrypt the data when received.

Authentication   The authentication component of VPN technology ensures that data can be read only by its intended recipient by using Pre-Shared Key (PSK) or RSA signatures.

Summary

This chapter provided you with a very basic introduction to security, but it covers all the CCENT objectives.

I started this chapter with an introduction to security on an enterprise network and then discussed the various types of attacks seen on networks today.

I then discussed how to mitigate password and hardware attacks on Cisco routers and switches.

The chapter ended with a brief introduction to virtual private networks and IPsec.

Exam Essentials

Describe a DoS attack.   A denial-of-service attack is a flood of packets that are requesting a TCP connection to a server.

Know what the first part of a comprehensive network security plan is.   The first part of your comprehensive network security plan is to physically secure network equipment from potential access by unauthorized individuals.

List the recommended ways of protecting network devices from outside network security threats.   Use a firewall to restrict access from the outside to the network devices, and use SSH or another encrypted and authenticated transport to access device configurations.

Know the command placed under the VTY lines to enable SSH.   The command to enable SSH on your router and switch under the VTY lines is `transport input ssh`.

Remember the `switchport port-security` commands.   Switch port security is very important on the CCENT exam. You must remember how to enable switch port security, the options you can configure, and why you'd use switch port security.

Written Lab 9

Write the answers to the following questions:

1.   What type of attack is a flood of packets requesting a TCP connection to a server?
2.   What command under the VTY lines will enable SSH on a device?
3.   What are the two recommended ways of protecting network devices from outside network security threats?
4.   What is the first part of your comprehensive network security plan?
5.   What would define a denial-of-service attack?

   (The answers to Written Lab 9 can be found in Appendix A.)

Review Questions

You can find the answers in Appendix B.

 The following questions are designed to test your understanding of this chapter's material. For more information on how to get additional questions, please see this book's introduction.

1. Why would a network administrator configure port security on a switch?
    A. To prevent unauthorized Telnet access to a switch port
    B. To limit the number of layer 2 broadcasts on a particular switch port
    C. To prevent unauthorized hosts from accessing the LAN
    D. To block unauthorized access to the switch management interfaces over common TCP ports

2. You need to allow one host to be permitted to attach dynamically to each switch interface. Which *two* commands must you configure on your catalyst switch to meet this policy?
    A. `Switch(config-if)#ip access-group 10`
    B. `Switch(config-if)#switchport port-security maximum 1`
    C. `Switch(config)#access-list 10 permit ip host 1`
    D. `Switch(config-if)#switchport port-security violation shutdown`
    E. `Switch(config)#mac-address-table secure`

3. What should be part of a comprehensive network security plan?
    A. Allow users to develop their own approach to network security.
    B. Physically secure network equipment from potential access by unauthorized individuals.
    C. Encourage users to use personal information in their passwords to minimize the likelihood of passwords being forgotten.
    D. Delay deployment of software patches and updates until their effect on end-user equipment is well known and widely reported.
    E. Minimize network overhead by deactivating automatic antivirus client updates.

4. What are *two* security appliances that can installed in a network?
    A. ATM
    B. IDS
    C. IOS
    D. IPS

5. What are *two* recommended ways of protecting network device configuration files from outside network security threats?

A. Allow unrestricted access to the console or VTY ports.

B. Use a firewall to restrict access from the outside to the network devices.

C. Use SSH or another encrypted and authenticated transport protocol to access device configurations.

D. Always use Telnet to access the device command line because it is automatically encrypted.

6. What is the effect of using the `service password-encryption` command?

A. Only the enable password will be encrypted.

B. Only the enable secret password will be encrypted.

C. Only passwords configured after the command has been entered will be encrypted.

D. It will encrypt the secret password and remove the enable secret password from the configuration.

E. It will encrypt all current and future passwords.

7. Which type of attack is characterized by a flood of packets requesting a TCP connection to a server?

A. Denial of service

B. Brute force

C. Reconnaissance

D. Trojan horse

8. What is the effect of this configuration?

```
line vty 0 4
password todd
login
transport input ssh
```

A. It configures SSH globally for all logins.

B. It tells the router or switch to try to establish an SSH connection first and if that fails to use Telnet.

C. It configures a Cisco network device to use the SSH protocol on incoming communications via the VTY lines.

D. It configures the device to use only Telnet on the VTY lines.

9. What is the result of the following switch port commands?

```
Switch(config-if)# switchport port-security maximum 1
Switch(config-if)# switchport port-security mac-address 0001.1234.ABCD.12ED
```

   A. It ensures that only the device with the MAC address 0001.1234.ABCD.12ED will be able to connect to the port that is being configured.

   B. It informs the switch that traffic destined for MAC address 0001.1234.ABCD.12ED should be sent only to the port that is being configured.

   C. It will act like an access list, and the port will filter packets that have a source or destination MAC of 0001.1234.ABCD.12ED.

   D. The switch will shut down the port of any traffic with source MAC address of 0018.DE8B.4BF8.

10. What are *two* characteristics of Telnet?

   A. It sends data in clear text.

   B. It is no longer supported on Cisco network devices.

   C. Is it more secure than SSH.

   D. It requires that the destination device be configured to support Telnet connections.

11. Which *two* of the following are considered to be denial-of-service (DoS) attacks?

   A. TCP SYN flood

   B. Application layer attacks

   C. Ping-of-death attacks

   D. Autorooters

12. A company has placed a networked PC in a lobby so guests can have access to the internet. A security concern is that someone will disconnect the Ethernet cable from the PC and reconnect it to their laptop computer and have access to the corporate network. For the port servicing the lobby, which *three* configuration steps should be performed on the switch to prevent this?

   A. Enable port security.

   B. Create the port as a trunk port.

   C. Create the port as an access port.

   D. Create the port as a protected port.

   E. Set the port security aging time to 0.

   F. Statically assign the MAC address to the address table.

   G. Configure the switch to discover new MAC addresses after a set time of inactivity.

13. What is the purpose of an IDS?

   A. To perform stateful firewall functions

   B. To block suspicious network activity from entering the network

   C. To detect malicious traffic and send alerts to a management station

   D. To hide the private IP addressing structure from outside attackers

14. An administrator has connected devices to a switch and, for security reasons, wants the dynamically learned MAC addresses from the address table added to the running configuration. What must be done to accomplish this?

    A. Enable port security, and use the keyword `sticky`.

    B. Set the switchport mode to trunk, and save the running configuration.

    C. Use the `switchport protected` command to have the MAC addresses added to the configuration.

    D. Use the `no switchport port-security` command to allow MAC addresses to be added to the configuration.

15. Which of the following makes a service unavailable by overwhelming the system that normally provides it?

    A. Application layer attacks

    B. Autorooters

    C. Back doors

    D. Denial-of-service attacks

16. Which *two* of the following are two data integrity algorithms commonly used in VPN solutions?

    A. AES

    B. ESP

    C. HMAC-SHA-1

    D. RSA

17. When confidentiality is required, which IPsec security protocol should be used?

    A. ESP

    B. RSA

    C. AES

    D. HMAC-SHA-1

18. Which of the following would you install at a branch office to enable and manage an IPsec site-to-site VPN?

    A. Cisco switch

    B. Cisco Adaptive Security Appliance (ASA)

    C. Cisco 2500 series router

    D. ESP

19. Which component of VPN technology will ensure that data is unaltered between the sender and the recipient?

    A. Authentication

    B. Peer-to-peer RSA

    C. Data integrity

    D. Encryption

20. Which component of VPN technology ensures that data can be read only by its intended recipient?

    A. Authentication

    B. Peer-to-peer RSA

    C. Data integrity

    D. Encryption

Chapter 10

Introduction to Wide Area Networks

THE CCENT EXAM TOPICS COVERED IN THIS CHAPTER INCLUDE THE FOLLOWING:

✓ **Implement and verify WAN links**

- Describe different methods for connecting to a WAN
- Configure and verify a basic WAN serial connection

The Cisco IOS supports many different WAN protocols that can help you extend your LANs to other LANs at remote sites. Connecting company sites together so that information can be exchanged is imperative in today's economy. But it wouldn't exactly be cost-effective to put in your own cable or connections to connect all of your company's remote locations yourself. A better way to go about it is to use service providers that will lease or share connections they already have installed and save you huge amounts of money and time.

I'm not going to cover every type of Cisco WAN support in this chapter—again, this book's purpose is mainly to give you everything you need to pass the exam. For that reason, I'm going to focus on HDLC and PPP, although I'll touch on other technologies, like Frame Relay. But first, I will look at WAN basics, including cabling a WAN.

For more detail on WAN technologies, above and beyond the Cisco ICND1 (CCENT) objectives, please see my *CCNA: Cisco Certified Network Associate Study Guide, Seventh Edition (Sybex, 2011)*.

For up-to-the minute updates for this chapter, please see www.lammle.com/ forum and/or www.sybex.com/go/ccent2e.

Introduction to Wide Area Networks

What is it that makes something a *wide area network (WAN)* instead of a local area network (LAN)? Distance is the first thing that comes to mind, but these days, wireless LANs can cover some serious turf! So, is it bandwidth? Here again, in many places really big pipes can be had for a price, so that's not it either. Well, what then? Perhaps one of the best ways to tell a WAN from a LAN is that you generally own a LAN infrastructure, but you lease a WAN infrastructure from a service provider.

I've already talked about a data link that you usually own (Ethernet), but now I'm going to talk about the data links you most often don't own but instead lease from a service provider.

The key to understanding WAN technologies is to be familiar with the different WAN terms and connection types often used by service providers to connect your networks.

> Many new WANs are available today, but again, this chapter is focusing on the Cisco ICND1 exam (CCENT) objectives only.

Defining WAN Terms

Before ordering a WAN service type, it is a good idea to understand the following terms, which are commonly used by service providers and shown in Figure 10.1.

FIGURE 10.1   WAN terms

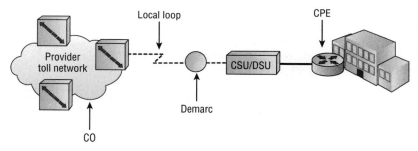

Customer Premises Equipment (CPE)   *Customer premises equipment (CPE)* is equipment that's owned by the subscriber and located on the subscriber's premises.

Demarcation Point   The *demarcation location* is the spot where the service provider's responsibility ends and the CPE begins. It's generally a RJ45 plug in a telecommunications closet owned and installed by the telecommunications company (telco). The customer is responsible for the cable (extended demarc) from this box to the CPE, which is usually a connection to a CSU/DSU. The CSU/DSU in the diagram (Figure 10.1) plugs into the demarcation location (demarc) and is the service provider's last point of responsibility for the circuit.

Local Loop   The *local loop* connects the demarc to the closest switching office, called a central office.

Central Office (CO)   This point connects the customers to the provider's switching net-work. A *central office (CO)* is sometimes referred to as a *point of presence (POP)*.

Toll Network   The *toll network* is a trunk line inside a WAN provider's network. This network is a collection of switches and facilities owned by the ISP.

It is important to familiarize yourself with these terms, because they are crucial to understanding WAN technologies.

WAN Connection Types

A WAN can use a number of different connection types, and this section will provide you with an introduction to the various types of WAN connections you'll find on the market today. Figure 10.2 shows the different WAN connection types that can be used to connect your LANs (DTE) over a DCE network.

FIGURE 10.2   WAN connection types

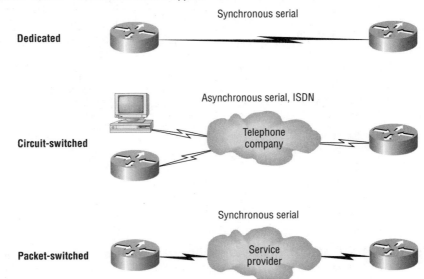

The following list explains the WAN connection types:

Leased Lines   Typically, these are referred to as a *point-to-point connection* or dedicated connection. A *leased line* is a preestablished WAN communications path from the CPE through the DCE switch to the CPE of the remote site, allowing DTE networks to communicate at any time with no setup procedures before transmitting data. When cost is no object, it's really the best choice. It uses synchronous serial lines up to 45Mbps. HDLC and PPP encapsulations are frequently used on leased lines, and I'll go over them with you in detail in a bit.

Circuit Switching   When you hear the term *circuit switching*, think phone call. The big advantage is cost—you pay only for the time you actually use it. No data can transfer before an end-to-end connection is established. Circuit switching uses dial-up modems or ISDN and is used for low-bandwidth data transfers.

Packet Switching   This is a WAN switching method that allows you to share bandwidth with other companies to save money. *Packet switching* can be thought of as a network that's designed to look like a leased line yet the cost is more like the cost of circuit switching. There is a downside: if you need to transfer data constantly, forget about this option. Just get yourself a leased line. Packet switching will work well only if your data transfers are bursty in nature. Frame Relay is a packet-switching technology. Speeds can range from 56Kbps to T3 (45Mbps).

WAN Support

Cisco supports pretty much every WAN service available, and you can see this with the encapsulation ? command from any serial interface (your output may vary depending on the IOS version you are running).

```
Router#config t
Enter configuration commands, one per line.  End with CNTL/Z.
Router(config)#int s0/0
Router(config-if)#encapsulation ?
  atm-dxi         ATM-DXI encapsulation
  bstun           Block Serial tunneling (BSTUN)
  frame-relay     Frame Relay networks
  hdlc            Serial HDLC synchronous
  lapb            LAPB (X.25 Level 2)
  ppp             Point-to-Point protocol
  sdlc            SDLC
  sdlc-primary    SDLC (primary)
  sdlc-secondary  SDLC (secondary)
  smds            Switched Megabit Data Service (SMDS)
  stun            Serial tunneling (STUN)
  x25             X.25
```

You cannot configure Ethernet or any type of LAN technologies as an encapsulation on a serial interface.

In this section, I will define the most prominent WAN protocols used today: Frame Relay, DSL, HDLC, PPP, and ATM. Usually, though, the only layer 2 WAN protocols configured on a serial interface these days (or for the exam) are HDLC, PPP, and Frame Relay.

Frame Relay   A packet-switched technology that emerged in the early 1990s, *Frame Relay* is a Data Link and Physical layer specification that provides high performance. Frame Relay is a successor to X.25, except that much of the technology in X.25 used to compensate for physical errors (noisy lines) has been eliminated. Frame Relay can be more cost-effective than point-to-point links and can typically run at speeds of 64Kbps up to 45Mbps (T3). Frame Relay provides features for dynamic bandwidth allocation and congestion control, replacing leased lines with permanent virtual circuits (PVCs) through a packet-switching network.

Frame Relay can be used when a router that connects to a LAN has only one WAN Interface but multiple virtual circuits are needed.

DSL   *Digital subscriber line (DSL)* is a technology used by traditional telephone companies to deliver advanced services (high-speed data and backward compatibility to analog video) over twisted-pair copper telephone wires. It typically has lower data-carrying capacity than Hybrid Fiber and Coax (HFC) networks, and data speeds can be limited in range by line lengths and quality (fiber backbone from the provider and cable to the home or business). Digital subscriber line is not a complete end-to-end solution but rather a Physical layer transmission technology such as dial-up, cable, or wireless. DSL connections are deployed in the last mile of a local telephone network—the local loop. The connection is set up between a pair of DSL modems on either end of a copper wire that is between the customer premises equipment (CPE) and the digital subscriber line access multiplexer (DSLAM). A DSLAM is the device located at the provider's central office (CO) and concentrates connections from multiple DSL subscribers.

HDLC   *High-Level Data-Link Control (HDLC)* was derived from Synchronous Data Link Control (SDLC), which was created by IBM as a Data Link connection protocol. HDLC is a protocol at the Data Link layer, and it has very little overhead, so it is the recommended WAN encapsulation (and the default) if you have two Cisco routers on point-to-point links. HDLC wasn't intended to encapsulate multiple Network layer protocols across the same link. The HDLC header carries no identification of the type of protocol being carried inside the HDLC encapsulation. Because of this, each vendor that uses HDLC has its own way of identifying the Network layer protocol, which means that each vendor's HDLC is proprietary for its equipment.

PPP   *Point-to-Point Protocol (PPP)* is an industry-standard protocol. Because all multiprotocol versions of HDLC are proprietary, PPP can be used to create point-to-point links between different vendors' equipment. It uses a Network Control Protocol (NCP) field in the Data Link header to identify the Network layer protocol. It allows authentication and multilink connections and can be run over asynchronous and synchronous links.

ATM   *Asynchronous Transfer Mode (ATM)* was created for time-sensitive traffic, providing simultaneous transmission of voice, video, and data. ATM uses cells instead of packets that are a fixed 53 bytes long. It also can use isochronous clocking (external clocking) to help the data move faster.

PPP and ATM can be configured on an asynchronous serial connection. HDLC and Frame Relay cannot.

Cabling the Wide Area Network

You need to know a couple of things in order to connect your WAN. For starters, you have to understand the WAN Physical layer implementation provided by Cisco, and you must be familiar with the various types of WAN serial connectors.

Cisco serial connections support almost any type of WAN service. Typical WAN connections are dedicated leased lines using HDLC, PPP, and Frame Relay. Typical speeds run at anywhere from 56Kbps to 45Mbps (T3), but many new services can get much higher speeds today.

In the following sections, I'll discuss the various types of connections and then move into the nitty-gritty of the WAN protocols specified in the ICND1 (CCENT) objectives.

Serial Transmission

WAN serial connectors use *serial transmission*, which takes place 1 bit at a time over a single channel.

Parallel transmission can pass at least 8 bits at a time, but all WANs use serial transmission.

Cisco routers use a proprietary 60-pin serial connector that you must get from Cisco or a provider of Cisco equipment. Cisco also has a new, smaller proprietary serial connection that is about 1/10th the size of the 60-pin basic serial cable. This is called the *smart-serial*, for some reason, and you have to make sure you have the right type of interface in your router before using this cable connector. The type of connector you have on the other end of the cable depends on your service provider or end-device requirements. The different ends available are as follows:

- EIA/TIA-232
- EIA/TIA-449
- V.35 (used to connect to a CSU/DSU)
- X.21 (used in X.25)
- EIA-530

Serial links are described in frequency or cycles per second (hertz). The amount of data that can be carried within these frequencies is called *bandwidth*. Bandwidth is the amount of data in bits per second that the serial channel can carry.

Figure 10.3 shows a typical router setup that has both an Ethernet and a serial interface. The serial interface can be used for a T1 connection, for example.

FIGURE 10.3   A router connecting a LAN to a router with a WAN serial interface connected to the Internet

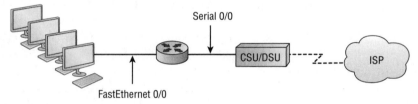

To connect a T1 to your serial interface, you must use a CSU/DSU as shown in Figure 10.3, which I'll discuss next.

Data Terminal Equipment and Data Communication Equipment

Router interfaces are, by default, *data terminal equipment (DTE)*, and they connect into *data communication equipment (DCE)*—for example, a *channel service unit/data service unit (CSU/DSU)*. The CSU/DSU then plugs into a demarcation location (demarc) and is the service provider's last responsibility. Most of the time, the demarc is a jack that has an RJ-45 (8-pin modular) female connector located in a telecommunications closet.

You may have heard of demarcs if you've ever had the glorious experience of reporting a problem to your service provider—they'll always tell you that it tests fine up to the demarc and that the problem must be the CPE, or customer premises equipment. In other words, it's your problem, not theirs.

Figure 10.4 shows a typical DTE-DCE-DTE connection and the devices used in the network.

FIGURE 10.4   DTE-DCE-DTE WAN connection

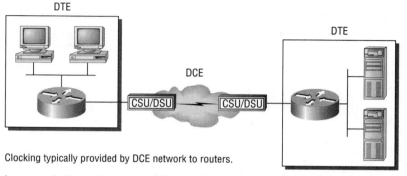

Clocking typically provided by DCE network to routers.

In non-production environments, a DCE network is not always present.

The idea behind a WAN is to be able to connect two DTE networks through a DCE network. The DCE network includes the area from the CSU/DSU, through the provider's wiring and switches, all the way to the CSU/DSU at the other end. The network's DCE device (CSU/DSU) provides clocking to the DTE-connected interface (the router's serial interface).

As mentioned, the DCE network provides clocking to the router; this is the CSU/DSU. If you have a nonproduction network and are using a WAN crossover type of cable and do not have a CSU/DSU, then you need to provide clocking on the DCE end of the cable by using the clock rate command, as I discussed in Chapter 4, "Cisco's Internetworking Operating System (IOS)."

Please remember for the CCENT objectives: routers are typically DTE devices connecting to a DCE device from a serial interface. The DCE (typically a CSU/DSU) provides clocking of the line to the router (DTE interface). If your router serial interface connecting to the WAN is acting as a DCE interface, you'll need to use the clock rate command under the serial interface configuration. This was covered in depth in Chapter 4.

High-Level Data-Link Control (HDLC) Protocol

The High-Level Data-Link Control (HDLC) protocol is a popular ISO-standard, bit-oriented Data Link layer protocol. It specifies an encapsulation method for data on synchronous serial data links using frame characters and checksums. HDLC is a point-to-point protocol used on leased lines. No authentication can be used with HDLC.

In byte-oriented protocols, control information is encoded using entire bytes. On the other hand, bit-oriented protocols may use single bits to represent control information. Bit-oriented protocols include SDLC, LLC, HDLC, TCP, IP, and others.

HDLC is the default encapsulation used by Cisco routers over synchronous serial links. Cisco's HDLC is proprietary; it won't communicate with any other vendor's HDLC implementation. But don't give Cisco grief for it—*everyone's* HDLC implementation is proprietary. Figure 10.5 shows the Cisco HDLC format.

FIGURE 10.5   Cisco HDLC frame format

Cisco HDLC

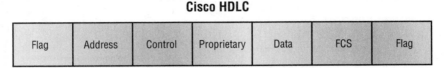

• Each vendor's HDLC has a proprietary data field to support multiprotocol environments.

HDLC

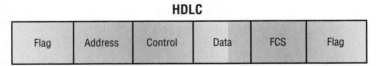

• Supports only single-protocol environments.

As shown in Figure 10.5, the reason that every vendor has a proprietary HDLC encapsulation method is that each vendor has a different way for the HDLC protocol to encapsulate multiple Network layer protocols. If the vendors didn't have a way for HDLC to communicate the different layer 3 protocols, then HDLC would be able to carry only one protocol. This proprietary header is placed in the front of the data field of the HDLC encapsulation.

Let's say you have only one Cisco router and you need to connect to a different vendor's router because your other Cisco router is on order. What would you do? You couldn't use the default HDLC serial encapsulation because it wouldn't work. Instead, you would use something like PPP, an ISO-standard way of identifying the upper-layer protocols. In addition, you can check RFC 1661 for more information on the origins and standards of PPP.

Before we move on to PPP, let's take a look at how simple HDLC is to implement and verify. First, I'll start by showing the configuration.

```
Router#sh run
Building configuration...
[output cut]
!
```

```
interface Serial0/0
 ip address 192.168.1.1 255.255.255.0
 no fair-queue
!
```

Notice the absence of any mention of HDLC under the active configuration file? That's right! If you're using the default HDLC encapsulation on your serial interfaces, the configuration does not display HDLC! So, let's try another command.

```
Router#sh int s0/0
Serial0/0 is up, line protocol is up
  Hardware is PowerQUICC Serial
  Internet address is 192.168.1.1/24
  MTU 1500 bytes, BW 1544 Kbit, DLY 20000 usec,
     reliability 255/255, txload 1/255, rxload 1/255
  Encapsulation HDLC, loopback not set  Keepalive set (10 sec)
```

Nicely, you can use the show interface command to verify the HDLC encapsulation on your serial interfaces at any time. It is important that you can look at the previous output and understand what you are seeing.

So, you need features such as multilink and authentication on your serial interfaces. Well, HDLC is not what you can use, because HDLC is basically featureless. So, let's take a look at the nonproprietary HDLC encapsulation that will provide you with features: PPP.

Point-to-Point Protocol

Point-to-Point Protocol (PPP) is a Data Link layer protocol that can be used over either asynchronous serial (dial-up) or synchronous serial media. It uses the Link Control Protocol (LCP) to build and maintain data link connections. Network Control Protocol (NCP) is used to allow multiple Network layer protocols (routed protocols) to be used on a point-to-point connection.

Since HDLC is the default serial encapsulation on Cisco serial links and it works great, when would you choose to use PPP? The basic purpose of PPP is to transport layer 3 packets across a Data Link layer point-to-point link. It is nonproprietary, which means that if you don't have all Cisco routers, PPP would be needed on your serial interfaces—the HDLC encapsulation would not work on non-Cisco routers because it is Cisco proprietary. In addition, since PPP can encapsulate several layer 3 routed protocols and provide authentication, dynamic addressing, and multilink, this may be the encapsulation solution of choice for you over HDLC.

Figure 10.6 shows the PPP protocol stack compared to the OSI reference model.

FIGURE 10.6   Point-to-point protocol stack

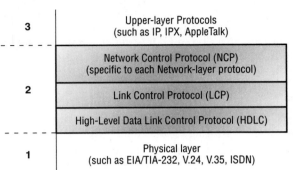

PPP contains four main components.

EIA/TIA-232-C, V.24, V.35, and ISDN   The international Physical layer standards for serial communication.

HDLC   A method for encapsulating datagrams over serial links.

LCP   A method of establishing, configuring, maintaining, and terminating the point-to-point connection. This protocol provides all the great services that you find with PPP that HDLC does not provide by itself.

NCP   A method of establishing and configuring different Network layer protocols. NCP is designed to allow the simultaneous use of multiple Network layer protocols. Some examples of protocols here are Internet Protocol Control Protocol (IPCP) and Internet Protocol version 6 Control Protocol (IPv6CP).

It is important to understand that the PPP protocol stack is specified at the Physical and Data Link layers only. NCP is used to allow communication of multiple Network layer protocols by encapsulating the protocols across a PPP data link.

Remember that if you have a Cisco router and a non-Cisco router connected with a serial connection, you must configure PPP or another encapsulation method, such as Frame Relay, because the HDLC default won't work!

In the following sections, I'll discuss the options for LCP and PPP session establishment, but first you need to understand how PPP session establishment takes place when a data link comes up.

PPP Session Establishment

When PPP connections are started, the links go through three phases of session establishment, as shown in Figure 10.7.

FIGURE 10.7   PPP session establishment

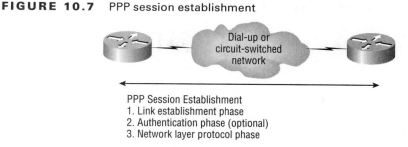

PPP Session Establishment
1. Link establishment phase
2. Authentication phase (optional)
3. Network layer protocol phase

Link Establishment Phase   LCP packets are sent by each PPP device to configure and test the link. These packets contain a field called Configuration Option that allows each device to see the size of the data, the compression, and the authentication. If no Configuration Option field is present, then the default configurations are used.

Authentication Phase   If required, either CHAP or PAP can be used to authenticate a link. Authentication takes place before Network layer protocol information is read. It is possible that link-quality determination may occur at this same time.

Network Layer Protocol Phase   PPP uses the *Network Control Protocol (NCP)* to allow multiple Network layer protocols to be encapsulated and sent over a PPP data link. Each Network layer protocol (for example, IP and IPv6, which are routed protocols) establishes a service with NCP.

PPP Authentication Methods

There are two methods of authentication that can be used with PPP links.

Password Authentication Protocol (PAP)   The *Password Authentication Protocol (PAP)* is the less secure of the two methods. Passwords are sent in clear text, and PAP authentication is performed only upon the initial link establishment. When the PPP link is first established, the remote node sends back to the originating router the username and password until authentication is acknowledged. That's it.

Challenge Handshake Authentication Protocol (CHAP)   The *Challenge Handshake Authentication Protocol (CHAP)* is used at the initial start-up of a link and at periodic checkups on the link to make sure the router is still communicating with the same host. After PPP finishes its initial link-establishment phase, the local router sends a challenge request to the remote device. The remote device sends a value calculated using a one-way hash function called MD5. The local router checks this hash value to make sure it matches. If the values don't match, the link is immediately terminated.

Configuring PPP on Cisco Routers

Configuring PPP encapsulation on an interface is a fairly straightforward process. To configure it, follow these router commands:

```
Router#config t
Enter configuration commands, one per line. End with CNTL/Z.
Router(config)#int s0
Router(config-if)#encapsulation ppp
Router(config-if)#^Z
Router#
```

Of course, PPP encapsulation must be enabled on both interfaces connected to a serial line to work, and several additional configuration options are available by using the help command.

Configuring PPP Authentication

After you configure your serial interface to support PPP encapsulation, you can configure authentication using PPP between routers. First set the hostname of the router if it's not already set. Then set the username and password for the remote router connecting to your router.

Here is an example:

```
Router#config t
Router(config)#hostname RouterA
RouterA(config)#username RouterB password cisco
```

When using the hostname command, remember that the username is the hostname of the remote router connecting to your router. And it's case sensitive. Also, the password on both routers must be the same. It's a plain-text password that you can see with a show run command. And you can encrypt the password by using the command service password-encryption. You must have a username and password configured for each remote system you plan to connect to. The remote routers must also be configured with usernames and passwords.

After you set the hostname, usernames, and passwords, choose the authentication type, either CHAP or PAP.

```
RouterA#config t
RouterA(config)#int s0
RouterA(config-if)#ppp authentication chap pap
RouterA(config-if)#^Z
RouterA#
```

If both methods are configured on the same line as is shown here, then only the first method will be used during link negotiation. The second is a backup in case the first method fails; however, it is extremely unlikely you will ever use PAP in today's networks.

 See Hands-on Lab 10.1 for an example of PPP authentication.

Verifying PPP Encapsulation

Now that PPP encapsulation is enabled, let's see how to verify that it's up and running. First you can verify that PPP encapsulation is set by looking at the active configuration file.

```
RouterA#sh run
Building configuration...
[output cut]
!
username RouterB password cisco
!
[output cut]
!
interface Serial0/0
 ip address 192.168.1.1 255.255.255.0
 encapsulation PPP
 PPP authentication chap pap
 no fair-queue


!
```

Since you're no longer using the default HDLC encapsulation, the active configuration file will show the configured encapsulation of the serial interface, in this example, PPP. Remember, you need the local database of the remote routers that your local router will have a layer 2 (data link) connection with. If the remote router's hostname is not in the local database, then your local router will not have a data link session with the remote router when using authentication. In addition, the passwords must match on both the local router and remote routers' local database.

You can verify the configuration with the show interface command.

```
RouterA#sh int s0/0
Serial0/0 is up, line protocol is up
  Hardware is PowerQUICC Serial
  Internet address is 192.168.1.1./24
```

```
   MTU 1500 bytes, BW 1544 Kbit, DLY 20000 usec,
      reliability 239/255, txload 1/255, rxload 1/255
   Encapsulation PPP, loopback not set Keepalive set (10 sec)
 LCP Open
  Open: IPCP, CDPCP
 [output cut]
```

Notice that the sixth line lists encapsulation as PPP, and the next line shows that LCP is open, which means that it has negotiated the session establishment and is good! The eighth line tells you NCP is listening for the protocols IP and CDP. If you had an authentication failure, then LCP would display listening and then eventually give up and say closed.

It is important to understand that you cannot configure just one side of a point-to-point link with PPP. For example, take a look at the following output:

```
Pod1R1#sh int s0/0
Serial0/0 is up, line protocol is down
```

There are of course numerous reason that the previous output could occur, but one thing you can decipher is that the local physical layer is not at fault because `Serial 1/0 is up` defines the physical layer, meaning that the local interface is receiving clocking from the CSU/DSU. The problem must be either the ISP or the remote end. For the CCENT exam, it is advised to keep "encapsulation mismatch" in mind as a possible reason for an up/down status on your WAN data link.

> You cannot have PPP on one side of a serial link and HDLC on the other!

Summary

This chapter covered the difference between the WAN services Frame Relay, DSL, HDLC, and PPP. Although I talked in depth only about HDLC and PPP, the most prevalent WAN technologies for the Cisco ICND1 exam (CCENT) objectives, don't skip the small but all-so-important section on Frame Relay!

You must understand High-Level Data-Link Control (HDLC) and how to verify with the `show interface` command that HDLC is enabled. This chapter provided this important HDLC information to you as well as how the Point-to-Point Protocol (PPP) should be used if you need more features than HDLC or you are using two different brands of routers. This is because HDLC is proprietary and won't work between two different vendor routers.

In the discussion of PPP, I showed you the various LCP options as well as the two types of authentication that can be used, PAP and CHAP, and how to verify the authentication process with the `debug ppp authentication` command.

It is important that you remember that Frame Relay is also a layer 2 serial WAN encapsulation, that Frame Relay can provide permanent virtual circuits (PVCs) through a packet-switching network, and that you need only one serial interface on you router to connect to multiple remote locations.

Just a few more practice questions, and you're done with this book! Hang in there!

Exam Essentials

Remember the default serial encapsulation on Cisco routers.   Cisco routers use a proprietary High-Level Data-Link Control (HDLC) encapsulation on all of their serial links by default. You cannot see that a serial interface is configured with HDLC with a `show running-config` command because if a serial interface is set to the default, it doesn't display the encapsulation method of HDLC. To verify HDLC is enabled, use the `show interface` command.

Remember the PPP Data Link layer protocols.   The three Data Link layer protocols are Network Control Protocol (NCP), which defines the Network layer protocols; Link Control Protocol (LCP), a method of establishing, configuring, maintaining, and terminating the point-to-point connection; and High-Level Data-Link Control (HDLC), the MAC layer protocol that encapsulates the packets.

Remember the WAN Data Link encapsulations.   The most common Data Link serial encapsulations—HDLC, PPP, and Frame Relay—are all layer 2 encapsulation methods for WANs.

Remember that Frame Relay is layer 2 and how it works.   Frame Relay, as well as HDLC and PPP, is a layer 2 encapsulation WAN method, but Frame Relay works by sending packets through a shared packet-switching network. It does this by using permanent virtual circuits (PVCs). One serial interface can be configured on your router to connect to multiple remote sites.

Remember the three phases used to set up a PPP session between routers.   The three phases, in order, are as follows:

- Link establishment
- Optional authentication
- Network layer protocol phase

Written Lab 10

Write the answers to the following questions:

1. Write the command to see the encapsulation method on serial 0 of a Cisco router.

2. Write the commands to configure s0 for PPP encapsulation.

3. Write the commands to configure a username of *todd* and password of *cisco* on a Cisco router.

4. What does PPP mean?

5. What are common Data Link WAN encapsulations?

6. Which type of port on a router is used for a T1?

7. If you had one serial interface on your router and needed to connect many remote locations, which Data Link encapsulation should you use?

8. What is the default serial encapsulation on a Cisco router?

9. What are the PPP Data Link protocols?

10. What is a good command to verify your serial interface on a router?

   (The answers to Written Lab 10 can be found in Appendix A.)

Hands-on Labs

In this section, you will configure Cisco routers in two different WAN labs. (These labs are included for use with real Cisco routers.)

   Lab 10.1: Configuring PPP Encapsulation and Authentication

   Lab 10.2: Configuring and Monitoring HDLC

Hands-on Lab 10.1: Configuring PPP Encapsulation and Authentication

By default, Cisco routers use High-Level Data-Link Control (HDLC) as a point-to-point encapsulation method on serial links. If you are connecting to non-Cisco equipment, then you can use the PPP encapsulation method to communicate.

The lab you will configure is shown in the following diagram:

RouterA   RouterB

1. Type **sh int s0** on RouterA and RouterB to see the encapsulation method.
2. Make sure each router has the hostname assigned.

   RouterA#**config t**
   RouterA(config)#**hostname RouterA**

   RouterB#**config t**
   RouterB(config)#**hostname RouterB**

3. To change the default HDLC encapsulation method to PPP on both routers, use the encapsulation command at interface configuration. Both ends of the link must run the same encapsulation method.

   RouterA#**Config t**
   RouterA(config)#**int s0**
   RouterA(config-if)#**encap ppp**

4. Now go to RouterB and set serial 0 to PPP encapsulation.

   RouterB#**config t**
   RouterB(config)#**int s0**
   RouterB(config-if)#**encap ppp**

5. Verify the configuration by typing **sh int s0** on both routers.
6. Notice the IPCP, IPXCP, and CDPCP. This is the information used to transmit the upper-layer (Network layer) information across the HDLC at the MAC sublayer.
7. Define a username and password on each router. Notice that the username is the name of the remote router. Also, the password must be the same.

   RouterA#**config t**
   RouterA(config)#**username RouterB password todd**

   RouterB#**config t**
   RouterB(config)#**username RouterA password todd**

8. Enable CHAP or PAP authentication on each interface.

   ```
   RouterA(config)#int s0
   RouterA(config-if)#ppp authentication chap
   ```

   ```
   RouterB(config)#int s0
   RouterB(config-if)#ppp authentication chap
   ```

9. Verify the PPP configuration on each router by using these two commands:

   ```
   sh int s0
   debug ppp authentication
   ```

Hands-on Lab 10.2: Configuring and Monitoring HDLC

There really is no configuration for HDLC, but if you completed Lab 10.1, then the PPP encapsulation would be set on both routers. This is why I put the PPP lab first. This lab allows you to actually configure HDLC encapsulation on a router.

    This lab will use the same configuration that Lab 10.1 used.

1. Set the encapsulation for each serial interface by using the encapsulation hdlc command.

   ```
   RouterA#config t
   RouterA(config)#int s0
   RouterA(config-if)#encapsulation hdlc
   ```

   ```
   RouterB#config t
   RouterB(config)#int s0
   RouterB(config-if)#encapsulation hdlc
   ```

2. Verify the HDLC encapsulation by using the show interface s0 command on each router.

Review Questions

You can find the answers in Appendix B.

 The following questions are designed to test your understanding of this chapter's material. For more information on how to get additional questions, please see this book's introduction.

1. What are the *two* PPP authentication methods?

   A. SLARP

   B. ARP

   C. CHAP

   D. PAP

   E. SLIP

2. Which Data Link encapsulation can be used if you have one free serial interface and many remote offices to connect?

   A. HDLC

   B. PPP

   C. Frame Relay

   D. Ethernet

3. Which of the following are considered common Data Link WAN encapsulation types? (Choose three.)

   A. PPP

   B. HDLC

   C. Frame Relay

   D. ISDN

4. Which are considered WAN connection types? (Choose three.)

   A. DLCI

   B. Packet switching

   C. Circuit switching

   D. Inverse ARP

   E. Leased lines

5. How do you configure a serial interface to use PPP encapsulation?

   A. `ppp encapsulation`

   B. `encapsulation ppp`

   C. `no hdlc encapsulation, ppp encapsulation`

   D. `encapsulation frame-relay`

6. Which encapsulations can be configured on a serial interface? (Choose three.)

   A. Ethernet

   B. Token Ring

   C. HDLC

   D. Frame Relay

   E. PPP

7. What is the default serial encapsulation used on Cisco routers?

   A. HDLC

   B. PPP

   C. SLIP

   D. Frame Relay

8. When a router is connected to a Frame Relay WAN link using a serial DTE interface, how is the clock rate determined?

   A. Supplied by the CSU/DSU

   B. Supplied by the far end router

   C. Supplied by the `clock rate` command

   D. Supplied by the physical layer bit stream timing

9. You are configuring a Cisco router and connect it with a serial interface to another vendor's router's serial port. Both routers are configured with HDLC. Which *two* statements are true regarding this configuration?

   A. The Cisco HDLC frame uses a proprietary Type field that may not be compatible with equipment of other vendors.

   B. HDLC requires a clock rate to be configured on the routers at both ends of the serial link.

   C. PPP encapsulation is recommended for serial links between equipment from multiple vendors.

   D. Usernames must be configured at both ends of the HDLC serial link.

   E. This data link will not establish a connection because HDLC is proprietary for each vendor.

10. When PPP connections are started, the links go through three phases of session establishment. What are the phases? (Choose three.)

A. Link establishment

B. High Definition Link Control

C. Authentication phase (optional)

D. Network layer protocol phase

E. Physical layer bit streaming timing

11. You have a Cisco LAN switch, and you need to connect your LAN to the Internet. Which device and interface configuration meets the minimum requirements for this installation?

A. A router with two Ethernet interfaces

B. A switch with two Ethernet interfaces

C. A router with one Ethernet and one serial interface

D. A switch with one Ethernet and one serial interface

E. A router with one Ethernet and one modem interface

12. The Acme Corporation is implementing dial-up services to enable remote-office employees to connect to the local network. The company uses multiple routed protocols; needs authentication of users connecting to the network; and, since some calls will be long-distance, needs callback support. Which of the following protocols is the best choice for these remote services?

A. 802.1

B. Frame Relay

C. HDLC

D. PPP

E. PAP

13. Which of that following is a packet-switching encapsulation?

A. PPP

B. Frame Relay

C. HDLC

D. ISDN

14. Which of the following layer 2 WAN technologies provide an optional authentication phase?

A. HDLC

B. PPP

C. Frame Relay

D. ATM

15. As shown by the following output, what is the reason the serial link between the Corp router and the Remote router will not come up?

```
Corp#sh int s0/0
Serial0/0 is up, line protocol is down
  Hardware is PowerQUICC Serial
  Internet address is 10.0.1.1/24
  MTU 1500 bytes, BW 1544 Kbit, DLY 20000 usec,
     reliability 254/255, txload 1/255, rxload 1/255
  Encapsulation PPP, loopback not set


Remote#sh int s0/0
Serial0/0 is up, line protocol is down
  Hardware is PowerQUICC Serial
  Internet address is 10.0.1.2/24
  MTU 1500 bytes, BW 1544 Kbit, DLY 20000 usec,
     reliability 254/255, txload 1/255, rxload 1/255
  Encapsulation HDLC, loopback not set
```

   A.   The serial cable is faulty.

   B.   The IP addresses are not in the same subnet.

   C.   The subnet masks are not correct.

   D.   The keepalive settings are not correct.

   E.   The layer 2 frame types are not compatible.

16. What is the problem between the two routers that is causing the lack of communication?

```
Corp#sh int s0/0
Serial0/0 is up, line protocol is down
  Hardware is PowerQUICC Serial
  Internet address is 192.168.10.1/24
  MTU 1500 bytes, BW 1544 Kbit, DLY 20000 usec,
     reliability 254/255, txload 1/255, rxload 1/255
  Encapsulation HDLC, loopback not set


Remote#sh int s0/0
Serial0/0 is up, line protocol is down
  Hardware is PowerQUICC Serial
  Internet address is 192.168.11.2/24
```

```
MTU 1500 bytes, BW 1544 Kbit, DLY 20000 usec,
    reliability 254/255, txload 1/255, rxload 1/255
Encapsulation HDLC, loopback not set
```

  A. The serial cable is faulty.

  B. The IP addresses are not in the same subnet.

  C. The subnet masks are not correct.

  D. The keepalive settings are not correct.

  E. The layer 2 frame types are not compatible.

17. If you have a T1, what must you connect from your router to a demarc?

  A. Ethernet switches

  B. CSU/DSU

  C. Air conditioning to keep the line cool

  D. A T2 to connect the DTE to the DCE

18. Which is true regarding HDLC as implemented on a Cisco router?

  A. It is an IEEE nonproprietary protocol.

  B. It is Cisco proprietary.

  C. It can be used with PPP on the same data link.

  D. It can be used with Frame Relay on the same data link.

19. Which PPP protocol provides link establishment?

  A. HDLC

  B. LAPD

  C. LCP

  D. NCP

20. Which statement is true for DSL?

  A. DSL is backward-compatible with analog voice.

  B. DSL transmission occurs within a frequency range of 330Hz and 3.3kHz.

  C. The DSLAM is installed at the customer site.

  D. Very-high-data-rate DSL is an example of SDSL.

Appendix A

Answers to Written Labs

Chapter 1: Internetworking

Written Lab 1.1

1. The Application layer is responsible for finding the network resources broadcast from a server and adding flow control and error control (if the application developer chooses).

2. The Physical layer takes frames from the Data Link layer and encodes the 1s and 0s into a digital signal for transmission on the network medium.

3. The Network layer provides routing through an internetwork and logical addressing.

4. The Presentation layer makes sure that data is in a readable format for the Application layer.

5. The Session layer sets up, maintains, and terminates sessions between applications.

6. PDUs at the Data Link layer are called *frames*. As soon as you see *frame* in a question, you know the answer.

7. The Transport layer uses virtual circuits to create a reliable connection between two hosts.

8. The Network layer provides logical addressing, typically IP addressing and routing.

9. The Physical layer is responsible for the electrical and mechanical connections between devices.

10. The Data Link layer is responsible for the framing of data packets.

11. The router searches the routing table to determine where to forward the packet.

12. The Data Link layer frames packets received from the Network layer.

13. The Transport layer segments user data.

14. The Network layer creates packets out of segments handed down from the Transport layer.

15. The Physical layer is responsible for transporting 1s and 0s in a digital signal.

16. Segments, packets, frames, bits

17. Transport

18. Data Link

19. Network

20. 48 bits (6 bytes) expressed as a hexadecimal number

Written Lab 1.2

Description	Device or OSI Layer
This device sends and receives information about the Network layer.	Router
This layer creates a virtual circuit before transmitting between two end stations.	Transport
This layer uses service access points.	Data Link (LLC sublayer)
This device uses hardware addresses to filter a network.	Bridge or switch
Ethernet is defined at these layers.	Data Link and Physical
This layer supports flow control and sequencing.	Transport
This device can measure the distance to a remote network.	Router
Logical addressing is used at this layer.	Network
Hardware addresses are defined at this layer.	Data Link (MAC sublayer)
This device creates one big collision domain and one large broadcast domain.	Hub
This device creates many smaller collision domains, but the network is still one large broadcast domain.	Switch or bridge
This device can never run full duplex.	Hub
This device breaks up collision domains and broadcast domains.	Router

Written Lab 1.3

1. Hub: One collision domain, one broadcast domain
2. Bridge: Two collision domains, one broadcast domain
3. Switch: Four collision domains, one broadcast domain
4. Router: Three collision domains, three broadcast domains

Written Lab 1.4

1. Convert from decimal IP address to binary format.

Complete the following table to express 192.168.10.15 in binary format:

Decimal	128	64	32	16	8	4	2	1	Binary
192	1	1	0	0	0	0	0	0	11000000
168	1	0	1	0	1	0	0	0	10101000
10	0	0	0	0	1	0	1	0	00001010
15	0	0	0	0	1	1	1	1	00001111

Complete the following table to express 172.16.20.55 in binary format:

Decimal	128	64	32	16	8	4	2	1	Binary
172	1	0	1	0	1	1	0	0	10101100
16	0	0	0	1	0	0	0	0	00010000
20	0	0	0	1	0	1	0	0	00010100
55	0	0	1	1	0	1	1	1	00110111

Complete the following table to express 10.11.12.99 in binary format:

Decimal	128	64	32	16	8	4	2	1	Binary
10	0	0	0	0	1	0	1	0	00001010
11	0	0	0	0	1	0	1	1	00001011
12	0	0	0	0	1	1	0	0	00001100
99	0	1	1	0	0	0	1	1	01100011

2. Convert the following from binary format to decimal IP address.

Complete the following table to express 11001100.00110011.10101010.01010101 in decimal IP address format:

Binary	128	64	32	16	8	4	2	1	Decimal
11001100	1	1	0	0	1	1	0	0	204
00110011	0	0	1	1	0	0	1	1	51
10101010	1	0	1	0	1	0	1	0	170
01010101	0	1	0	1	0	1	0	1	85

Complete the following table to express 11000110.11010011.00111001.11010001 in decimal IP address format:

Binary	128	64	32	16	8	4	2	1	Decimal
11000110	1	1	0	0	0	1	1	0	198
11010011	1	1	0	1	0	0	1	1	211
00111001	0	0	1	1	1	0	0	1	57
11010001	1	1	0	1	0	0	0	1	209

Complete the following table to express 10000100.11010010.10111000.10100110 in decimal IP address format:

Binary	128	64	32	16	8	4	2	1	Decimal
10000100	1	0	0	0	0	1	0	0	132
11010010	1	1	0	1	0	0	1	0	210
10111000	1	0	1	1	1	0	0	0	184
10100110	1	0	1	0	0	1	1	0	166

3. Convert the following from binary format to hexadecimal.

Complete the following table to express 11011000.00011011.00111101.01110110 in hexadecimal:

Binary	128	64	32	16	8	4	2	1	Hexadecimal
11011000	1	1	0	1	1	0	0	0	D8
00011011	0	0	0	1	1	0	1	1	1B
00111101	0	0	1	1	1	1	0	1	3D
01110110	0	1	1	1	0	1	1	0	76

Complete the following table to express 11001010.11110101.10000011.11101011 in hexadecimal:

Binary	128	64	32	16	8	4	2	1	Hexadecimal
11001010	1	1	0	0	1	0	1	0	CA
11110101	1	1	1	1	0	1	0	1	F5
10000011	1	0	0	0	0	0	1	1	83
11101011	1	1	1	0	1	0	1	1	EB

Complete the following table to express 10000100.11010010.01000011.10110011 in hexadecimal:

Binary	128	64	32	16	8	4	2	1	Hexadecimal
10000100	1	0	0	0	0	1	0	0	84
11010010	1	1	0	1	0	1	1	0	D6
01000011	0	1	0	0	0	0	1	1	43
10110011	1	0	1	1	0	0	1	1	B3

Chapter 2: Internet Protocols

Written Lab 2

1. 192–223, 11000000–11011111
2. Host-to-Host
3. 1–126
4. Loopback or diagnostics
5. Turn all host bits off.
6. Turn all host bits on.
7. 10.0.0.0 through 10.255.255.255
8. 172.16.0.0 through 172.31.255.255
9. 192.168.0.0 through 192.168.255.255
10. 0–9 and *A*, *B*, *C*, *D*, *E*, and *F*

Chapter 3: IP Subnetting, Troubleshooting IP, and Introduction to NAT

Written Lab 3.1

1. 192.168.100.25/30. A /30 is 255.255.255.252. The valid subnet is 192.168.100.24, broadcast is 192.168.100.27, and valid hosts are 192.168.100.25 and 26.
2. 192.168.100.37/28. A /28 is 255.255.255.240. The fourth octet is a block size of 16. Just count by 16s until you pass 37. 0, 16, 32, 48. The host is in the 32 subnet, with a broadcast address of 47. Valid hosts 33–46.
3. 192.168.100.66/27. A /27 is 255.255.255.224. The fourth octet is a block size of 32. Count by 32s until you pass the host address of 66. 0, 32, 64. The host is in the 64 subnet, broadcast address of 95. Valid host range of 65–94.
4. 192.168.100.17/29. A /29 is 255.255.255.248. The fourth octet is a block size of 8. 0, 8, 16, 24. The host is in the 16 subnet, broadcast of 23. Valid hosts 17–22.

5. 192.168.100.99/26. A /26 is 255.255.255.192. The fourth octet has a block size of 64. 0, 64, 128. The host is in the 64 subnet, broadcast of 127. Valid hosts 65–126.

6. 192.168.100.99/25. A /25 is 255.255.255.128. The fourth octet is a block size of 128. 0, 128. The host is in the 0 subnet, broadcast of 127. Valid hosts 1–126.

7. A default Class B is 255.255.0.0. A Class B 255.255.255.0 mask is 256 subnets, each with 254 hosts. You need fewer subnets. If you used 255.255.240.0, this provides 16 subnets. Let's add one more subnet bit. 255.255.248.0. This is 5 bits of subnetting, which provides 32 subnets. This is the best answer, a /21.

8. A /29 is 255.255.255.248. This is a block size of 8 in the fourth octet. 0, 8, 16. The host is in the 8 subnet, broadcast is 15.

9. A /29 is 255.255.255.248, which is 5 subnet bits and 3 host bits. This is only 6 hosts per subnet.

10. A /23 is 255.255.254.0. The third octet is a block size of 2. 0, 2, 4. The subnet is in the 16.2.0 subnet; the broadcast address is 16.3.255.

11. Overloading (PAT)

12. A registered address that represents an inside host to an outside network

13. Ping

14. arp -a

15. 192.168.2.65–126

16. 4,094

17. 172.16.156.0

18. 10.16.2.0

19. 10.16.3.255

20. The routers' interfaces are in different subnets. 192.168.10.80 and 192.168.10.84; they must be in the same subnet to communicate.

Written Lab 3.2

Classful address	Subnet mask	Number of hosts per subnet (2x – 2)
/16	255.255.0.0	65,534
/17	255.255.128.0	32,766

/18	255.255.192.0	16,382
/19	255.255.224.0	8,190
/20	255.255.240.0	4,094
/21	255.255.248.0	2,046
/22	255.255.252.0	1,022
/23	255.255.254.0	510
/24	255.255.255.0	254
/25	255.255.255.128	126
/26	255.255.255.192	62
/27	255.255.255.224	30
/28	255.255.255.240	14
/29	255.255.255.248	6
/30	255.255.255.252	2

Written Lab 3.3

Decimal IP address	Address class	Number of subnet and host bits	Number of subnets (2x)	Number of hosts (2x − 2)
10.25.66.154/23	A	15/9	32,768	510
172.31.254.12/24	B	8/8	256	254
192.168.20.123/28	C	4/4	16	14
63.24.89.21/18	A	10/14	1,024	16,384
128.1.1.254/20	B	4/12	16	4,094
208.100.54.209/30	C	6/2	64	2

Chapter 4: Cisco's Internetworking Operating System (IOS)

Written Lab 4

1. `router(config-if)#clock rate 64000`

2. `router#config t`
   `router(config)# line vty 0 4`
   `router(config-line)# no login`

3. `router#config t`
   `router(config)# int e0`
   `router(config-if)#  no shut`

4. `router#erase startup-config`

5. `router#config t`
   `router(config-line)# console 0`
   `router(config)# login`
   `router(config-line)# password todd`

6. `router#config t`
   `router(config)# enable secret cisco`

7. `router#show controllers serial 0/2`

8. `router#show terminal`

9. `router#reload`

10. `router#config t`
    `router(config)#hostname Chicago`

Chapter 5: Managing a Cisco Internetwork

Written Lab 5.1

1. `copy flash tftp`
2. `copy start tftp`
3. `copy start run`
4. `config mem`
5. `show cdp neighbor detail` or `show cdp  entry *`
6. `show cdp neighbor`
7. Ctrl+Shift+6 and then X
8. `show sessions`
9. `copy tftp flash`
10. Either `copy tftp run` or `copy start run`

Written Lab 5.2

1. Flash memory
2. ROM
3. NVRAM
4. ROM
5. RAM
6. RAM
7. ROM
8. ROM
9. RAM
10. RAM

Chapter 6: IP Routing

Written Lab 6

1. Router(config)#**ip route 172.16.10.0 255.255.255.0 172.16.20.1 150**
2. It will use the gateway interface MAC at L2 and the actual destination IP at L3.
3. Router(config)#**ip route 0.0.0.0 0.0.0.0 172.16.40.1**
4. Router(config)#**ip classless**
5. Stub network
6. Router#**show ip route**
7. Exit interface
8. False. The MAC address would be the router interface, not the remote host.
9. True
10. Router(config-if)#**clock rate *speed***
11. (config-router)#**network 10.0.0.0**
12. (config-router)#**passive-interface s1**
13. Route poisoning
14. Split horizon
15. Router# **debug ip rip**

Chapter 7: Layer 2 Switching

Written Lab 7

1. show mac address-table
2. Flood the frame out all ports except the port it was received on.
3. Address learning, forward/filter decisions, and loop avoidance
4. It will add the source MAC address in the forward/filter table and associate it with the port the frame was received on.
5. Spanning Tree Protocol (STP)

6. Flood the frame out all ports except the port it was received on.
7. Port security
8. Collision
9. The switch has failed the post, and it is typically fatal.
10. The port is experiencing errors.

Chapter 8: Wireless Technologies

Written Lab 8

1. 11Mbps
2. 54Mbps
3. 54Mbps
4. 2.4GHz
5. 2.4GHz
6. 5GHz
7. DSSS
8. Three
9. The IEEE 802.11i standard has been sanctioned by WPA and is termed WPA version 2.
10. 12

Chapter 9: Security

Written Lab 9

1. Denial of service
2. `transport input ssh`
3. Use a firewall to restrict access from the outside to the network devices, and use SSH or another encrypted and authenticated transport to access device configurations.
4. Physically secure the equipment.
5. A denial-of-service attack is a flood of packets requesting a TCP connection to a server.

Chapter 10: Introduction to Wide Area Networks

Written Lab 10

1. show interface serial 0
2. Config t, interface serial 0, encapsulation ppp
3. username todd password cisco
4. Point-to-Point Protocol
5. HDLC, PPP, and Frame Relay
6. Serial
7. Frame Relay
8. HDLC
9. HDLC, LCP, NCP
10. show interface

Appendix B

Answers to Review Questions

Chapter 1: Internetworking

1. D. A receiving host can control the transmitter by using flow control (TCP uses Windowing by default). By decreasing the window size, the receiving host can slow down the transmitting host so the receiving host does not overflow its buffers.

2. A, D. An Ethernet frame has source and destination MAC addresses, an Ether-Type field to identify the Network layer protocol, the data, and the FCS field that holds the answer to the CRC.

3. C, D. Not that you really want to enlarge a single collision domain, but a hub (multi-port repeater) will provide this for you.

4. D. The Transport layer receives large data streams from the upper layers and breaks them up into smaller pieces called *segments*.

5. A, C, E, G. Routers provide packet switching, packet filtering, internetwork communication, and path selection.

6. B. Routers operate at layer 3. LAN switches operate at layer 2. Ethernet hubs operate at layer 1. Word processing applications communicate to the Application layer interface but do not operate at layer 7, so the answer would be none.

7. C. The encapsulation method is data, segment, packet, frame, bit.

8. A, D. The main advantage of a layered model is that it can allow application developers to change aspects of a program in just one layer of the layer model's specifications. Advantages of using the OSI layered model include, but are not limited to, the following:
   - It divides the network communication process into smaller and simpler components, thus aiding component development, design, and troubleshooting.
   - It allows multiple-vendor development through the standardization of network components.
   - It encourages industry standardization by defining what functions occur at each layer of the model.
   - It allows various types of network hardware and software to communicate.
   - It prevents changes in one layer from affecting other layers, so it does not hamper development.

9. B, C. Bridges break up collision domains, which allow more bandwidth for users.

10. A, D. Unlike full duplex, half-duplex Ethernet operates in a shared collision domain, and it has a lower effective throughput than full duplex.

11. D. Fiber-optic cable provides a more secure, long-distance cable that is not susceptible to EMI interference at high speeds.

12. C. A reliable Transport layer connection uses acknowledgments to make sure all data is transmitted and received reliably. A reliable connection is defined by a virtual circuit that uses acknowledgments, sequencing, and flow control, which are characteristics of the Transport layer (layer 4).

13. A, C, D. The common types of flow control are buffering, windowing, and congestion avoidance.

14. B, C, E. Hubs cannot run full-duplex Ethernet. Full duplex must be used on a point-to-point connection between two devices capable of running full duplex. Switches and hosts can run full duplex between each other, but a hub can never run full duplex.

15. C. Flow control allows the receiving device to control the transmitter so the receiving device's buffer does not overflow.

16. A, B, E. Full duplex means you are using both wire pairs simultaneously to send and receive data. You must have a dedicated switch port for each node, which means you will not have collisions. Both the host network card and the switch port must be capable and set to work in full-duplex mode.

17. B. To connect two switches, you would use a RJ45 UTP crossover cable.

18. B, E. Once transmitting stations on an Ethernet segment hear a collision, they send an extended jam signal to ensure that all stations recognize the collision. After the jamming is complete, each sender waits a predetermined amount of time, plus a random time. After both timers expire, the senders are free to transmit, but they must make sure the media is clear before transmitting and that they all have equal priority.

19. D. To connect to a router or switch console port, you would use an RJ45 UTP rolled cable.

20. B. You must be able to take a binary number and convert it into both decimal and hexadecimal. To convert to decimal, just add up the 1s using their values. The values that are turned on with the binary number of 10110111 are 128 + 32 + 16 + 4 + 2 + 1 = 183. To get the hexadecimal equivalent, you need to break the eight binary digits into nibbles (4 bits), 1011 and 0111. By adding up these values, you get 11 and 7. In hexadecimal, 11 is *B*, so the answer is 0xB7.

Chapter 2: Internet Protocols

1. A, D, E, G. To send mail, the protocol SMTP is used at the Application layer. SMTP uses TCP at the Transport layer to create a reliable virtual circuit. IP is used at the Network layer to provide routing, and Ethernet is the typical Network Access (LAN) connection type. Although ARP can be used at the Network layer, it is not mandatory because the destination MAC address may already be known.

2. C. Proxy ARP can help machines on a subnet reach remote subnets without configuring routing or a default gateway.

3. C. Dynamic Host Configuration Protocol (DHCP) is used to provide IP information to hosts on your network. DHCP can provide a lot of information, but the most common is IP address, subnet mask, default gateway, and DNS information.

4. B. Address Resolution Protocol (ARP) is used to find the hardware address from a known IP address.

5. A, C, D. This seems like a hard question at first because it doesn't make sense. The listed answers are from the OSI model, and the question asked about the TCP/IP protocol stack (DoD model). However, let's just look for what is wrong. First, the Session layer is not in the TCP/IP model; neither are the Data Link and Physical layers. This leaves us with the Transport layer (Host-to-Host in the DoD model), Internet layer (Network layer in the OSI), and Application layer (Application/Process in the DoD).

6. C. A Class C network address has only 8 bits for defining hosts: $2^8 - 2 = 254$.

7. A, B. A client that sends out a DHCP Discover message in order to receive an IP address sends out a broadcast at both layer 2 and layer 3. The layer 2 broadcast is all *F*s in hex, or FF:FF:FF:FF:FF:FF. The layer 3 broadcast is 255.255.255.255, which means all networks and all hosts. DHCP is connectionless, which means it uses User Datagram Protocol (UDP) at the Transport layer, also called the Host-to-Host layer.

8. B. Although Telnet does use TCP and IP (TCP/IP), the question specifically asks about layer 4, and IP works at layer 3. Telnet uses TCP at layer 4.

9. C, D. Internet Control Message Protocol (ICMP) is used to send error messages through the network, but it does not work alone. Every segment or ICMP payload must be encapsulated within an IP datagram (or packet).

10. B, D, E. SMTP, FTP, and HTTP use TCP.

11. A, C, F. DHCP, SNMP, and TFTP use UDP. SMTP, FTP, and HTTP use TCP.

12. A, B, E. UDP does not have reliability, so it will not sequence, acknowledge, or use flow control (windowing). UDP, however, will use port number and a checksum, just like TCP.

13. C. You should know easily that only TCP and UDP work at the Transport layer, so now you have a 50/50 shot. However, since the header has sequencing, acknowledgment, and window numbers, the answer can only be TCP.

14. A. Both FTP and Telnet use TCP at the Transport layer; however, they both are Application layer protocols, so the Application layer is the best answer for this question.

15. C. The four layers of the DoD model are Application/Process, Host-to-Host, Internet, and Network Access. The Internet layer is equivalent to the Network layer of the OSI model.

16. C,E. Class A private address range is 10.0.0.0 through 10.255.255.255. Class B private address range is 172.16.0.0 through 172.31.255.255, and Class C private address range is 192.168.0.0 through 192.168.255.255.

17. B. The four layers of the TCP/IP stack (also called the DoD model) are Application/Process, Host-to-Host, Internet, and Network Access. The Host-to-Host layer is equivalent to the Transport layer of the OSI model.

18. B, C, F, G. The hard part of this question is remembering the terms Cisco uses in the answer. Step 1 is a discover broadcast, step 2 is an offer unicast from the server, step 3 is a request broadcast from the client, and step 4 is an acknowledgment unicast from the client.

19. C. The TCP header has a sequence field that helps provide reliable transmission. Sequencing numbers each segment as it creates the TCP header so that the data stream can be put back together again in the correct order on the receiving host.

20. D. DNS uses TCP for zone exchanges between servers and UDP when a client is trying to resolve a hostname to an IP address.

Chapter 3: IP Subnetting, Troubleshooting IP, and Introduction to NAT

1. D. A /27 (255.255.255.224) is 3 bits on and 5 bits off. This provides 8 subnets, each with 30 hosts. Does it matter if this mask is used with a Class A, B, or C network address? Not at all. The amount of host bits would never change.

2. D. A 240 mask is 4 subnet bits and provides 16 subnets, each with 14 hosts. You need more subnets, so let's add subnet bits. One more subnet bit would be a 248 mask. This provides 5 subnet bits (32 subnets) with 3 host bits (6 hosts per subnet). This is the best answer.

3. C. This is a pretty simple question. A /28 is 255.255.255.240, which means that the block size is 16 in the fourth octet: 0, 16, 32, 48, 64, 80, and so on. The host is in the 64 subnet.

4. F. A CIDR address of /19 is 255.255.224.0. This is a Class B address, so that is only 3 subnet bits, but it provides 13 host bits, or 8 subnets, each with 8,190 hosts.

5. B, D. The mask 255.255.254.0 (/23) used with a Class A address means that there are 15 subnet bits and 9 host bits. The block size in the third octet is 2 (256 − 254). So, this makes the subnets in the interesting octet 0, 2, 4, 6, and so on, all the way to 254. The host 10.16.3.65 is in the 2.0 subnet. The next subnet is 4.0, so the broadcast address for the 2.0 subnet is 3.255. The valid host addresses are 2.1 through 3.254.

6. D. A /30, regardless of the class of address, has a 252 in the fourth octet. This means you have a block size of 4 and your subnets are 0, 4, 8, 12, 16, and so on. Address 14 is obviously in the 12 subnet.

7. D. A point-to-point link uses only two hosts. A /30, or 255.255.255.252, mask provides two hosts per subnet.

8. C. A /21 is 255.255.248.0, which means you have a block size of 8 in the third octet, so you just count by 8 until you reach 66. The subnet in this question is 64.0. The next subnet is 72.0, so the broadcast address of the 64 subnet is 71.255.

9. A. A /29 (255.255.255.248), regardless of the class of address, has only 3 host bits. Six hosts is the maximum number of hosts on this LAN, including the router interface.

10. C. A /29 is 255.255.255.248, which is a block size of 8 in the fourth octet. The subnets are 0, 8, 16, 24, 32, 40, and so on. 192.168.19.24 is the 24 subnet, and since 32 is the next subnet, the broadcast address for the 24 subnet is 31. 192.168.19.26 is the only correct answer.

11. A. A /29 (255.255.255.248) has a block size of 8 in the fourth octet. This means the subnets are 0, 8, 16, 24, and so on. 10 is in the 8 subnet. The next subnet is 16, so 15 is the broadcast address.

12. B. You need 5 subnets, each with at least 16 hosts. The mask 255.255.255.240 provides 16 subnets with 14 hosts—this will not work. The mask 255.255.255.224 provides 8 subnets, each with 30 hosts. This is the best answer.

13. A, E. First, if you have two hosts directly connected, as shown in the graphic, then you need a crossover cable. A straight-through cable won't work. Second, the hosts have different masks, which puts them in different subnets. The easy solution is just to set both masks to 255.255.255.0 (/24).

14. A. A /25 mask is 255.255.255.128. Used with a Class B network, the third and fourth octets are used for subnetting with a total of 9 subnet bits—8 bits in the third octet and 1 bit in the fourth octet. Since there is only 1 bit in the fourth octet, the bit is either off or on—which is a value of 0 or 128. The host in the question is in the 0 subnet, which has a broadcast address of 127 since 128 is the next subnet.

15. A. A /28 is a 255.255.255.240 mask. Let's count to the ninth subnet (you need to find the broadcast address of the eighth subnet, so you need to count to the ninth subnet). Starting at 16 (remember, the question stated that you will not use subnet zero, so you start at 16, not 0), 16, 32, 48, 64, 80, 96, 112, 128, 144. The eighth subnet is 128, and the next subnet is 144, so the broadcast address of the 128 subnet is 143. This makes the host range 129–142; 142 is the last valid host.

16. C. A /28 is a 255.255.255.240 mask. The first subnet is 16 (remember that the question stated not to use subnet zero), and the next subnet is 32, so our broadcast address is 31. This makes our host range 17–30. 30 is the last valid host.

17. E. A Class C subnet mask of 255.255.255.224 is 3 bits on and 5 bits off (11100000) and provides 8 subnets, each with 30 hosts. However, if the command `ip subnet-zero` is not used, then only 6 subnets would be available for use.

18. E. A Class B network ID with a /22 mask is 255.255.252.0, with a block size of 4 in the third octet. The network address in the question is in subnet 172.16.16.0 with a broadcast address of 172.16.19.255. Only option E even has the correct subnet mask listed, and 172.16.18.255 is a valid host.

19. D,E. The router's IP address on the E0 interface is 172.16.2.1/23, which is a 255.255.254.0. This makes the third octet a block size of 2. The router's interface is in the 2.0 subnet, and the broadcast address is 3.255 because the next subnet is 4.0. The valid host range is 2.1 through 3.254. The router is using the first valid host address in the range.

20. D. Option C looks like a good answer because of the word *global*; however, it also has the word *private*, which would make it an inside address. Inside global is defined as a registered address that represents an inside host to an outside network. In other words, you're looking for a translated address. Inside local is before translation; inside global is after translation.

Chapter 4: Cisco's Internetworking Operating System (IOS)

1. C. The exec-timeout command is set in minutes and seconds.

2. D. The auxiliary port can be configured with modem commands so that a modem can be connected to the router. It lets you dial up a remote router and attach to the auxiliary port if the router is down and you need to configure it *out-of-band* (meaning out of the network).

3. C, D. To configure SSH on your router, you need to set the username command; the ip domain-name, login local, and the transport input ssh under the VTY lines; and the crypto key command under global configuration mode. However, SSH version 2 is not required but suggested.

4. C. The show controllers serial 0 command will show you whether either a DTE or DCE cable is connected to the interface. If it is a DCE connection, you need to add clocking with the clock rate command.

5. C. The default locations of the files are IOS in flash memory, start-up configuration in NVRAM, and running configuration in RAM.

6. B. The command service password-encryption, from global configuration mode, will encrypt all current and future passwords.

7. B. From global configuration mode, use the line vty 0 4 command to set all five default VTY lines.

8. C. The enable secret password is case sensitive, so the second option is wrong. To set the enable secret password, use the enable secret *password* command from global configuration mode.

9. C. The typical banner is a message of the day (MOTD) and is set by using the global configuration mode command banner motd.

10. C. The prompts offered as options indicate the following modes:

    router(config)#—global configuration mode

    router>—user mode

    router#—privileged mode

    router(config-if)#—interface configuration mode

11. D. To copy the running-config to NVRAM so that it will be used if the router is restarted, use the `copy running-config startup-config` command in privileged mode (`copy run start` for short). Option C is wrong because it's at the wrong prompt.

12. D. To allow a VTY (Telnet) session into your router, you must set the VTY password. Option C is wrong because it is setting the password on the wrong router.

13. D. The erase startup-config command erases the contents of NVRAM and will put you in setup mode if the router is restarted.

14. B. If an interface is shut down, the `show interface` command will show the interface as administratively down. (It is possible that no cable is attached as well, but you can't tell that from this message.)

15. C. With the `show interfaces` command, you can view the configurable parameters, get statistics for the interfaces on the router, verify if the interfaces are shut down, and see the IP address of each interface.

16. C. If you delete the startup-config and reload the router, the router will automatically enter setup mode. You can also type **setup** from privileged mode at any time.

17. D. You can view the interface statistics from user mode, but the command is `show interface serial 0/0`.

18. B. The `% ambiguous command` error means that there is more than one possible `show` command that starts with *ru*. Use a question mark to find the correct command.

19. B, D. The commands `show interfaces` and `show ip interface` will show you the layer 1 and 2 status and the IP addresses of your router's interfaces.

20. A. If you see that a serial interface and the protocol are both down, then you have a Physical layer problem. If you see `serial1 is up, line protocol is down`, then you are not receiving (Data Link) keepalives from the remote end.

Chapter 5: Managing a Cisco Internetwork

1. B. The default configuration setting is 0x2102, which tells the router to load the IOS from flash and the configuration from NVRAM. 0x2102tells the router to bypass the configuration in NVRAM so that you can perform password recovery.

2. E. To copy the IOS to a backup host, which is stored in flash memory by default, use the `copy flash tftp` command.

3. B. The command `traceroute` (trace for short), which can be issued from user mode or privileged mode, is used to find the path a packet takes through an internetwork and will also show you where the packet stops because of an error on a router.

4. C. Since the configuration looks correct, you probably didn't screw up the copy job. However, when you perform a copy from a network host to a router, the interfaces are automatically shut down and need to be manually enabled with the `no shutdown` command.

5. B. The `show flash` command will provide you with the current IOS name and size and the size of flash memory.

6. C. Before you start to configure the router, you should erase the NVRAM with the `erase startup-config` command and then reload the router using the `reload` command.

7. D. The command `copy tftp flash` will allow you to copy a new IOS into flash memory on your router.

8. C. The best answer is `show version`, which shows you the IOS file running currently on your router. The `show flash` command shows you the contents of flash memory, not which file is currently running.

9. C. All Cisco routers have a default configuration register setting of 0x2102, which tells the router to load the IOS from flash memory and the configuration from NVRAM.

10. C. If you save a configuration and reload the router and it comes up either in setup mode or as a blank configuration, chances are you have the configuration register setting incorrect.

11. D. To keep open one or more Telnet sessions, use the Ctrl+Shift+6 keystroke combination and then press X.

12. B, D. The best answers, the ones you need to remember, are that either an access control list is filtering the Telnet session or the VTY password is not set on the remote device.

13. A, D. The `show hosts` command provides information on temporary DNS entries and permanent name-to-address mappings created using the `ip host` command.

14. A, B, D. The `tracert` command is a Windows command and will not work on a router! A router uses the `traceroute` command.

15. D. Since the question never mentioned anything about a suspended session, you can assume that the Telnet session is still open, and you would just type **exit** to close the session.

16. C. To see console messages through your Telnet session, you must enter the `terminal monitor` command.

17. C. The `show version` command provides you with the current configuration register setting.

18. E. Although option A is certainly the "best" answer, unfortunately option E will work just fine, and your boss would probably prefer you to use the `show cdp neighbors detail` command.

19. B, D, E. Before you back up an IOS image to a laptop directly connected to a router's Ethernet port, make sure the TFTP server software is running on your laptop, that the Ethernet cable is a "crossover," and that the laptop is in the same subnet as the router's Ethernet port, and then you can use the `copy flash tftp` command from your laptop.

20. C. The default configuration setting of 0x2102 tells the router to look in NVRAM for the boot sequence.

Chapter 6: IP Routing

1. A, E. There are actually three different ways to configure the same default route, but only two are shown in the answer. First, you can set a default route with the 0.0.0.0 0.0.0.0 mask and then specify the next hop, as in option A. Or you can use 0.0.0.0 0.0.0.0 and use the exit interface instead of the next hop. Finally, you can use option E with the `ip default-network` command.

2. C. The `(config-router)#`**passive-interface** command stops updates from being sent out an interface, but route updates are still received. It is not executed in interface configuration mode, but in RIP configuration mode (accessed by typing **router rip**), and the interface is specified at the end of the command in the form *interface_type number*.

3. A, B. Although option D almost seems right, it is not; the mask is the mask used on the remote network, not the source network. Since there is no number at the end of the static route, it is using the default administrative distance of 1.

4. C, F. The switches are not used as either a default gateway or other destination. Switches have nothing to do with routing. It is very important to remember that the destination MAC address will always be the router's interface. The destination address of a frame, from HostA, will be the MAC address of the Fa0/0 interface of RouterA. The destination address of a packet will be the IP address of the network interface card (NIC) of the HTTPS server. The destination port number in the segment header will have a value of 443 (HTTPS).

5. C, D. The route to 192.168.50.0 is unreachable (a metric of 16 for RIP means the same thing), and only interfaces s0/1 and FastEthernet 0/0 are participating in the RIP update. Since a route update was received, at least two routers are participating in the RIP routing process. Since a route update for network 192.168.40.0 is being sent out Fa0/0 and a route was received from 192.168.40.2, you can assume a ping to that address will be successful.

6. A. A split horizon will not advertise a route back to the same router it learned the route from.

7. A, D. RouterC will use ICMP to inform HostA that HostB cannot be reached. It will perform this by sending a destination unreachable ICMP message type.

8. B, E. Classful routing means that all hosts in the internetwork use the same mask and that only default masks are in use. Classless routing means that you can use variable-length subnet masks (VLSMs) and can also support discontiguous networking.

9. B, C. The distance-vector routing protocol sends its complete routing table out all active interfaces at periodic time intervals. Link-state routing protocols send updates containing the state of its own links to all routers in the internetwork.

10. B. The debug ip rip command is used to show the Internet Protocol (IP) Routing Information Protocol (RIP) updates being sent and received on the router.

11. B, E. RIPv2 uses the same timers and loop-avoidance schemes as RIPv1. Split horizon is used to stop an update from being sent out the same interface it was received on. Hold-down timers allow time for a network to become stable in the case of a flapping link.

12. B. RIP has an administrative distance (AD) of 120, while EIGRP has an administrative distance of 90, so the router will discard any route with a higher AD than 90 to that same network.

13. C. You cannot have 16 hops on a RIP network by default. If you receive a route advertised with a metric of 16, this means it is inaccessible.

14. A. RIPv1 and RIPv2 only use the lowest hop count to determine the best path to a remote network.

15. A. Since the routing table shows no route to the 192.168.22.0 network, the router will discard the packet and send an ICMP destination unreachable message out interface FastEthernet 0/0, which is the source LAN from which the packet originated.

16. C. Static routes have an administrative distance of 1 by default. Unless you change this, a static route will always be used over any other dynamically learned route. EIGRP has an administrative distance of 90, and RIP has an administrative distance of 120, by default.

17. C. The network 10.0.0.0 cannot be placed in the next router's routing table because it already is at 15 hops. One more hop would make the route 16 hops, and that is not valid in RIP networking.

18. B. When a routing update is received by a router, the router first checks the administrative distance (AD) and always chooses the route with the lowest AD. However, if two routes are received and they both have the same AD and differing metrics, then the router will choose the one route with the lowest metrics or, in RIP's case, hop count.

19. D. Another way to avoid problems caused by inconsistent updates and to stop network loops is route poisoning. When a network goes down, the distance-vector routing protocol initiates route poisoning by advertising the network with an unreachable metric of 16 (for RIP), sometimes referred to as *infinite*.

20. C. RIPv2 is pretty much just like RIPv1. It has the same administrative distance and timers and is configured similarly.

Chapter 7: Layer 2 Switching

1. A, D, E. Microsegmention is created by having every network segment be its own collision domain, and not a shared medium. Microsegmentation provides full-duplex, no collisions, and more bandwidth for users.

2. C. The command `show mac address-table` displays the forward/filter table on the switch.

3. A, E. Bridges break up collision domains, which would increase the number of collision domains in a network and also make smaller collision domains.

4. C. To stop unauthorized users from accessing the LAN, you can configure port security on your switch.

5. A, E. When you plug a correct Ethernet cable type into a switch port, the port will turn amber and then turn green after the loop detection mechanism (STP) has converged. The port light should blink green as it is forwarding or flooding frames.

6. A, C, E. Layer 2 features include address learning, forwarding and filtering of the network, and loop avoidance.

7. A. When you connect to a switch port, at first the link lights are orange/amber, and then they turn green, indicating normal operation. If the link light is blinking, you have a problem.

8. B. Switches break up collision domains, and routers break up broadcast domains.

9. E. From global configuration mode (not interface mode), you set the default gateway with the `ip default-gateway` command, which allows you to manage the switch remotely.

10. D. Switches flood all frames that have an unknown destination address out all ports, except for the port the frame was received on. If a device answers the frame, the switch will update the MAC address table to reflect the location of the device.

11. C. Since the source MAC address is not in the MAC address table, the switch will add the source address and the port it is connected to into the MAC address table and then forward the frame to the outgoing port.

12. B, E, F. To troubleshoot a switch problem where no lights are showing on the ports, you need to ensure that your cabling is correct. Routers and PCs use straight-through cables into a switch. You should also verify that the switch is powered up and then reseat all the cables.

13. A, C. Each port on a switch is a separate collision domain (microsegementation). Also, ports can be configured into separate bridge groups, which are called virtual LANs (VLANs). Although VLANs are outside the CCENT objectives, you should understand their meaning.

14. C. The command `show mac address-table` will display the forward/filter table, also called a *CAM table* on a switch.

15. B, C. Layer 2 switches are much better than hubs because switches segment the network and hubs just connect network segments together. Switches segment the network by filtering frames based on the MAC address. And unlike a hub, switches allow for simultaneous frame transmissions.

16. A. A switch can have multiple MAC addresses associated with a port. In the illustration, a hub is connected to port Fa0/1, which has two hosts connected.

17. A, B, C, D. Switches, unlike bridges, are hardware based. Cisco says its switches are wire speed and provide low latency, and I guess they are low cost compared to their prices in the 1990s.

18. B. Since the destination MAC address is in the MAC address table (forward/filter table), it will send it out port Fa0/3 only.

19. B, D. `switchport port-security` is an important command, and it's super easy with the CNA; however, from the CLI, you can set the maximum number of MAC addresses allowed into the port and then set the penalty if this maximum has been passed.

20. A. If the system LED is amber, reboot the switch, and if it does not go green, the switch has probably gone bad and needs to be replaced.

Chapter 8: Wireless Technologies

1. C, E. WPA uses PSK to perform authentication and can use either static or dynamic encryption keys. The benefit of WPA over static WEP keys is that WPA can change dynamically while the system is used.

2. C. The IEEE 802.11b and IEEE 802.11b both run in the 2.4GHz RF range.

3. D. The IEEE 802.11a standard runs in the 5GHz RF range.

4. C. The IEEE 802.11b and IEEE 802.11b both run in the 2.4GHz RF range.

5. B. 802.11b uses Direct Sequence Spread Spectrum (DSSS) technology.

6. A. The IEEE 802.11g standard provides three non-overlapping channels.

7. A. The IEEE 802.11b standard provides three non-overlapping channels.

8. A, B. Instead of bounded media using digital signaling, 802.11 wireless LANs use unbounded media, and analog signaling uses a radio frequency or infrared signaling, although infrared is not as popular as RF.

9. B. The IEEE 802.11b standard provides a maximum data rate of up to 11Mbps.

10. B, E. If you have more than one access point in an area, the APs need to have overlap of at least 10 percent or more to allow for roaming, the APs should be in different channels (frequencies), and they must use the same SSID. This setup is called an ESS.

11. A, B, D, E. The IEEE 802.11b data rates are 1, 2, 5.5, and 11Mbps.

12. B, D. The IEEE 802.11 standard provides 14 channels for the 2.4GHz range, with 11 configurable channels in the United States. CSMA/CA helps with the 802.1b half-duplex nature by using a RTS/CTS mechanism.

13. A, D. The Wi-Fi Alliance tests devices engineered by manufactures to verify that they are within the IEEE standards, which means that they will interoperate with other vendors' equipment.

14. D. WEP uses a static key, and WPA uses a pre-shared key, but the actual key transmitted changes throughout the session. This is called *broadcast key rotation* and is part of the TKIP protocol suite.

15. C. If an AP does have SSID broadcasting disabled, the client needs to set the SSID value of the AP on the client software in order to connect to the AP.

16. A. WPA2 uses the Advanced Encryption Standard (AES) known as the Counter Mode Cipher Block Chaining-Message Authentication Code (CBC-MAC) Protocol (CCMP).

17. C. If you have more than one access point in an office and they all connect to the wired network (infrastructure), set each AP with the same SSID, but set all APs to different channels with at least 10 to 15 percent overlap of coverage.

18. B, D, F. Both APs should be configured to operate in separate channels and have at least a 10 percent overlap of coverage. You don't have to connect them both to an Ethernet connection, but for best service, your APs should be configured with the same SSID name, and both should be connected to the same Ethernet network or virtual LAN (VLAN). This is called an extended service set (ESS).

19. A. *Extended service set ID* means you have more than one access point and they all are set to the same SSID and all are connected together in the same VLAN or distribution system so users can roam.

20. C, E, F. The 2.4GHz band can have interference from microwave ovens, cordless phones, and Bluetooth devices because they operate in similar frequencies. Keep your access points away from devices that contain metal, such as metal filing cabinets. And of course, any type of wireless connection is dependent on the type and direction of an antenna.

Chapter 9: Security

1. C. To stop unauthorized users from accessing the LAN, you can configure port security on your switch.

2. B, D. `switchport port-security` is an important command, and you can set the maximum number of MAC addresses allowed into the port and then set the penalty if this maximum has been passed.

3. B. Your first step in creating a comprehensive network security plan is to physically secure all your network equipment.

4. B, D. Intrusion detection systems (IDSs) and intrusion prevention systems (IPSs) help prevent threats by watching for trends, particular patterns, and other factors.

5. B, C. You should always have a firewall on your network to block access from outside devices. In addition, Cisco recommends always using Secure Shell (SSH) instead of Telnet to configure your devices in-band.

6. E. As long as the `service password-encryption` command is enabled, it will encrypt all current passwords and any passwords you change.

7. A. If you flood a server with TCP requests, all the available TCP ports will be used, and the server will stop responding.

8. C. The command `transport input ssh` configures a device to allow only Secure Shell (SSH) to be used when you're connecting to it in-band.

9. A. The answer to this question is assuming that the switch port is an access port and that switch port security has been enabled. With that said, the specified commands will allow only the source MAC address 0001.1234.ABCD.12ED into the switch port to be configured. Any other source MAC address would be dropped.

10. A,D. Telnet sends all data in clear text, so it is not more secure than SSH. Also, the destination device must be running as a Telnet server.

11. A, C. The four typical types of denial-of-service attacks are TCP SYN flood, ping of death, Tribe Flood Network, and stacheldraht.

12. A, C, F. To provide port security on a LAN switch, which stops unauthorized users from connecting, you first need to make your switch port (or ports) an access port, enable port security, and then set your options, which in this example were statically assigning the MAC address of the PC.

13. C. An intrusion detection system (IDS) does not stop any type of attack but instead documents and logs them. It can send alerts to a management station or even page an administrator.

14. A. Again, the first thing that must be configured is that the switchport mode must be set to access. Then enable switch port security and add your options. In this question, the best option is using the `sticky` keyword to save the source MAC addresses into the `running-config`.

15. D. Denial-of-service attacks make a service unavailable by overwhelming the system that normally provides it, and there are several different versions of this type of attack.

16. C, D. HMAC-SHA-1 provides hashing of the data so it is not altered along the way, and RSA provides encrypted key exchange between two peers so that each host has the key to unencrypt the data when received.

17. A. When confidentiality is required, the Encapsulating Security Payload (ESP) IPsec security protocol should be used. ESP encrypts the payload of the IP packet.

18. B. The Cisco Adaptive Security Appliance provides security for small to very large enterprise networks. The ASA has IDS and IPS components as well as a VNP module.

19. C. Data integrity provides authentication and encryption of the data across a VPN.

20. A. The authentication component of VPN technology ensures that data can be read only by its intended recipient by using Pre-Shared Key or RSA signatures.

Chapter 10: Introduction to Wide Area Networks

1. C, D. The two authentication methods built into PPP are CHAP and PAP.

2. C. If you have only one free serial interface on your router, you can use Frame Relay to connect multiple remote sites using PVCs (subinterfaces).

3. A, B, C. ISDN is considered a layer 3 WAN technology and is completely outdated. Cisco considers PPP, HDLC, and Frame Relay the most common WAN technologies.

4. B, C, E. Leased lines, circuit switching, and packet switching are the typical WAN connection types.

5. B. You cannot use the no encapsulation command on a serial interface. To enable a certain encapsulation or to change to a different encapsulation type, use encapsulation ppp, for example.

6. C, D, E. Ethernet is a LAN technology and cannot be configured on a serial interface. PPP, HDLC, and Frame Relay are layer 2 WAN technologies that are typically configured on a serial interface.

7. A. Cisco, as do most router vendors, uses HDLC as the default serial encapsulation, but remember that each vendor uses a proprietary HDLC.

8. A. Clocking on a serial interface is always provided by the CSU/DSU (DCE device). However, if you do not have a CSU/DSU in your nonproduction test environment, then you need to supply clocking with the clock rate command on the serial interface of the router with the DCE cable attached.

9. C, E. High-Level Data-Link Control (HDLC) was derived from Synchronous Data Link Control (SDLC), which was created by IBM as a Data Link connection protocol. It is unlikely that two different vendors' routers will communicate because of a proprietary LLC layer. Option A is wrong because the Type field is used in an Ethernet frame, not a serial encapsulation; option B is wrong because you use the clock rate command only in nonproduction networks; and option D is wrong because you don't have usernames or authentication with HDLC.

10. A, C, D. When PPP connections are started, the links go through three phases of session establishment: link establishment, the authentication phase, and the Network layer protocol phase.

11. C. This question is looking for today's typical connection type, which would be an Ethernet connection to a router and then a serial interface to the Internet. Certainly there are other options, but option C is the best answer to this question.

12. D. PPP is your only option because HDLC and Frame Relay do not support these types of business requirements. PPP provides dynamic addressing, authentication using PAP or CHAP, and callback services.

13. B. A packet-switched technology that emerged in the early 1990s, Frame Relay is a Data Link and Physical layer specification that provides high performance.

14. B. PPP has a three-phase setup when you bring up a data link using PPP. These are session setup, optional authentication, and the network layer protocol phase.

15. E. This is an easy question because the Remote router is using the default HDLC serial encapsulation and the Corp router is using the PPP serial encapsulation. You should go to the Remote router and set that encapsulation to PPP or change the Corp router back to the default of HDLC (assuming both routers are Cisco routers).

16. B. Since each subnet mask is a /24 (255.255.255.0) and the IP addresses are Class C, each IP address is in its own subnet. The two interfaces will never communicate.

17. B. Router interfaces are, by default, data terminal equipment (DTE), and they connect into data communication equipment (DCE)—for example, a channel service unit/data service unit (CSU/DSU). The CSU/DSU then plugs into a demarcation location (demarc) and is the service provider's last responsibility. Most of the time, the demarc is a jack that has an RJ-45 (8-pin modular) female connector located in a telecommunications closet.

18. B. The version of HDLC as implemented on a Cisco router is Cisco proprietary, and you cannot have HDLC on one side of a link and any other version of HDLC on the other side of the link. Nor can you have HDLC of any type on one side and PPP or Frame Relay on the other.

19. C. LCP provides a method of establishing, configuring, maintaining, and terminating the point-to-point connection. At start-up, LCP provides link establishment.

20. A. Digital subscriber line is a technology used by traditional telephone companies to deliver advanced services (high-speed data and backward-compatible to analog video) over twisted-pair copper telephone wires and is backward-compatible with analog voice.

Appendix C

About the Additional Study Tools

In this appendix:

- Additional Study Tools

- System Requirements

- Using the Study Tools

- Troubleshooting

Additional Study Tools

The following sections are arranged by category and summarize the software and other goodies you'll find from the companion website. If you need help with installing the items, refer to the installation instructions in the "Using the Study Tools" section of this appendix.

> **NOTE** The additional study tools can be found at www.sybex.com/go/ccent2e. Here, you will get instructions on how to download the files to your hard drive.

Sybex Test Engine

The files contain the Sybex test engine, which includes two bonus practice exams, as well as the assessment test and the chapter review questions, which are also included in the book itself.

Electronic Flashcards

These handy electronic flashcards are just what they sound like. One side contains a question, and the other side shows the answer.

Study Sheets

I have added two Excel study sheets that will help you study for the CCENT exam. This includes a file called `Lammle_CCNA_Answer_Sheet.xlsm` and another file called `Test_Booklet.xlsx`. These sheets will provide valuable study information, as well as test your foundation. You'll have to enable macros in order to take the tests in these Excel files. It's worth the time to take a look at these great study tools.

Todd Lammle Videos

A series of videos can be purchased in either DVD or online streaming format from www .lammle.com. However, as a bonus, the first module of this series is included with this book.

Todd Lammle Audios

One full section from Todd Lammle's CCNA audio series—nearly one hour of audio—is included with this book. The full CCNA audio series has a value of $199 and can be found at www.lammle.com.

PDF of Glossary of Terms

We have included an electronic version of the glossary in .pdf format. You can view the electronic version of the glossary with Adobe Reader.

Adobe Reader

We've also included a copy of Adobe Reader so you can view PDF files that accompany the book's content. For more information on Adobe Reader or to check for a newer version, visit Adobe's website at www.adobe.com/products/reader/.

System Requirements

Make sure your computer meets the minimum system requirements shown in the following list. If your computer doesn't match up to most of these requirements, you may have problems using the software and files. For the latest and greatest information, please refer to the ReadMe file located in the downloads.

- A PC running Microsoft Windows 98, Windows 2000, Windows NT4 (with SP4 or later), Windows Me, Windows XP, Windows Vista, or Windows 7
- An Internet connection

Using the Study Tools

To install the items, follow these steps:

1. Download the .ZIP file to your hard drive, and unzip to an appropriate location. Instructions on where to download this file can be found here: www.sybex.com/go/ccent2e.

2. Click the Start.EXE file to open the study tools file.

3. Read the license agreement, and then click the Accept button if you want to use the study tools.

The main interface appears. The interface allows you to access the content with just one or two clicks.

Troubleshooting

Wiley has attempted to provide programs that work on most computers with the minimum system requirements. Alas, your computer may differ, and some programs may not work properly for some reason.

The two likeliest problems are that you don't have enough memory (RAM) for the programs you want to use or you have other programs running that are affecting installation or running of a program. If you get an error message such as "Not enough memory" or "Setup cannot continue," try one or more of the following suggestions and then try using the software again:

Turn off any antivirus software running on your computer. Installation programs sometimes mimic virus activity and may make your computer incorrectly believe that it's being infected by a virus.

Close all running programs. The more programs you have running, the less memory is available to other programs. Installation programs typically update files and programs; so if you keep other programs running, installation may not work properly.

Have your local computer store add more RAM to your computer. This is, admittedly, a drastic and somewhat expensive step. However, adding more memory can really help the speed of your computer and allow more programs to run at the same time.

Customer Care

If you have trouble with the book's companion study tools, please call the Wiley Product Technical Support phone number at (800) 762-2974, or email them at http://sybex .custhelp.com/.

Index

Note to the reader: Throughout this index **boldfaced** page numbers indicate primary discussions of a topic. *Italicized* page numbers indicate illustrations.

X

Y

Free Online Study Tools

Register on Sybex.com to gain access to a complete set of study tools to help you prepare for your CCENT Exam

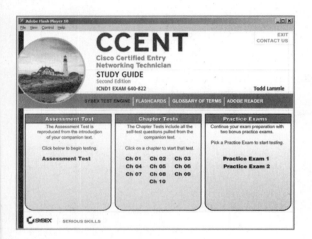

Go to www.sybex.com/go/ccent2e to register and gain access to this comprehensive study tool package.

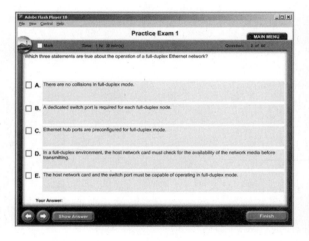

Comprehensive Study Tool Package Includes:

- **Assessment Test** to help you focus your study to specific objectives

- **Chapter Review Questions** for each chapter of the book

- **Two Full-Length Practice Exams** to test your knowledge of the material

- **Electronic Flashcards** to reinforce your learning and give you that last-minute test prep before the exam

- **Searchable Glossary** to give you instant access to the key terms you'll need to know for the exam

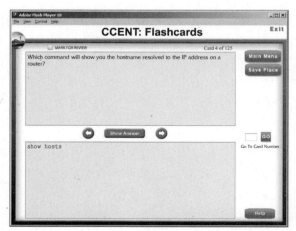